THE WATER CLOSET

Ipswich River Watershed and Beyond

Pike Messenger

All profits from sales of this book will go to the following organizations: Middleton Stream Team, Middleton Historical Society, Ipswich River Watershed Association and Essex County Greenbelt.

Front cover photo: River otters playing above and below thin ice, Willowdale State Park, Ipswich, MA., courtesy of Winston Ajce.

Back cover photo: Paddlers passing abutments of Log Bridge, gone since 1972, Ipswich River, Middleton. Courtesy of Judy Schneider.

For Chitose, my dearest critic who came across the sea with me.

Chitose's Hands

Worn white maple table
Scrubbed clean a thousand times
By her square hands and grit.

Round wool rugs
Braided taut from 100 scraps
By her strong hands and will.

Fine brown baskets
Twisted tight up tens of rows
By her deft hands and eye.

Three honest kids
Raised two decades long
By her kind hands and love.

Wondrous varied meals
Cooked cleverly with art
By her quick hands and soul.

Ten brown fingers
Wired finely to stout character
By the unseen hands of gods.

~ Pike Messenger

The Ipswich River Watershed

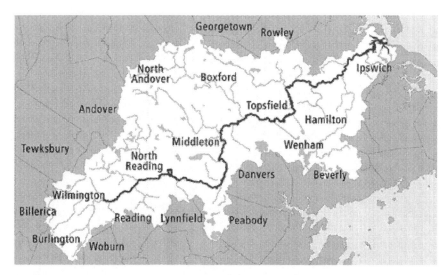

The Ipswich River Watershed, also called a basin, catches the rain and snow that falls on 160 square miles. Some water evaporates and returns to the air as vapor, some runs off into streams, and some permeates the soil. All in its various forms constitutes the basis of life in the watershed. Beaver dams—there are more than forty in Middleton alone—slow the flow to the sea at Plum Island Sound. Precious water is thus kept longer in wetlands and the ground.

Foreword

Welcome to a rich and enjoyable assortment of water-related essays written for a weekly column, "The Water Closet," by the Middleton Stream Team and published from January 2006 through December 2011 in the *Tri-Town Transcript*, a community paper serving the Ipswich River watershed towns of Middleton, Boxford and Topsfield, Massachusetts. The essays were accompanied by current United States Geological Survey weekly data on Ipswich River flow rate, and recent and accumulative precipitation amounts for the area. Many people outside the tri-town communities also receive the Water Closet through email, the Ipswich River Watershed Association's home page, and the Town of Middleton's internet site. The Middleton Stream Team is an active volunteer group with the broad purposes of environmental stewardship, conservation, advocacy, public service and education. The essays and information provided span all these purposes.

This group of over 300 issues of the Water Closet is published as a gift to Pike Messenger, author of all the essays, from the Middleton Conservation Commission, which he served from 1995 to his retirement in 2009. The commission put this collection together to honor his quiet but continual contributions in education and environmental stewardship to the communities, not only through the Water Closet, but through his work as Conservation Commission Agent and through the many projects of the Middleton Stream Team.

For various periods Pike has served on the Essex County Greenbelt Association and the Ipswich River Watershed Association boards of directors. Prior to becoming conservation agent, he taught biology and other sciences at Melrose High School and Triton Regional High School. Before his teaching career he served as a naval line officer aboard two United States Navy ships in the Pacific. He is known locally as an amateur naturalist, with knowledge of the topography, ecology and history of the tri-town area, and of Massachusetts coastal wetlands.

~Katharine Brown and John Bacon, Middleton Stream Team

Introduction

In 2005 Katharine Brown of the Middleton Stream Team asked Carol Ball, editor of the *Tri-Town Transcript*, a weekly newspaper serving Boxford, Middleton and Topsfield, if her paper would publish a column of Ipswich River flow rates and area precipitation data as well as water conservation and water-related recreation tips. Editor Ball agreed and a column dubbed "The Water Closet," Brit for toilet, has been flushed on the paper's readers ever since. We Stream Teamers thank the *Tri-Town Transcript*, Editor Ball and her successors David Rogers and Kathryn O'Brien for giving us space to air our interests and to educate folks on a much taken-for-granted natural resource: water, the living essence of us animals, plants, soil and air.

As the weeks rolled on tips gave way to water-related mini-essays. Fans of the WC have often encouraged the Stream Team to publish its columns in book form. This was started as a retirement gift after I, author of the essays, left my job as Middleton Conservation Agent in July 2009. Derek Fullerton, Middleton Health Director and Conservation Administrator; John Bacon, Middleton Stream Team Leader; and Joan Caulfield, recently Conservation Commission secretary and friend, became the publishers. I can't think of people I'd like to be more associated with on such a project. Since the column's inception, John has gathered river flow rate and precipitation data and reviewed early drafts of the essays to meet our never-ending Tuesday evening deadlines. Without John there would be no Water Closet. My cousin Karlene Pettengill Johnson, former English teacher and retired newspaper reporter, reviewed also. And then there have been the candid comments of Katharine Brown, former biology student of mine and stalwart of the Stream Team, who let me know right up front what she thought and felt.

Judith Schneider, Stream team photographer, and friend and photographer Pamela Hartman have often in the last few years provided The Water Closet with fine photos that greatly added to the essays. Many were obtained after late requests, a few hours before weekly press deadlines. We are also fortunate in having well known Ipswich artist Dorothy Monnelly let us use her striking black-and-white salt marsh photographs. Some of these ladies' photos grace this book. I also want to thank Winston Ajce, a photographer never met, who several years ago sent the Stream Team remarkable close-ups of otters playing in ice water at Willowdale State Park (see cover).

I also add the names of a few readers who have given much encouragement over the years. Their past comments kept me going as deadlines loomed. For this, I thank Bob Lemoine, Francis Masse, Joan Cudhea, Sandy Rubchinuk, and Glenice and Galen Kelley, fellow Stream Teamers; Ira Singer, Middleton Town Administrator; Kerry Mackin, executive director, Trish Aldrich, and Jim MacDougall, naturalist, Ipswich River Watershed Association; Jim Berry, ornithologist; friends Shirley Raynard, Pamela Beaubien and husband, the late David Beaubien; and others who liked an essay now and then and said so. My dearest critic has been wife Chitose, who reads the published version each week and gently, but firmly, lets me know what she thinks. Her reactions tell me much.

The essays, found here in chronological order, have little sequential connection, except perhaps seasonal at times, so may be read in any order. Most were inspired by area hikes, clamming trips, paddles along our Ipswich River and its tributaries and estuaries, or from hearing about water issues somewhere else that could be related to local waters. Much New England, Massachusetts and Essex County history is woven into them.

Since we never use the first person singular in the Water Closet, I imagine helpers and me as a group, "Closeteers" or "Stream Teamers," of old colleagues, members of an environmental choir, who retire now and then to the Water Closet, an imaginary shack on the bank of the Ipswich River, a small building not unlike Thoreau's real one near Walden Pond. There we discuss the waters of the world. Now and then a column floats forth.

~ Pike Messenger, July 2012

2006

WATER RESOURCE AND CONSERVATION INFORMATION FOR MIDDLETON, BOXFORD AND TOPSFIELD

Precipitation data for month of	Sept	Oct	Nov	Dec
30 Year Normal (1971-2000) Inches	3.71	4.12	4.48	3.96
2006 Central Watershed Actual	3.36	4.86	6.68	2.48

IPSWICH RIVER FLOW RATE (S. MIDDLETON USGS GAGE) IN CUBIC FEET PER SECOND (CFS):

For January 6, 2006	Normal...53 CFS	Current Rate...107 CFS	*

JANUARY 2006

WATER WIZARDS

On the edge of a large red maple swamp, one of many in the vast unspoiled woods of northern Middleton, southwestern Boxford, and southeastern North Andover, we hikers happened upon a bust in white oak recently sculpted by a beaver. A foot above the base of this 10-inch diameter tree is the neck, a deep unfinished notch all round; above it is a beaver head. The tree, felled from just above this head,

Another beaver-sculpted bust in the making. Photo, courtesy of Stream Team.

* The table above, with essay, is how The Water Closet appears weekly in the *Tri-Town Transcript*.

lies in the beavers' impoundment. Why did the unknown artist stop cutting the lower notch if she just wanted to fell the tree? Perhaps she cut the top notch first, saw the possibilities of a head, and then carved the neck. Features in the resulting head can be imagined. The sculptor, not a slave to realism, had made a rough Picasso. No doubt some of you are muttering "nonsense" as well you might. However, this beaver is one of a clan who has made a 70-acre impoundment in which hundreds of trees are dying, the result of dams they have built down-drainage in a funnel-shaped intermittent stream. Perhaps we are hopelessly anthropomorphic in considering them engineers and skilled contractors. Yet, if engineers, why couldn't some be artists?

We'll leave these farfetched speculations and look at the facts. This swamp's clan has built four dams, all across the same narrowing stream in a 500-foot stretch flowing from the swamp. Let's look at each from downstream up in the order we think they were built. The first is 10 feet long, the second 15, the third 40, and the fourth, 100. The upper two are curved upstream the way we make our biggest dams. The impounded water is slowly making what is called a "beaver meadow." As the trees succumb to year-round flooding the light will pour through the leafless corpses and give rise to herbaceous plants. We guess that if they can make a rich new wildlife habitat, a simple wooden bust is easy.

WATER HIGHS AND LOWS

At year's end a Stream Teamer suggested a Closet overview of the Ipswich River's non-tidal highs and lows for 2005. Upon reflection it was agreed that this might involve more than just rates of flow. Not only does the water fluctuate in depth and flow, but also in temperature, dissolved oxygen, light absorbed and reflected, ice coverage, runoff receipt, turbidity, biological activity, etc. It reminds us of "cold-blooded" organisms with annual life cycles, such as insects, fish, amphibians, reptiles and other groups. James Lovelock, English atmospheric chemist, in 1979 gave us the Gaia Hypothesis, which has the earth as an organism, a living thing. Certainly the earth has its cycles, balances, energies, life and correcting mechanisms. If Lovelock can do it for the planet why can't we ask if the river and its tributaries are alive? Lets review last year's fluctuating vital signs, at least some highs and lows. The flow rates are from the gauge in South Middleton. Temperatures, dissolved oxygen amounts, and depths are from Thunder Bridge, just upriver from Masconomet near the point where Boxford, Topsfield and Middleton meet.

Flow (CFS) (mg/l)	Depth (ft.)	Temperature (C)	Dissolved Oxygen
410 on 3/29	8.5 on 10/30	21 on 7/31	12.6 on 3/20
0.014 on 9/13	4.1 on 9/26	0 from 1/7 to 3/20	3.1 on 9/26

Numbers, numbers, what do they mean!? They certainly show a complex system; Lovelock might say an "organism." The Ipswich River Watershed Association would probably say "patient," one about which it constantly frets; members make head-to-toe checks each month to measure metabolic signs. (Can you old-timers remember when doctors came to us?) In the 19th century, agriculture might have been their main concern; now, it is runoff from ever expanding asphalt. In subsequent Closets we'll look more closely at some of the variables separately. Alas, there is some danger here; they aren't unrelated (find some relationships above) and must eventually be thought of as a whole, or dare we say as an organism?

WATER WALLS

Last year the Ipswich River, at a point near where our three towns meet, fluctuated in depth from 4.1 to 8.5 feet. The land between high and low water is defined as "bank." Banks, because of their contact with water, are rich habitats for organisms and are given special status under the Massachusetts Wetlands Protection Act. We've all seen the richness of life along these edges. It is where otters and children play, and ducks, herons, frogs and turtles hang out. A water sweep with a fine net among bank plants will yield insects, crustaceans and many other organisms too small to see. These need surface which banks provide in abundance with their soil grains, stones, decaying leaves, sticks and great jungles of plant stems and roots. A few feet up from water's edge or a few out into it, biodiversity decreases as water or surface diminish. For years TV nature shows have taken us to mangrove swamps along our tropical waters to see the diversity there. We have our mangroves here in the form of maples, buttonbushes, swamp dogwoods, and pickerel weeds. These plants and many more provide substrate, shade, hideaways, and food. Endless variations can be seen in a paddle down the Ipswich to the sea. Go very quietly some early morning or evening after the ice is gone. You'll likely see muskrats, beavers, mink, birds, turtles, fish, mussels; the list goes on.

Most species are unseen because they are too small, water covered, or hidden in the millions of crannies provided by the stuff of banks. These unseen inhabitants are the bases of food chains. If the bank is dry too long many die or go dormant until water returns. Bank organisms have adapted to survive seasonal fluctuations. Excessive withdrawals by man at the wrong times do harm. We should regulate our activities with the natural cycles there; follow our own advice and "go with the flow."

RIVER RIFFLES

Wind ruffles feathers and water from above, riverbed stones riffle from below; both increase air-water interface. 'Twixt moving water molecules are others such as those of life-giving oxygen (O2). In this year's first Closet we noted the high and low dissolved O2 measurements for last year just below the river's surface at Thunder Bridge. They were 12.6 mg/l on March 20 and 3.1 mg/l on September 26. The water ran fast and cold, 0° C in early spring and sluggish and warm, 19° C in early fall. Had we measured at different points in our streams and river there would have been significantly different concentrations. Boston Brook above Mundy Bridge, Middleton, is one of the area's few stretches of "white water," the drug of rafters. A little kid on a board could do this one. The brook there drops over 15 feet in a few hundred, traversing a bed of stones that cause breaking riffles at fast flow. This week, at these mini-rapids, the dissolved O2 concentration was 12.2 mg/l, while just downstream in slow-moving Prichards Pond, an impoundment of Boston Brook, it was 11.0 mg/l. If you are an active predator or forager, riffles are the place to live. (The poor miners at Sago needed lots of O2, alas for them, it was displaced by carbon monoxide, CO;. Both bond to the hemoglobin of red blood cells; however, the O in CO is unavailable. Animals, especially active ones, need much O2 for respiration. We read of bicycle racers "blood doping" to increase it.) Cold water holds much more O2 than warm, and riffles, rapids, and breaking waves absorb more O2 than places where the water is quiet and air-water contact is less. Is it any wonder that thrill-seeking rafters, artists, fishermen and other animals flock to places where cold water dances with air?

WATER WORRIES

How strange to have January, the coldest of months, not cold or even close so far. Even vernal pools have little ice. The soil, some years rock hard to three feet, can now be spaded. Our flowing Ipswich, always reluctant to freeze and never really safe for walking, has been largely ice-free bank to bank this winter. This week's snowstorms have fallen gently through warm air. In eight of 27 days this month, temperatures have risen to points of competing with all-time records. We hear of severe cold in Russia; perhaps our share is there. Almost a month of continuous rain in western Washington and Oregon, floods in California, drought and fires in the Dust Bowl, from all around come reports of water excess or absence. The Wisconsin continental glacier, waning for the past 12,000 years in one of 40 or more interglacial periods during the last million years, now seems to be accelerating due to our activities. For decades, reports of retreating glaciers and shrinking ice caps have literally poured in from 'round the world. Water is on the move from ice to liquid; the oceans are rising, climate patterns changing. We New Englanders are long used to January thaws and fickle weather. Robert Frost said it best in his "Two Tramps at Mud Time":

> *You know how it is with an April day*
> *When the sun is out and the wind is still,*
> *You are one month on in the middle of May.*
> *But if you so much as dare to speak,*
> *A cloud comes over the sunlit arch.*
> *A wind comes off a frozen peak,*
> *And you're two months back in the middle of March.*

Alas, what he describes is happening now in January! While Yankees take a perverse pride in their rambunctious climate, now with fewer "frozen peaks," worry lurks under the "sunlit arch." What will rising waters bring?

FEBRUARY 2006

ATLANTIC'S WHIRLING WATER

They came boldly powered by wind and riding a mighty current. *The New World*, now at local movie theatres, authentically shows the lovely tidewater settings, if not the history, of Jamestown. The horror not shown was the "time of the great dying" for the area's "naturals." Few fell to English musket balls or swords, most were laid low by germs neither their foreign vectors nor their new hosts had any notion of. The former died mostly from incompetence in diplomacy, hunting and fishing, and agriculture. They kept coming and eventually, with the help of indentured servants and slaves, prospered by raising tobacco. Those who taught them how were gone.

How did they so readily get here in small and often less-than-seaworthy vessels? The ships of the period sailed south from England and picked up the latitudes Columbus had crossed on. Upon reaching the "Indies" they continued on the warm current north and northeasterly by Florida to the Virginias and New England. They rejoined the warm easterly flowing waters upon returning home. Benjamin Franklin, whom we celebrated this past month, on his diplomatic trips to England and France passed his time taking water temperatures, examining charts, and talking with experienced seamen; from his studies came the first good chart of the Gulf Stream. A century later Joshua Slocum, first round-the-world solo navigator, sailed east from the severe cold of mid-winter Maine in his small sloop *Spray* and after a few days was reading on deck in shirt sleeves. We on cold Massachusetts Bay are just out of that great clockwise-flowing "river," yet our history is intimately tied to it. The English, French and Portuguese rode it here long before Plymouth, to fish the banks where the cold Labrador Current mingles with the warm "stream," and cod once thrived. "So distant in time and space!" you say. Not so, the waters in our back yards are continuous with the Gulf Stream via the river.

WORKING WATER

The Closet, here each Friday, moves about the river basin in between. This past week it was on a tiny island in Boston Brook just upstream of the riffles descending to Mundy Bridge. The fast-flowing brook it divides, upon close examination, looks manmade, as do the berms to the north and south across the stream branches. In the 1680s the Thomas Fuller family built a mill dam here. We can envision that earthen dam; one branch was the sluiceway, the other the overflow channel. We imagine harder and wipe away the trees; there is the mill pond surrounded by rough pasture. Teams of oxen and horses hauling in logs are commanded by farmers speaking Elizabethan English. Other logs are being floated downstream to the pond where they wait their turn at the slow up-and-down saw, run by a water wheel. Old deeds indicate this mill, then in Boxford near the Salem line, later Middleton, only operated a generation or two. The earthen ruins of thousands of such small seasonably run mills, dependent upon the volume of their ponds, can be found. The oldest houses in the tri-town area may well have boards from this mill. These clean sources of power were superseded by season-independent steam and, later, electricity. Just a third of a mile down from Mundy Bridge is a much larger concrete dam built by Charles Prichard about century ago to make "Prichards Pond" on which a summer cottage was built. He neither sawed nor ground corn. Most small dams are on the way out, as we so dramatically saw in Taunton. Time and ice will reduce them all. While a good clean source of energy in a country "addicted to oil," they have a major fault. They block the passage of water animals in their yearly migrations, especially those of spawning anadromous fish such as alewives, shad, sturgeon and salmon. Will any survive the demise of dams? Damned if we don't, damned if we do.

MORE WATER WORK

Mundy Bridge was mentioned here last week. It now consists of two four-foot diameter steel culverts that allow Boston Brook, down from Boston Hill in North Andover, to proceed under North Liberty Street on to the Ipswich River. Until Middleton was incorporated in 1728 it was practically on the Boxford-Salem line. All that is geography; what about the name? Some have guessed Mundy might be a misspelling of Maunday as in Maunday Thursday from the old Christian tradition of washing feet of the poor on that day. Just above what was probably once a broad stone culvert or wooden bridge are riffles descending over a 200-yard stairway of stones, a fine place for the washing and cooling of sweaty feet. John "Red" Caulfield, who lives nearby, remembers a story told him by lifelong Middletonite Jim Martin of a woman who lugged her laundry each Monday, the traditional wash day of old, to the gentle rapids here. The clean water flowing over washboard stones was an ideal place to scrub and rinse. Imagine a time when the woman in John's story is young and surrounded by other launderers happily gossiping while washing their precious hours—free from household chores—away. Young children wade and splash nearby. They meet at Mundy Bridge each Mundy; and isn't this spelling more correct, the way we say it? We in the Closet have no records of any of this; we do know that up to the time of crude washing machines, women gathered at such places. How much more pleasant than bending over tubs of dirty water pushing cloth across corrugated boards. And isn't this a far better source of the name than some yarn about a rum-soaked Mr. Mundy falling off his horse and bridge into the brook there?

NOTE: We have since found out that a Mrs. Mundy lived close to the bridge. The cellar hole of what we think was her small house is still there. You can ignore our theories about the bridge's name.

WATER HITCHHIKERS

As we sit around the WC stove awaiting true spring, not the tease experienced these past seven weeks, we discuss a new book entitled *Out of Eden,* by Alan Burdick, who writes very well of worldwide invasions of species, with concentration on those spread by humans. In his extensive research he hung out with biologists who devoted their lives to studying "invasive-exotic" species. Many worry deeply about homogenization and loss of diversity. Movement by introduced organisms is usually the result of unplanned hitchhiking on ships, planes and other vehicles. (Note for younger readers: old-timers remember when raising one's pointed thumb toward oncoming cars, hitchhiking, was a common and acceptable means of travel.) Early wooden ships had lush zoological gardens growing from their rotting hulls. Such ships are largely gone, yet we can get a hint of what they were like by going to the Gloucester and Salem waterfronts and peering down at wooden pilings; mussels, barnacles, seaweeds and crabs are but a fraction of the organisms covering them. Imagine the whale ships out of New England ports on two- to four-year voyages. They'd wallow home with scarce headway enough to maintain steerage due to the drag of two-foot layers of seaweeds and their denizens. Many of our marine organisms were probably so introduced. Now, on fast-moving steel ships coated with antifouling toxins, little is carried externally; rather, vast volumes of foreign waters are carried within as ballast. Tens of thousands ships, many a thousand times the displacement of the *Mayflower,* now criss-cross the oceans; those without full cargoes ballast down with seawater that is pumped out along with foreign inhabitants in places where they shouldn't be. A few survive, thrive, and compete with native species. Do we in the Ipswich River basin, where water comes from snow and rain without hitchhikers, need to worry? Alas, we have water invaders introduced by other means; next WC we'll fret about a few.

MARCH 2006

WATER IMPORTS

Last week we considered "introduced" species. People have long introduced themselves to new lands, yet now, while spreading, get ever closer though cyberspace. There is another network, an ancient one of trade and transport. It too is expanding in volume, number, length of routes, and speed. Columbus took six weeks, modern ships six days, and jets six hours to cross the Atlantic. Viruses, bacteria, seeds, insects, and whole plants and animals now travel more easily with people and their goods. They end up where they didn't evolve. Some adapt. Consider the tiny zebra mussels (*Dreissena polymorpha*), which arrived in the Great Lakes in 1988 from Europe, probably via ballast water, and now pave bottoms with their spectacular populations. The changes to ecosystems there must be enormous as these filter feeders sweep basic plankton from the waters, which in Lake Erie are now disturbingly clear. They've moved quickly down and up the Mississippi and are now as far east as the Hudson River, poised for leaps into the Berkshires. (Next week we'll look at the chinese mystery snail, an import discovered in Johnson Pond, Boxford, last spring.) In the summers of 2003 and 2004, Essex County Greenbelt Association and New England Wildflower Society volunteers fought hand to stem against water chestnuts (*Trapa natans*) in Upper Mill Pond on the Ewell Reservation in Rowley. These battles may have eradicated this prolific invader there or at least slowed it down; however, its large, very hard, spiny fruit/seeds are known to remain viable for years. Introductions of species raise a host of questions like: why do some of the newcomers survive and thrive in competition with well-adapted natives? The standard answer used to be that the "invaders" have no natural enemies in the new area. 'Tis much more complicated, but at least the questions are now being asked. In the meantime, inspect and wash down your vessels when traveling between ponds. There may be hitchhikers.

WATER WEED

Last week we billed the chinese mystery snail for this; however, a giant invasive grass has again raised its beautiful head in TV and print and should be addressed. We'll let the oriental snail lie dormant in

Boxford/Georgetown's Johnson Pond until after a site visit there for further information of its status. Nova Scotian Jef Achenbach, formerly of Boxford, has returned for another look at *Phragmites australis,* "common reed grass," uprisings here on the fringes of our salt marshes and in wetlands alongside our roads. It likes a pinch of salt as do we. He wants to remove it from the wetlands, where it shades out native species, and raise it to our rooftops in the form of thatch. We had thatch roofs here up until fire codes did them in about the time of the Revolution. Then, there was no "phrag," as Jef calls it; rather, the smaller, native "cordgrass" along our estuarine river and creek banks was used. Thatch was an important seasonable industry here in our coastal towns. John Adam's grandfather is said to have ordered him to the Quincy salt marshes when he was on the verge of deciding on Harvard or the family farm. After several days with sickle in August heat and greenheads, he went to Harvard. Jef has cut over 10,000 bundles of "phrag" from the Newbury salt marshes as he builds up inventory for a hoped-for market. He says his roofs will last 40 years. One of the Closeteers visited a Japanese farmhouse a half century ago and was impressed by the beauty and insulating qualities of its half-meter-thick roof. On that hot summer day it was cool within. There are still thatchers in Europe; why not here? We'll end here this week and continue the story of this majestic invader and gutsy "Herring Choker" Jef, our would-be thatcher and marsh savior, next.

WATER WEED RETURNS

Inspired by news of thatcher Jef Achenbach's plans for "exotic" and "invasive" *Phragmites,* we have thatched the Closet with it, cut from a swamp nearby. It gives the drafty Closet a warm and cozy look, like a Beatrix Potter cottage. We expect Mouse and other characters will soon take up residence within its thick cap. Historically, such large grasses have had other uses; perhaps the most famous were the reeds of Moses' tiny cradle/ark made to hide him from the Egyptians. He was launched among papyrus along the Nile. Thor Heyerdahl, after viewing small vessels such as those of the Iraqi Marsh Arabs, built a seagoing ship of lashed papyrus bundles that he and colleagues successfully sailed across the Atlantic. Perhaps builders here can use *Phragmites* to start biodegradable boat businesses. Replacing plastic vessels and asphalt shingles might be appropriate in a country "addicted to oil." Is the adjective "exotic" true for this disturbing invader of our wetlands? Yale biologist Kristin Saltonstall, painstakingly using DNA analysis, has shown the invading "monster phrag" to be an Old World variety that is very effectively wiping out the very similar, less competitive, native variety; the latter is almost gone. One Closeteer, who as a lad roamed the Salisbury marshes, never saw *Phragmites* there 55 years ago. Now, he returns to his old haunts where visibility is unlimited over short native grasses—salt hay of yore—and finds patches covering acres with thick stands, eight to 14 feet high with no other plants. Visibility within is only a few feet. Each plant produces thousands of wind-blown seeds. Stout underground stems grow out from patch edges and give rise to shoots asexually. Cutting, burning and grubbing just slow it down. Will Jef's thatch scheme successfully part the economic Red Sea and at the same time save the marshes, as Moses did his people? We, protected by our new *Phragmites* roof, can only wish him well. In the meantime, aerial spraying of herbicide from the Carolinas to the Maritimes is, in places, underway.

WATER WIND WORK

What do Joseph Ignazio, retired engineer, and the late Timothy Fuller have in common? The answer is that they have both stood before Middleton townspeople and spoken of hydropower. Last week, the selectmen received Mr. Ignazio with enthusiasm as he described a plan to install small helical turbines in the Ipswich River. Mr. Fuller in 1770 requested of Town Meeting that he be allowed to "narro" a fish opening in his mill dam on Middleton Brook to increase the size of his mill pond, hence its potential energy, and was denied.* He must have been lectured on the necessity of providing access for fish, probably alewives and shad, to their spawning grounds. One wonders what the citizens would have done a century later when the industrial revolution was in high gear and "progress" was a national slogan. We can easily guess: the anadromous fish are gone, but ironically so are many of the dams. Our modern engineer was with a group called Citizens Advocating Renewable Energy, led by selectmen William Mugford and retired school superintendent Frank Fitzgerald. They touted what we all know should happen as the need for cleaner energy becomes ever more apparent. The selectmen and Town Administrator Ira Singer didn't poo-poo their proposals, but rather expanded on them. Closeteers present could sense a fresh breeze of hope over

Bare Hill (jail site) where the wind 75 feet above the ground is said to average 15 mph, perhaps enough for a wind turbine. The helixes are tentatively planned for a place near the Bostik Dam in south Middleton. They are turned by water flow passing through them like air through pinwheels. The elegant looking helical blades run an electric generator. How good to see and hear our town mothers and fathers listening intently to those whom, a few years ago, would have been dubbed dreamers. It is high time for the return of water, sun, and wind as sources of energy, i.e.– water wheels, photovoltaic cells, wind turbines and sails. We once sawed our wood, evaporated seawater for salt, and powered our ships with them.

* Watkins, Laura Woodside, Middleton Massachusetts: A Cultural History, page 50

WINGS OVER WATER

Above the beaver impoundment where North Andover, Boxford and Middleton join there is a little-known development of 24 aerial units, all with wonderful views of Pond Meadow Pond and immersed surrounds. The builders started four years ago without permits from the Essex County Greenbelt Association, landowner, or town boards. These flighty newcomers were attracted by the needleless white pines towering above 40 acres of standing Atlantic white cedar and red maple copses. A beaver dam killed them all by raising the water of their swamp less than two feet. The dam was built in 1998; in only four years all the trees were without leaves. This winter's wind has taken its toll on the rotting maple trunks. The decay-resistant cedar skeletons may be around for another 40 years. The pine trunks and branches might support the squatters for another half-dozen seasons. These are the spring-summer child-rearing homes for the otherwise solitary giants. Child may be the wrong word here; the fast-growing young are covered with down at first and soon feathers. By summer they are three to four feet tall, rivaling harassed parents who spend most of their time stalking prey, which they regurgitate into these fledging Great Blue Herons. Human witnesses of the returning parental providers are rewarded, not with regurgitated snakes, mice, fish and frogs, but with a crescendo of clamorous croaks and cries from both parents and kids. Gracefully flying parents signal from some distance; kids joyfully respond. Please forgive the anthropomorphisms. You can feel what is going on; after all, we do share their genes. Soon two, three, or even four are standing precariously on their stick nests, giving and receiving. In the background, frogs, potential victims, provide a chorus, perhaps in mourning. As you can see, there is no getting away from unscientific interpretations. We must enjoy such visits while we can; soon, the supporting pine trunks will follow the maples and the herons will move on to newly devastated forests. Isn't that what we do, new kids on the evolutionary block, once hunter-gatherers also? These magnificent relatives of the dinosaurs have done so 50 times longer. *We* should live so lightly!

APRIL 2006

RIVER WATER WOES

It is Tuesday morning; rain that started last evening continues. This is our first significant precipitation in seven weeks. Weather folks tell us this March was the driest since 1915! In the Closet we are worried about the low water in our vernal pools, wetlands and river. Last night's *PBS News Hour* reported that the Pacific Northwest salmon fleet is being kept at the docks because stocks are so low. Conditions in the Klamath and the Columbia Rivers were featured. Upriver hydroelectric dams without fish ladders and withdrawals for irrigation have kept the rivers too low, slow, and warm for riverine fish. In addition, erosion from excessive logging has done great sedimentation damage. Sound familiar? It all happened here two centuries earlier. The land was clear-cut for agriculture; livestock overgrazed right down to the river where they waded and defecated; there was sediment-laden runoff from cultivated floodplain fields, and dams were built to provide power. How very sad that truly living streams and rivers were made ill by us, their admirers. Long ago, the Charles, Mystic, Ipswich, Parker and Merrimack Rivers teemed with shad, alewives, smelt, salmon and even mighty sturgeon. At Pawtucket Falls, now Lowell, there were great gatherings of Native American clans during spring salmon runs. Spawning migrations of shad up the Schuylkill River to Valley Forge saved thousands of Washington's men after a terrible winter of protein and fat starvation. Along the Ipswich, colonists bid for town licenses to seine alewives. Here too damming, erosion, and pollution quickly put an end to those vibrant times. With this morning's welcome rain, hope comes again that we will protect and restore our watersheds. We finally understand; now is the time to earn redemption through action. As of this writing plans for river restorations on both coasts are being debated. Here at home, our active Ipswich River Water Association has just formally established a River Restoration Program. Would that all rivers were so lucky!

WATER WINDOWS

Window, as in "window of opportunity," has become a common metaphor. There are windows for courting and family raising; last month at "ice-out" in our vernal pools the breeding window opened for certain salamanders and small frogs. If they don't metamorphose from the aquatic stage with gills and tail into their terrestrial form with lungs and legs before the ponds dry up, they'll miss 2006's window. The past couple weeks we've been visiting vernal pools and have found them only partly full or in some cases dry due to the severe yet little noticed late February and March drought. Even if there are normal spring rains from now on, the shallow pools may dry up early while the tadpoles are still fish-like. Far away on Ellesmere Island, paleontologists recently discovered fossil fish in rocks one-third billion years old. In their fins are the pro-leg bones of us tetrapods. These extinct fish, called tiktanlik, "large shallow water fish," may be missing links between fish and land dwellers. Here in our vernal pools, small descendants with short life cycles show the transition each year in living color. Too many dry years, or filled vernal pools, and they'll be gone the way of tiktaalik. Last week a Closeteer, while attending a master plan committee meeting, was jokingly asked, "How are our swamps doing?" He fretted about the low water in our vernal pools, prompting good-natured chuckles and sarcasm. Alas, almost all of our temporary pools, whether bathtub size or isolated shallow swamps of several acres, places without fish, are vernal pools essential for mole salamanders, wood frogs and other small creatures. Many new egg masses were found in them this past week. We, who can close windows, in this case by clearing surrounding habitat and filling, must think hard about what we do. Once closed, the opportunities may not come again and future paleontologists of another species may find our fossils in ancient strata along with those of bulldozers and cars.

WATER WAYS

Our streams and river here drop gently to their destination, the sea. Beaver dams, absent well over three centuries, further slow descent, keeping water in the basin longer. These waterways were once the ways

Painted turtles basking on log floating in the Ipswich River. Photo, courtesy of Stream Team.

of wildlife, people, and numerous fish. Before the colonists and their devastating livestock, they were accompanied by narrow foot paths. Any bridges were fallen logs; low temporary dams were of sticks and mud. Then the English came along and paid for pelts. The beavers and their trappers were soon gone, the latter from novel diseases. Newcomers built bridges and higher dams of stone. Paths along banks and floodplains became cart ways and, over time, roads for transport and for cattle and hog drives. Those were rough affairs, passable most seasons by oxen and horse-drawn sleds or wagons. Seasonal high waters provided transport for logs. Former beaver impoundments called "beaver meadows" were drained, creating "farmer meadows" for late season hay. "Bottoms" (periodic floodplains) were cultivated much more intensely than the Algonquian speakers had. Uplands above floodplains became largely pasture interspersed with small woodlots. People still descended to river roads for travel. We can drive them today on Lockwood Lane and Middleton Road hugging Fish Brook in Boxford, on Coppermine Road near Nichols Brook in Topsfield, and on Essex Street paralleling Boston Brook in Middleton. The railways also followed them for their gentle grades; alas, those behemoths' great momentum needed long, straight runs so wetlands were filled in creating right-of-ways. Finally, dynamite, huge earth-moving equipment, and fast cars in ever greater numbers led to straight wide roads like Routes 1 and 114; wetland and hill topography be damned! Waterways crossed at right angles all but disappeared to fast travelers. Paved roads became fast, efficient and comfortable, but unnatural. In our hurry, we perhaps have lost our way. Yet, some deep urge lingers on. Witness our return in canoes and kayaks, descendants of those ancient craft of log, bark and skin.

WATER WORKERS, *CASTOR CANADENSIS*

North American explorer David Thompson is quoted as saying in 1784, the land "may be said to have been in the possession of two distinct species of beings: man and the beaver." The ever increasing beavers, mentioned often in the Closet, can no longer be ignored. They are fast changing our lower landscapes. On Patriot's Day, Francis Masse led a canoe trip down the Ipswich River; his mother started this yearly paddle as a family tradition over 60 years ago. Family have dispersed or passed on so now he invites old friends, including a couple Closeteers. This year's group put in at Farnsworth Landing, Route 114, and leisurely paddled, with a stop for dinner, to Thunder Bridge near the Boxford and Topsfield lines. So far, this little story has been of humans, but all those involved soon realized they were deep into beaver territory. Just downstream from launch they came upon a new lodge, seven feet high and 25 feet across at the base! All along the river on both sides trees were chewed on or completely girdled, hence doomed, or felled as were hundreds of channel-flanking bushes, such as swamp dogwood. The canoers, despite two months of drought and relatively low flows, were able to proceed because beaver dams were keeping the water higher, thus navigable. One high dam encountered was safely slid over by the first three of four canoes; the fourth got stuck mid-passage. The two paddlers unwisely rose to the occasion by standing and pushing on the dam with paddles. One of our group fell, briefly entering the beavers' domain, alas without a beaver suit. No harm was done; the wet one and crew mate were greeted with good-natured kidding. Any beavers within hearing were probably chuckling also. Some realized while passing that this lovely corridor of floodplain trees might soon be gone and the sun would pour in on a beaver meadow of shorter herbaceous water plants. The river may soon look more like the one Masconomo and his people knew and lost.

MAY 2006

WIDE WATER VIEWS

The brain is wider than the sky,
For, put them side by side,
The one the other will include
With ease and you beside.

The brain is deeper than the sea,
For, hold them, blue to blue,
The one the other will absorb,
As sponges, buckets do.

These, the first two stanzas from one of Emily Dickinson's famous poems, hail our capacity to think large. A scientist-philosopher—no one in the Closet can remember his name—said something like: "My mind is but a tiny speck in space, yet with it I can embrace the Universe." Recent reports of NASA's surprisingly long lived Rovers, searching for signs of water on Mars, remind us that people do more than think big; they act. Back on Earth last Saturday, the Ipswich River Watershed Association (IRWA) held its 10th annual training session for volunteer water quality monitors who have been testing, measuring and reporting monthly for almost a decade. While both NASA and IRWA are concerned with water and its relationship to life, the former may spend 10 million dollars to IRWA's one. We now understand the far reaching dimensions of adequate water to the quality of the environment in which we live and its very finite limits. In recent months, a more enlightened view has emerged in settlements reached on water withdrawal limits set by the Massachusetts Department of Environmental Protection for Ipswich River Basin communities. As is still the case with gasoline, demand and consumption traditionally had been given much higher priority in the economy than conservation, although citizens polled give strong lip service to the latter. We started here with large ideas and have traversed to practical ones having to do with taken-for-granted water. We need to think of water from river basin points of view rather than parochial and narrow user or town self interests. Expanding again, we can see what thinking nationally rather than globally is doing to our planet. Groundwater, streams and rivers are no respecters of town bounds; air and oceans give not a hoot for arbitrary national borders. We must set aside greed and pride and join hands for the good of all including our fellow creatures and plants.

WATER TO WATER

On a recent afternoon wander down the old Essex railway right-of-way between branches of Boston Brook a Closeteer came upon a "spotted turtle" en route on the other side. Both stopped, the turtle withdrew its head, tail, and feet and was picked up by the old man, a perfect handful, its smoothness and heft remembered from such pickups over 65 years before. The then boy would carry his prize around for a time; take it home to show other boys, or even sisters. All liked spotted turtles, as most do ladybugs or giraffes, perhaps it is their spots. And then on mother's say-so he'd return to the place where found so it could get on about its business. Now *Clemmys guttata* is on the endangered species list, classified as of "special concern." Concern, despite its bureaucratic origin, is a good word here. It arose out of worry for the fate of the smallest and more helpless among us, and for the much larger fate of habitat loss. These turtles, wood frogs and salamanders, little known or seen, should be the canaries of our minds, bad pun intended. If they go out, many other lights of life may soon follow. The season of turtle crossing time is upon us. This one, found on a rail bed abandoned in 1926, had little to fear. The man did not pocket for later showing, rather put it gently down and went his way, also "concerned," knowing he'd soon find scores of turtles—not spotted—dead along our fast-traveled roads. Their cryptic paths from wet to wet cross ours from dry to dry at angles only we might straighten out or at least provide for. After all, they've been on earth a hundred times longer than we have. You might say they have the right of way.

WRENCHES IN WATER WORKS

Animals, including us, are mostly water. We are about 65 percent; jellyfish, over 96 percent. Our ancient ancestors, many thousands of forms removed, were aquatic. Is it any wonder that children return to puddles and adults to beaches? It used to be, when we humans were far fewer and innocent of chemistry, that our pollutants were natural wastes that had evolved with us. With our great, largely water, brains we have learned of molecules and their manipulation. Our genius results in novel forms that appear in test tubes. If they are useful, or just desirable, we synthesize them on vast scales; they and the by-products of their creation are released to the land, water and air. Alas, these wondrous new molecules didn't evolve over millennia along with species. Their shapes and electrical nature don't always fit with the "natural" ones of tissues. Remember the old fear in WWII defense plants, that saboteurs may "throw a wrench in the works"? Imagine ultramicroscopic wrenches, our manufactured molecular tools, in the delicate molecular machinery of living cells. In most cases, we have no clue as to what they do. We only test a fraction on certain mammals for toxicity. The late Rachel Carson, mid-20th-century zoologist, became alarmed about these chemicals, particularly pesticides and herbicides, and the harm they were causing. She wrote the much praised and damned book *Silent Spring* in warning. Our heroes in science are usually in the medical field, such as Louis Pasteur and Jonas Salk, not quiet woman naturalists. Carson's pleas for action resulted in a vast movement of testing, and even in banning useful chemicals, such as the insecticide DDT. That was a start, yet some didn't heed, and sprayed hundreds of tons of Agent Orange, a powerful plant killer, on the jungles draining to rice paddies in Vietnam. Human maladies four decades later are blamed on those biological-chemical attacks. Carson has been proven correct in many of her dire predictions, so dramatically and eloquently given. Let's not let our brilliant creations loose before we truly know them.

ONE WEEK'S WATER

At April's end, after almost three months of drought, the Ipswich River and its tributaries were feeling down. Light snows and rains had been few and far between; water tables were down; vernal pools were dangerously low for wood frog tadpoles and salamander larvae. Spring rains finally came on May second and third, providing the tri-town area with one and a half inches of water, enough to dampen the dry topsoil. On Tuesday, May ninth, dark clouds brought more. Vast, swirling water-laden air masses stalled over us and cold winds off the ocean kept us in periods of drizzle, alternating with heavy rain. By Wednesday morning two inches had fallen. Thursday was damp and cool; the new May leaves dripped onto wet soil. Friday evening, the rain resumed in earnest and left another inch overnight. Saturday, it intensified; by Sunday morning the Closet rain gauge showed another five inches. Sometime Saturday, the water table reached the soil surface;

saturated, it could take no more. Additional rain then flowed parallel with the ground, "runoff" as from impervious manmade surfaces, to low areas. These quickly filled and overflowed to fill our streams and river. More and more fell on Sunday; by early Monday about 14 inches had fallen since the previous Tuesday! All our water bodies were now full or overflowing. Their ultimate collector here, the Ipswich River, was a quarter mile wide in places and flowing fast. Monday evening it crested at the South Middleton USGS gauge where it had risen seven and a half feet in just one week, reaching a new high of eight and a half since regular recording began in 1938. Eight miles downriver at Thunder Bridge, just up from the Boxford/Middleton line, water flowing over a 200 yard front across East Street reached the second bridge rail, one and a half feet higher than the previous record flood on March 23, 2001. Our river and streams, usually scarce seen within their lush vegetation, had once again risen up and were giving notice. We strip the living skin of land, absorbing plants and topsoil, at our peril.

JUNE 2006

WONDROUS WATER

Is it any wonder that people have long thought water holy, sacred, a gift from gods and spirits? It falls from the skies, flows down pure from mountain heights, and gathers in great life-giving rivers; White Mountains give rise to the Merrimack, Rockies to the Missouri, Himalayas to the Ganges. Water starts its land journey clean and cold. Early folks, not knowing of atmospheric highs and lows or even distant lands and mountains, saw its comings and goings as truly magical. Our several-centuries-old knowledge of air and water currents and world geography have moved these phenomena from the realm of the magical to the truly wondrous. We use the expression, "The devils are in the details." Why couldn't it just as well be "Good spirits are in the details." Early this spring, Middleton teacher and Stream Teamer Sandy Rubchinuk took a vial of Ipswich River water to the sacred Hopi villages in Arizona. There, it was mixed with samples from the Colorado, Rio Grande and many other rivers. Runners carried this blessed mix to Mexico City 1,500 miles away. This "Run for Agua" ceremony was to dramatize its importance and protection. Now, playing in some theaters is the Indian movie *Water*. Alas, the movie is shown in the Hindu language, so it probably won't get the play it should. This story of a child-widow in the late '30s, when Gandhi was peacefully rising to power, unfolds on a broad, unnamed river. People in their daily rounds visit its banks to pray, bathe and meditate. Water from it is fetched to anoint the dying. Bodies are burned on pyres along its banks. Their ashes are launched upon it, accompanied by prayers. This film, enthusiastically recommended by a couple of Closeteers, is not about water, yet water is as important to every scene as is light. A minor character, a Hindu priest, simply explains to a troubled woman, "The river is alive." We, who anoint and baptize with, pray to and for, and sing of water, and who have understanding of meteorology and chemistry, also know that water is far more than just H-O-H.

WALLS TO WATER

Last week, three septuagenarians inspected a damaged dam on Prichards Pond in Middleton. Two Stream Teamers and pond co-owner Joan Prichard Cudhea, here on semi-annual visit from distant San Diego, boarded a tiny aluminum punt and rowed down the eight-or-so-acre pond to the 75-year-old dam. There, the Great Flood of May 2006 overwhelmed Boston Brook with runoff from North Andover, Boxford, and northern Middleton and flowed over and against its concrete wall. A southerly section of concrete about 30 feet long, one and one-half feet deep, and two feet wide broke away and is now lying just downstream, a reminder of the ultimate fate of all manmade dams from Hoover to the now-championed Three Gorges in China. The one-third-mile long pond is now one and one-half feet lower because of the loss, just the thickness of that added by Joan's late father Charles Prichard, Jr. to the dam built by his father to provide the family a lakeside summer retreat four generations ago. That much bank, so important to so many animals, is now exposed to air. Joan is hoping to repair the dam so the pond is as it was. The Prichards, in building the dam on a major tributary of the Ipswich River, created a fine pond/woodland ecosystem for more than just their children. It has long been a place for fishing and skating. Herons, ducks, muskrat, beavers, otters, mink, turtles, snakes and other creatures attracted to ponds frequent this undeveloped haven. Alas, dams are walls across stream and river habitats that are continuous for many animals along their lengths and beyond. Some species populations traveling them are isolated from winter and summer ranges. Anadromous fish are kept from their spawning grounds. This is an example of good works by humans brought into question. Prichard's Dam is just one of thousands built in the last three centuries here in New England. What is to be done? Repair, or let ice and time lay it low as when beavers were the only dam builders?

WASHING WATER

Usually, we think of washing with water. Let's look for a moment at washing water. Such an important substance certainly needs cleaning now and then. Since the beginning, this gift from the seas has scrubbed the skies of particles and gas molecules from volcanoes, dust storms and fires. Upon cooling, water laden with its burden falls upon land as rain and snow. There, it runs off vegetation, shingles, and pavement, into the ground. For new subdivisions, we design swales and detention ponds so runoff doesn't bypass the soil and go directly into water bodies. Soils are of rocks ranging in size from gravel to microscopic silt and clay. Incorporated with these are decaying plant debris. These are the dark topsoils ranging here from a half foot thick on dry uplands to three feet thick in wetlands. The parts we can't see, or don't notice, are the living bacteria, fungi and insects. There are millions of bacteria per teaspoon of healthy soil. These microorganisms, like us, need water and food. They absorb water and break down molecules carried for energy and growth. Methane, alcohols, pesticides, and herbicides and those of our wastes are largely digested to water and carbon dioxide. Boards of health and septic system engineers are well aware of these living filters. The latter design systems requiring sand with optimum surface area for bacterial populations. By the time the polluted rain or sewage has passed through countless layers with their microorganisms it is clean or nearly so. The oceans eventually receive it pretty much in the condition it left. Boxford, Middleton and Topsfield are covered with about 45,000 acres of this living filter. If we very roughly calculate the manmade leaching fields of these towns, without municipal sewage systems, we get the equivalent of about 300 football fields of vital filter/reactors. Healthy soils and leach fields, as with all living things, are always in jeopardy of being overloaded with food and poisons. Our stores, garages, workshops and bathrooms contain compounds that may sicken or do in the very filters that clean our cleaner. Frightening, misleading ads for disinfectants would have us kill them all.

Reviving Rivers

Last week a Closeteer and classmate of over 50 years ago explored the valleys of the Berkshire Mountains near where they had gone to school. The latter, now a semi-retired dairy farmer, was born in these foothills. They drove leisurely, as they do most everything now, up the Deerfield River and its tributaries. Pastures and hayfields once covered 80 percent of these mountains. The English cleared and let their livestock have most of the land, except for a few acres set aside for cultivation and woodlots. Down in the rivers, dams were built to power saws and grind grain. In a century, they'd tamed the land and streams, the latter often brown with silt and clay runoff from overgrazed fields. As young men, the old-timers had seen some remaining high fields; now, the mountainsides are heavily forested, only the best bottoms host a few surviving farms. The narrow roads following them are shaded. On shortcuts over the hills, there are few open views. There are still people, but their fields are reduced to lawns without calves and chickens. Now and then the roads abruptly turn across fast-running streams. The speckled bottoms of clean stones are quite like the beautiful speckles of trout backs, which have copied them through time. Despite recent rains, there was no sediment, the renewed soil and growth filtered well before it reached the flow, quite like 300 years ago when moccasined folks without devastating livestock and dams lightly walked these routes. There are still signs of dams; most have succumbed to floods and ice. It is nice to see recovering watersheds. We now understand what our well-meaning, struggling ancestors had done to them. Let's look further back and set aside vast areas to be owned by all, or, better still, by none, such as those Algonquian-speaking inhabitants knew. They didn't "set aside," but rather were a part. Now, there are many more of us; we have the benefit of lessons learned. We know what should be done.

Movie Review

Albert Gore Jr., senator, environmentalist, vice president, and twice—so far—would-be president, has a film out about global warming and Al Gore. *An Inconvenient Truth* is playing now in local theaters. This is an unusual movie in which Mr. Gore lectures, using slides, photographs and many graphs, to focus on the truths of increasing atmospheric CO_2, rising air and water temperatures, and waning glaciers and polar ice caps. With sincerity and enthusiasm, he does well summarizing the data scientists have gathered these past four decades, interlacing graphs with aerial, satellite and spacecraft photos. Alas, his director includes campaign footage of his star's boyhood on family Tennessee farm, family tragedies, and too many brisk purposeful walks through air terminals and arrivals before admiring crowds around the world. He has done this essential slide show before a thousand or so groups since his 1992 book *Earth in the Balance*. In the planes en route we are shown our hero deep in thought and study, laptop at the ready, as he contemplates the world's woes.

How sad that this long dedicated, obviously very bright public servant puts himself in the hands of PR people and directors. The Closeteers who recently saw this film recommend it because it is about water, ever more changing from solid to liquid, and a crisis that should, in their opinions, have priority over terrorism. If there is a connection between carbon dioxide increases and global warming, then we Americans are, more than any others, responsible and should want to be leading in efforts to reduce its effects. According to Mr. Gore and many others we are hardly even following. Go see for yourselves; 75 percent has a sound science base. Rest your eyes and ears during the emotional parts that have their place in campaigns but are questionable in what many would call a documentary. This movie is a strange hybrid. *The Boston Globe*, that other paper, gives it three stars. Without the fluff, we might give it three and a half; for importance, four.

JULY 2006

SOURCES TO SEA INVITATION

Summer is a good time to "go with the flow." Try the Ipswich River's lovely, long green corridor amongst civilization largely unseen and unheard. The river is still high from May and June's record rains. All you have to do is paddle enough to steer in current descending gently to the sea. The most calories you'll burn will be getting the canoe, kayak, or even tube in and out of the water and, now and then, over or around a fallen tree. It is all downhill on a liquid conveyor belt. Last week, a Closeteer and friend rode from the North Reading/Middleton line to Plum Island Sound in six leisurely, two-hour sessions. The only breaks were a 30-yard portage around Foote's Dam and a fifth-mile one around Sylvania Dam and flood-damaged Choate Bridge, both in downtown Ipswich. After each, they hid their battered old aluminum canoe in bushes. We'll skip their glowing accounts of the peaceful wonders of each section, except to say all are different. This report is to urge you out on the now-warm water to see for yourselves. In doing so you'll get a Masconomo view of our river basin. Its fluid highways through lush growth meander, unlike asphalt ones; if not for flow signs and sun you'd quickly become lost. The Native Americans followed the same routes as today's paddlers, only in birch bark and dugout canoes or along the banks by foot. Their summer villages and gardens were in the rich bottoms. Again, after 300 years, there are no livestock clearing down to the water's edge and wading. For those seeking exercise, go against the flow, the old-timers mentioned above did it for stretch from the Ipswich town landing to Route 1A so they could say they'd gone all the way. If you don't have their flexible schedules, go early in the morning or evening; you'll see more wildlife.

ROBBED RIVERS

The water cycle is wondrous in its effects. On its way through the soil and then back to the sea much water is absorbed by plants which clothe the land with food, fiber and beauty while taking in CO2 and giving off O2. During dry periods, the water table sinks slowly, only to be "recharged" when the rains return. Enter people, now seven-or-so billion, and their enterprises, who want more for their needy agriculture. In many areas they grow water-guzzling cash crops such as alfalfa and cotton, instead of traditional food crops. They tap water from rivers and pump from the earth, thus lowering the water table faster than rains can replenish. Then, they pump ever deeper until the cost becomes prohibitive. This is the story the world over in dryer regions where evaporation leaves behind trace amounts of minerals that, over the years, accumulate until the land becomes poisoned with salts. Millions of acres are lost each year due to such intensive irrigation. The people move on to crowded cities. Some great rivers are so affected they don't reach the sea; the once mighty Colorado and Rio Grande are examples. Dams and irrigation upriver have done them in; folks, especially in the lower reaches, look elsewhere for work. Water warehouses, mountain snow and ice caps, are the great providers at key times for floodplain agriculture. The most far-reaching example is the Himalayas, which provide melt water in season for India, Pakistan, Iran, China and several countries watered by the Mekong. Here, there are great warehouses on the high Rockies and Sierra Nevada the latter water California, one of the world's richest fruit and vegetable baskets. Environmentalist Al Gore and others show us that such ice warehouses are fast diminishing due to global warming. We recommend a recent book by water writer Fred Pearce, *When the Rivers Run Dry* , which is now making the rounds of the Closet. He describes the plight of desert rivers around the world. Our Ipswich River still reaches the sea, but in some months very feebly due to upriver withdrawals.

SALAMANDERS VERSUS SPECULATORS

Radiating out from the point where North Andover, Boxford and Middleton meet are about 4,000 undeveloped acres, thanks to Harold Parker and Boxford State Forests, substantial Boxford Land Trust and Essex County Greenbelt parcels, and rough terrain, vernal pools, swamps and streams. Beeline three miles northeast from the southerly loop of Boston Brook near School Street, Middleton, to Fish Brook in Boxford and you'll encounter no houses. Here, long-frozen igneous rock peeps forth as granite ledge through thin, new skin formed since the glacier flayed the prior one. From it grow oaks and huckleberries. The soil was a little thicker before the English and their hard-hoofed livestock stripped the vegetation, thus allowing the rains to carry much off. In low, wet areas, dark soils are several times the thickness of those above. These "mucks" have little oxygen, so the organic debris rots slowly and accumulates. Red maples, highbush blueberries, and a dozen other wetland plants dominate. These glacier-carved ups and downs are the varied habitats of myriad organisms; a big wildlife area that has horizontal depth larger mammals and certain birds need. In the loop of Boston Brook mentioned there is an area hatch-marked on the National Heritage and Endangered Species Program map for Middleton—each town has one—that shows the habitats of endangered plants and animals. This one has blue-spotted salamanders. Speculators have their eyes on substantial lots flanking protected Greenbelt land there. These "legal" owners never lived on or even spent time on them. One applied to the conservation commission to cross Boston Brook and was denied, in part because of the blue-spotted who have lived there for generations. They breed in the numerous vernal pools. Alas, the courts don't recognize their claim. Humans, who made the laws, have more clout as well as chainsaws and bulldozers. The denied would-be mansion builder is before the commission again with a new plan showing an access bridge just up stream from the first. Will he be allowed to clear the oaks, huckleberries and salamanders' soil? Woody Guthrie eloquently wrote: "This land is your land. This land is my land . . ." We in the Closet like to think he meant "your" to apply to all creatures. We certainly know he was for the little guy, spots and all.

WATER WARS

As everywhere else, the newest Mideast war has reached the Closet. The hodgepodge of names flowing through time come back from Sunday school lessons and news over the last half century. Canaan, Judah, Israel, Palestine, Israel again; Syria, Galilee, Nazareth, River Jordan, Jerusalem, Bethlehem, Dead Sea, and, of course, now-suffering Lebanon. We watch as the Holy Land again becomes a place of rockets and refugees. We, in the Closet, gather around a map, trying to put the images received in a water context. Mountains inland just a few miles from the Mediterranean parallel it from north to south. Moisture-laden air wafts in from the warm sea and ascends the Lebanese and Palestinian Mountains, the Golan Heights and the West Bank, and cools, condenses and falls as rain to recharge deep aquifers, or runs off back to the sea or to the Jordan River. Just east of the heights is a vast rain shadow like that formed by our Sierra Nevadas and Rockies where water is truly precious and much sought. The Israelis, who politically control the Golan Heights and West Bank, also ride herd on much of the water. Alas, amidst all the fighting we hear little of water as a root cause of these miseries. Ariel Sharon, then commander of Israeli forces, candidly said, "The Six-Day War really started on the day Israel decided to act against division of the Jordan [river] . . . While the border disputes were of great significance, the matter of water division was an issue of life and death." Diversions and interceptions of mountain runoff have resulted in pumping from aquifers along political borders. Sewage from settler villages is seeping into the underground water as its level drops. There is little water, so competition is intense. We, here in the Ipswich basin, have much more, yet even here strains of competition are being felt. Let's hope that water, the very basis of our existence, will in time bring us together to husband and to share. In the land Jesus and his fisher followers wandered let there be cooperation and the sky be a source of real treasure, not missiles. May the mountains be forever baptized with gentle rain. We think Christ and Mohammed would have had it so.

AUGUST 2006

WINGS OVER WATER

Imagine on this hot day a back country, winding road flanked by arching trees. Such green corridors are cool, or seemingly so. The other afternoon a group of Stream Teamers in kayaks and canoes paddled down the Ipswich in the shade of silver maples and swamp white oaks. Their smooth road was cool in the fine shade and contrasted nicely with the leaf-tossed light above. The paddlers' eyes were soon drawn to the many dragonflies and damselflies darting, scarce seen, hovering, and perching on twigs, protruding snags, gunnels, and even heads and arms. Voracious predators, one man counted 60 mosquitoes in the gut of a dragonfly; to us human visitors they were nothing but delight. No mosquitoes were seen or felt on the two-hour trip, thanks perhaps to them. The damselflies species seen, when alight their four wings vertically pressed back over long slender electric-blue and green abdomens, are a beautiful translucent black, daytime fireflies glowing in the filtered light; ballerinas on unseen floors of air. The heftier dragonflies hold their four wings plane-like when hovering or resting. These remarkable wings are variably pitched and can move independently of one another. Both have great compound eyes and short antennae; sight must be their thing. We were only enjoying the shorter aerial phase of their lives. They metamorphose from aquatic larvae, predators of the water where they swim and crawl about for months and even years. These long-lived larvae will be the topic of a future Closet. Here, we've gone on about the aesthetic pleasure these 250-million-year-old creatures give. They are much more, another reason for not spraying our two-centuries-old manmade chemicals. We may inadvertently kill the very predators of our target species. In wars, this is called "collateral damage," a phrase much in the news lately. Let's heed the old saying "Live and let live."

WATER WAYS

Our ways are of asphalt from oil—metamorphosed plant material, a million-plus years old. It is lain in strips on subsoil, courtesy of the Wisconsin glacier just 12,000 years ago, and on cut granite ledge that cooled 350 million years ago under three-mile-high volcanic mountains. In ways that better suit our human sense of time, let's leap forward to the written historical period here. The English came in ships 400 years ago and clung precariously to the coast for a century before moving slowly inland. They built rough cart paths town to town, yet water remained the main transport until the railroads came along in the mid-19th century. If you wanted to go from Salem to Andover, just 12 miles west, with goods, you'd sail around Cape Ann to the Merrimack and then up it on the tide. A trip to Portsmouth or Falmouth, Maine, by colonists was done by sailing "down east," rarely by the miserable roads. Folks knew more of Bristol, England, Amsterdam, and Lisbon than they did of towns just a few miles inland. Waters were the ways. The early shipbuilders from tree-starved England must have thought they were in heaven; here were large white oaks, the favored wood, growing right down near the shore. There were straight white pines, six feet in diameter and over 120 feet tall, along rivers and streams. Kings lusted after them for masts for their men-o'-war and had agents axe mark them with the king's broad arrow. These giants were not used for the smaller, local ships, but floated to England, sometime as great sailing rafts. How did they get enormous logs out of the woods and down to shipyards and seaports? At first they cut those along riverbanks and floated them down at ice-out in the spring. As they ventured deeper inland, oxen and horses hauled them to streams, which carried them onto rivers then down to Newburyport and lesser towns. Join us in the Closet next week and we'll travel up against the flow deep into the interior and the 19th century.

WHITE WATER WAYS

River Dance, the famed Irish group, has tapped furiously around the world for a decade now. They were long preceded in New England by little-known "River Rats" who jumped from log to log above icy whitewater roaring down from the deep woods. Those acrobats, many speaking French, were our spring cowboys riding herd on logs, not cattle, en route to downriver mills, saw and pulp, and waiting ships. Down the great tributaries of the Penobscot, Kennebec and Saint Johns those daredevils came on loose rafts of rolling wet logs and in rugged bateaus. Those double-ended work boats were their cow-ponies. The logs often went astray or stampeded through narrows where they formed great jams. No solid wooden stage of boards for these little-known performers, a misstep found them in frigid water between fast-moving timber. They were responsible for getting a long winter's harvest down to where it could be processed and used. This occurred ever deeper into the interior in the late 18th and 19th centuries and continued in Maine right up until 1978, when environmentalists got the legislature to ban drives on Maine waters because of the damage they did. An ever growing network of gravel roads and great trucks took over. One Closeteer and his young family were tenting at the convergence of the West Branch of the Penobscot and Abol Stream down from nearby Mt. Katahdin in the early summer of 1978. One morning, they watched as a bateau appeared on the fast flow. Several wiry men with poles stepped in and out of their vessel, pushing stray pulp logs out into the current from bank crannies where they'd gotten hung up. The campers learned later that they had witnessed the end of the last drive there. Water roads run log free again. Log-laden trucks roar down roads of gravel. Sedentary truck drivers have replaced the river dancers.

NAMES OVER WATERS

Several years ago, Middleton Stream Teamers decided to install name posts for the seven streams and river crossed over by town roads. It seemed a relatively simple task. Alas, their research found several major streams with two or more names, while one of note had none. After examining maps and plans, they chose. You've no doubt seen some of the 24 green signposts with vertical yellow lettering that resulted, e.g., Boston Br., Ipswich R. and so on. For the one without, the selectmen approved recommended "Flint Brook." While we like our signs, for some of us there is lingering discomfort, perhaps caused by the spirits of Native Americans who had other names. The English, with their Puritan baggage, incorrectly called the people in the area Agawam, and largely ignored native names. There are no Algonquian names, except Masconomo, left in the river basin that we could find. We do know their place names were descriptive and not after people. For example: Nashua signifies "beautiful stream with pebbly bottom." Merrimack roughly translates to "place of strong current." So, what were the native names here? Unless ghosts come forth and whisper to sympathetic souls, I guess we'll never know and must settle with the names of long-dead colonial farmers or English places. We were reminded of all this last week when a stalwart Stream Teamer and friend reversed the stream naming process and installed street name signs for Ipswich River paddlers at five bridge crossings, e.g., Boston,

South Main, Maple, Peabody and East Streets. There is one on each side so canoers and kayakers can tell whether they are coming or going. We thank them and recommend such naming to folks in neighboring towns, especially for bodies of water. If you can, try to do as we could not, and find some original names. When passing over or under here in Middleton we sometimes sense disturbed whispers on the breeze.

OIL AND WATER DON'T MIX

We in the Closet are obsessed with water. Is this admission what is called "coming out of the closet"? A greater concern by far should be our addiction to another liquid, one we share with many Americans. President Bush, hardly an environmentalist, recently admitted we are "addicted to oil." As president, shouldn't he now lead us to treatment centers on foot or bicycle? Perhaps it would be wiser and fairer not to wait for him, but rather admit to our dependence since hooked as teenagers and then fight to overcome. Even more than alcohol abuse, excessive gasoline usage hurts others far beyond our ken. The breakdown products of our drug poison the planet. Let's 'fess up to our problem. Isn't that what they do at AA meetings? Three weeks ago, a Closeteer and wife drove 90 miles oneway to a beautiful New Hampshire mountaintop where they picked 12 quarts of blueberries they didn't need. The same couple has twice meandered on blue highways across the country and back on vacations. Like many Americans, we drive long distances on frivolous trips, such as to L.L. Bean's, way "down Maine," to shop for things they'll mail or that are readily available here. We go nowhere at the drop of a hat, or just to buy a hat! Why? Because during the past three generations it has been easy; wages have been good, gasoline cheap. We complain about three dollars per gallon, yet this is half the world price. It will be tough kicking this lifelong habit. Which is the more important liquid in our lives, water or gasoline? It might be argued that we can't have a clean quantity of the essential one without using less of the other. Shopping, made easy by cars, is another addiction many admit to. Until we live more lightly on the land with less our environmental woes will continue.

SEPTEMBER 2006

WHERE FRESH AND SALT WATERS MEET

Every week or so, "red tides" permitting, an old Stream Teamer and friends drive to the mouth of the Ipswich River to dig clams from the same lowtide flats where squaws dug four centuries ago. There is record of a selectmen's meeting circa 1636 at which a group of them asked the town fathers to keep their clam-digging English hogs off the flats. The old-timer who told us this can't remember what, if anything, was done. Wide-ranging, prolific pigs were serious problems in the early colonies. Sorry, we digress; this week's Closet is about a place, not cloven-hoofed pests and clams. A place readily viewed from the heights of the Ipswich necks and Castle Hill, a wondrous one where fingers of ocean intertwine with those of land. Those of the ocean pull back and extend twice daily, allowing access to wide mud flats, low beaches, sandbars, and the bottoms of creeks interlacing the salt marshes, Whittier's "low green prairies of the sea." One Closeteer as a child played and swam within them most summer days. Here, salt water, chemically akin to our blood, intermingles with fresh from rivers off the land. The early explorers, Samuel de Champlain and John Smith for two, marveled at these estuarine mosaics of forests, beaches, dunes, marshes, fresh waters and fish-laden tides. Now the fish are far fewer, the squaws and their families gone without traces, and the once open, savannah-like uplands—due to controlled annual burns—are now forested or built upon. We can still paddle or take a short drive downriver and glimpse this once semi-wild Eden where fields of wild berries surrounded patches of corn, beans and squash within sight of the rivers and sea. Places vacationers now jet across oceans and continents to visit, our early forebears braved weeks of seasickness and starvation in leaky, wooden ships to come. They had one-way tickets.

WINGS OVER WATER

Gloucester again celebrated its famous fishing schooners on Labor Day weekend. The highlight of "Schooner Days" for Stream Teamers present was the parade of sail on beautiful Monday morning. A dozen so schooners, mostly yachts or museums/schools now, from up and down the East Coast, ranging in size from a 19-foot dory with schooner rig to Canada's 161-foot beauty, *Bluenose II*, tacked out of the harbor into a westerly breeze. In the 1800s and early 1900s, hundreds of working schooners, after which these descendants were modeled, sailed from here for fishing grounds as far away as Greenland. Only a century ago, wind was still a serious source of power. A Maine lighthouse keeper, circa 1900, kept count of coastal schooners, mostly three- to five-masted cargo ships. He tallied about 10,000 passings between March and November! The "coasters," unlike Gloucester's two-masted schooners, were the trailer trucks of trade along our coast, the Gulf Stream and Labrador Current their I-95 and Route 1. This lovely promenade prompted one Stream Teamer to wonder if sail wouldn't return as oil got scarcer and more expensive. A lively discussion followed about hollow alloy spars, new strong light fabrics, and decay-resistant synthetic lines that would replace wooden masts and yards, heavy short-lived canvas, and decay-prone manila rigging of yore. These are already used in modern yachts. Sails and spars with sensors could be controlled by computers to take advantage of variable winds. Auxiliary propulsion powered by batteries charged en route by solar panels, perhaps part of the sails themselves, could take over in shallow waters and ports. There are numerous stories from the days of sail about ships returning from long voyages only to tack sometimes for several days off Newburyport and Boston, waiting for a shift in the westerlies to allow entry. Imagine wind-powered cargo ships again, with neither greenhouse gases nor oil spills! The frosting would be the aesthetics of sail, air and water, again in concert. We hope our grandchildren will enjoy such symphonies.

WATER UPS AND DOWNS

Earth's fragile film, with water only about 10 miles thick on rough average, including the atmosphere, covers our 4,000-mile radius sphere of rock, which orbits the sun, as the moon does around it. These bodies' gravitational forces pulling on the water give us tides. So? Nothing so remarkable, you say; they have always done it, and it would be surprising, at least to physicists, if they didn't. "Wonderful" then might be the better word. We, near the sea, essentially have two coasts with continuous gradations in between. Twice daily, we can wander among rocky tide pools, on vast clam flats and far out across low beaches. When sun, earth, and moon or sun, moon, and earth are in line we can go farther out on lows and not so far on highs. When the moon, in its 28-day rounds, is perpendicular, the highs are lower and lows are higher; clammers and walking marine biologists have less range. We, here in New England, exult in our wild weather that makes life so interesting. How about our ever changing, yet remarkably predictable tides? One old Closeteer goes on about his boyhood in Salisbury. On summer days, children, free from chores and school, biked and walked, some several times a day, to the "dock," a place on the salt marsh of tidal "cricks," to swim and play. On the highs, the banks were full or overflowing with clean, cold ocean water. On the lows, the water was warmer and muddy where children stirred the crick bottoms. There was never a dull moment in that hourly changing place. Sometimes on the hotter days there might be a score of naked boys running crick to crick engaged in savage peat-mud throwing fights. As girls approached the marsh to swim, before emerging from the woods, they'd loudly yell "girls!" and the boys would race for their bathing suits or pants. The tides there still come and go. Children do so no longer. They are home in pools of tepid, chlorinated water.

WORTHY WATER WEEDS

Have you noticed in our three towns and beyond that many swamps and ponds are a brilliant green? Take a closer look and you'll find their emerald mantles are only skin-deep. What we are looking at is "duckweed," Lemna, and "watermeal," Wolffia, the tiniest of flowering plants. Scoop up a handful and you'll find each is a separate, or nearly so, flat-oval spot of green, ranging from pinhead-size watermeal to a couple millimeters, duckweed. The latter have one or several translucent hairs from the undersides that project down into the water, thus acting as unanchored roots and keels. Flowering is rare; most reproduction is by simple asexual budding. Buds grow out from these floating fronds and become separate, new plants. By midsummer and on into late fall there are great rafts of countless billions of these mini solar panels enriching the water with food and oxygen. Their photosynthetic products are high in protein and nucleic acids, e.g., DNA, and make excellent animal food. In some countries, they are skimmed and fed to livestock. If you really want to pry into the lives of these diminutive yet important plants, place a few in a glass dish or depression slide and examine under a microscope. You'll find, especially on the undersides, that they harbor a host of protozoa, algae and many other small creatures. Each cluster is a zoo of symbionts, organisms that live together. They provide surfaces, flotation, shelter, food and oxygen. These annual skins of quiet waters are truly alive and of great biological diversity! Some folk see them as invasive pollutants in their pools. Quite the contrary, they filter out pollutants, break them down, and are a rich source of nutrients for far more than ducks. Take a deep breath. Some of the oxygen molecules now working wonders in your cells are from these largely ignored plants that now brighten thousands of acres.

OCTOBER 2006

WATER TURNOVER

Look at our fall lakes and try for a moment not to be distracted by the dazzling colors along their shores; rather, send your mind into their depths. Bring a thermometer to measure temperatures from surface to bottom in the deepest part. You'll find the water cooling now in the upper few meters due to the daily lower sun, perhaps down to about 16 degrees C, by now. At some point in your descent, you'll find it quickly getting colder. Past this thermocline layer, it will be close to an uncomfortable five degrees C. This stratification, i.e. warm, changing, and cold layers, is very stable in the summer due to a wondrous property of water, which becomes steadily denser upon cooling, but only to a point, four degrees C, and then, with further cooling, it becomes less dense! So at freezing, zero degrees C, it is lighter and floats. Good thing. You wouldn't want to have to don scuba gear to go skating. At zero degrees C, water molecules bond into crystals, called ice. As the temperature in the epilimnion (G. epi = above, limne = pond) drops, the layers become unstable as temperatures top to bottom (and thus densities) become the same. Wind then influences, causing mixing. The oxygen produced by water plants and algae near the surface, where there is more light, is mixed throughout the water column; plankton animals needing oxygen thrive and reproduce despite reduced temperatures. In this turnover, nutrients from decay on the bottom rise to the surface, fertilizing the photosynthesizers and causing them to become active; animals eat them and each other. At a time of leaf death above, life within our lakes peaks! In the winter the water again becomes stratified the upper layer under four degrees C, ice or nearly so, is resting on the denser four degrees C hypolimnion. Ice prevents wind influences and mixing. Each spring, as the buds of the plants in the warming air above start to swell, there is another turnover. From the above information can you explain why?

WATERSHEDS COMPARED

A recent TV article proclaimed that about one-fifth to one-third of the world's fresh water daily enters the oceans from the Amazon. The Spanish and Portuguese explorers early on learned that, 200 miles out to sea from its mouth, the water was fresh enough to drink! Let's play with some numbers and compare with our Ipswich in an effort to appreciate the Amazon's size and importance. The former, straightened out, is about 40 miles long and drops 110 feet from its headwaters in Woburn to the sea. The Amazon descends 15,000 feet from the Andes to the Atlantic, 4,000 miles away. The Ipswich drains 155 square miles, the Amazon about 2,800,000. The rate of flow at the mouth of the Amazon ranges from four to seven million cubic feet per second (CFS). At the Willowdale dam gauge, the Ipswich averages about 200 CFS. There are thought to be 4,000 species of fish in the Amazon basin and about 25 in ours. We could go on, but as you can readily see there is no comparison; one drains 40 percent of a continent and the other half a county. One is important to a few million people, the other to eight billion plus. We've known for decades that the lush tropical jungles and marshes of the Amazon have great effects on CO_2, O_2 and water vapor in the atmosphere. World climates and weather are directly and continually related to what happens there. Leaders like to sagely say, "in our country's self interest," to justify their military and economic actions and threats. Here is a clear case of "self interest" for all nations. Ours now pours two billion dollars a week into the Tigris and Euphrates watershed, the "cradle of civilization." Wouldn't the money do far more for the self-interest of all if used to protect the threatened Amazon habitat, truly a cradle, rather than allowing its destruction to provide beef for our burgers, exotic hardwoods for our yachts, and coca and coffee for our addictions?

FIELDS ABOVE THE RIVER

Middleton's Friday morning Conservation Commission/Council on Aging-sponsored walking group recently hiked the lovely Topsfield loop around Ipswich River bottom from Trinity Church along River Road by Coolidge Estate to Salem Road under Wheaton's Hill, then up Rowley Hill Street into high country on Cross Street, once home of Meredith Farm's famous Ayrshires. The cows are gone; the fields that sustained them are still mowed or cultivated. From the heights the hardy old-timers descended to the river's wooded floodplain on Rowley Bridge Road. (Note the names—nothing fancy; roads were named by where they went.) It was mid-October and all around the dormant fields hardwoods were ablaze. Down along the river, swamp maples, their season having peaked in late September, were half dressed in fading reds. Here, the river sweeps in great curves from south of Masconomet to beyond the fairgrounds.

A few years ago a Closeteer brought in a century-old book entitled *The Physical Geography, Geology, Mineralogy, and Paleontology of Essex County* by John Henry Sears. Sprinkled among the rocky descriptions are poorly printed black-and-white snapshots of stone formations and glacier-carved topography. One shows a view from Ferncroft Heights of then-pastoral Topsfield and Boxford with trees few and far between. We walked a remnant of that scene, one of the last portions of open farmland with such panoramic views in the county. As agriculture faded westward after the Civil War the trees returned in most places. The river probably has a better plant buffer than at anytime since the English arrived four centuries ago. Imagine the sediment load the river must have carried in the days of overgrazed fields and hundreds of eroded cow paths right down to the channel. That silt and clay in suspension is gone. We now hope for the return of the anadromous alewives, shad, salmon and sturgeon, once so abundant. Alas, our rivers, small and large, were damned, not by gods, but by industrious, not always wise, Yankees.

NOVEMBER 2006

RIVERS JOIN AT SEA

Caleb was raised in nearby Groveland near the Merrimack River. When a teenager he joined the Rings Island Rowing Club at the river's mouth in Salisbury. As a young man he attended Maine Maritime Academy on Penobscot Bay. Meanwhile, in distant Pennsylvania's anthracite coal country in the valley of the mighty Susquehanna, Rebecca, daughter of a Navy man, grew into a spunky young woman. She, too, was called to the sea and signed as volunteer crew on a seaworthy replica of

H.M.S. Bounty built for the movie *Mutiny on the Bounty*, the version that starred Marlon Brando. Caleb, too, heard of the opportunity and applied for a berth. You can probably guess the rest. These young sailors, unlike mutineer Christian Fletcher and Captain William Bligh, hit it off. We like to think they first huddled and flirted in the lee of the main mast after a dangerous hour aloft reefing sail. That was three years ago; last week a Closeteer, member of Caleb's rowing club, and wife attended the formal splicing of these shipmates in a church overlooking the river of her girlhood.

We in this column have often gone on about the water cycle: sea to sky, sky to land, land to rivers, rivers to sea. Evolution from water to land over unimaginable time has also been marveled at here. We have seawater in our blood because our ancestors, if we go back far enough, were part of it. More recent forebears came in ships like the *Bounty* and even smaller. Our lives, even landlubbers, are immersed in water, one way or another. In the case of our romance-finding sailors, their rivers may have drawn them to Mother Sea. Reckless Christian and bold and able Bligh have no idea of the ripples down two centuries their unhappy separation has caused. It has resulted in many books, bringing together millions of moviegoers, and certainly the union of the newlyweds in our story.

YEAR'S WATER REVISITED

As the mid-October light of a clear day waned, Middleton Stream Teamers, friends and photographers gathered in the fine old upstairs meeting room of Memorial Hall. The low light through the west-facing windows fell on 42 pictures entered in the team's fourth annual photography contest. Winners had been selected several days before for this awards ceremony.

Scenes, restricted to Middleton's waters, could be submitted by people from Topsfield, Nigeria, anyplace. It was fun admiring each and trying to figure where it had been taken from and when. Most were somewhat familiar yet different because of light, season, camera angle and souls of the photographers.

Judy Schneider's second-place winner of the Ipswich River, chock full of water and 10 times wider than usual during the record flood of May 15th, vividly captures the mood and dynamics of that day. Pam

Hartman's third-place entry reminded us of winter with her starkly white-black-white view of Prichards Pond. Ice covers the northern third, softer snow-covered ice the southern side; both flank the seemingly deep black of the open channel. Above this cold scene the somber grays of naked hardwoods blend with the sky. Pam's first-place photo is of bright leaves, mostly red maple, floating on Pond Meadow Pond Brook, which carries water down from distant Boxford. Here, she has caught their last hurrah before they sink, decay and are recycled.

Many of the fine entries caught our eyes and might have been our selections as winners. We are thankful for independent judges. Each contestant had selected the scenes to shoot and their best one or two to share. Spread out on the long wooden tables they reminded us of our wonderful seasons and basic underlying water that makes them and us possible. The recorded light had passed not only through glass lenses, but the aqueous humor of eyes into the watery mysteries of the brain.

WOOING WATER WARNING

Soon, the siren songs of ice will again lure us to places we've wanted to explore, fish through, or play on.

John James Audubon, athlete, dancer, superb naturalist and artist, as a teen was skating fast down a Pennsylvania river in the lead of several companions. He went through an opening and disappeared for a bit, only to pop up, fortunately for the world, through another hole downriver.

In uplands, above the still, open waters of swamps, ponds and streams, soils are filling with rising groundwater. Soil particles lose heat more quickly than water to the cooling air. This cools the soil water and soon its molecules, without enough energy to maintain their independence, bond and stitch each other and the soil particles into rock. All fall the ground and turf have been forgiving to football players; one late November day they'll find it concrete hard.

As frost penetrates deeper into the soil, open waters remain liquid, except for thin surface coatings quickly whisked away by morning sun. It takes many days of below-freezing temperatures before ice will bear us. Flowing water has considerable energy and is slow to freeze. We see open water above the channels of our Ipswich and its tributaries even after long cold spells. Under our shallow ponds and swamps are springs and other places with decaying organic matter. Spring water oozes up from the earth at 55 degrees F and heat emanates from the respirations of bacteria and fungi, keeping the ice above thin. If you go in, body heat at 98.6 degrees F will be quickly conducted out to the 32 degrees F water.

Alas, the urge is strong to try, especially among boys and even foolish old men, as one Closeteer has admitted. He went through, chest deep, and could not crawl out on the breaking ice edges. An elm sapling, just barely reached, saved him. Adults are supposed to know better; the trouble with some old guys is they forget.

SOLAR CELLS IN THE SEA

Marine biologists have long known of algae large and small in our oceans and fresh waters. They have also greatly underestimated the degree to which they are present. In 1988 researcher Dr. Penny Chisholm of MIT and her team found in their ocean water samples very tiny chlorophyll-containing bacteria in enormous numbers. They were found to depths of 200 meters where only about 0.1 percent of the light entering the sea is left. Some samples had populations of as many as 20,000 per drop of seawater. These newly found cyanobacteria (the old name was blue-green algae), dubbed Prochlorococcus, are doing what the green leaves of giant redwoods and corn do: photosynthesis. Their chlorophyll molecules absorb light, which is the energy used in their cells to make food and oxygen gas from carbon dioxide and water. Dr. Chisholm and others estimate that these hard-to-see—except with the best of light microscopes—and little-known organisms carry on half the earth's photosynthesis! (A *Prochlorococcus* cell is about one-tenth the diameter of our red blood cells.) By the way, she might call the world "Ocean" rather than earth, since it covers three-fourths of its surface and carries on the vital function of our planet's CO2 and O2 balance.

So, the next time you are knocked down by a wave at the beach and come up sputtering, know you have probably taken in a few thousand Prochlorococcus. Don't worry; you've killed them with no harm to self. A liter of seawater might contain up to 100 million of these minute solar-powered food factories. However, they are more than factories;

they reproduce themselves by simply dividing when conditions are right.

For decades now, we've known of the essential importance of our oceans. Chisholm's discovery and subsequent work have increased this realization many fold. Yet, around the world we continue to use our seemingly limitless oceans as dumps.

Water Calls

The other day, after substantial rain, a Closeteer descending Wills Hill passed two little girls kneeling, heads together, over a streamlet on the edge of the street. They were happily manipulating water on its way to the distant sea. Dams and side channels were being made; sticks were launched.

The Closeteer and friend just up the hill have cars so their quests to be near water are broader. Every couple weeks they drive downriver, the route the girls' water takes, to the low tide flats where they dig clams and rake oysters. These ancient, easily gathered animals are their excuses to be among creeks, marsh and sea. This urge, deeper than hunger or need for mollusk flesh, is so strong they go throughout the year, rain or shine, hot and buggy, windy and cold.

Millions 'round the world flock to rivers, lakes and ocean edges each year, some say, "to get away." We suspect it may be something deeper in the DNA, signaling "return to where your fish ancestors began." We each started life in a sac of warm salt water; our ancestors evolved in seas of such, the amniotic sacs of evolution. Throw in unimaginable stretches of time, and the great diversity of life forms arising from the world's waters can, with difficulty, be imagined.

The girls were playing as we all did as children. Soon, as teenagers, they'll be frolicking and courting on lake shores and ocean beaches. We old-timers, who no longer admit to playing, will be making up excuses like going fishing and clamming. However, when no one is watching we, too, wade through puddles and, with boot or stick, make little dams and sluiceways. And then, who can forget Gene Kelly in the throes of love, splashing in and out of flowing gutters while singing and dancing in the rain? It's in the genes.

DECEMBER 2006

WATER, SOLID TO LIQUID

On December 1, there was no frost in or on the ground, just some speculations in the forecasts; the temperature all day was over 60 degrees F! In the Closet, we huddled around the computer screen in an effort to keep cold. Friend, prize-winning photographer Pam Hartman, had just sent us, via the Internet, beautiful shots from Churchill, Manitoba, of polar bears on ice.

Hudson Bay is freezing over; soon, these great white beauties will venture forth on the sea ice as they have done for thousands of years to stalk and kill seals. The problem in some areas, not for the bears of Churchill Pam reports, is that the ice on average comes later and thinner each fall as the planet warms and its total ice volume diminishes. That in refrigerators and freezers has, no doubt, greatly increased in the past few decades; however, we are talking caps here, not cubes. The Arctic's, Greenland's and Antarctic's caps are melting more than they are adding. Photos from space of their too-rapid decline are alarming. We are glad the bears don't watch TV or Al Gore's movie *An Inconvenient Truth.*

While Pam was taking her photos, the United States Supreme Court was hearing arguments from Massachusetts' lawyers who want to sue the Environmental Protection Agency for not doing its duty in regulating vehicle emissions. One of their strongest arguments, in the opinion of many, is the many miles of Massachusetts coastline vulnerable to sea rise from ice melt caused by global warming. Responses from half the justices for taking the case so far have been cool. The EPA is desperately training seals to sign; environmental groups are doing the same with polar bears. The hope is that they'll testify as friends of the court. The film stars of Churchill can't bear the thought of diminishing ice. They fear it will seal their fate.

WATER, WARMTH AND LIFE

Lately, we've learned that there is life in seemingly lifeless rock. We've long known that rock contains some water, even to great depths. Miners, dependent upon pumps, are well aware of this. Deep in the diamond mines of South Africa, where our planet's inner heat is wetly felt, continuous pumping and ventilation are required. Some primitive bacteria can reproduce in temperatures close to boiling. We have but to look at the abundant microbial flora in the very hot springs of Yellowstone to appreciate this. We further know that more than just surface soils and shallow waters are inhabited. Here, a couple weeks ago, we reported that there are up to 20,000 cyanobacteria per drop of seawater. Estimates of bacteria in fertile topsoil are 10 billion cells per gram, truly a living mix! And now we have evidence that microscopic life continues on down between particles and in cracks of rock to depths of two miles, wherever there is water and it is not excessively hot.

Biologists find this new knowledge comforting. If the earth's surface species are wiped out by nuclear warfare's fire and radiation or by the collisions of asteroids, deep life forms with water-based cells of proteins and nucleic acids (RNA, DNA), as ours are, will survive. In time—millions of years—these might, through evolution, give rise to novel organisms. Why not? It has happened here before.

We live in a thin layer of the universe where there is water and the temperatures are right for life. On a line drawn from the earth's center outward into space, life is only found from about two to seven miles below the surface, through five miles of atmosphere above, roughly one four-hundredths earth's radius, and then nothing, perhaps, forever. It is the only such place we know of. This fragile film of life, three billion years in the forming, already shows signs of fraying due to our actions. We tamper with it at our peril. Now that we understand, let's not rend it further.

WHERE WATER AND LAND INTERTWINE

Often these last two years here in the Closet, we've marveled at our lower river's estuary where ocean and lowlands merge. Twice daily, cold plankton-laden seawater fills the creeks and twice, monthly, on new and full moons, rises over the salt marshes. Marshes, banks, flats and channels and their clams, oysters, mussels and scores of smaller species are fed and provided oxygen on each flood tide. Cold water holds more dissolved oxygen. Wastes, gill-clogging clay particles, carbon dioxide, and infusions of fresh water with nutrients from streams and rivers are gently flushed out to sea on the ebb. Animals, such as oysters on the creek bottoms and flats, are fed and cleansed by this flow and ebb. In each tidal cycle of 25 hours, they experience two periods of colder saltier water and two lows of brackish, almost fresh water. Bivalves live out their long, sedentary lives filtering out plankton in habitats of constantly shifting variables.

Last week, bearing three bushels of Ipswich oyster shells, two Closeteers and friend drove to Jackson Estuarine Laboratory, University of New Hampshire, a good day's sail up the coast to Great Bay in the Piscataqua River estuary. The car took one hour. The lab had put out a call for shells to provide substrate for the young oysters they raise by the millions through their early vulnerable stages. Oyster larvae, for the first few weeks after conception, drift with the currents as plankton. Then, they metamorphose into tiny "spat" that attach to almost any hard surface, including other oysters on the bottom. There, they remain perhaps for as long as 80 years if the Closeteers and other "rakers" don't get them.

In a future Closet we'll revisit oysters, perhaps at spawning time in July and August when they are safe from humans, and tell more of their life cycle and of the important research at Jackson Lab. Today, we just wanted to once again hail the wonders of the daily intertwinings that connect us with the ocean, oysters and estuaries along the coast.

Rising Water

At the mouth of the Ipswich, Parker and Merrimack Rivers lie vast, flat salt marshes, Whittier's "low green prairies of the sea," at the same elevation as mean high water. The gravities of distant moon and sun, using earth's water, sculpt our estuaries with their tides. These marshes have been forming for about 3,000 years, no time at all geologically speaking. As the sea level has slowly risen the marsh surface has thickened apace by grass-trapped sediments. Geologists tell us that if the water was to rise a little faster the marshes would drown; their stabilizing salt grasses would soon die. The twice-daily tides would then erode the accumulated soft peat and sediment away. On the other hand if the sea subsided, the salt species could not compete and would soon be replaced by upland plants. With global warming due to slow natural and now faster manmade changes, it looks like their fate might be the former. Lowlands on the continents' margins will be immersed. Katrina reminded us of just how low the delta marshes and floodplains of the lower Mississippi are. The whole of south Florida, except where man has built up, is only several feet above mean high tide. Here nor'easters, combined with full or new moon high tides, cover the salt marshes a foot or more. At such times look north from Castle Hill above Cranes Beach across the Ipswich River and you'll see what appears to be a great bay all the way to the Merrimack flanked by the dunes of Plum Island to the east and the low hills of Ipswich, Rowley and Newbury to the west. The next time the weather woman warns of coastal flooding when high tides and east winds are due to coincide, go see this preview of possible permanent coming attractions for yourself.

2007

January 2007

Precipitation 2006 and Before

Since precipitation in the year 2006 set new single month and annual records, we thought we should take a look back to see how the year just past compares with the record books. The latter have been painstakingly built each day by the Danvers Water Department for the Middleton Pond site used for Closet precipitation data and for monthly reports to the U.S. Weather Service going back to 1926. With the aid of Don Bancroft, Filtration Plant Manager, we looked at data back 62 years to 1944.

The records show 2006 with the highest annual precipitation of 62.82 inches in the entire period; the next five highest years (ranging from 53.27 inches to 59.89 inches) occurred in 1972, 1983, 1996, 2004 and 2005; all in the later part of the period. The lowest annual rainfall in the period was 25.63 inches in 1965. Our great flood, cresting on May 15, 2006, and producing the highest local flood levels on record, was associated with the highest single month rainfall of 17.26 inches in the entire period.

We looked for an indication of long-term precipitation trend in the six-decade record by comparing 30-year overlapping precipitation intervals and found averages have increased about 10 percent in the 30 years since 1976:

- 2006 to 1977 Average annual rainfall 46.53 inches
- 1996 to 1967 Average annual rainfall 45.25 inches
- 1986 to 1957 Average annual rainfall 43.14 inches
- 1976 to 1947 Average annual rainfall 42.20 inches

In a subsequent Closet we will take a similar look at the USGS mean annual river flow data over the same period and its correlation with annual rainfall.

If this strange non-seasonable weather keeps up, as it has since October, we anticipate new winter high temperature/low snow records may be established.

Let us hope that salamanders and buds aren't fatally fooled. Dances calling for cold and snow are being conducted nightly around the Closet.

SNOW AND ICE

Closeteers read somewhere that the Inuit in northern Canada have 28 words for snow, depending on its characteristics. Now that ice is finally part of our winter, we might go out and see how many types we can find. Cross-country skiers have a dozen waxes for various snow conditions. We've long used adjectives like fluffy, slushy, granular, crusty and black to describe forms of ice and snow.

Stream Team photographer Bob Lemoine returned from a very cold winter's hike a couple winters ago with fine pictures of ice as decorative fringe hanging from plates of surface ice along the edges of fast-moving Boston Brook. Hundreds of tiny icicles, transparent stalactites, hung above the dark water just below where the water surface had fallen away from its ice. On warmer afternoons, trickles from the snowmelt above, along with nightly cold, crocheted these curtains seen sparkling in the morning sun. Next time you walk along our winter brooks and river, look closely and you'll see ice in a spectrum of guises. We can look forward to wondrous mornings after, when the icy coats of a trillion twigs catch the rising sun, their dazzle hard to take. Gentle storms of dry snow will give us fluff-covered worlds that, chameleon-like, reflect the sky moods above. Between these marvels will be periods of slush and mud to make us appreciate the gifts of fresh storms even more. Then, every generation or so will come the great one that leaves us quietly stranded for a week, despite our powerful plows. The late local bard John Greenleaf Whittier left us his childhood storm in *Snow Bound*, perhaps the best of his many poems. In the Closet we harken back to "The Blizzard of '78" when over three feet of snow slowed the rat race here for a whole week. We even found ourselves and neighbors walking!

Snowbirds, down there in your semi-tropic daily doldrums, watch TV weather and eat your hearts out!

February 2007

Waterlines

During the torrential rains last May we forlornly huddled around the Closet stove and cast occasional glances out the window at the rising Ipswich River. Someone put on a Johnny Cash record and we listened to his famous question, "How high's the water, Mama?" over and over. A somewhat related question, "Where is the river's edge?," has been asked over and over around the state ever since Governor Bill Weld dove into the Charles River back in 1996 after signing the Rivers Protection Act, which significantly restricts work within 200 feet of rivers and perennial streams. It would seem intuitively obvious to any rational being that the edge is where the swimmer enters or leaves the water. Ahh, but the Act, a law, must define so people know where to measure the 200 feet from. In the Great Flood of May 2006, the Ipswich River, where the tri-towns join, just south of Masconomet, was 1,700 feet wide; in September, it was 50.

Two weeks ago, the Middleton conservation agent, an engineer and a wetland specialist representing a developer, and river expert Heidi Davis from Massachusetts DEP walked along the Ipswich River, south of Peabody Street, to determine the river's edge. Alas, there were two being described. The developer's representatives had the edge along the bank of the main channel, where most folks would say it is. The conservation commissioners had said "no" at a hearing, insisting it was much further out and up at the mean annual high water level. The distance between the two determinations ranges from 10 to 150 feet along 1,500 feet of river, very significant differences to both sides. Ms. Davis, DEP's lady Solomon, listened patiently with little comment to the arguments of both sides as she looked for signs that met the regulations' criteria. Now and then she'd tie a piece of pink surveyors' ribbon around a tree or bush. She was considering signs of erosion, sedimentation, vegetation present and topography. Her newly flagged line was being ruled the edge.

Young Cash, remembering a childhood flood, didn't get all this attention and double talk from his mother who answered, "Well, its five high and risin'." The commissioners and developer's folks might well have sung this at the site during the May flood, the commissioners singing high, the developers low, with maestro Davis striving for some harmony between.

WAILS UPON THE WATER

Fishermen Sean Cone and Dave Miller, two young fishermen lost recently when their vessel, *Lucky Lady*, went down last month off Cape Elizabeth, were said by family and friends to have loved the ocean. Many love the ocean especially from its edges, yet how many will venture forth in small ships in mid-winter to engage in commercial fishing, a most dangerous occupation? Engine and body heat and souls were immersed in 40 degree F seawater and quickly became one with the sea.

While poring over a chart of the Gulf of Maine, Closeteers discussing the loss noticed Boon Island off Kittery, about 50 miles south-southwest of the Cape, and were reminded of the famous story of the *Nottingham Galley.* On a stormy December night in 1710, en route Boston from England, she, blown well off course, slammed into a protruding acre of ledge, later dubbed Boon Island. Captain John Deane, passengers, and crew of the tiny ship scrambled in darkness off the broken hull and rigging onto the spray-drenched rocks. Deane and 10 of 14 survived their continuously wet, month-long struggle there and left a story well worth reading. Kenneth Roberts, in his overly dramatic historical novel *Boon Island,* greatly expanded on Deane's straightforward report, "A Narrative of the Ship-Wreck of the Nottingham Galley." We recommend the latter and first mate Langham's contrary account and leave it to you to do as Roberts did, to the degree imagination takes you. As we recount the tale around the Closet stove we find ourselves unconsciously wrapping arms around our chests and shivering.

We know the *Nottingham Galley*'s story, yet may never know the *Lucky Lady*'s. Some of us like to think, despite 14 generations of separation, that Cone, Miller, and Captain Deane are kindred souls. The sea was their livelihood and no doubt much more. They dared the winter waters, returning to the place, if we go back far enough, we all came from.

WALKING ON WATER

Just seven months ago this shallow, beaver-inundated swamp appeared black; the bottom beneath the transparent water took the light. The surface was laced with the emerald greens of duckweed and watermeal, the smallest of flowering plants. Bass bullfrog choruses filled the warm air.

On a recent afternoon under a clear, cold sky, Closeteers and friends visited the same latitude and longitude, yet found a very different world of foot-thick ice frosted with thin snow. Beavers had built a large dam down drainage on Pond Meadow Pond Brook that backed the water up over 100 acres, almost to the point where North Andover, Boxford and Middleton join. That was eight years ago, and now the few white pines and many water-loving red maples and Atlantic white cedars are dead. The maples and cedars like water, but not all year 'round. Their gray copses stand starkly above the ice. Several springs ago, Great Blue Herons found the needleless white pine branches and built nests high up upon them. Each year since there are more nests; previous ones have gained new layers of sticks. Against the light blue winter sky they appear as dark starbursts. There are now a score or more that remind of desolate summer cottages awaiting their season. It won't be long now; the first herons will arrive in late March. At times, after the young hatch, this becomes a lively, noisy place. Last week, it was silent except for an arctic west wind strumming the dead cedars. There were thousands of deer, fisher, coyote, fox, and otter tracks criss crossing the thin snow. We walkers, a talkative group, saw none; their time comes when the sun goes down.

We wondered, as we wandered o'er the ice, if beavers don't sometimes climb nearby knolls and marvel, as we do from hills above our farms, at the changes wrought by their dam husbandry. Do they consciously seek to "dominate" the land as Genesis would have us do? We do know that they will, like the Indians they once shared the land with here and who rotated their garden patches every few years, move on.

MARCH 2007

RAIN FOREST RESPIRING

Candice Millard's new book *The River of Doubt* exudes water, cover to cover. The reader, like the people and forest this story is about, never feels dry. Theodore and Kermit Roosevelt, marvelous Brazilian Candido Ronlon, and the men of their exploring party, have us suffering in sympathy as they descend a tributary of the Amazon in rough dugout canoes. For 300 miles they had no idea what the next mile would bring. Millard, who has done her homework and more, writes beautifully and in honest prose gives us the best description of the rainforest some of us Closeteers have encountered. We've long heard of TR endeavors as brilliant student, cowboy, naturalist, boxer, policeman, warrior, fine writer, governor, and activist president. Now, we can include explorer. Many in Cuba and the Philippines might add imperialist to this list.

Millard truly brings alive the pristine forest the men traveled through. She tells of its "breathing" exhaling water vapor by evaporation-transpiration from millions of billions of leaves until the air above is saturated. Evaporation of liquid to gas absorbs heat and cools the air around the leaves just as it does our skin when we leave the shower. This cooling lowers the temperature of the air above the lush forests until the dew point is reached, resulting in condensation and released heat coming back as rain in warm air. The adventurers and their surroundings were never dry, despite the high temperatures.

We'll not say more of this fine account of a terrible adventure, except to highly recommend.

The Amazon basin, absorber of much of the world's carbon dioxide and producer of much of its oxygen gas, has been explored and exploited too much. Many wise men and women now know that this vast area the size of the United States greatly affects world climate. Naturalists for decades have realized that perhaps most of the planet's species reside there. Let's proceed slowly, or even retreat, before we reach a point of no return.

MOOSE TALE

A story comes down from the very top of Maine, where the second language of moose is French. Brothers Jacques and Gaston Leroux of Escourt Station still log the old way, with teams of horses. Three years ago, a cow moose started hanging out with the off-duty horses. Soon, she bore a bull calf; no, it wasn't a hoose as some of you might suspect, but a purebred moose. The Leroux took him under their wings: groomed, fed, and, after a year, tried harness on him. He took to it and followed the teams to work. Gradually, and gently, they had him twitching out logs. This third-hand story includes a photo of a bull moose in harness.

This yarn of the largest wild aquatic mammal in New England besides whales prompted a great deal of discussion in the Closet. We swapped stories of sightings reported and signs seen here. A decade or so ago, while hiking on the ice of a beaver-flooded swamp below Stearns Pond in North Andover, we found the impressive incisor scrapes of bull moose on two red maples four feet above the ice. When made in the fall, the moose must have been wading and reaching up seven feet. In 2003, a pile of moose scat was found in the woods north of Peabody Street, Middleton, where a mansion is now. Last summer, in northern Maine, a Closeteer watched one grazing on wild salads in a beautiful flower-flanked stream. It had head under water much of the 20 minutes watched. We read that they will swim up to 12 miles, crossing large lakes. Anxiously, we await the arrival of more here to liven things up and to take advantage of the thousands of acres of wetland we have in the tri-towns. We wonder if some might fraternize with Richardsons' cows or folks' riding horses.

Whether the tale passed on is true or false, we bet moose parents are warning their calves and yearlings to stay away from horses and loggers at the risk of ending up in harness.

SPRING MELTDOWN

The northern half of earth recently started bowing in obeisance to the sun. Our star's radiant energy now shines more directly on the ice that formed the previous months. The heated molecules vibrate faster; ice crystals crack. Ice, in a word "melts" and flows as liquid water! Proteins, amino acids, carbohydrates, fats and salts of once-dormant cells interact in their liquid matrix, allowing the cells to feed, breathe and reproduce.

Even in transparent waters there are millions of bacteria per teaspoon that carry out all life's activities, including death, thus producing food, oxygen, carbon dioxide, etc. for themselves and for larger animals and plants. Our ponds, vernal pools, puddles, streams and swamps truly become alive. They were idling; now, with heat, their lives shift into high gear.

And in the recently frozen topsoil, unseen in the crannies between clay, silt and sand particles, water is also released. Microorganisms, as the moist soil warms, become active and provide for worms, insects, roots and seeds. A soil expert might easily stretch this rough list to one of several pages. The soils we so carelessly take for granted and douse with chemicals are alive! Charles Darwin and others who looked at them carefully guessed this was so because of all the larger organisms they could see. Alas, they didn't then know much about bacteria. In all of recorded history, about 10,000 years, we have only been aware of bacteria and viruses for the last 150.

We now know they are almost everywhere, in unimaginable numbers, wherever there is water and some heat. Most of the many thousands of species are beneficial, even essential, to our ecosystems. The late, great Rachel Carson, poetic naturalist, who gave us *The Sea Around Us*, angrily, yet effectively in her book *Silent Spring*, warned us that we spread manmade chemicals amongst waters and organisms at their peril and ours. The TV ads we are bombarded with hustling unnecessary disinfectants must have her soul wailing in the wind she so tried to protect.

APRIL 2007

SERIOUS SPRING BREAKS

There is a new black structure in Middleton that is 1,700 feet long and two feet high. What can it be? It is a fence of plastic cloth imbedded in woodland topsoil. Every 20 or so feet wooden stakes hold it perpendicular to the ground. Is it art, a smaller version of Christo's 24-mile, 18-foot-high "Running Fence" that ran from the open California highlands to the Pacific? Here are more hints. Every 50 feet along the fence are two five-gallon plastic buckets, one on each side, embedded to their lips in the ground. Such a fence is only built to stand in the latter half of March and first half of April. Give up? Enough teasing; it is an expensive trap designed to catch adult salamanders en route to their trysting pools.

You might ask what sadistic joker would raise this barrier to such harmless creatures at this critical time; after all, the hormone-driven participants have no other in the year. Each morning naturalists doing the study go out and lift the animals from the buckets and put them on the opposite side of the fence so, come evening, they may continue on their way. In this case, a developer wants to build houses on 20 acres he owns in possible "listed" species habitat. The National Heritage and Endangered Species Program of the Massachusetts Division of Fisheries and Wildlife has requested this study because blue-spotted salamanders have been found in the area; on the list, they are of "special concern," thus giving their habitat some protection.

After two weeks of checking, counting and releasing each morning the naturalists conducting this breeding migration study have found a few dozen blue-spotted as well two to three times as many common yellow-spotted salamanders. This proves they live where houses, driveways, septic systems and road are planned. Who will win this contest with manmade rules for habitat, the ancient amphibians who must return to water to reproduce, or us advanced mammals, relative newcomers, who needn't leave our beds? Some of us will hail a salamander victory here as one for us all.

Ups and Downs

The other evening, two Closeteers and friend searched along the lower Ipswich River for Jenning's flat. We arrived too early, before low tide. This plus a brisk east wind was keeping the flats covered. Old-timers with plenty of time, we visited Little Neck, Great Neck and Pavilion Beach. From the beach we admired a long line of "Oldsquaws" stretched along the channel of Plum Island Sound. These small ducks, to be politically correct, are now called Long-tailed Ducks. As kids, we were told by men that the old name was from the reputation women had for incomprehensible chatter. Perhaps the Indians and English who took up the name didn't realize that both males and females are vocal. Their songs, not quacks, in quiet weather often fill a bay with not unpleasant sounds. Anyway, we stick with the Algonquian name from old habit.

This story started with the subject of tide, a twice-daily wave that allows us access to a wide strip of beach, tide pools and flats, where mollusks, worms and birds abound. We, ostensibly after oysters, soft-shelled clams, and now and then on low lows sea clams, really visit because it is a marvelous place where sea, beach, river, and salt marsh intermingle with the pulls of sun and moon causing low water waves with 12,000-mile wave lengths that rise and fall as our planet spins. The crest of these waves, upon approaching the coast at 1,000 miles per hour, encounters the shallows and increases in height as much as 11 feet above the low of the wave's trough, arriving about six hours later. The lows allow clammers a few hours to revert to hunter-gatherers.

A trip down to the estuaries several hours later finds full bays and creeks; another crest has come. Commercial clammers on long days will sometimes work two lows. We older gatherers only do one and miss the following while happily eating our passive prey and harkening back to our recent visit to the place where squaws once dug with sticks.

Thoughts at Ice-Out

As winter too slowly wanes, thoughts strangely turn to ice. Stream Teamers with a summer place way up north in New Sweden, Maine, recently received a report that the ice on their lake is three feet thick. Another who ice fishes on nearby Putnamville Reservoir, Danvers, says he had to drill through 17 inches of ice there last month. Older members remember the tail end of the great ice industry here that they caught glimpses of as small children. In those days icemen peddled their cold product door to door in summer. On the tailgates of their trucks, with ice picks, they'd make lines of holes in great transparent blocks and then split off kitchen-icebox-sized chunks. Shards of ice that would fall from these breaks were quickly snatched by waiting kids. Generous icemen would purposely cut a few small pieces for their fans. How quaint this must all seem to folks with freezers and cube makers. A couple of us can recall the late winter cutting on local ponds. Men scored lines on the surfaces and would then with great saws cut perfect rectangular blocks that were floated in open channels and pushed with poles to a conveyor belt that lifted them up into large double-walled, pondside wooden icehouses, insulated with sawdust. Those of us who still cut firewood in the winter will sometimes find patches of ice buried under sawdust near our sawhorses in June and beyond.

Before refrigeration, ice from New England lakes and ponds was shipped far and wide in schooners from ports all along our coast. It was packed in sawdust in the holds. From Richmond to Rio, restaurants and bars preserved food and chilled drinks with it.

When a kilogram of water freezes 80 kcal (1 kcal = 1 food calorie) of heat energy is lost from it. When that kilogram of ice melts 80 kcal is taken in from the surrounding air and food, which is thus cooled.

Don't you love the idea of a cold Yankee product cooling Rebel punch 300 leagues away? The ice ships would then return laden with molasses, cotton or southern yellow pine. Cool!

A Western River's Tale

The Closet essays are often of rivers, usually our much beloved Ipswich. This week's is about a boy who grew up where two great western Massachusetts rivers converge, the feisty Miller's and the mighty Connecticut. His town was Millers Falls, where falling water once powered the famous tool factory of that name. The boy's unusual nickname arose from this mix of man and water. Here is his true story as remembered by a classmate.

David becomes Hacksaw

The Miller's was covered with skin of ice
Bridge road above was paved with snow.
A truck from factory slipped and tipped
Boxes of tools slid to river below.
The ice, for rescuers, not thick
Drew crowd to puzzle of their fate.
The Village Wizard David heard
Sensed his Goliath near at hand.
Boldly he descended on the scene
His sling a battery, stout wire.
The lad stood on the bridge above his prey
Open mouthed the peasants watched.
Slowly, slowly, magnet swung 'ere down
Until it nudged a hacksaw case
Which hero and helpers pulled ashore
The people roared, not "David"! "David"!
"Hacksaw! Hacksaw!" their clever cry
They knew a thing or two of tools.
That's how David in tender years
Lost Bible name to fickle fame.
Old now he's back to Dave and David
His old friends on Hacksaw do insist
We've long loved the legend dearly
Though our batteries corrode, and wires rust.

David "Hacksaw" Beaubien, inventor, electrical engineer, pied piper to his classmates, and much, much more, and, by the way, a friend of the Water Closet, died last week at the age of 73. His funeral mass will be tomorrow morning in Turners Falls, just a couple miles downriver from the site of his early triumph.

MAY 2007

RIVER RITE

In the Boston area we hail the Patriot's Day marathon as a rite of spring. On our Ipswich River there is another that for 62 years has been faithfully followed by Middleton's Francis "Frank" Masse. His mother, the late Rita Huntoon Masse, remembered spring family canoe trips down the river, sometimes all the way to Plum Island, since her teenage years. Frank recalls his first with family at the age of 16. In later years he kept the Patriot's Day tradition going with friends.

Two Saturday mornings ago, a beautiful warm day, his 2007 group of eight in four canoes got underway from Farnsworth Landing off Route 114. The voyage had barely begun on unusually high water under the 114 Bridge, when there was a surprise complete immersion baptism. A steel snag, projecting down from the bridge girders above, caused the crew of one canoe in the fast-flowing current to duck. The starboard rail rolled under and gave their life jackets our wise leader insisted all wear a good test in the still cold water. The two men, far too old to be swimming in April, did so and were soon safely ashore. Their gear and canoe were recovered and within half an hour the journey resumed. For such never really unexpected events, Frank had brought waterproof bags of dry clothing. He remembers past spills in freezing water when there was still snow on the banks.

We could go on about this and other trips on the beautiful Ipswich River we in the tri-town area are lucky to live near. At Thunder Bridge take-out, while loading the canoes that somehow seem heavier each year, we septuagenarians marveled at how privileged we were to have experienced the sights and sounds enjoyed by five generations or more of Huntoons, Masses, and no doubt, many other groups from Wilmington to the sea. We were reminded of Tevye in *Fiddler on the Roof* as he, with great gusto, sang "Tradition! Tradition!" We, tired, old paddlers understood.

WATER SOUNDS

We often tell each other while on the fly in this fast-paced world we've made, "Stop and smell the roses! Take it easy!" Once, there was a time without engines, when legs, horse and sail were our ways around. A voyage to England took a month. Emerson and Hawthorne once spent two days walking the 20 miles from Concord to the town of Harvard, deep in conversation both ways. Goods hauled by horse or oxen bounced on a rough cart path in a long day's journey from Salem to Andover. Larger loads between these colonial towns sailed more easily in shallops and sloops around Cape Ann and up the Merrimack. What did the passengers, drovers and sailors think and talk about in those hours? They must have been very aware of their natural surroundings and each other during those slow passages.

Perhaps this is why people often escape on the water with paddle, oar or sail. Two weeks ago on a Sunday afternoon, a Greenbelt group of 19 folks in 13 canoes and kayaks paddled up the Parker River's meandering channel though the wide flat brackish marsh of Newbury. In three hours the only sounds were of water stirred by breeze and paddles and human and bird voices. Even a cell phone ring was not heard. For a time, it was as it used to be with our ancestors and the Indians who preceded them. We could contemplate the tides, winds, birds, flanking banks of dark peat, husks of last year's plants, new shoots of this year peeping forth, each other, or nothing at all.

Water provides a different place, an old, old one whence we came, one cheaply and readily available here if we are willing to mix our sweat with the medium. Let's leave the noisy engines and cell phones behind; let others wonder where we are. We will be more missed and welcomed upon return.

FIRE WATER

Last week, fire, on a gentle westerly breeze, swept through oak woods from First Pasture off North Liberty Street halfway to "Old Boxford Road." Had the breeze been a little stiffer and more southerly much of the protected forests in southern North Andover and Boxford might also have had their floors blackened. "Recycled through" might be a better metaphor than "swept." The fire burned the dry leaves, sticks, bushes and small trees; it didn't sweep them into piles and windrows.

While walking the perimeter of over 200 acres of charred woodland floor, thoughts turned to the seeming magic of burning and rotting. The basic chemical equation for both that you may remember from high school biology and chemistry is: organic matter + oxygen yields carbon dioxide + water + energy.

If enough heat is applied to start, oxygen combines with organic fuel to explosively produce the products CO2 and H2O. Bacteria and fungi do much the same, only more subtly and slowly. "Cool," we might say. Whether our flesh is cremated or rots, the products of the reactions are the same. Recyclable common molecules are formed.

Walks around the aftermaths of fire, especially barn and house fires, understandably depress. Harken back to the great Yellowstone fires of more than a decade ago. Many thought, wrongly, the park ruined for generations. In walks around last week's fire there were no such worries. The thicker-barked trees suffered little; their May leaves are still a live green canopy above the ashes. We know they are taking in water and carbon dioxide, products of fire and decay, in the process of photosynthesis, another equation your teachers once laid on you. Simply reverse the direction of the arrow in the one above and substitute sugars (food) for organic matter and light for energy. How very wondrous is this world that recycles despite us. The trite old saws, "ashes to ashes and dust to dust" and "what goes around comes around," we now understand.

SILENT SPRING

This year too few will celebrate the hundredth birthday of the late naturalist, Rachel Carson, who gave us gutsy influential *Silent Spring*. She also wrote poetically of water and left for posterity *The Sea Around Us*.

Monday, on a visit to check the Great Blue Heron rookery of 20 or so nests above the large beaver impoundment near where North Andover, Boxford and Middleton join, a Closeteer, eagerly anticipating the sights and sounds of parents and young as heard before on monthly spring visits these past five years, was met with silence. There were no raucous croaks as mother and father flew in carrying food, or answering squalls from waiting young. There were only the sounds of a gentle west wind playing the new oak leaves. Swallows flitted among the dead trunks of red maples, Atlantic white cedars, and tall nest-bearing white pines. Not a heron was seen or heard during the half hour search of each nest through binoculars. Each spring and just three weeks ago, there were sentinels standing over or sitting on each nest and others coming and going. On this lovely day after five of cold nor'easter rains there was only silence. The herons were gone.

Here is one hypothesis as to what might have happened. Two weeks ago, a large forest fire a third of a mile south of the rookery was fought with the help of helicopters bringing in water. The low-flying machines roared up from Middleton Pond again and again and probably turned around over the rookery. Did they scare away the herons? If they did, the corpses of abandoned chicks and fledglings must be rotting in the nests. The visiting Closeteer is too old to wade thigh deep into the high nest trees to climb and look.

We love our many, many machines because they make things comfortable and easy. Road kills, egg-laying turtles' time soon, attest to the harm they cause our fellow creatures. Did the choppers silence the rookery? The silence there is now as deafening as the noise must have been during the fire.

June 2007

Deep Reservoir of Hope

World-renowned naturalist/writer Edward O. Wilson frets eloquently in old age about the loss of biodiversity. Species are becoming extinct at an alarming rate on our continents. Ant expert Wilson has spent a productive lifetime looking closely with one eye at our smallest creatures. From these observations, those of others, and much thought, have come large explanations on the evolution of behavior as well as biodiversity. Charles Darwin, over a century earlier, also looked closely at small things like beetles as a boy; his observations led to the theory of natural selection, the basic explanation for the existence of all species.

In the Closet we read last month with great interest and renewed hope reports of deep ocean studies off Antarctica in which hundreds of new species were discovered in the cold dark depths near or on the ocean floor. As with most expensive deep water studies the area and samples were small. Researchers reporting in *Nature*'s May 17 issue expect to add greatly to their aquatic species lists as they explore further. In these cold (4 degrees C) and most ancient and unchanging of habitats, there is life in abundance and great unexpected diversity.

We trust Professor Wilson is pleased and heartened by the hope these findings provide for life on our planet. There is still a vast reservoir of forms where our surface effects have been relatively unfelt, a place largely unknown and not yet exploited. In the past, farmers, loggers and miners ran roughshod on and under the land without much knowledge or thought. Since the oceans are largely international, let's hope collective wisdom and cooperation may arise to temper our evolving brilliance, avarice and technology. How ironic it is that the future of earth's life may reside in the DNA of simple, mostly microscopic, aquatic organisms, rather than in that of its advanced intelligent forms. If the latter succumb these are the basis for a new beginning on land.

FOOD FROM WATER

April, May and June are the main months of woody growth. In April, the buds swell and give hint last year's sugars accumulated in the roots rise to them. In May, they shuffle off their protective scales, and embryonic leaves expand in a spectrum of muted shades of green, brown and red. Their stems grow and orient these solar panels to best receive gifts from the sun. People, now worrying about fossil fuels, emulate them and talk more and more of light-to-electricity transforming shingles. Now, nearing summer, the leaves grow to full size and optimum efficiency while there is still plenty of groundwater, one of the two basic reactants of photosynthesis. The other, carbon dioxide, is in the air around them. We'll repeat the basic equation marveled at a dozen times before here in the Closet. (Just as folks repeat prayers over and over, why not remind ourselves repeatedly of the basis of almost all life on our planet.)

light + water + carbon dioxide produce carbohydrates + oxygen

With these sugars and starches, cells can synthesize almost all the other compounds needed, from proteins to fats. Trees, bushes, weeds, flowers and crops grow higher and stouter. We animals, fungi, and most bacteria, who can't do photosynthesis, eat them.

On a recent early morning while the sun was still well below the trees a Closeteer and friend paddled down the Ipswich River through a quiet canyon of working greenery. Not far away, yet out of sight and hearing, were houses and roads. On the smooth relatively fast-flowing river people and their works were forgotten. A century ago, according to old photographs, the travelers would have looked out on pastures. The cows are gone; swamp white oak, river birch, red and silver maples, and a score of other plants shade the ancient water road. Ducks and herons are spooked on rounding bends, each turn promising a novel scene. You needn't visit our river to revel in this time of rapid growth, just walk on your lawn grasses and beyond into the bushes and trees. Their cells are using water to make cellulose, wood, for us all.

LOW WATER

Last week, we left you with head in the leaves and the promise that we'd explain how they obtain water from the soil far below. As too often happens in human affairs, the promise is being postponed. Something has come up that Middleton Stream Teamers think takes priority over the Cohesion-Tension Theory you've been so anxiously anticipating all week.

We've only had about 0.2 inch of rain since the substantial two-inch storm of June third and fourth. May and June is when the greatest growth by bushes and trees occurs; the time when plants take in massive amounts of water from the ground. Most of the water taken up is lost by transpiration to the air. We have but to look at our river to see the dramatic results of no rain. John Bacon, leader of the Stream Team, has on several occasions calculated the decrease in flow on each day without rain. Just three weeks ago at the gauge in South Middleton the flow rate was 200 cubic feet per second (CFS). John's calculations have shown a 13 percent decrease of the previous day's flow each day without rain. As of this writing, June 25, it is 20 CFS. Twelve paddlers doing the Ipswich River Watershed Association's "Source to Sea" voyage, Middleton section, last Saturday found the river inconveniently low; the nine or so miles took five hours rather than the usual three.

Last week, flow at the gauge dropped to 29.8 CFS, triggering the Town of Danver's Water Division Level 3 Drought Conditions, water restrictions that Middleton also goes by. Outdoor watering is allowed only Tuesday, Thursday and Saturday, between the hours of 7 p.m. and 8 a.m. This applies to all residents, even those with private wells.

Don't fret. Lawns don't need additional water. The holes in their leaves called stomates close down in drought conditions, thus conserving water. Growth will slow and the blades even turn brown for a bit. You'll be relieved of mowing. When the rain returns the cells will make new chlorophyll and all will be green again.

JULY 2007

WATER CHAMPIONS

This week's mini-essay is not about Olympic or English Channel swimmers. Our topic arose after reading last week's *Tri-Town Transcript*'s front page article entitled "Judge tosses Topsfield's water appeal." Put too simply, the Ipswich River Watershed, Essex County Greenbelt, and Charles River Watershed Associations asked the Department of Environmental Protection (DEP) in court to enforce its water withdrawal regulations. Towns who take water from the Ipswich River counter-sued and asked that a 2003 revised DEP regulation not be enforced. Superior Court Judge Patrick Brady agreed with the environmental groups and denied Topsfield's request.

This long litigation had us Closeteers discussing the wisdom of our political jurisdictions. Before the English, there were loose confederations of Indian clans who lived along our watersheds. They hunted, fished, and grew corn, beans and squash. Then along came the English into a people wasteland; it has been estimated that as many as 80 to 90 percent of the natives had died in the previous decade from Old World poxes. The English quickly formed strong largely autonomous towns with the bounds we have today, lines largely unrelated to topography.

A frivolous "What if?" question arose in the Closet. What if our ancestors had divided our land here into watersheds instead of states, counties and towns? Would these have been protected more if each had representatives in the Great and General Court and in Congress? They were not so divided, yet in the last few decades we have seen a movement in that direction by non-governmental groups, such as watershed associations.

Kerry Mackin, Executive Director of the Ipswich River Watershed

Association, and her small staff have little power except that of persuasion and the help of members. If you have ever found yourself involved in civil litigation you know how much time and perseverance are involved to see it though. Gertrude Ederle, first woman channel swimmer, had nothing on water champion Kerry, who, in turn, credits Margaret Van Deusen of the Attorney General's office, who might be likened to the coach and Gertrude's tender.

WATER IN ANCIENT PACKAGES

This morning, there was an empty plastic bottle in the Closet yard. Under the label's brand are the words "Pure Water. Perfect Taste." Some littering stranger had bought the water despite access to a tap. A discussion ensued, while sitting on the bank of the now low, slow Ipswich, about the exploding bottled water phenomena. Our ancestors upon arrival here three centuries ago must have marveled at the clear waters after drinking English water and beer for weeks from moldy casks. We imagine them now along our streams cupping water to lips. With the industrial revolution, people left the scattered farms and crowded into the towns where sewage ditches and wells got too close. Pasteur and others taught of microorganisms and water-borne diseases, which led to engineering marvels involving distant reservoirs, aqueducts, tunnels, and, wonder of all wonders, pipes to each building. We can now go to one of our several taps and drink safely to our blood's content.

In the last century, a little sugar and flavoring were added to water and sold in glass bottles as "pop," "tonic," and "soda." Then, some canny entrepreneurs had the bright, if not environmentally wise, idea of putting groundwater into bottles with fancy unoriginal names like "Crystal Aqua." The unspoken message here is that their water is cleaner and tastes better. This has led to tens of thousands of large trucks on the roads each day carrying water above municipal pipes that carry the same thing. Ships transport bottled water from as far away as distant Fiji around the world to people who can afford and have fallen for the scam. Our supermarkets fill whole aisles with water, plain and sugared. Our schools sell it to the kids, who have water bubblers in every corridor.

Despite availability elsewhere, we buy water in plastic containers made from ancient fossil fuels. These bottles, which require energy to process, flood our landfills and increase traffic and litter on our highways. We Yankees pride ourselves on "common sense." How the water hucksters must be laughing. Next they'll be selling air in plastic bags.

WATERSHED WANDERINGS

Stream Teamer Joan Cudhea in distant San Diego loaned a fellow member Helen Cruikshank's *Thoreau On Birds*, a compilation with commentary of many of Henry David Thoreau's bird notes. "Thoro," as family pronounced the name, roamed just two watersheds west of ours, Shawsheen and Concord. Throughout his life, he did what we old-timers did as kids; that is, explore our neighborhoods, circles ever widening with age. Those were the years before 24/7 parental supervision. Rafts were built and launched on ponds, huts were constructed of branches and scrap boards, lookout seats were installed in the tops of high trees for the purpose of spotting German bombers. We were free after chores and meals until we were old enough to do serious work from which we'd escape at every opportunity for nearby swimming holes and ice; no boring chlorinated pools or indoor rinks for us. We enjoyed Thoreauvian lives until the workaday world caught us up.

Thoreau carefully figured out how much time he'd have to devote to odd jobs and surveying to earn base room and board. One of seven days was his tally, the other six he "sauntered," often 20 miles a day, in earth-colored clothes with large pockets for lunch, notebook, knife, string, compass, etc. In this camouflage, he became intimate with the wild inhabitants of Concord. He found no need to travel farther; the wonders of nature were readily at hand and always changing. Patient observer, he watched his fellow creatures and plants through time, and to the great good fortune of us all, recorded his findings and ponderings in a most entertaining and original style. Modern ecologists as well as poets still seek inspiration from his voluminous notes.

His writings have us in the Closet wondering what might have been, if our teachers and parents had had us read Thoreau and encouraged his lifestyle rather than the drudgery of office, store and factory.

Old now, we notice that many our age are reverting. Clamming, canoeing, fishing, hunting and just sauntering take up more and more time as we leave the paved roads and return to woods and waters whence we came.

AUGUST 2007

CHANGES AROUND THE BAYS

In the Closet's two and a half years, we have often imagined what we think it might have been like here in Indian and colonial times. When the newcomers first arrived, the natives were mostly gone. Historians guess 70 to 90 percent died between 1615 and 1619 from Old World poxes brought by pre-colonial fishermen who'd been along the coast in the warmer months for a century or so. Last year we were much impressed by Charles Mann's new book, simply titled *1491*, about America before Columbus. Our image of great wilderness sparsely populated by Indians is falling under an increasing body of evidence that indicates there were lots of people here who managed the land with agriculture and fire.

One of the most intriguing of all the early accounts are 80 or so pages, *New Englands Prospect*, left us by young William Wood who was here 1629 to 1633. He roamed the new land around Massachusetts and Narragansett Bays, and with amazing candor for the time, wrote of what he saw. He seems to have carried no Puritan baggage and to have ignored the colonists' many prejudices. He became an admirer of the native peoples whom he often visited. Historians value his account as a welcome glimpse into how it truly might have been.

South of us, the citizens of Middleborough and area Wampanoags with some Indian inheritance, once an Indian tribe of the South Shore and Rhode Island, are now contemplating a casino to do what Wood reports was a favorite pasttime of Indian men: gambling. Instead of dice-like games on the ground, reed-and-bone pieces, there will be a couple hundred acres of gaming floors, guest rooms, parking lots and roads. Dollars, not wampum and goods, will be the medium of exchange. Where once there were transitory wigwams, there may soon be a permanent, high-rise city on the new nation's ground.

There were once many "nations" (our word) here, ever-shifting ones on bays, estuaries, and up watersheds. During King Philip's War (1675-

1677) there must have been an alarm cry in fledgling Middleborough something like, "Beware, the savages are coming!" There seem fewer such cries now; wampum has changed to cold, hard cash.

Dam Dilemma

What should we do with all the old dams we have inherited? There are thousands in Massachusetts, many now only ruins, others succumbing to ice and flood pressures. Many have lake-size mill ponds; those waters are no longer used for power, yet are rich habitats of beauty.

Last week, the question was asked about the steel/rock dam across Fish Brook in Boxford, just upstream from the ancient stone dam off Lockwood Lane. Water has washed around the dam's east end, producing a deep but narrow gully, which has lowered the third-mile-long impoundment two feet. The once lovely lake is quickly becoming vegetated wetland as it was centuries ago before the millers. In its stead is a sinuous brook channel flanked by flats, perhaps not what Boxford might have wanted to protect when obtaining it and the fine rolling land along its easterly bank.

In Middleton, there are two somewhat similar dams that have worried owners and neighbors in the past few years. Prichard's concrete dam across Boston Brook, built early last century to provide a lake for a summer cottage, lost a 30 by 2 by 2-foot chunk last year in the great Mother's Day Flood. Prichards Pond is a now a couple feet lower and water lilies and pickerel weed are thriving in the shallower water. Just a half mile downstream is Curtis Dam built of concrete in the 1930s to power a new sawmill. Ice and only four decades, since the last logs were sawn, have lowered a wide portion six feet. Curtis Pond is gone.

Mother Nature doesn't like walls across her streams and rivers that thousands of creatures are adapted to. She must be astounded at the hubris of one species to make high barriers across them, other species be damned.

We have long fretted about what do with old dams here that block our spawning alewives and shad. And what about the folks, other animals, and plants in Louisiana who are losing the whole protective southern part of the state due to perpendicular and lateral dams on the upper Mississippi?

The wise answer, before the dam building, was "do nothing." Maybe, this is still the proper one. Let ice, floods and time do their things.

DOWNS AND UPS ALONG THE RIVER

Sixty-five years ago a Closeteer, then a boy, visited kin in West Virginia. He came away with vivid memories of strip mines where lush green mountaintops were decapitated for coal. Rains ran off the tailings and yellowed the rivers with clay and poisoned them with unseen sulfuric acid. The boy was taken to favorite swimming holes by a cousin and warned not to open his eyes. He from the clear seawater of the Massachusetts coast forgot and couldn't open his red eyes to the sun for an hour after.

In that same period, strip miners were here in southeast town of Middleton within the great elbow bend where the Ipswich River swings north. They were after good gravel, which was trucked off to Logan for runways. Uplands that had been pasture for two centuries were lowered down to the water table. Much of the area between Route 114, River Street and Hilldale Avenue became a moonscape of craters. A half century of good rain and high groundwater have hidden the devastation with diverse plants and rich wildlife habitat despite the absence of topsoil. One of the deeper pits is a pond with fish, herons and turtles. Several more are inundated much of the year. In the midst of this large pockmarked area connected to the river's floodplain is a 10-acre island of upland with a bare two feet of freeboard on which an industrial park is planned. The miners lowered the land down to elevations that are now protected wetland. Much of the monetary value of the earth once there is now under tarmac in East Boston.

Conversely, five miles downriver near where the tri-towns join is a great hill of fill, topped by glacial moraine clay from the bowels of Boston, brought here in the late '90s from the Big Dig to cap a landfill that had smothered five acres of wetland in the '70s with debris from the great fires of Chelsea, Lynn and Lowell. The hillside fields, mowed once each year, provide habitat somewhat akin to the pastures lost upriver. How very strange, the things we do.

WATER FLOATERS AND WADERS

What a summer it has been for the very smallest of flowering plants, watermeal and duckweed. It looks as if the surfaces of our shallow ponds and swamps have been painted with veneers of emeralds. There are scores pressing single leaf to single leaf per square centimeter, each absorbing light and making food and oxygen. On their nether sides are zoos of protozoa, algae and bacteria.

Towering above these tiny plants and their communities are some of our area's tallest animals, the herons. Their long legs wade through the shallow waters; their muscular long necks terminate in long, sharp beaks mounted between even sharper eyes that search for fish, frogs, crayfish, snakes, mice and insects.

The largest, two-thirds our height with wingspans greater than our outstretched arms, is the Great Blue Heron, now common here in our wetlands and sky. Recently, a Sunderland man was heavily fined for shooting 275 over the years as they visited his trout hatchery to snack. There are several rookeries in the tri-town area; one, on the North Andover/Boxford line, had over 50 active nests a couple years ago. The heron perhaps most often noticed here because of its brilliant white plumage is the Great Egret, not much less lofty than Great Blues. Then there are shorter Black-crowned Night Herons, the males rather dandies with shiny black tuxes and wide gray-white waistcoats. Even smaller is the Green Heron that, perhaps because shy and blending, is not often seen.

All four species were seen together recently when spooked by Middleton board members on a site visit. As they rounded a dense-green screen of alders a dozen herons arose from an area of open water in a buttonbush swamp and flew to trees just out of range. Human chatter was replaced by oohs and aahs. Talk returned as these descendants of dinosaurs waited to resume fishing.

The humans responsible for deciding the fate of upland nearby were, we hope, reminded of these deedless owners by right of long usage. The herons, like the bygone Indians, probably don't have the word "own" in connection with land.

SEPTEMBER 2007

LOONACY ON OUR LAKES

Reports of declining loon populations on our New England lakes are much in the news this summer as counts come in on the dearth of nesting pairs. Loons are truly water birds that can scarce take off from it; their best flying is done in the denser medium below. These beautiful, big birds have long entertained us with their antics on the surface and their most wondrous of cries.

Their decline, even loon lovers say, is little understood. Yet, people say the same thing of our turtles even though their crushed shells litter our road shoulders each nesting season. Couldn't powerboats, jet skis, and other motorized water toys buzzing around our lakes be adversely affecting loons? They certainly do many less-noticed creatures.

Researchers suspect that many die from ingesting lead sinkers. The bottoms of water bodies are littered with them. We've known for almost two centuries that lead is poisonous, yet we continue to use it. We've finally gotten the lead out of paint and gasoline. Alas, it still resides in our posteriors "getting the lead out" might lead to corrective action.

Wouldn't it be nice if our lakes were refuges from motors? Paddle, oar and sail could be our power sources there. People who work on or near machines all week, then drive SUVs, RVs, and pickups to lake retreats would find some respite from exhaust fumes, noise and even speed.

It is loony, perhaps un-loony a better word, to inflict engines on wildlife habitats now we know the harm they do. Psychiatrists might say we are in denial. Even the loon researchers and wildlife folks do their surveys from powerboats. Strange? No, just Americans "doing our thing."

We in the Closet wonder if loons cried so hauntingly before we polluted their lakes with excess feces, urine, oil, lead sinkers and shot. The sound, of course, is no doubt ancient and even joyful. Thoreau from Walden Pond described "wild laughter." It only rings sadly now that it becomes ever more lonely.

WATERS ON THE MEND

An old Closeteer too often tells us stories of his boyhood years on the Merrimack River. One still stinks even after 60 years. The mighty river's water, then the recipient of sewage and industrial wastes from the cities of Concord, Manchester, Nashua, Lowell, Lawrence, Haverhill, arrived at Newburyport in foul condition. In the warmer months menhaden, or "pogies," sometimes entered the river in great schools. Children playing in the cleaner tidal waters splashed excitedly among them, trying unsuccessfully to catch with bare hands. Commercial fishermen used torches to attract them to their nets. Children and fishermen were minor hurdles compared to the oxygen-depleted water laced with poisons and massive populations of bacteria encountered. The hapless herring suffocated; windrows of their corpses rotted in the human flotsam along the banks.

Two decades later in August of 1964 the same Closeteer and young family held their noses as they drove along the murky water of Maine's Androscoggin River in Brunswick, just above its tidal flows. The water had received its noxious loads from the paper mill towns upriver.

Those shared memories came flooding back recently upon watching a public television documentary that featured a happy fisherman waist deep in the Androscoggin enthusiastically exclaiming several times, "A river is a living thing!" Our Closeteer might say, "the river has been restored to health." He had seen and smelled it when very ill.

Upon passage of the Clean Water Act in 1972, cynics, who thought our species collectively—as in government—could do no good, proclaimed it was too late for our rivers. In less than two generations they were proven wrong. The feds, using sticks (regulations) and carrots (money) have largely cured the Merrimack, Androscoggin and other rivers. They stopped the introduction of wastes directly into our water bodies. Sewage systems were built. We can now row down from Haverhill breathing freely, occasionally pausing for a dip.

A POEM LEFT

Dear Readers, Have you ever wondered what our Water Closet is? It is, of course, nothing but a weekly column, only an ink layer deep. However, here is what we imagine:

Our one-room shack is inspired by the famous house Thoreau built by Walden Pond. Ours, without plaster wall and stone foundation, is even simpler. The untreated sills are also skids used to drag it to a half-dozen rafted canoes when the water is high. These float it to a new site on the Ipswich River. A true WC our building is not, that moniker is just a fading joke. We don't need a water closet, our retreat has a shovel beside the door and woods all around. Water for cooking is carried a few steps up from the river. Don't try to find our ephemeral place. If, on a woodland wander, you happen upon it, enter, the door is never locked. Old issues of the *Transcript* and matches will allow you to build a fire in the stove. There is a pile of driftwood just outside. A laptop powered by solar panels is our concession to technology. This allows access to river depth and flow data from the gauges in South Middleton, Ipswich, and the waters of the world beyond.

September rains slowly have our wetlands and river recovering after the record August drought. On this, the first day of fall, while looking out the Closet's recycled windows and admiring the red maples now living up to their name, we remember a poem left on our tiny table last fall by an old Closeteer.

Fall Rain

The rain came in the dark
Still falls while I await
Some light to do my chores.
Drops are taken by the too dry soil.
From the stove's heat I listen
To their arrival on the leaves.
Descent and absorption are more felt.
I should go forth and lie
Gratefully with ear to ground,
The other catching fresh cold drops.
There my heat drains to the soil and air
I join all that was before
And that will come again.
Yet here by the fire is pleasant
I'll wait until the fires go out.

ECO-WORDS AT ODDS

Economy and ecology, both with the Greek root *oikos* meaning house, have become broad, ever more important words; the first having to do with "management of a household or state," and the second "the study of the relations between living organisms and their environments." Ecosystems, houses for communities of plants and animals, are of special interest to Closeteers, especially those of our wetlands, ponds, rivers and oceans.

Hundreds of times each day from the media we hear the phrases "the economy" and "the environment," even in our own conversations. Since the industrial revolution, the first has clearly dominated the second is catching up in speech, but not in action. We speak of environmental problems yet ignore them in daily commerce. Just drive to Peabody on crowded Route 114 and see acres of gas guzzling Hummers and SUVs in the car lots and on the road. Go to our supermarkets and walk long aisles of bottled water we don't need. Roadsides are littered with empties. In some countries, there are fast, clean public buses and trains connecting communities; sidewalks and bicycle lanes flank motor roads. Gasoline, over twice the cost of ours, encourages conservation.

In polls, we claim to be environmentalists with knowledge of ecology. The latter is true, we now know a great deal from media, books and school. However, when solutions to environmental problems are proposed, the movers and shakers say they will hurt the economy. We acquiesce. To paraphrase Lincoln, "A house divided against itself cannot stand." How about, "A mind divided against itself cannot stand"? Can we maintain our self respect if we think and speak one way and hourly act another? We'll go crazy. Mother Nature might say, "You are crazy. Look what you are doing to my house, our planet"; maybe, she already has, in not-so-subtle ways.

Isn't it high time we managed our economy wisely while learning more and more about its brother, ecology? Presently, an economy of excess is adversely affecting the environment. We are fouling our own *oikos*.

OCTOBER 2007

HIGH HOPES

Last week, Closeteers gathered around a map of Asia while listening to visitor Tenzing's story. He, a 34-year-old Tibetan who has never seen his beloved country, enthusiastically told us of it as learned from his parents who fled the Chinese Army in 1959; his refugee camp schools; Indian and, later, American media. He and five siblings were born and raised in a camp in hot southern India. Tenzing, a devout Buddhist, grew up on stories of "the roof of the world," where the air is clean and cold. The Himalayas, stretching 2,000 miles, west to east, have the water-laden clouds of the monsoons from the Indian Ocean climbing, cooling and precipitating. Water is stored as ice and snow on the mountaintops. Melt runoff flows down spectacular valleys to a thirsty continent below. Parents and countrymen have imbued Tenzing with the wonders of their pure, high homeland. We, much interested in watersheds, traced with fingers the well-known rivers that flow from it: Indus, Ganges, Brahmaputra, Mekong, Yangtze, and Yellow. His unseen land, so yearned for as we could sense in voice and eyes, provides water for a billion people. Is it any wonder many worship those endless flows from above?

As a teenager attending a Tibetan boarding school in India near Nepal, Tenzing tried to visit the land of his DNA and dreams. He was rudely stopped at the border. His dreams go on, as do those of the Dalai Lama. Our surprise guest, a man with four languages, now lives with his homesick parents in Cambridge, where he works as a carpenter's helper. They, with no interest in TV, English, or our culture, spend many hours each day spinning prayer wheels, their minds among the distant peaks.

We tell him of our Ipswich River watershed here, only a leisurely hour's drive in length and an unrealized climb of 110 feet from sea to source. He, half listening, sadly smiles, perhaps thinking he has 10,000 and then several vertical miles to go. We hope that when the border opens to him, the snow and ice will still be there.

RISING EXPECTATIONS

Evidence of global warming pours in from around the world. Liquid water literally pours from polar ice caps and mountain glaciers. We can't directly see the rising oceans, so must rely on the data from those who measure. Closeteers often speculate on a planet with increasing liquid water and less dry land. One recalls approaching Bikini and Eniwetok, Marshall Island atolls of nuclear bomb test infamy, and not being able to see the low ground of their islands until his ship was only a few miles off. A couple meters rise would have the waves of the northeast trades washing over them. They and other low islands like the Maldives of the Indian Ocean will disappear first. In our country the southern half of Florida and the Gulf Coast, flooded by Katrina, will follow. And nearer home our beautiful salt marshes from Gloucester to Rye, Whittier's "low green prairies of the sea," will be inundated. Their stabilizing salt grasses will drown, and 3,000 years of accumulated peat and sediment will erode away on ebb tides.

If you'd like a preview of coming attractions for your grandchildren, go downriver to the heights of Great Neck in Ipswich at low tide. Look out across the tidal flats and marshes that have turned from the vivid greens of a month ago to the rich caramel colors of fall. Upon return home, check the tide chart again and look ahead for the highest. Pick a daytime high of about 12 feet and then revisit. You'll find a very different scene dominated by seawater; the hidden flats and marshes will seem a great bay from Ipswich to the Merrimack and beyond. The weekend after October 26's full moon has good "high-runner tides" at about 1 p.m.

When the vast, deep Greenland ice cap is gone, perhaps in our grandchildren's time, they'll look out on such shallow bays rather than grassy marsh. Plum Island, Salisbury-Seabrook-Hampton beaches will be characterized by breaking waves over submerged bars rather than buildings and dunes; Great Neck, Little Neck, and Castle Hill will be offshore islands. Maybe.

WATER WORKS

Leaves, no longer green, flutter down around the Closet. The ground is lightly shingled in rich yellows, reds and browns and all mixes in between. When dry, our comings and goings rustle in accompaniment.

When wet with dew or showers, they glow, even in the residual light, filtered through the clouds. The quiet Ipswich River outside our door ferries a thin layer of this fall's harvest. Breezes arrange featherweight rafts into swirls and sweeping lines. Last year's golden pine needles form patches that remind of Maine's lakes and rivers of yore filled with logs as seen from hills. This year's needles will stay on and provide winter greenery among naked, deciduous neighbors.

Let's don microscopes and visit the innards of these ephemeral factories that provide food, oxygen and ever-changing colors. Factories in which the machines are protein molecules operating in watery solutions. Dry leaves, as all you mowers know, don't function. In processes not fully understood, chemical reactions affected by day length, temperature, humidity and water availability from the soil cause two adjacent cell layers at the base of a leaf stem to change. Their cell walls thicken and block vessels while weakening the glue between their two layers. This so-called abscission layer cuts off the movement of water from the ground, the diffusion of sugars to stems and roots, and finally, the leaf factory from twig. As metabolism changes, so do colors. Green chloroplasts break down, revealing yellow carotenes, pigments there all summer. The glut of sugars in drying leaves causes red pigments, anthocyanins, to form. As any of you crayon wielders know, combinations of yellows and red give orange and all shades in between. The death pigments, brown tannins, follow, either on the tree or later on the ground.

On moist ground, bacteria and fungi receive these bright gifts, which they break down to basic molecules for all to share. They too must have water. We are all waterworks. The green photosynthesizers provide food. The microscopic decomposers recycle. We, who cannot do either, should go forth and protect our benefactors' habitats with might and main.

NOBEL CHAMPION

Our land "from sea to shining sea" is, despite its deserts, truly water country. The people who aggressively took it over came in ships. They quickly repopulated the coasts and navigable rivers. From there they moved inland, up watersheds. Even dryer areas didn't stop them. They built dams, canals, and dug wells for irrigation. Where these were not possible, they ran cattle waterhole to waterhole. In their much-hailed hubris they went further and constructed hundreds of miles of levees and enormous dams for flood control.

Now and then, bold politicians lobbied by naturalists would attempt to call a halt. Theodore Roosevelt, naturalist in his own right, spurred on by John Muir, is the most famous example. He, using considerable charisma and forceful speech, reined in miners, ranchers and loggers over vast areas of designated federal land. Later, in mid-century, another was born in Tennessee to Albert and Pauline Gore. Young Albert followed his father, gutsy civil rights champion, into a life of public service. He, like father, was thoughtful, scholarly and ambitious. Three decades ago, he listened to scientists and even read many of their dense papers. He, an American politician in an age of jet setters and space exploration, contemplated the whole planet. I suppose TR had also. He sent his smoky, coal-burning Great White Fleet, his big stick, around it to show the flag. Al, Jr. didn't send ships, rather, warnings of quite a different kind. He worried a whole generation before most political leaders about what we might be doing to the biosphere. He gave us his book *Earth in the Balance: Healing the Global Environment* in 1992 and a decade later the film *An Inconvenient Truth*, read and seen in many more countries than Teddy's battleships. He became the scientists' political voice.

Earlier this month, Harvard scholar/Vietnam veteran/Representative/ Senator/author/Vice President/filmmaker Albert Gore Jr. was awarded the Nobel Peace Prize. He has long understood, without having to say so, that clean air and water are fundamental for peace of mind and peace between peoples. The Nobel committee also understands and has spoken.

DAM STRANGE

The time was 8:40 a.m., October 26, when the phenomenon occurred. There were 11 human witnesses. Middleton's Council on Aging/ Conservation Commission Friday morning walkers left the Peabody Street landing at 8:20 a.m. They strolled on a path along the Ipswich River, and although their average age is about 70, they chatted like school kids on an outing. They didn't, however, dart around as much. Upon being blocked by a tributary, they quickly made a bridge of dead logs and precariously crossed, joking all the while.

The group was off to solve a riddle, one it had an answer for that needed confirmation. River flow has been significantly below its 69-year average since mid-July. Why, then, was the water so deep? River watchers suspected a beaver dam downriver. Several hundred yards up from Thunder Bridge, the gentle sound of trickling water flowing through the top branches of a dam was heard. Suddenly, there it was, three feet high, 70 long, bank to bank. It had raised the level back up a half mile to another dam. The old-timers gathered on the bank a few yards downriver and admired the recently built structure. Then, at 8:40, the top branches two-thirds the way across started moving very slowly eastward. They accelerated as we oohed and aahed. The impounded water soon gushed down through a 12-foot gap. No one had touched the dam; there had been no wind, wave or earth tremor. Flow, barely detectable a moment before, was now a torrent gushing seaward. A physicist, if present, might have lectured us on potential energy becoming kinetic. A colonial sawyer would have thought of a water wheel and work. We, continuing downriver, just marveled at having been there. We made anthropomorphic cracks about a beaver conference soon to be convened where blame would be brought down on the engineers.

Witnesses returned the following two days and found repair progressing. There were freshly cut winterberry and arrowwood bushes, fruit and leaves still on, stuck in the breech. Drifting leaves were piling up against them. The water level, which had fallen two feet, was rising. We suspect there had been no meetings or hearings, just a team's quick response. There may be a beaveromorphic lesson here.

NOVEMBER 2007

WOODEN WATER BUCKETS

A walk down to the Ipswich River for a bucket of washing water got an old Closeteer going on about the wooden buckets of his boyhood on the farm. Some wag quietly played Louis Armstrong's classic "My bucket's got a hole in it" as background. For those of you who have never used anything but light plastic pails, a wooden bucket was like a small half barrel with a wire or wooden handle called a bail. It was made of about a dozen staves, beveled on the edges so that when put together they formed a round container held together by hoops of steel or wood, like an inside-out wooden boat, only the ribs—hoops—were on the outside, holding the planks in against the water pressure.

Those working buckets, used by him to carry water to hen houses some distance from the faucet in the cow barn, were heavy and clumsy. If they dried, the planks shrunk and seams opened up like in a wooden boat out of water. When picked up while very dry they sometimes fell apart. Buckets, relatively valuable then, could be painstakingly put back together, resurrected, then filled with water that swelled the staves back against the hoops. Water-logged buckets turned black with bacteria and fungi as they rotted.

Our colleague grumbled on and told us of carrying water in the winter, bucket full in each hand, out through deep narrow paths in the snow, his swinging tormentors banging against legs and water spilling over on pants, where it quickly froze. The walk back after filling the chickens' water buckets was a stiff-legged slog. Buckets filled again, he was off to another hen house.

He, despite his old ways, praises modern five-gallon plastic pails. They are lighter, stronger and much cheaper. However, we notice he comes to life when telling about carrying man-fashioned, not stamped-out, containers. He had gotten down and dirty with mud, snow, manure and thirsty chickens that he knew, fondly remembered, and wanted to lay on us. There would be no story from one who has only to turn a valve to send water through pipes to chickens rarely seen as in modern poultry factories.

Fish, Then and Now

Recent commentary about herring and the increase in mid-water trawler numbers, with "nets the size of football fields" to catch them, caused much consternation in the Closet.* We remembered the '70s, before the 200-mile limit, when foreign factory ships wreaked havoc on our fisheries. Herring, consumers of plankton, many of whom used to come up the Ipswich to spawn in legendary schools, are the basic food for larger fish, such as cod, haddock, halibut, tuna, striped bass and blue fish. Eliminate the alewives, shad, menhaden and sardines from the base of the food pyramid and all above would soon collapse.

The Indians here lived in a wonderland of diverse fish. Archeologists have found signs of weirs in estuaries up and down the coast. Imagine their excitement after a hungry, deep-snow, thick-ice winter when the fish returned to the rivers now called Mystic, Saugus, Danvers, Ipswich and Parker. At Pawtucket Falls on the Merrimack, now Lowell, widespread clans gathered peacefully in great numbers and joyfully caught salmon, sturgeon, lamprey eels and herring. Many of the smaller fish were used for fertilizer. Centuries later at Valley Forge, Washington's starving men were saved in the spring by shad in the tens of thousands coming up the Schuylkill River.

The best historical evidences we have for the unbelievable numbers of fish are Old World merchants' tallies and colonial anecdotes. Brave men speaking Portuguese, French and English fished off our coasts May through October a whole century before the Pilgrims. They came in tiny, wooden ships, ballasted with salt, and returned before the bitter November winds, loaded with dried/salted cod. Perhaps largely iliterate, they left no logs. We know they were here from first colonists' reports of meeting natives who spoke their languages.

Those early fishermen fished with hand lines that, when dropped for cod and haddock, barely dimpled the bottom. Today's massive trawls rake rich bottom habitat like corn belt harrows.

Perhaps it is high time to take some lessons from the Indians and fishermen of the 17th through 19th centuries who used weirs, hooks and lines. We might start by curtailing the use of factory ships with sonar-computer guided mammoth nets and by razing dams, walls to herring spawning.

* *Boston Globe* commentary by Peter Baker and Ray Kane, November 6, 2007

Dark Cloud

Last week, Governor Sonny Perdue of Georgia and others stood on the state house steps in Atlanta and prayed to God for rain to relieve the southeast and southwest from drought. Later, in the Closet, we discussed what we had seen and heard on TV and tried to imagine God's response thundering down from a large black cloud passing overhead. "My children, I have given you this wondrous planet with plentiful, once clean, air and water, and through evolution, a multitude, now fewer, of diverse plants and animals. You have squandered my precious gifts by using wasteful irrigation methods, by growing crop monocultures with little resistance to disease and insects and that require excessive amounts of water, by maintaining extravagant water-wasting, chemically doused lawns, by showering your bodies too often, too long, and by using massive amounts of your clever chemicals that did not evolve along with my creatures. I sent Rachel Carson to warn you of the harm your novel molecules were causing. You ridiculed her, paid little heed; all this, despite your amazing powers to reason. Now, you have the gall to ask me for relief so you can carry on your profligate ways." As the cloud drifted to the east, dropping no rain, God was heard softly muttering, "Conserve. Protect. Conserve. Protect . . ."

We Yankees can't smugly criticize those devout Georgians. We also waste and poison. Our days of drought will come. Here in the tri-town area, we borrow over 60 gallons of water per person per day. Visualize twelve five-gallon buckets, more than many third world families use in a week. The water we return to the ground and air is tainted with mined and man-made compounds. In many cases we have no idea what their effects are on us, our fellow creatures, or on life-sustaining plants.

Whoever that was in the passing cloud, God or Mother Nature, she clearly put the ball in the court of us *Homo sapiens*, the animal with the brilliant, yet unwise, mind.

WATER CHALLENGES

This past week, we Closeteers crowded around our atlas in an effort to understand poor, long-suffering Bangladesh, a south-facing funnel with Indian and Burmese walls that concentrate monsoons and typhoons. Low lying, the storm surges sweep over its southern half as Katrina did over our similarly situated Gulf Coast. There are other comparisons to help us imagine. The Ganges river delta region making up much of the country receives massive amounts of fresh melt water down from the Himalayas, the basis of a rich agriculture. Here, we have the once-fertile/prolific Mississippi floodplain and delta. Bangladesh is the recipient of life-giving water from the mountains and life-taking salt water from the Indian Ocean and the Bay of Bengal; in the United States, the Rockies, western Appalachians, and the Atlantic and Caribbean correspond.

Now, the great looming threat to all the delta regions around the globe is warming, with resultant rising water. Some climatologists say it is already too late for these areas and that the frequency of immersions will increase. A few say we've crossed a red line and it may be too late even to adapt, as the ice caps of Greenland and Antarctica melt and storm activity increases.

The United States and China are now being pointed at by the rest of the world as the worse polluters responsible for many of the planet's woes. Isn't it high time for our rich country to again take bold action for the sake of the world as it did in WWII? Only, this time, peacefully using our and our allies' remarkable technologies, free governments, and flexible economic systems. Such initiatives would again involve many countries. The challenges accompanying climate change are even more widespread than those of fascism in the last century, when we used our industrial might and altruistic will to successfully meet them.

Let our children and grandchildren gently grasp those pointing fingers in their own and embrace their owners in groups, cooperating scientific teams, without bombs and battleships. Hopelessly naïve you say? What have they got to lose? What other choices do they have?

DECEMBER 2007

BETWEEN SUN AND MOON

The other evening, one night before full moon, we, a group of old men from up the Ipswich River, paused from our clamming in a wide, low tide Ipswich creek near Essex, to admire the already plenty-full moon, rising onto a salt marsh stage. It was reflecting goodbyes from the setting sun. The clear, cold air let the scene's colors, tinged with red, play fully out, a moment photographers stalk. We stood and called out quietly to each other to take a look. The clouds in the west above the trees were trying to steal the show with their golds, reds, and a dozen other shades we could not name.

In this mood, we washed our clams in the creek's darkening salt water. The moon, early blush subsiding, was rounding up after its low, oval entrance. We climbed the creek banks and headed toward the sun, now below the horizon, still very much with us. The marsh grasses, once "salt hay," were a light-caramel color, flowing flat in all directions until they met the dark uplands carved by glaciers, polished by time and decorated with trees. We knew the salt marshes would, in just six hours when the moon was overhead, be immersed in a clean ocean bath. We would miss that act. Scene sated and happy we could only take so much. The act we'd been a part of, theater-in-the-round, was enough to last us for a long, long time.

Later, we tried to remember our physics. There was talk of light wave lengths and their differential bending as they enter the atmosphere at low angles. The reds, upon going from space to air, are bent downward more and dominate for a while, hence the red hues reflected. The gravitational forces of the moon and sun pulled the earth's waters, the crests 90 degrees of longitude east and west of us. The trough of the great half-the-earth's-diameter wave was here allowing access to the flats. All that beauty was much more than in the eyes and feelings of the beholders. Mathematics allows us to go beyond.

Pick a twilight moonrise and sunset when the tide is low and go out on our marshes and see for yourselves.

WALKING ON WATER

December, after the complaining snowbirds have flown south, is a grand time. Some, like this December, have access ice on our shallow swamps early, due to below-average temperatures. Last Friday morning, Middleton Council On Aging/Conservation Commission (COA/CC) hikers explored the beaver impoundments near where North Andover, Boxford, and Middleton join. In that large, undeveloped area, thanks to Harold Parker and Boxford State Forests, Boxford Trails Association/Boxford Open Land Trust, and Greenbelt, you can walk for miles without seeing a paved road or house.

A month ago, the shallow water of the beaver impoundments, as seen from surrounding knolls, appeared black. Where light entered the transparent water and was absorbed by the black muck of the bottom, there are now four inches of white ice. We walked on it beneath the barkless trunks of dead red maples, white pine and Atlantic white cedars that, less than a decade ago, shaded a woodland swamp. Now, most of the maples and pines have fallen; the corpses of the tough cedars still stand. This may sound like the new habitats due beaver dams are lifeless places. The criss-crossing tracks of birds, deer, fishers, foxes, coyotes and otters in the snow covering the ice belie this, as did duck quacks, heron croaks, and bullfrog choruses last summer. We spotted woodpeckers, flickers, nuthatches, creepers and chickadees flitting among the dead trunks. High in the still-standing pines are two dozen Great Blue Heron nests. This impoundment, we call the rookery, is interesting, even beautiful, in its flat openness with tree-covered uplands all around. One colorful feature among the winter grays and whites are maroon patches of sweet gale, thigh-high bushes with fruit that smell like its relative, the bayberry.

Three impressive dams there have created three vast impoundments. One stretches north halfway to Boxford center, another east almost to Thomas Road, and the oldest, the rookery, covers 100 acres of the Pond Meadow Pond floodplain, which drains south down long Pond Meadow Pond Brook to Boston Brook then onto the Ipswich River.

We urge you to seek out nearby beaver impoundments, so easily recognized as flooded areas of dead maples. They are becoming "beaver meadows," light-filled places wildlife are attracted to. We wondered on our walk if the beavers appreciate the devastation and renewal they wrought.

Cheers to a Champion

Two winters ago a Closeteer walked along snow-flanked Fish Brook, below Mill Street in Boxford. From a distance, the channel appeared as a black path in the snow. Standing on a bank and looking down through transparent water he discovered the pebble-covered bottom. The rounded stones displayed a spectrum of browns, greens, reds, blacks and whites. In the shallows, water riffled over the smooth stones. He, who had done biological monitoring for water quality along the Ipswich River, recognized this as a place probably high in dissolved oxygen with a whole array of insect larvae and crustaceans. The labyrinth of passageways between the pebbles provides substrate, protection and food such as microscopic algae and bacteria.

Back in the Closet, he described the beauty of what he had seen through the lovely window between banks of white. We were reminded of the Nashua River, big sister of the Ipswich to the west flowing to the Merrimack. Nashua in Algonquian means "stream with beautiful pebbly bottom." Almost four centuries ago, the English came with their diseases, livestock and land-owning ways. The Indians were soon gone; the newcomers claimed the rich bottomland and their prolific cattle and hogs overgrazed stretches of bank and floodplain. At times, the river was laden with sediment, the pebbly bottom fish so love, obscured. In the 19th and 20th centuries industry and cities, especially Fitchburg, used the river as a sewer, which was often colored with dyes from paper factories. The water became poisonous and stunk.

In 1962 Marion Stoddart, housewife raising a family in Groton, opened her eyes and nose to these outrages and then her very persuasive mouth against them. She and followers formed a cleanup committee. They effectively lobbied all levels of government and industries along the 52 miles of river. By the late 1980s, a river many thought had died was resurrected; pebbles were seen again, odors gone, and trout back.

On a canoe trip not too long ago, Stoddart, now 79, happily paddled by several rope swings hung by swimmers from trees. Her goal had been to see people swimming there again. We hope she lives to see her beloved Nashua and our Ipswich also drinkable. We'll scoop a pitcher and raise our glasses to her. Cheers, Marion! Well done!

WHITE CHRISTMAS

Last Friday morning, we broke trail through deep snow from Sharpners Pond Road, North Andover, south to where Essex Street crosses Emerson Brook in Middleton. Had we gone that way a century ago we would have had easy going, despite the snow. Essex railway trains would have cleared our path. The rails are long gone, the ties part of the soil. There is no need now to step aside and wave to passing passengers en route Salem or Lawrence. The wetland of Boston Brook on either side of the rail bed is the home of red maples, ducks, herons, muskrats, otters and turtles.

Single file, on foot, we swapped point now and then to share the work of breaking through the gifts of four storms. The top four inches had fallen the day before; bushes and trees, thanks to cold and clouds, were still coated making for a quiet wonderland. The new snow showed few tracks. Here and there, shrews had barely dented the meringue-soft snow with their delicate feet and tail marks. We saw a squirrel trail come down a pine and venture out to a leaf-cluttered hole, where it had probably stashed an acorn. There were no fresh deer tracks. Midway on our slow trek, we came upon a beaver lodge where there had been much commotion in the snow and an open hole through the thick ice above where the beaver's underwater entrance should be. On closer examination we found no large beaver tracks; also, the hole was too small for them. There were fresh otter tracks obviously coming up from the icy water. They had emerged to slide down the rail bed shoulder. Toboggan-like belly marks were clear. After several slides they returned under the ice. We did not follow, as gutsy Alice would have their hole was too small, the water under gray-sky black.

Our legs, tired from the long slog, had been given no thought en route, such were of people, oxen and horses who had built the bed across wetland and through upland ledge, of those who rode the trains, of farmers who worked the flanking meadows, and of the wild things that replaced them. If we had gone back further, we might have found ourselves in soft, fur boots, our upper bodies wrapped in deerskins.

Winter's Water

This December just past, lots of water fell in novel form, at least quite different than that from May to November; still HOH, but fluffy, white and cold. Imagine a great crowd (water molecules) intimately dancing in a city square. Enter cruel General Drillmaster Cold, sweeping in on a north wind. He doesn't like the hugging, slide and cuddle, and orders, as soldiers will, the participants to rigidly extend their arms; the only contact allowed with fellows are hands to shoulder. He takes the heat right out of their play. The mass expands with arm-length gaps between the now freezing dancers. The crowd is less dense, and this is why ice floats. Most substances upon cooling become ever more dense; water is an exception. At four degrees C (39 F) it starts to expand and continues to zero C (32 F). Ice is crystalline; we have but to look at fresh flakes to imagine the molecules unseen, arranged somewhat like "Bucky balls." Chemists have nicknamed spherical, hollow molecules of carbon atoms after Buckminster Fuller. You know his geodesic domes, so light yet strong and rigid. But let us leave the world of molecules we never really see and return to welcome snow.

We who stayed may look forward to other storms and the new white worlds they give us. Many snowbirds have left; more will leave. Let them fly; they don't know what they will be missing. Alas, here our dance metaphor collapses. We warm-blooded types will be playing in the snow, moving all the more. We'll tell the tanned returnees, but they won't listen. For them, water is only warm, blue and liquid. Maybe they were afraid the dance would never resume. We here know that with warmth the once dancing molecules will move again under and within swelling buds to new spring songs.

Photo, courtesy of Alison Colby Campbell.

2008

JANUARY 2008

BLOOD ON SNOW

While perusing a copy of Sidney Perley's *The History of Boxford*, Closeteers stumbled upon a winter tale that made our warm blood run cold.

In 1724, Captain John Lovewell of Dunstable made a proposal to Massachusetts for an Indian hunt to be conducted by a company he would raise. He asked for five shillings per man per day. If none were killed he'd ask for nothing for their "time and trouble." A deal was struck. Sixty-two men were mustered, a dozen or so from our area. In January 1725, the company set forth on snowshoes, and within a few days found the tracks of a small band of Indians, which they followed north to frozen Lake Winnipesaukee. On trackless ice, they lost their prey for a bit until they saw ravens flying above an island. Soon, they were within earshot of Abenaki speakers; signs indicated that they had had a successful day of hunting. Lovewell told his men that they would wait until midnight when the meat-sated Indians were asleep. At one in the morning they quietly attacked. Nine of only 10 Indians were quickly killed; the tenth ran and was dispatched by Lovewell's dogs. The murdered, our word not Lovewell's or Perley's, were relieved of their scalps, the rest left for the ravens. All 62 of Lovewell's company, still intact, looped around via Cocheco, now Dover, eventually to Andover where they were "entertained." Their bloody trophies were later cashed in.

We tried to find original sources for this account. Kindly librarians in Middleton and Dunstable helped. We found two other secondary accounts differing slightly in dates and places; however, the essentials are the same.*

At first light on a recent Sunday, a wandering Closeteer came upon boot prints in the snow on a swamp, deep in Boxford State Forest. Mingled with them were diffuse blood droplets and slide marks where a deer had been dragged out. He followed them for one and one-half miles to Middleton Road with thoughts of blood dripping from fresh scalps and wondering, to his horror, if he as a young English farmer in Lovewell's time might have signed on.

* Try The Scalp Hunters by Alfred Kayworth and Raymond Potvin, a balanced, but wandering account of the English-Iroquois and French-Abenaki skirmishes from King Philip's War to the end of the French and Indian War.

CONSTRICTIONS

Last Friday morning in 10-degree air, members of the Middleton COA/CC's walking group crunched along in snow down the Essex railway bed from Emerson Brook to the Ipswich River. At the river we came to an abrupt halt; the bridge over which the trains had traveled from Salem to Lawrence several times daily until 1926 has been long gone. We stood on the great granite blocks of the abutment and looked down across the 30-foot gap. It was obvious from our high vantage point that the natural river, channel and floodplain, was once about 100 yards wide. The railroad builders, circa 1846, built a causeway of fill across the floodplain to the channel, which could then be crossed with a short bridge. Imagine the hubris needed to constrict a river system to one-tenth its former width. Some might say they lacked the environmental knowledge we now have. We shouldn't let them off so easily. Less than a century before, Timothy Fuller, who had a sawmill a mile or so upriver on Middleton Brook, was denied his request to narrow the fish passage in his sawmill dam by Town Meeting. Citizens well knew the importance of shad and alewives spawning runs. Later, the much-touted industrial progressives were in the saddle, other folks, animals and plants choking in their dust.

Downriver where it passes under I-95, near where the tri-towns join, road builders in the 1950s reduced the river width from about 400 to 70 feet. Floods upriver have been higher ever since.

Perhaps the worst example that comes to mind is the bridge from Newburyport to Plum Island. A few decades ago, there was a long one perched on wooden pilings. On higher marsh-covering tides, the seawater easily flowed among them. The Army Corps of Engineers (ACOE) allowed the river-friendly bridge to be replaced with a concrete one that greatly reduced flow width. Several square miles of estuary, some of the world's richest habitat, have been affected.

There is reason to hope the worst of the bad old days of road building are over.

The ACOE in 2005 promulgated a new policy, requiring that new bridges span 1.2 times the width of rivers and streams. The Middleton Conservation Commission recently required it be followed for a planned access road over Boston Brook.

Valley Vapors

We generally don't think of our topography as having valleys, yet many, now largely hidden by trees, have been brought to our attention, found by beavers. Just a century back farmers and livestock intimately knew these low lands with water-providing streams flanked by ledgy uplands of poor pasture. Here and there, small patches of trees were maintained as woodlots. Scattered few and far between were trees spared to provide some shade. Late 19th century photographs show pastoral scenes like those of Old England.

On an afternoon during the recent January thaw, when the glass read 40 degrees higher than the week before, we, Closeteer, son and granddaughter, walked north up the valley of little known Watkins Wallow, a mile-long swamp and intermittent stream draining south between uplands characterized by poor soil and granite outcroppings shaded by mature, slow-growing oaks. Parts of the wet valley floor are strewn with boulders, courtesy of continental glaciers. The brook, once rarely over ankle deep, now has our attention due to four water-retaining beaver dams. Where once water trickled quickly south to Boston Brook, there is now a broad stairway of impoundments.

It was these dams and ponds, no longer hidden by summer leaves, we went to see. While descending the valley's easterly ridge though a half foot of rapidly waning snow we felt the valley's chill. Balmy southwest wind delivering 60-degree air was losing heat to melting snow and vaporizing melt water. Chemists tell us 619 calories are absorbed in melting and evaporating one gram of water, ice to vapor. No matter. Increased blood flow from rough going kept us cozy.

At the mini-valley's bottom, we walked upstream past the dams to a large swamp. On our moist hike we were reminded of what a water world ours is: melting snow, evaporating melt water, water audibly trickling through the tops of dams, watery blood coursing, vapor cooling hands and faces, and above, floating clouds of Gulf moisture.

Just above the highest dam, producer of 80 acres of flooded swamp, we walked on wet ice and thought how much beavers are in tune with water in all its forms. We were in what has been beaver territory for the last decade and was for 10 millennia before the English. The valleys are theirs again.

Layers of Snow and Ice

Harken back a couple weeks ago when about a half foot of fluffy snow fell in the night on wet trunks, branches and twigs. A front came through, wet at first, then very cold. The soft snow froze and the following morning a new world greeted us. Our roads were canyons of white, from tree tops to ground. Each weed had become an ornament, glistening even in cloud-filtered light, and dazzling in full sun.

Off North Main Street, Middleton, opposite Meritor Academy, Emerson Bog's buttonbushes and dead Atlantic white cedars, disguised in snow, were a striking tableau. The cedars, 40 years since killed by flooding, and long reduced to bleached heartwood and a few remaining branches, stood up from the ice, resembling frosty horsetail plants only 20 times as tall. Below and all around were spiky buttonbushes, their deer antler-like branches coated with an inch of snow. All rose above a frigid blue-white carpet, its pile from ice warp floating on a couple feet of liquid water. We had to imagine the latter, an active life layer insulated by flake-trapped air.

These lovely shows we are blessed with several times each winter last only a few hours. Warmth and wind usually quickly take away. Earlier December cold and that following the storm and its lingering display left us with thousands of acres of ice-covered swamps, bogs and ponds.

The other afternoon on ice we explored a usually inaccessible vast swamp among beaver-drowned red maples. The opaque aerated ice, except on the swamp's shallow edges, was safe. Here and there were transparent patches of so-called black ice, black because the light enters these windows and doesn't return. Laying flat, we pressed our noses to cold panes and gazed down at plants and the detritus and mud of the bottom. There, in 32-degree clear water we peeping Toms saw tadpoles, small fish, insects and crustaceans slowly going about their wintry business in oxygen-poor water. The netherworld of ice is very much alive.

Above us peekers, on the dead maple trunks, woodpeckers noisily mined for dormant prey. The aquatic creatures, ancient kin, in their stable stratum seemed oblivious to both us and the hungry drummers.

FEBRUARY 2008

FINDING WATER

Recently, around the Closet stove, the subject of finding water came up. One old Closeteer harkened back to his boyhood when his farmer uncle asked Sherb Eaton to divine for water in one of his fields. Sherb, a diviner, farmer, clammer, boat builder, hunter, ocean fisherman who couldn't swim, and finder of lost property bounds, was held in awe by Salisbury folks for his many practical skills.

Sherb arrived one summer morning and immediately cut a fresh chokecherry branch. This, he then held tightly out in front of his chest, base up by its arm ends. The boy cut a similar Y-shaped "divining rod" and slowly followed Sherb. He'd been told that upon crossing above a good source of water the rod would twist uncontrollably down, pointing to the prize. Silent Sherb soon found two separate places where this happened. The boy wanted his rod to follow suit, and after Sherb left he practiced this wondrous strange skill. At times the stick did seem to be mysteriously pulled down. Later, he expressed his skepticism to adults who championed Sherb and other diviners and extolled examples of their valuable finds.

That September, as a high school sophomore, the boy took biology. Popular teacher and coach Sandy Roy harangued his students in the first class about science over superstition. He gave divining for water as an example of the latter. The boy took the bait and rose in defense of Sherb. Mr. Roy asked him to bring a divining rod in the next day. He did, and the whole class was led to the athletic fields for a demonstration. The diviner was blindfolded and led for a half hour around the fields. Near third base, he found water in a place he had passed over unknowingly 20 minutes before with no result. Mr. Roy took off the blindfold and said in effect, "So there. Superstition."

The only mildly humiliated student was not at all convinced. He had enjoyed being the center of attention. Perhaps a divine girl, there were several in class, would recognize his unproven potential. He would find water for her.

Later in life, he came to the conclusion that Sherb, expert in the lay of land, was seeing a lot more than his divining rod was feeling, and signals from his experienced brain subconsciously told the stick to confirm his divinations.

WATER THEN OIL

Last week, somebody brought in a large map of Iraq and surroundings. MESOPOTAMIA is printed in faint letters northwest to southeast down the axis of the Fertile Crescent between the two great rivers we learned about in school. We were taught this was the "cradle of civilization," nourished by and rocked in the arms of the Tigris and Euphrates, bringers of water from the high Persian mountain chain to the east and the snow-covered heights of Turkey. This gift, certainly once thought descending from the heavens, gave rise to agriculture, towns, writing and art.

Now bombs, theirs and ours, rock the cradle crazily in an Eden turned hellish.

None of us Closeteers have been to Iraq. Our taxes have, along with a tiny fraction of the sons and daughters of others. We who pay carry on as if there were no war; rather, we shop as urged by our commander in chief. Each evening, TV brings us scenes from the country we have adopted: image after image of desolate, treeless streets, their buildings pockmarked with the scars of bullets and shrapnel, of gutters with escaped sewage flowing around vehicle carcasses, and of market pavements stained with blood. Rarely are we given views of gardens or the mountains and famous rivers that provide water for them.

We Closeteers, who see the world through watery lenses, studied the map and tried not to think of politics, religion and war, but rather what was and might be in a fertile land with endless streams of water. Perhaps the problems have literally risen in the form of another ancient liquid, one released from the underworld and piped and shipped around the world in exchange for money never fairly shared. Thoughts of oil depressed, ours turned again to what the Crescent and other such places might be without it. We imagine children playing in the rivers, tributaries and irrigation ditches, towns with functioning sewage systems, clean water piped to each house, and fisheries restored.

Let's leave ancient fossil oil and coal fuels be and look to the sun and wind for higher forms of energy. With great drills and diggers, *Homo technicalis*, seduced by those powerful black genies, have released them. Burned, they just don't disappear. Their products poison. We've long proclaimed oil and water don't mix, perhaps its time to listen.

WATER WRITTEN IN WOOD

In medieval times, what is now southwestern United States was populated by a people dubbed Anasazi (alien ancient ones) by the late-coming Navahos. Scattered throughout the dry canyons and plateaus are numerous ruins of adobe, stone, and wood-raftered houses. The most spectacular hang from cliffs like barn swallows' nests. In the late 13th century the Anasazi went missing. Despite extensive study of their buildings, baskets, pots and petroglyphs, their fate remains a mystery.

In the past few decades, researchers, with no written language to decode, have turned to water-written climate records locked in the trunks of old trees. The code consists of annual growth rings, the oldest at the center. You needn't be a botanist to roughly read them. When a tree is cut in your neighborhood, gather up the family, go forth to the stump and count the rings. After you have determined the age look for patterns. You'll find some rings significantly thicker than others, indicating good growing seasons. Almost all tree growth here takes place in May and June. Other things being equal, the more water in the soil the greater the growth. Last year, wet until July, was a good tree year. The wood cells, which die and become vessels, grow fast and large in the spring; you can almost see them with naked eye. As summer progresses new cells are smaller and densely packed. The line between "summer wood" and the following year's "spring wood" is clear.

Tree readers of the semi-desert do the same with old trees in dry habitats near ruins. Under lenses, a record of growing seasons can be easily seen. Core samples from rafter poles can be slid along those of old trees until their patterns coincide, e.g. four thin, three very thin, and eight wide, the latter indicating a wetter period. From this, you can tell when the pole was cut.

The record shows a significant period of drought about the time* the Anasazi either died of starvation and disease, emigrated, a combination of these, or did each other in competing for scarce resources. In dry places, folks dependent upon agriculture and hunting live on the edge.

* See Drying of the West, this month's "National Geographic", in which computer climate modelers and tree ring readers predict a dry 21st century.

Hard Water Industry

Old-timers fondly remember the iceman who cut smaller blocks from huge ones with an ice pick on the tailgate of his truck and let cold splinters fall into the hands of waiting youngsters. Popsicles cost money; there wasn't much around then. Our hero would then, with tongs, heave a block onto his burlap shoulder protector and carry it to his customer's icebox. An icebox was a wooden cupboard with three or four insulated zinc compartments. A block of ice was put in one, perishables in the others. The icebox was usually in an unheated entryway so ice was not needed in the winter.

One old Closeteer vividly remembers a scene from when he was six when Uncle Bill took him up to Stevens Pond to see his father and grandfather harvesting ice. All was white, black and gray that very cold day. There were Dad and Grampy with about a dozen other men cutting and moving ice, part-time winter work for thousands throughout coastal New England and the Maritimes. The snow-covered ice contrasted starkly with the black water of the cut ice canals. Some men were cutting with great chisels and saws; others, armed with spike-ended poles, were pushing floating blocks toward a huge, ugly wooden building on the bank. There they pushed the great cubes onto a conveyor, which lifted them up through a high door. The boy later learned that inside the icehouse other men were stacking and covering the blocks with layers of sawdust. The storage house was double walled with the same good insulation in between.

From rivers, ponds and lakes near seaports ice was hauled to great insulated warehouses on the docks and riverbanks. There were several hundred along the Hudson and Kennebec Rivers. Sailing ships from our ports carried their cool cargo around the world. For 50 years there was a very profitable ice trade in Calcutta for ice-cream making and to cool the drinks of the rich. The South and Caribbean, closer home, were a big market for the new, circa mid-1800s, ice craze.

After WWII, artificial refrigeration became available to the masses and by the 1950s the famous Yankee industry had melted away; empty icehouses burned or rotted.

MARCH 2008

WIDENING NORTHWEST PASSAGE

We anxiously look north and worry about the nature of the water there. Will its yearly ratio of solid to liquid continue to decline?

In the 19th century, British minds were also focused on the then unknown Arctic. Their Royal Navy, after two centuries of successful exploration and colonization, was at loose ends. Surplus officers, without war, were hankering for fame, glory and promotion. The mysterious poles were opportunities for further exploration, so the Navy sent forth wooden ships and inexperienced crews to again seek an elusive Northwest Passage. Those brave and often foolish sailors learned from whalers and earlier explorers that their window through the ice was at best three months, often only two or none. They left England in June and, after rounding southern Greenland, sailed on northward through the Davis Straight among dazzlingly beautiful icebergs and then westerly toward Lancaster Sound. There, they encountered ever more ice, some free and drifting, much in great impassable packs. By then, it was usually August, and they knew there was only another month for exploration before increasing cold would stitch together loose bergs, floes, packs and, all too often, their frail ships. Thus trapped, they would face a long dark winter among ice-covered seas, peninsulas and islands they didn't know. Poor food, inadequate fuel, clothing and insulation would be their lot until the ice broke up and released them, or not, the following June.

Lucky crews encountered Eskimos who generously provided them with friendship and fresh meat, thus reducing stress and scurvy, the scourges of all seamen. What astounds the modern reader of these adventures is the terrible arrogance, snobbery and stubbornness of the newcomers who could readily see the natives were healthy and relatively happy due to fresh food, clothing, snow houses, and light sleds pulled by dogs. They were well adapted after millennia and freely shared their knowledge. Few British officers would descend to allow themselves or their men "to go native," to do things the non-British way. Suffering and death were often the result.

How ironic that coal- and oil-fired industrial countries led by Britain have melted an ever-widening passage with their pollutants. There are no equivalents of Victorian crowds cheering this accomplishment. The stimulating fears of an unknown land of ice have been replaced by fears of climate change and rising seas.

ICE WATER BEAUTIES

March fifth on a sunny afternoon, two mild days after a warm rain, we, an old Closeteer and bluebird-house-maker friend, stopped by a long, lovely woodland pool. Covering most of its one-quarter acre surface was a half foot of white ice. Around its edge, due to groundwater seepage, was liquid water at 32 degrees F. We stared down into the perfectly clear melt water and there, just above a rich brown floor of last year's oak leaves, were several red-orange spots. A closer look revealed the fairy shrimp we had hoped we might see.

These beautiful crustaceans, less than an inch long, were gracefully swimming upside down, propelled by 10 pair of feathery legs, preceded by a head with large eyes on stalks. Translucent, the dark guts in some were clearly seen. These tiny relatives of sea shrimp, crabs, and lobsters live in ponds where predator fish cannot. Such places, ranging in size from puddles to large ponds without streams that dry up most years, are called vernal pools. If certified, they are protected by law. One must simply find fairy shrimp, wood frogs, or certain salamanders in some stage of their fast life cycles to certify. In a few days or weeks after mating, fairy shrimp females will drop their eggs; dormant on the pond floor, they may survive the dry season and not hatch until the pond is again flooded and cold, usually in the winter or early spring. Studies have found that with some species the eggs will not hatch for many years; this extended dormancy is called "bet hedging." "Egg banks" on the soil may last many years.

We knew this isolated, unspoiled pond from past visits. In another month, we'll return expecting to see wood frog and salamander eggs and tadpoles, plus numerous insects. These pools—there may be a thousand in the tri-town area—are essential to their inhabitants as well as for the adult frogs, toads, and salamanders who spend most of their year in nearby uplands and visit only in early spring to breed.

Visit one near your home on a warm, moist night in the next few weeks; bring flashlight and family. You are quite likely to observe what naturalists call a "Big Night," one of a few each year, when vernal pool amphibians are perhaps too busy mating and spawning to even notice scrumptious fairy shrimp.

PEOPLE INCREASE, WATER DECREASE

In the American Southwest one-story cities creep out across desert valleys and up flanking hills. Many of the washes and rivers are dry except for a few weeks each year. A Closeteer and wife now in Arizona report back that the desert is relatively green and its flowers blooming from this winter's extra rain. His Arizona sister, resident of Phoenix for the past 43 years, tells that when she arrived in her new city it had one-third million people; now, there are 12 times that. An area roughly three times that of greater Boston is now covered with pavement, roofs and water-guzzling lawns.

Aye, water, there's the dry rub. Only about 10 inches falls per year; 95 percent of that is lost to the air by evaporation and transpiration, leaving only about a half an inch to enter the ground. Needed and unneeded water is canalled in from the distant Colorado River and used extravagantly; the poor Colorado, after further thefts by Las Vegas and agriculture in southern California, doesn't make it to the sea. The Mexicans on the downriver end used to complain to no avail.

Lake Mead, great reservoir for Las Vegas, creation of Hoover Dam, is running low. Its water has recently been found to have trace amounts of hormones, antibiotics and numerous other chemicals associated with people.

Tucson, southeast of Phoenix, is growing apace; some predict the two cities 120 miles apart will some day join. To the north, the high desert town of Prescott is exploding out over the surrounding dry hills toward Phoenix 80 miles to the south. Millions more people are flocking to places where there isn't enough water now and the promise of even less. Climate modelers are predicting an ever drier 21st century in our southwestern states.

East of Scottsdale, in the northeast corner of greater Phoenix, is a relatively new city by the name of Fountain Hills. The other day, Arizona sister, while passing many miles to the north, pointed out to brother a tower of water shooting high into the sky. She said the huge fountain was built before the city as a real estate come-on. Perhaps the developers were inspired by the fountains of Las Vegas, where daring gambles are being made with Mother Nature. We wonder if the planned casinos here will have such in-her-face outrages.

CHEMICALS ON THE LOOSE

CoCo Key Water Resort patrons complained about rashes and breathing problems due to excessive chlorine in the indoor playground's water and air. The Middleton Board of Health ordered everyone out of the pool for a few days until doses were lowered and brought under control. As of this writing, applications for private pools are being received by area building departments. Many will receive chlorine.

Around these pools are lawns. An article in the March *Kiplinger's Personal Finance* shared with the Closet this week estimates there are 32 million acres of lawn in the United States. Fertilizers, pesticides and herbicides are added to many. Some of these and their breakdown products leach into groundwater.

Reports of pharmaceuticals found in groundwater and reservoirs from those flushed down toilets have been much in recent news. In Colorado's Boulder Creek, a tributary of the mighty South Platte River, fish have been found with gender and reproductive cycle abnormalities thought due to disposed birth control pills. This month trace amounts of hormones, antibiotics, and dozens of other manmade chemicals were found in Lake Mead, reservoir for Las Vegas.

In 1962, the late Rachel Carson warned us about our synthetic chemicals in her angry book, *Silent Spring*. She, a zoologist, was in a barely controlled rage because manmade pesticides and herbicides used by farmers and homeowners were harming the wild animals she had devoted her life to.

Carson's plea to stop poisoning was read by then-President Kennedy who ordered his government look into the uses and abuses of manmade chemicals. The problem is they have not evolved over generations with organisms. Many of these novel molecules just don't fit in the machinery of cells. Carson, as a biologist, knew this and tried to explain. Her enemies, many in agricultural and chemical circles whose short-term interests were in jeopardy, called her strident, unscientific, and even hysterical. Research in subsequent decades has shown she was for the most part right. Our chemicals from air, fields and lawns were and are being flushed into the waters of the world.

Responsibly maintained lawns do not need chemicals or additional water in most cases. Nothing except natural organic substances, such as feces, urine and food residues should be flushed down our toilets and sink drains.

APRIL 2008

NATURAL LEVEES THREATENED

The other morning while washing clams at the clammers' landing, Eagle Hill, Ipswich, an old Closeteer overheard a returning young clammer saying to another something like, "They're afraid the ocean might wash through Plum Island." A brisk east breeze carried the rest of his words away. The next morning, last Friday, *The Boston Globe* had an article entitled "On the Edges." The *Newburyport Daily News* of the day before had one with the byline: "Next storm may wash out houses and roads."

This is not news to old-timers brought up in the Salisbury-Ipswich area. Each winter, northeast storms come in hard and carry portions of our beaches out aways to offshore bars. In calmer summer months the sand is slowly returned. This back-and-forth migration makes up a beach's annual cycle. As a boy the Closeteer was hired by a carpenter after one big nor'easter to help repair a Plum Island beach front cottage that had lost two neighbors to storm waves. A little higher and the ocean would have cut through to the marsh.

Alas, the problem is that our beaches, Texas to Maine, have little freeboard, as a sailor might say. Freeboard is the vertical distance between gunwale and water. In most of Maine and Cape Ann, high granite ledge harshly greets the waves. In a great gentle arc from Rye to Wingaersheek Beach, there are only dunes of loose sand. Behind them are salt marshes of soft peat, dependent on the shifting beach barriers for protection.

The ominous threat, not mentioned in the articles about storms breaking through the barrier at Plum Island and leaving hundreds of north-end cottages on an island, is more rapid seawater rise due to global warming. To paraphrase a cliché from business and government, "It is the big white bear in the room." Some obviously are aware, levees are being built by cocky New Orleanians and stilts are required under new buildings at Plum Island and some Cape Hatteras towns.

If the water rises faster than the marshes' vertical growth by sedimentation and plant accumulations, and if sand receipts from rivers don't keep up with ocean rise and erosion, both beaches and marshes will be drowned. Inland ancient ledge will be the new shoreline here. Will we add planks to raise freeboard, bail, or move to higher ground?

THOSE BEFORE

Some archeologists and historians now say there were tens of thousands of people here before the English and the "years of the great dying," 1616 to 1619, when estimates are that 75 to 95 percent died of Old World diseases they had little resistance to. Earlier estimates were much lower.

The land, due to annual controlled burns and agriculture, was Savannah-like, berry fields between trees. The newcomers, with colony in mind, just moved in. One of the most revealing hints about population change has been given us by William Wood, Englishman here 1629 to 1633, who wrote of Naumkeag, Beverly-Salem, waters:

"There, they [English] cross these rivers with small canoes, which are made of whole pine trees, being about two feet and a half over, and 20 foot long. In these, likewise, they go afowling, sometimes two leagues six miles to sea. There be more canoes in this town than in the whole patent, every household having a water horse or two."

Dugout canoes were not easy to make by men without iron tools. The

English, then only at Salem five years, must have taken those left by the deceased.

Suffice it to say there were many substantial tribes along the coast from the Piscataqua River to the Connecticut, where agricultural lands intertwined with fish-laden estuaries and bays.

One old Closeteer, who played in the Merrimack River estuary, remembers his boyhood there and the imagined natives, hardly "Indians" or "Americans," he never knew, but somehow wished some kinship with. He has written:

Looking For Arrowheads

We often did this fallow field
Eyes in competition down
Sharp out for glint of flint
A chip, a flake, a sign
Or perhaps the product still intact
We'd found them here before.
Every time in passing by
Hope rose anew and held us
To our random downcast wander.
Perhaps just to be there was enough
Salt hay smells joined those of the woods
Across the marsh the river shone
Always beckoning to us boys.
After rains we sought again
Surface rocks stood in relief
Each must be checked for telltale marks.
I still look down in kindred fields
Without the hope of much to find
But out of habit from another time
When cool spring soil met naked feet
My full attention on its skin,
Seeking signs from those before.

SEA TURTLES AND CHILDREN

Water Closet friend Felipe Gonzalez and his large family, Spanish language Mayan DNA, were small-boat scuba fishermen in Isla Mujeres off Cancun. A few years ago, he fell in love with a Massachusetts tourist. They now live landlubbers' lives in Greenfield with bilingual daughter Aisha. Felipe, once daily intimate with the creatures of the coral reefs around his small island, wrote, illustrated, and published a book for Aisha. We are sorry we cannot share his nine pages of fine, colored sketches with you. Here is what he wrote in English.

Lupita la Tortuguita

Once upon a (future) time, in the great Caribbean Sea, there was a turtle named Lupita. Lupita was born in Cancun's beach in 1970, as every turtle has to lay its eggs in the same place as it was born. Lupita is 70 years old and she needs to lay her eggs, but there is a big problem. The place where she was born has a big hotel. Lupita was angry with this case, so she decided to talk with older turtles of the Caribbean Sea. After Lupita and the older turtles had talked about this case they decided to go to Cancun and talk with the owner of the hotel.

Then, 26 big turtles went to Cancun. On Main Street they blocked the cars to show the owner of the hotel who built in their spot where their ancestors were born and where a new generation will need to be born.

The people from Cancun felt sad. The turtles went to talk with the owner of the hotel and the owner said, "Okay. I don't need any more money and will order the destruction of the hotel. Let the sand come back from the sea. You and your future babies can lay your eggs on the same beach.

~

Naturalists tell us that sea turtles, now endangered, once grazed the oceans in enormous numbers, rivaling the bison in now North America. Evolved from land reptiles about 100 million years ago, they never lost their need to lay eggs on land hence the dangerous returns to beaches every couple years. At Cancun, rich Gringos have taken their places.

Let's try to hear as Aisha might. This simple but powerful tale makes perfect sense if one is fair. Somehow, in growing up, we lose this virtue.

FIRE AND WATER

On a hot afternoon last May, a fire somehow started just east of North Liberty Street, Middleton, the dirt road leading north to North Andover and Boxford. The duff of the floor of the oak forest on high ledge was dry. The fire burned hot as it rode a gentle breeze from the west toward Thomas Road. When the breeze slackened it burned deep in places and took the organic matter out of the upper layer of soil. Bushes, dominated by huckleberries, young trees, and herbaceous plants just peeping forth, were killed, at least the parts above the ground. Roots and seeds in the moist deeper soil survived. Leaves up to 40 feet above the ground were wilted and set back a couple weeks. Many thin-barked saplings, especially those of pine, succumbed. The thick barks of older oaks got a good scorching, especially on their lee sides where the flames slowed and rose up their trunks.

Firemen from several towns fought mightily on the fire's flanks. Helicopters roared up from Middleton Pond with great buckets, hanging California style, and splashed their loads along the eastern front. A front that might well have ended up at Middleton Road in Boxford if the breeze had been a little brisker and the beavers hadn't flooded 70 acres of water in its path.

We were reminded of that 200-acre fire this past week upon hearing warnings of forest fires on several hot, dry days. The week after that fire, we had walked its sooty half-mile-wide swath and found that it abruptly ended at the red maple swamp a large beaver dam across Cudhea's Crick had drowned.

When you come right down to it, our existence here is all about water: water coursing through the firemen's veins and oozing from their skins, water riding in the buckets from Middleton Pond, water ascending the sapwood from roots to leaves, and water just beneath the leaves and sticks in soil. We civilians, non-firefighters, watched the smoke, mostly water, rise to join the water clouds.

At this writing, we Closeteers are sitting on an Ipswich River bank, raising our water-filled glasses in a toast to water. After, we will vow again to love, cherish, and conserve 'til death do us join.

WHERE FROM?

Two weeks ago, our asparagus shoots were not yet above their thin blanket of salt grass mulch. Last week, after unusual late April heat, we cut a dozen ankle-tall spears. Nearby rhubarb plants, recently nubs of dirty green, are now rosettes of dark green leaves a foot across. In school we learned the law of conservation of matter; our experiments convinced us that matter can neither be created nor destroyed. Where then does the stuff making up asparagus and rhubarb come from? It has mass and is therefore matter. Did it condense from the very air? Did some of the soil transform? Early farmers thought the latter. They knew that manure added to the soil resulted in better growth and any fool could see that plants arise from the ground.

Four centuries ago, Dutchman Jan Baptiste van Helmont carefully weighed 200 pounds of oven-dried soil and put in a very large clay pot. In it he stuck a willow shoot weighing five pounds. He left it in an open courtyard so the tree could receive rain and sunlight. At the end of five years he very painstakingly removed the whole tree, including all roots, from the soil. He again dried and weighed the soil and found it only a few ounces under 200 pounds. The tree weighed 169 pounds. He concluded that 164 pounds (169 minus five) of stems, leaves, and roots "had arisen from the element of water alone." In his day, scientists thought there were only four elements (earth, water, air and fire), not the 92-plus we know now, and that they could somehow transform into different forms of matter. He ignored the air surrounding the plants because he couldn't measure its mass.

Thus, van Helmont clearly showed that plant flesh is not transformed soil. Since water was the only thing added, he thought the tissues were of transformed water; pretty good but only partly correct.

Along the Ipswich River, on a recent canoe trip between West Peabody and Maple Street, Middleton, we admired acres of new reed canary grass leaves arising a foot above the water of the floodplain; tons of new fodder for ducks, geese and mammals. Thanks to van Helmont and scientists who followed, we now know it largely comes from carbon dioxide and water energized by light in leaf processes called photosynthesis.

MAY 2008

FODDER, THATCH, MULCH, INSULATION

A half hour down the Ipswich River by pickup truck, seven or so in Agawam moccasins, and a day by canoe, there is a grand estuary where the Ipswich, Chebacco, Rowley, Parker, Plum Island, Merrimack, and Hampton Rivers join Atlantic waters. The soft peat marshes, grass covered, are protected by barrier beaches from ocean waves. Draining the marshes of twice-daily doses of seawater are labyrinths of meandering cricks. Laid upon these by 19th- and 20th-century man are grid-like patterns of straight "mosquito ditches." The edges of the natural cricks and rivers are steep cuts, gradual slopes, and jumbled affairs of collapsing banks. On their upper slopes, between half tide and mean high water, grows a tall grass with fat stems called *Spartina alterniflora*, "cordgrass," or "thatch," after its colonial use. By August, thatch is breast high. Just above, on the high marsh, elevation of mean high tide, are finer *Spartina patens*, "saltmeadow cordgrass" and *Juncus gerardii*, "blackgrass," botanically, a rush. These calf-high plants are the dominant salt hay species. Thousands of acres were once mown every year for fodder and bedding. One old Closeteer brought up on a Salisbury farm says they only fed the cows salt hay once a week; more, and the milk tasted of its name. No one feeds it anymore. Now, a few hundred acres are cut here and there and sold for mulch, much desired by landscapers and gardeners, because the seeds won't sprout in upland soils.

Last week, two old Stream Teamers, also gardeners, borrowed a pickup truck and fetched several loads of free mulch from the edge of the Ipswich marshes. Winter storms, especially nor'easters, accompanied by high tides, float it in and deposit in great wide windrows along low roads. Moving ice on the high marsh and banks had cut it; wind and water delivered.

Only a few generations back, folks all along the coast gathered this bounty and banked it up against their outside cellar walls until the sills were covered to keep the cold winds from stealing heat. In the spring, it was used for mulch.

What have these random reminiscences to do with anything? Not much, they are just gentle reminders of our connection with the sea from whence we came.

LOG BRIDGE EN ROUTE SALEM TO ANDOVER

Log Bridge across the Ipswich River is no more. The large abutment stones on the Danvers and Middleton sides are still there. The current is swift in the constriction formed. In the 1970s, after three centuries of service, the bridge, probably the latest of several, was removed. The street from it to South Main Street, Route 114, and once to West and Green Streets across the river, has kept the name Logbridge Road.

In early colonial times, this was the way one would go overland on foot, horseback, or horse- and ox-drawn carts from the busy port of Salem to the fertile fields of Andover. By all accounts, and Middleton's late historian Lura Woodside Watkins has left a few, the cart path was rough, slow going. An easier way, especially with any load, was to sail around Cape Ann and up the Merrimack. Much of the winter and spring the road must have been impassable.

Middleton-Masco lad Xavier Chambers has been working on a project for the past year to transform the dumping ground the west bank at the crossing had become, from a littered parking area to an attractive mini-park. Xavier is doing this as an Eagle Scout project, the most ambitious we've known. He has gotten many volunteers (fellow scouts, friends, parents, Stream Teamers) to help, particularly contractor Tim Willey with his workers and machines. The place has been transformed. Next month Xavier, Middleton Scout Troop 19, and the Stream Team, which sponsored the project, will dedicate the park to Middleton for the use of passersby on Logbridge Road and canoeists on the river.

The Town has provided a sturdy picnic table. If you see it occupied, no bother; sit on one of the great river stones Tim has provided. While dozing after lunch, if lucky, you may sense the rumble of steel-tired wooden wheels as they cross a wooden bridge and hear the cries of drovers as they urge their teams across. They may even stop to water and rest their animals and sit with you a bit. Don't say anything or peek.

Red Tide Returns

How very magical the natural world seems. Magical and natural don't jibe in the minds of many. As we study nature, it loses some of its magic, but certainly not its wonder. Evolution has performed miracles, which turn out to be something else, never-ending mysteries scientists feel compelled to solve. The rest of us ooh and aah, are enlightened, or ignore. Ignorance and ignore must have the same root.

This idle speculation arises out of yet another red tide bloom now drifting in from the sea on easterlies that have caused health officials to close the clam flats. The cysts of a tiny, tiny dinoflagellate stimulated by some combination of light, temperature, and available nutrients have risen from the ocean bottom and doubled every few hours as single-celled organisms sometimes do, millions become zillions. Clams in the shallows along the coast suck them into their filters and concentrate the minute amount of nerve toxin each contains in their livers. The clams, apparently unaffected, become poisonous to larger creatures, including us, who eat them. Despite this fear, we've heard of no one locally having been killed, despite several blooms since the early '70s, when first noticed here. There was a reported case of tingling lips and fingertips after a plate of steamers, the beginning of paralysis, up Newbury way.

The Essex County flats since last Friday are closed to clammers. The previous time there was a big bloom in the summer of 2005, they lost work for two months; bad for them in the short run, good for both clams and clammers in the long.

What, you ask, is so wondrous or seemingly magical in all this? Those who have to ask might not understand any answer. Unicellular photosynthesizing algae rise after long quiescence from the dim light of the ocean's bottom. They, each one-one hundredth the size of the period at the end of this sentence, influenced by a dozen variables, most unknown, drift and multiply. Innocent ancient clams take them in and become poisonous to their predators. Some seagulls and ducks die, many folks worry, a very few show signs of paralysis, and clammers find other work. Shellfish vendors truck clams down from the Maritimes above the bloom. Wow.

DRIP... DRIP... DRIP... DRIP

Through television and other media, we all know the world is warming faster than it should and that we humans are probably to blame. Reports daily trickle in of Greenland's thick ice shield melting, of the Arctic ice cap shrinking and becoming thinner, of the Antarctic's edges breaking off in state-sized chunks, and of the Indian Ocean's Maldive Islands losing freeboard. All this might happen anyway in this intercontinental glacial period, but not this quickly.

Drip, drip, drip, as the earth's frozen water changes from solid to liquid and the seas rise. In the tundra and boreal forests, the permafrost follows suit; spruce in mushy soils tilt before the winds. And speaking of winds, great cyclones roar ashore from Louisiana to Bangladesh to Myanmar. Whirling tornadoes skip across our southern and central states, and last week Colorado and Minnesota, at much greater frequencies than before. Many meteorologists say this is from increased atmospheric heat.

The following may seem farfetched, but isn't it is high time to stop warring against one another and start concentrating our efforts on appeasing Mother Nature and not getting her so hot and bothered? Just think of what might be done if we in the rich industrial countries got serious and traveled along green paths together. The billions spent in fear of one another could go to capturing direct sunlight and wind energy. On the hills above each town would be windmills. In deserts, there would be vast arrays of solar panels and smaller patches on appropriate roofs. Along our roads would be wide sidewalks and bicycle paths both sides. Green industries would spring up everywhere if encouraged, subsidized, as are agriculture and fossil fuels. Humankind could rejoice in its cooperative accomplishments. Even if the drip, drip, drip continued, there would be good feelings for having done right things together. Our fellow animals and plants would certainly benefit.

This idealistic rant may sound all wet. Yet, how much wetter will things become if we don't chill a bit and get our two-century oil, gas and coal binge behind us.

JUNE 2008

QUIETLY ON EDGE

An old Closeteer recently stood quietly for half an hour on the edge of the large beaver impoundment near where North Andover, Boxford and Middleton join. Their unseen bounds had no meaning on that late afternoon, bathed in soft light so sought by photographers. Stretching out from his feet were over 100 flooded acres of black water supporting a patina of emerald green. The water is transparent; black, decaying plant debris on the nearby bottom absorbs most of the light. Minute duckweed plants make up the floating emeralds. Ducks and geese swim among them. On arrival, he spooked a pair of Wood Ducks. Above, in dead white pines, are the large nests of Great Blue Herons. Parents flew gracefully to and from their rapidly growing chicks with food, which they regurgitated into them.

After about 15 minutes without movement, except to lift binoculars to eyes, the Closeteer lost himself in the scene, become a part. He recalled similar boyhood experiences over 60 years before. His fellow creatures sang and moved about him unaware of his presence. A pair of Red-winged Blackbirds, the male robustly singing, flitted above on beaver-drowned red maples. A rare treat was a bush-hopping Scarlet Tanager just feet away. The brilliant red, unlike that of any other, contrasts sharply with black wings. His greenish-brown mate checked out the duff below him. High, high above, on the sphere's pale blue ceiling, two Red-tailed Hawks soared on late day thermals. The light seemed to magnify them. In this precious area, no cars were heard; distance and lush green filters silenced. Only bird, breeze and frog sounds were heard.

The Closeteer, entranced even in the telling, told us he hadn't wanted to leave, but worries of a loved one waiting with supper stole into his blissful state. The more he stood the more he saw and knew this was as things should be and perhaps once were.

Visit one of our many beaver impoundments at dawn or twilight. Don't be put off by the gray, dead trees. Beaver dams kill whole red maple forests, keep the water in once fluctuating swamps high, and allow light to pour in. So-called "beaver meadows" in time arise, one

Return to the Rookery. Photo, courtesy of Pamela Hartman.

of the very richest of wildlife habitats. Go alone; don't move; just watch and listen.

KNIGHTS OF THE FISH TABLE

Last Friday, a dozen or so little-known knights sat at a large square table for four hours discussing the fate of fish. The meeting, held at the Ipswich River Watershed Association's new headquarters, which overlooks its charge, was arranged by the association's local naturalist of reknown, Jim MacDougall. The women and men assembled were without swords, armor, awaiting valets or horses. Their Grail is the restoration of fish in our coastal rivers. These scientists, toilers in the vineyards of truth, champion the voiceless descendants of our most ancient vertebrate ancestors. Their rewards be neither treasure nor fair prince's or damsel's kiss. They want to see the alewives, salmon, shad, trout, smelt, and sturgeon back in our streams and rivers, and devote much of their lives to this goal. Perhaps the urge is unconscious and somehow arises deep from the large amounts of DNA both share. This may also explain the avid angler's yen to catch them at every away-from-work hour, an obsession that sometimes leads to domestic woes.

We know this tortured analogy is ridiculous, yet as perhaps wiser, older folks, whose heroes were once knights and other warriors, we have replaced them with scientists and their helpers, many volunteers, who work mightily to understand the habitats and habits of organisms other than themselves in an effort to save us all; all this, and their subjects never even ask.

There was no hand ringing, cries of rage, political grandstanding, or plans of midnight raids on dams with dynamite at this meeting. The patient participants simply shared the knowledge that their studies and those of others had found. Like knights, they need the encouragement of their fellows and allies.

An old Closeteer, invited as Middleton Stream Team representative, got lost at times in the earnest scientific jargon and daydreamed a bit. He harkened back to the Indians here before the English. He saw them sitting silently and patiently around the table, politely smiling and perhaps thinking, "What are these talkative men and women so concerned about? In the spring, our rivers and streams are teeming with fish; wading children can catch them with their hands." Awaking, he, also with Old World genes, realized these modern warriors, armed with curiosity, educated eyes, and instruments, just wanted what his ghosts had had.

DEATH ON THE HIGHWAY

Last week an old Closeteer took a macabre midday hike up busy North Main Street (Route 114) in Middleton, from Emerson Brook to the North Andover line and back on opposite sides. He had just read articles about June turtle movements in the *Tri-Town Transcript* and the Massachusetts Fish and Wildlife newsletter. For years, he had noticed road kills, especially turtles, in this stretch, much of which is flanked by wetlands. On this walk, he counted the flattened carcasses of five painted turtles, one snapper, six frogs, two muskrats, two squirrels, one chipmunk, one mink, one beaver, and one woodchuck on the narrow shoulders devoid of vegetation. He made no attempt to search the weedy lower shoulders for casualties. He wondered how many had been wounded, been pressed into uncountable stains in the asphalt, been dragged off by scavengers, or were roaming, disoriented, in the woods, suffering PRCS (post road crossing syndrome). In three weeks, after the height of turtle egg-laying, he plans to repeat this four-mile walk.

Our paved roads, which allow for high speeds, have been here less than one century. Turtles have been on earth two million centuries. Roads fragment the land in unnaturally straight lines that are barriers for animals following their ancient comings and goings. Fish encounter dams and forbidding small dark culverts. The uplands and wetlands of amphibians are separated. Female turtles seeking suitable soil nesting sites are particularly vulnerable; their speed is one one-hundredth those of shell-cracking tires. At night, the sudden onslaught of light freezes the movements of mammals. We, in the name of progress, have laid down a deadly grid upon the land.

Lucky are the turtles that live near Butch Cameron's secluded sunny garden and sandy lawn by the Ipswich River. He counted nine turtles, seven painted and two snappers laying eggs there this season. Mary Jane Morrin stumbled upon a "frying pan size" snapper doing the same in her garden. "Since she looked about as happy as any woman in labor, I quickly went away." Her guest must have come up from nearby Boston Brook across busy Essex Street.

The old Closeteer told us that the refrain of an old country song by Dorsey Dixon kept running through his mind on that grim hike, which goes something like, "I heard the crash on the highway but I didn't hear nobody pray."

AMONG THE FISH BROOK FERNS

Last week, Middleton's Council on Aging/Conservation Commission Friday morning walking group hiked in the Fish Brook, Boxford, watershed. We left our cars on Lockwood Lane near the sluiceway of the long gone gristmill. From there, we proceeded easterly on a well-used trail maintained by the Boxford Trails Association. We'd done its rougher lovely path around Crooked Pond the week before.

In the shade of a cathedral-like grove of hemlocks above a great bend in the brook we descended to its pathless floodplain where we quickly found ourselves head-high in cinnamon and royal ferns. Their impressive growth, though hardly that of the dinosaurs' tree ferns, was twice the density and height of most wetland stands. The leaders in our column could barely see the stragglers. Lingering morning dew dampened our clothing. There, scarcely 200 yards from the road, we pushed through wondrous plants whose ancestors have been around 200 million years. In open patches between the fronds, Joe-Pye weed's striking maroon-speckled green stems and leaves brushed against our knees. We will return in August to see these relatively modern beauties rise above their ancient neighbors and put forth large clusters of tiny purple flowers, a rich color like no other.

Why are the plants in the floodplain flanking Fish Brook so spectacular? The answer is probably a combination of year-round high water table, the partial shade of nearby upland trees to the south, and the nature of the thick topsoil added to by floods. Only a century or so ago livestock ate all plants, including tree seedlings. These rich places, farmers call bottoms, also yielded late summer hay and were cultivated in dryer years.

Mosquitoes, which had bothered some in the woods above, were not noticed. Perhaps the electric-blue-green damselflies, that alighted, and delighted, on the fronds around us, and their larger kin, the dragonflies, had eaten most.

We pushed on through the clumps of ferns, experiencing another world, one our ancestors had left long, long ago. Although kidding and mildly complaining about the damp resistance to our passage, we were obviously happy in our unexpected surroundings. There are many such places, always changing, scattered throughout the tri-town area and beyond. We have but to leave our roads a bit to stumble upon them. Soon it will be Joe-Pye weed time.

July 2008

Floods Again

During one of our recent showers, while the rain did a comforting drum roll on the Closet roof, we discussed the Mississippi floods that TV had inundated us with in June. Just outside, the Ipswich River's usually smooth surface was pocked with raindrop splashes. We dusted off our atlas and turned to the map of North America. Those of Iowa and Missouri just wouldn't do for such a continental phenomenon. The Mississippi River basin, defined by high divides over 1,200 miles apart, Rockies to the west, Appalachians to the east, and the Canadian Shield across the north, is a watershed we roughly calculated to contain over 12 million square miles.

Imagine billions of rivulets braided into millions of streams converging into thousands of Ipswich-sized rivers, which give rise to hundreds of large rivers, many longer than the Merrimack. The Monongahela and Allegheny become the Ohio. Far to the northwest the Milk, Jefferson and Yellowstone flow down from the high Rockies to join the Missouri. The mighty Ohio and Missouri, added to each mile, enlarge the Mississippi. Melt water and rain of half a continent mix and meander to the sea.

Every few years the distant snow packs are thicker and melt quickly; rains are frequent and prolonged. Rising waters overflow banks and spread out over vast floodplains, where sediment-laden water slows and releases suspended silt and clay, adding to already deep soils. That was how it was for thousands of years.

Then, along came brave immigrants from the east. They cultivated the wide, rich bottoms, heavenly land compared with the thin, rocky soils of New England and the ever tinier patches in crowded countries across the Atlantic. They built towns in the floodplains. Periodic floods led to protective levees, and so it has gone for 150 years.

The waters constricted in huge, yet vulnerable, walls rise higher and flow faster. Here and there, they breach, and the works of folks are flooded. Crops are drowned. Some levees are later elongated and raised yet again.

Our cocky flood control systems have gone too far. We build in deserts, in floodplains, and on coastal beaches well knowing that we shouldn't. In the meantime, snow and rain falls or doesn't, glaciers melt, seas rise, and climate changes. Regional and global planning seem our only hope; both depend on peace and cooperation.

Thoughts While Rowing on the Merrimack

Last Saturday morning, a Closeteer and his niece from distant Arizona rowed up the Merrimack on the tide. En route, he thought of Henry David Thoreau and brother John here in a skiff they'd built 169 summers before. In yearly lengthening stretches on each side from bank to channel are floating parking lots filled with plastic powerboats. On a fine mid-summer's weekend, almost all were at their moorings. The rowers wondered if the price of fuel was responsible. Some of the larger craft get only about two miles per gallon. A century ago on these waters there were numerous oar- and sail-powered work boats, ships and a few yachts. Steamships carried passengers up and down the river and port to port, along the coast. Rail and two- to five-masted schooners transported serious freight.

The rowers, with neither cargo nor lack of time, pulled up the "Back River," shielded from bustling Newburyport, by wooded Rams, Carrs, Eagle and Deer Islands. In the quiet calm of the Salisbury side, a gentle east breeze played the salt grasses. Now and then, unseen Marsh Wrens' chatter emanated from them.

Off Amesbury's Point Shore, home of once noisy shipyards, their dory homed in on venerable Lowell's Boat Shop, where thousands along the same lines had been built for two centuries. They drifted just below the high bank and fueled up on coffee and rolls while waiting for the tide to change and join the fresh water coming down from the old textile cities and White Mountains, far beyond.

The ebb soon came as it always does, and they rowed out to the channel's center to catch all they could. In what seemed no time at all they were back the three miles at their Salisbury town landing start. Their only expenditures were a few pounds of flesh and sweat, all too easily replenished.

The hundreds of tethered vessels passed going and coming where still at their moorings, economics far beyond our ken rendering them little more than floating rooms. The happy rowers smugly wondered if sail and oar power, so essential and important in the past, might not return. What a clean, quiet and efficient mix 'twould be if hooked up to solar panels and computers.

INFINITE DIVERSITY

We Closeteers often try to describe our river in its various moods and seasons. Two Stream Teamers and a good friend capture moods and moments beautifully in photos. One Closeteer tries prose and even poetry. Others share observations, anecdotes and measurements. Alas, all these combined don't begin to convey the complexity of their subject.

One Closeteer tried, while writing a report about last Saturday's "Source to Sea" group paddle on the Ipswich. He soon gave up, after the following start:

Paddlers who looked closely at the surface admired water striders skating on the molecule-thin water surface-tension layer. The striders' shadows were seen on the sandy bottom just below. These images were true except for the tiny feet, which appeared as six large snowshoe-like ovals. The strider's minuscule weight pushing down on the surface tension layer makes depressions, which act as concave lenses and spread the light.

Also on the surface were floating patches of tiny duckweed, each a mini-island habitat. Just beneath them in the clear water we could see great green soft beards of filamentous algae flowing downstream from where attached to anchored water plants.

The above observations haven't even scratched the life on just the

Reed Canary grass along the Ipswich River. Photo, courtesy of Judith Schneider.

surface. We could spend lifetimes just studying and trying to describe the multitude of creatures, plants and bacteria in a water column between the air and bottom. Our inventories would change with the seasons and with diurnal light and temperature changes. A few years ago some of us participated in an interesting study of the bottom fauna called biomonitoring. We stuck a wire-framed fine net, mouth at right angles to the flow, into the bottom gravel for a few seconds, and then stirred up the bottom just upstream. The few handfuls of debris, soil and pebbles sampled, when dumped into white trays, revealed hundreds of animals: tiny worms, insect larvae, mollusks, crustaceans, etc., and those were just the creatures we could see. Microscopes would have revealed many others. If we had tallied the bacteria in a teaspoon of our take, we'd have gotten millions. Natural waters and their bottom substrates are alive.

To understand enough to truly describe we'd need teams of scientists visiting year round or cruising up and down on floating labs. Until this is done it might be wise not to disturb these wondrous mixes of billions years of evolution, water, air and earth.

AERIAL WATER WARFARE

Is it any wonder the ancients, before instruments, were in awe of clashing gods in the sky? This past July, their thunder, lightening, and 10 inches of tears filled the air, soil and river with water. On an early morning last week after a night of heavy showers, a north-south band of blue sky opened; we looked up from the Closet's clearing to the east where spectacular, high cumulus clouds were moving quickly west. Their white jagged edges, backlit by the unseen rising sun, glistened like frost on winter windows. They soon met a front of darker, wetter behemoths up from the southwest. The whole sky darkened and the booming of another battle began. The already dripping plants and saturated soils were doused once again.

In the shelter of the Closet, just a shack beside the Ipswich River, those of us Closeteers not watching the storm and river from the windows went to the Internet and clicked on the United States Geological Survey's south Middleton automatic gauge that measures the river's depth (USGS Real-Time Water Data for USGS 01101500). Its data is transmitted and relayed by satellite to a USGS computer, which calculates rates of flow, the source of the weekly data we share here.

Runoff from the night's showers showed the flow rate plotted from measurements taken rising steeply as expected, right there before us on the screen. We then clicked on the downriver gauge near Willowdale Dam in Ipswich and found much the same, only with much higher numbers. River flow there is the accumulation of runoff from a much greater area (USGS Real-Time Water Data for USGS 01102000).

Put these sites on your desktop or list of favorites, as we have. Visit daily and take the pulse of your watershed. In a larger sense, it is as vital to all us animals and plants as our blood pulses are to us.

Don't linger in front of the 2D screen. Run outside and raise your eyes to the ever changing clouds of water; exult in the thunder that once caused so much consternation and even reverence. Lick the tears from the climbing, rubbing, jousting clouds as they roll down your cheeks. Wade barefoot into the river's shallows among the now blooming pickerelweed. Feel the water rising, perhaps even revere, but do not fear.

AUGUST 2008

CLINGING TO DARK DAMP WALLS

Red Caulfield, previously mentioned in this column for making and setting up bluebird houses in area fields, excitedly told a Closeteer of Chimney Swifts in Middleton's Memorial Town Hall's brick chimney. On July 28, about sunset he had counted about 53 entering.

The Closeteer wondered when they left in the morning. On August first, he went there 15 minutes before sunrise. The sky was completely overcast, the ceiling high. It was light yet no swifts were seen flying. A couple of minutes before sunrise at 5:38, swifts, singly at first, started to exit the four-by-four-foot-wide, 50-foot-tall chimney. In the next six minutes, leaving in ever shorter intervals, 91 were counted before the exodus abruptly stopped. The next morning, 60 were counted leaving, all within five minutes bracketing a 5:39 sunrise. Twenty-four entered during 20 minutes of watching. On August third, under yet another overcast sky, 115 exited between 5:33 and 5:41. Only 10 entered during 30 minutes of watching. Close to sunrise on August fourth, a clear morning, 79 exited. We've read that they spend daylight on the wing, catching insects. Were those entering bringing food for young? Is there a relationship between sunrise and the time of exit? Four mornings' observations strongly suggest there is. Do they have biological clocks or do they somehow detect UV light penetrating the clouds? Wouldn't trees and bricks in line with the sun preclude the latter?

We went to Edward Howe Forbush's venerable *Birds of Massachusetts*, three tomes published in 1927, and found a half-dozen interesting pages on Chimney Swifts. Forbush tells us of a very wet cold June in 1903 when these chimney dwellers died in great numbers. "Wheelbarrow loads" were removed from the bottom of a large mill chimney in North Billerica and "bushels" from another at Clark University. We wondered if our population had suffered this past month when a foot of rain fell in intense showers. Did town officials hear signs of distress from the tower so near their desks?

As with most such observations, more questions are raised than answered. Red and the Closeteer will seek access to the chimney and hope that the excess water didn't result in disaster. Imagine clinging to sooty, wet walls during torrential rains while fallen young and colleagues pile up below.

LOTS OF WATER

Can you remember such a wet summer? In July, three fold the average rain fell. Showers, some with much wind and lightning fanfare, continue. August's usually sterile, salty road edges and brown shoulders are green and graced with grasses and blooming chickory, Queen Anne's lace, St. John's wort, and goldenrod. These are but a few of the plants growing from pavement down into lush roadside ditches. Road salt has leached out; these plants, discriminated against as weeds, are thriving right up to the asphalt. Most years, there are bare strips of roadside sand between plants and pavement. The Ipswich and its tributaries are running higher thanks to higher water tables, runoff, and beaver dams that hold water in their basins longer. In home gardens cucumber and tomato vines spread beyond their cages and intertwine with neighbors. One Closeteer has Kentucky Wonder Beans overtopping 12-foot poles. He picks them from a stepladder. Tree leaves show no signs of the usual August fading.

Along the river's slow-flowing meanders through the wide floodplains just up river from Route 114 and downriver, north of Wenham

Swamp, silky dogwoods, fox grapes, buttonbushes, and silver maples are leaning out into the channel. Between patches of these bushes and trees are dense stands of reed canary grass and purple loosestrife. One of the showier river delights are deep red cardinal flowers. There seem many more this year.

During a recent walk on the Essex railway bed, flanked by Boston Brook on both sides, we marveled at growth that rivals that of semi-tropical gardens. Fragrant pepper bushes grow on the shoulders between century-old cinders and the now high swamp waters. Water hemlocks, mistaken for Queen Anne's lace, dot the water's edge. Emerging from the surface are patches of pickerel weed, sporting spikes of fine, blue flowers; blossoms of arrowhead and buttonbush are vanilla-white. To record all we saw would require several return trips with notebook and a botanist.

Railroad engineers of old crossed wetlands and floodplains to avoid grades. When the trains stopped running, level paths were left behind, accesses to our swamps. Along the river's edge in Peabody, one is now being converted to a user-friendly trail. Topsfield's "rail to trail," in the planning stages, runs along School Brook. Seek out one of these natural gardens and rich wildlife corridors.

Food and Water

Last week's column, "Lots of Water," pointed out lush plant growth, the result of this summer's rains. Our foods and those of the animals we eat are from plants. Plants and animals are found in places where there is water. Our food crops require a great deal. We were hesitant to include the previous sentences; they are so very basic.

Well-known authors Barbara Kingsolver and Michael Pollan provide abundant evidence in separate recent books that most Americans take food for granted and are disconnected from its sources. They teach us in very readable, well-researched books about our food systems, largely based on corn and soybeans. Pollan, who won literary fame with *The Botany of Desire*, a beautifully written, very popular work about four plants of great historic-economic impact, does so in his latest book entitled *The Omnivore's Dilemma*. For his research, he went to the vast fields of our Midwest and the feedlots of "agribusiness," no longer "farms," and beyond, to find the sources of our foods and trace them through their processing, marketing and transport systems.

Kingsolver and family left friends and a beloved home in Tucson, Arizona, for the southern Appalachians, where there is water. She was dismayed at having her family's food, or the water needed to grow it, brought from great distances at high environmental costs. She wanted to enjoy home-grown, good-tasting varieties in season. Her family of four decided to eat from their own and neighboring farms for one year. After their successful experiment that eschewed almost all food transported from a distance, they continue. In *Animal, Vegetable, Miracle* she, who knows biology and economics well, enthusiastically describes that year, and challenges us to do the same to the degree we can.

These important books are indirectly as much about oil as water and food. Much of the cost of our food is for transport from distant places so we can have all things at all seasons, regardless of the energy required. Both urge us to buy locally-grown food and to eat lower down on the food chain, e.g., less beef.

Dig up a sunny portion of your unproductive lawn and get the kids out there in the dirt. Show 'em what tiny seeds can do. Buy from local farms. Visit the farmers' market at the fairground this weekend.

WILD RICE AND GREEN HERONS

Wild rice, *Zinzania aquatica*, and Green Heron, *Butorides virescens*, are no more related than white rice, *Oryza sativa*, the tame world staple, and *Homo sapiens*. The noble grass and handsome heron are mentioned in the same breath because both were recently admired near where Middleton Brook joins the Ipswich River.

The grass, rising six feet above the water, was recognized by a canoeing Closeteer and his paddling companion as they passed sparse patches, each stem topped by a large flower without petals waving in a gentle breeze above those of more colorful and common purple loosestrife. The Closeteer remembered reading as a boy of Chippewa harvesting wild rice, an important food, from canoes around our Great and other northern lakes. They still do; the valuable shiny black, long, jewel-like seeds they don't eat are sold in organic food stores. The Middleton canoers were seeing the large, tassel-like inflorescences.

The grains formed in the upper, more closely held female parts had not yet ripened. Pollen from the more spreading, lower, spindly male parts below the female had probably already made its journey on the wind to the ovaries of neighboring rice plants. Think of pollination in corn where pollen drifts from tassels to ears. When most of the resulting grain is ripe, two Indians per canoe paddle through the vast watery fields; one with sticks gently shakes the inflorescences above their vessel; the weakly held grains fall into it. The few plants seen along the Ipswich will be visited again in the next few weeks in hopes of gathering some token fruit.

So where do the Green Herons fit into this account? They, our smallest heron, scarce two feet stretched out, were simply observed at the same time scouting for fish. We were impressed by their striking color changes as seen from different angles in the bright sunlight. Upon flying, they ruff up their feathers and suddenly appear a deep maroon. Green Herons are famous for fishing with feathers, presumably their own. They have been observed dropping them on the water's surface where they act as lures, you might say fly-fishing without a line. A harpoon beak, flung by a long, powerful neck does the catching. We hope these clever anglers are there when we return for rice. These are but two of the many wonders encountered on our summer river.

SEPTEMBER 2008

PLEASE NO "DRILL BABY, DRILL"

Last week, from TV sets around the world the chant "Drill baby, drill" was heard coming from a political convention hall on the banks of the Mississippi in Minneapolis-St. Paul. Feisty cheerleader Palin, down from Alaska where the permafrost is melting, was warming up the delegates and no doubt millions more around NASCAR nation. Some in the Closet, unabashed environmentalists, wondered how the rest of the world heard this cheer from in-your-face drivers of SUVs, Hummers, cigar boats, RVs, ATVs, and pickups, many without cargo and going nowhere necessary.

The rest of the planet's people might well be saying, "Now those arrogant Americans want to drill around the lands' fertile margins on continental shelves, fishing banks, and estuaries." They do already, yet want to expand even further, all the time knowing well that oil and water don't mix. This on a planet where the wind blows and the sun shines in abundance. Folks have known for centuries how to harness the wind with windmills and sails. Now we have a dozen clever ways to capture sunlight and transform it, and yet we hear "Drill baby, drill" coming from people who should know that their pollutants become ours. Nothing new for over two centuries now, the industrialized world's boardrooms have been chanting some version of "Burn baby, burn" with reference to coal.

There is no attempt here to point to the Republicans at their happy rally last week as sole villains. Democrats, who drive all the vehicles listed above, have as gas prices rose this past year been weakening their anti-offshore drilling rhetoric. The imaginations of many don't rise much beyond the fossil fuel-powered internal combustion engines we love and depend too deeply on.

We Closeteers don't think that Messrs. McCain and Obama, deep in their hearts and minds, want more drilling. Mrs. Palin might. Both recognize that global warming is a serious problem and are smart enough to know drastic things must be done to curtail our role in its causes. Alas, both want the votes of fellow gas-guzzling Americans. We environmentalists, also hypocritical guzzlers, hope that whoever is elected will boldly flip-flop once again and use his power to change our oily ways.

BLUEBERRIES AND WATER

Early morning light greeted us through clouds not forecast. We, an old Closeteer and friend, were off for the distant Berkshires and blueberries. Friend's sister Susan had invited us to pick from a hundred or so bushes set out a half century ago.

The drive west from the Ipswich River was largely on Routes 495 and 2. We soon passed over the placid Concord River, flowing north to the Merrimack. We thought of Thoreau and brother John rowing their homemade skiff down river en route to Plum Island. Near Leominster, we looked down on the cleaned-up Nashua River descending to the Merrimack in New Hampshire. The next river recognized was the lively Miller's, recently rejuvenated by five inches of rain, gift of Hanna. She flows bumpily down over rocks on her way to rendezvous with the mighty Connecticut. There, we walked out on the high arc of the magnificent French King Bridge that crosses from half-billion-year-old Paleozoic, metamorphic schist west over the Connecticut River to Jurassic conglomerate 50 million years younger. The river there has eaten a spectacular gorge between these venerable formations. We looked north, upriver, into the low clouds covering Vermont.

As we continued, a few drops of rain splashed on the windshield. We knew that any blueberries left this late in the season would be wet.

In gentle mountains beyond Greenfield we drove along the Deerfield River, its flow opposite ours. At Shelburne Falls, we turned south across the river and climbed along a shaded tributary, seemingly out of the now dark clouds. The waterfall-punctuated brook and lovely winding road took us up into a high valley where we came upon heavily laden dwarf apple trees, 17,000 we were soon told, of our destination.

After introductions with her in-laws Sue led us, buckets in hand, up through mature conifers and hardwoods to a half-acre highbush blueberry patch on a lovely hill overlooking a valley. It began to rain in earnest as we started to pick. Damp and with only a few wet berries we fled to our host's home.

In the afternoon, after a tour of orchards and surrounding woods, the sky partially cleared and we, still damp, returned to pick the last of this season's blueberries. Laden with berries and gift apples we leisurely retraced our routes along and across the rivers home. Excess water, now out of the sky, was on the trees and in the ground and streams. A wet yet wondrous day in forested land once mostly pasture left us with Brigadoon and Shangri-La-like memories.

MEANDERING ABOVE THE DAM

Down down the water comes, day after day, year after year toward its mixing place in Plum Island Sound. We along the Ipswich River can depend on it at least in human lifetimes. Thousands of people drink it. Millions of birds and mammals live in or visit its floodplain. Trillions of insects, worms, mollusks and crustaceans support the millions. Microorganisms in numbers raised to many more powers live in the waters, soils, and in and on the plants and animals, including us. They are fodder for the trillions.

The other morning in crisp clear air, harbinger of impending fall, a Closeteer and friend paddled upriver from the dam at Bostik, an adhesives plant on the river near the junction of Middleton, Peabody, Lynnfield and North Reading. The dam, for a long time unused, had been the site of working dams powering saw, fulling, grist and paper mills from about 1670 to 1920. The sluiceways and penstocks have long been blocked, but the millpond where we put in is still intact with 11 acres of potential energy lost now on the rocks below the dam where it resumes downstream as kinetic energy. There are no longer water wheels or leather belts connecting them to mill room drive shafts. Behind the dam, over three centuries of sediment from as far away as Wilmington have built up.

We paddled up the long mill pond between shallow edges covered with pond lilies. Mature forest on both sides, surprisingly lush for mid-September, seemed a green-walled canyon. The pond narrowed to river channel, one that gently meanders through a wet, heavily vegetated floodplain. Swamp dogwood, laden with clusters of blue fruits, and buttonbush, with perfect brown spheres of seeds, crowded out over the channel's edges within a few feet of our vessel. Rafts of flowering smartweed almost touched. The ever swifter water of our deep liquid road was clear and inviting. The peaceful sounds were those of breezes, birds and flow around fallen logs.

As we proceeded westward toward North Reading center, the meanders became more pronounced as the floodplain widened. Several times after a few minutes' paddle we found ourselves back close to a turn just left. Our sinuous path had us going three fish for every one crow mile. We didn't want our exploration in this delightful labyrinth to end; alas, frivolous time constraints and a beaver dam encountered had us stopping, resting, and then reluctantly turning to ride the current back. Try this lovely stretch we Closeteers have so long ignored.

WET WHIRLING WINDS

Images of the aftermath of Ike's devastation on the Gulf Coast stretching out from Galveston and Houston had one of the Closeteers doing a pretty good rendition of Glen Campbell's hit song whose sad refrain is "Galveston, Oh Galveston." Poor Galveston went under in September 1900 with the loss of over 6,000 people. This time the people got out in time and left their buildings to the storm. Ike's surge, predicted to rise well over 20 feet, came in at about two-thirds that. Still, this city of 57,000 folks was inundated.

The stories from the flooded areas led to a discussion in the Closet about hurricanes, their origins and increasing frequency, and reminded us of prior storms. A couple old Closeteers have vivid memories from the deadly colossus here in September 1938. It was followed over the decades by Carol, Edna, Andrew, Jeanne, Rita, Katrina and Ike, to mention but a few. The following poem by an old Closeteer that appeared in this column after Jeanne tells the basic story of most Atlantic hurricanes:

> Restless air off Africa
> Follows in Colombo's wake
> Plucking water as she goes
> In Caribbean gathers more.
> Now an angry swirl dubbed Jeanne
> Who slams her waving skirts ashore.
> Thousands in poor Haiti die
> Rage half spent she slows
> And weeps away the rest on north
> Here, a thousand leagues from start
> Her tears fall on my cheeks

The plucky people driven inland by Ike will return to their long, usually beautiful and peaceful, barrier island. The survivors and newcomers built anew after the 1900 blow as they are now doing in New Orleans after Katrina. Folks like to live near water. Plum Island shows signs of being cut through by winter nor'easters, yet no one is leaving.

Alas, the oceans under a warming atmosphere are rising; estimates range from two to eight feet, due to glacier and ice cap melting, by 2100. Warmer water is fuel for even larger storms.

The first lines of Glen's verses about a soldier in some distant place remembering his home there, not about hurricanes, go:

> Galveston, oh Galveston, I still hear your sea winds blowing

> Galveston, oh Galveston, I still hear your sea waves crashing
>   Galveston, oh Galveston, I am so afraid of dying.

Barrier islands and other lowlands around the world may soon see human habitat dying by drowning. Our ancient aquatic ancestors will move in.

OCTOBER 2008

SILVER MAPLE SWAMP

In 1638 Chief Masconomo put his mark on a deed selling the lower Ipswich River watershed and rights thereon to John Winthrop Jr. for 20 pounds. We doubt if he, though probably a wise leader in his own culture, had any idea what was happening. Winthrop and four cronies who witnessed surely did.

The other morning an old Closeteer and friend paddled with the flow around Masconomet Regional School for an hour and never saw the large campus where Masconomo's people no doubt planted corn, squash and beans. The canoeists, down from Middleton on high water thanks to four inches of rain gently given the previous Friday through Monday, passed through the tunnels under I-95 and entered a wide floodplain dominated by silver maples. Here, where Middleton, Boxford and Topsfield join the river's twists and turns, the low banks and lower floodplain were inundated. The channel, hidden in many places by leaning and fallen trees, was navigated by observing flow around emergent bushes and snags. The outer banks of these meanders erode; sediment builds up on the inner. Eventually, these growing loops meet and a short-cut channel forms. The cut-off loop, called an oxbow, becomes a pond that sediment fills in time.

We found ourselves in a pleasant jungle as we passed south near the school's fields from which came the tree-muffled cries of kids. We were in a silver maple swamp. As a tree-climbing lad, the Closeteer had learned the hard way to mistrust these beautiful yet brittle trees. Huge old specimens along the banks seem to lean on the water. Covered with snow and pushed by wind, they had fallen, half their shallow roots and soil raised high in the air; other roots, still anchored, sustained them. Come spring their branches grew upward. We were surrounded by these mini-groves of clones, perhaps with the exact same DNA of their ancestors, millennia before. These young from old compete with each other; many will die leaving one or two survivors to grow old and fall. Such gnarled bank sentinels become even more spectacular downriver in Wenham Swamp.

For three hours we never saw another human soul. The drone of the superhighway diminished. The sounds of play had fallen behind. We, so near civilization, had left it for a while. Our aluminum canoe could have been of birch bark or dugout pine.

WATER WORKS

Leaves, no longer green, flutter down around the Closet. The ground is lightly shingled in rich yellows, reds and browns, and all mixes in between. When dry, our comings and goings rustle in accompaniment. When wet with dew or showers, they glow even in the residual light filtered through the clouds. The quiet Ipswich River outside our door ferries a thin layer of this fall's harvest. Breezes arrange featherweight rafts into swirls and sweeping lines. Last year's golden pine needles form patches that remind of Maine's lakes and rivers of yore filled with logs as seen from hills. This year's needles will stay on and provide winter greenery among naked deciduous neighbors.

Let's don microscopes and visit the innards of these ephemeral factories that provide food, oxygen, and ever-changing colors. Factories in which the machines are protein molecules operating in watery solutions. Dry leaves, as all you mowers know, don't function. In processes not fully understood, chemical reactions affected by day length, temperature, humidity, and water availability from the soil, cause two adjacent cell layers at the base of a leaf stem to change. Their cell walls thicken and block vessels while weakening the glue between their two layers. This so-called abscission layer cuts off the movement of water from the ground, the diffusion of sugars to stems and roots, and finally, the leaf-factory from twig. As metabolism changes so do colors. Green chloroplasts break down revealing yellow carotenes, pigments there all summer. The glut of sugars in drying leaves causes red pigments, anthocyanins, to form. As any of you crayon wielders know, combinations of yellows and reds give orange and all shades in between. The death pigments, brown tannins, follow, either on the tree or later on the ground.

On moist ground bacteria and fungi receive these bright gifts, which they break down to basic molecules for all to share. They too must have water. We are all waterworks. The green photosynthesizers provide food. The microscopic decomposers recycle. We, who cannot do either, should go forth and protect our benefactors' habitats with might and main.

SOFT WATER

We generally take clouds for granted. As young children we looked up at them with awe and saw all sorts of creatures. We still do, even after knowing what they are. We from rich countries can board planes and pass through them to view from above. The other day an old Closeteer and wife stared out the window of a jet six miles high for an hour as it approached Boston over the Grand Banks. Far below were stratus clouds not being taken for granted. As far as the eye could see were snowy blankets rent with holes revealing the blue sea. The clouds of this patchwork were infinite in form and ever changing. We have hundreds of adjectives and phrases to describe clouds, yet few do them justice: cumulous, mackerel, leaden, wispy, nimbo, mushroom, sea smoke, sea turn, etc. After being told of God and heaven as a child the Closeteer thought, upon viewing ranges of cumulous mountains climbing high into the sky and glowing in the sun, that he was seeing heaven. Later he learned that they were only thin skin deep upon the earth. In the sixties the astronauts gave us their first marvelous photographs of a lovely green, brown and blue planet half frosted with white.

Clouds are of tiny water droplets, not water vapor, which is unseen until condensed around dust particles in the air. Mixed with the breezes and affected by scores of other variables, such as temperature, air pressure and smoke, they assume countless guises. From the plane they appeared as cultivated white fields, crooked furrows defined in shades of blue-gray. Around us, from time to time, was high cirrus we effortlessly passed through. Clouds, mists, fogs and unseen vapor are but a tiny fraction of our water, yet are as essential to us as the great mass from which they come by evaporation.

The Closeteer, having seen millions of clouds in infinite forms from below and now above, no longer imagines gods' works or heaven. Folk singer Iris Dement has a line in one of her songs, "Let the mystery be." Many won't and study to learn more; the mysteries only become more compelling. Blaise Pascal, 17th-century French mathematician-physicist-theologian, said something like "Knowledge is like an expanding sphere in space, the greater the volume the greater its contact with the unknown."

Meeting by the Water

After two hours of strenuous clamming, four old-timers sat in one's Suburban enjoying a drink of watered brandy and a light lunch of crackers. It was the way our group of Middletonites always ended raids upon the helpless mollusks. Our vehicle, perched on the shoulder between paving and salt marsh below Eagle Hill, Ipswich, was aimed north so we could take in the great expanse of flat, rising tide, caramel-colored salt marshes, and dunes of Plum Island. We were happily talking of practical and outdoor things between sips when from a car parked up the road came an old guy about our age. He approached our open window with friendly face, then after hellos all around, asked us about the Ipswich clam flats. He wanted a firmer flat he could more easily access. We, who were also slower now, thus experts on walking conditions on Ipswich flats, poured our knowledge on him.

Lonely, he rambled on for a whole half hour until we knew his life from A to Z. He, even more coastal than we, had lived his 70 years on Rings Island, Salisbury, a dozen miles north, on the Merrimack. He declined a drink and told us he'd sworn off 25 years before after a series of incidents we didn't want to know; he told us of several anyway. Most of our long back and forth was of local clamming, fishing and hunting. He finally said goodbye and limped away after having enriched us with another life story we could understand.

Over the years, our new friend had strayed far from his natural inclinations, as had we. Jobs for money had taken us indoors. Now retired, we return to our boyhood haunts. We hope the gravel flat that we call the "rock pile" suits our new acquaintance and will support his game leg well. He'd had polio as a young man. We didn't tell him excavating there is much harder than in the soft mud of the Plum Island cricks he knows. Of course, none of us, even the young commercial clammers who dig several times our yield in the same time, are there because it's easy. We bet that 400 years ago squaws on these same flats dug as they joked and gossiped for more than just clams.

November 2008

Paintings on Water Canvas

Flowering plants in the scheme—or non-scheme—of things and of time in numbers beyond our ken, have surpassed algae, mosses, ferns and conifers in their evolution. They are our crop plants, weeds, grasses, bushes and deciduous trees. We reluctantly use the word "weeds" here and do so only because we lack another word for the hundreds of species that bother fussy gardeners. Many of our so-called "weeds" have blossoms that rival those of the finest orchids. What better blue than common roadside chicory?

Flowering plants are so successful in part because fertilization after pollination is protected in an ovary that becomes a tough seed. Which species are the smallest? We are more familiar with the large such as mighty oaks. The Curtis white oak on Peabody Street, Middleton, is 17 feet in circumference and estimated to be four centuries old. You are also familiar with the smallest, although you may not know their names. That is a clue; want another? They completely cover many ponds in late summer. Algae you say. Pretty good, but remember algae evolved long before and are not flowering plants. Also, some algae, such as seaweeds, are very large. Here are a couple more hints. Each floating plant, the shape of a pancake, is less than one-eighth inch in diameter. Ducks like them. Give up? They are duckweeds, Lemna, and watermeals, Wolffia. The latter are but grains of green less than one-sixteenth inch across and yet both are so prolific they can cover acres of water surface in weeks by simple asexual budding.

In the fall they appear to disappear. Our ponds and slow-moving streams become clear. The other morning a Closeteer en route to pick up a friend passed by Curriers Pond on Forest Street in Middleton. The acre-plus manmade pond's surface was emerald green, bank to bank. Three windy hours later, upon passing by again, half the surface was visible clear water; the remainder decorated with wind-brush swirls of green. In the fall much sinks and goes dormant on the dark cold bottom. More probably dies and goes the way of fallen leaves. In spring, as temperature and light increase, some of the sleeping plants rise to become the beginning of a new crop, billions of tiny islands providing substrate and oxygen for even smaller organisms and pond paintings for us.

A LIFETIME LATER

We probably all remember rare moments when our spirits mysteriously soared. Now and then in the Closet we try to share, as people do everywhere, those times that can't be shared with mere words. One old-timer at least once a year lays on us the story of an evening early in April when he was 12 looking out across the low tide flats of the inner mouth of the mighty Merrimack. Decades later he wrote:

> Between the layers of spring that day
> All smells broke loose
> To buoy me up from where I lay.
> Out in front my warm grass hole
> Mud flats went and joined the tide,
> Which met the shore and then the sky,
> To curl back up o'er where I lie.
> Yellow legs, peeps, stout ducks and geese
> Plovers and curlews at muddy feast
> Their noises joined those of the air
> Of gulls and sea bound golden-eye.
> Delicate reds in the western sky
> Softened up and warmed the blues,
> Which left my rising singing blood,
> And had me join apart the flood
> That swept the coast that April eve
> And lingered as I took my leave.

The other evening at about the same hour he returned via Sweet Apple Tree Lane, Salisbury, to Morrill's Rock near the same spot on the river's edge. The sky, thick with fog, was a similar gray to that of the halftide water. There wasn't a hint of wave or ripple. The flat surface reflected all the little late light received and glowed like warm platinum. The air for several hundred feet between low sky and water was clear. Salt marsh grasses of rich red-browns had no breeze to stir them. This time the birds were somewhere else. No motor sounds were heard. Standing near the "warm grass hole," now red cedars and bushes, he didn't feel the elation of that spring 63 years before, just deeply good with its memory in such peaceful surroundings.

As the lights of distant Plum Island and Newburyport brightened in the growing dark he turned and walked the mile back to his late parents', now daughter's, house. He told us he might try again next April on an evening when the tide is out.

BYGONE WATER MILLS

We urge you to visit the remains of our water mills. Alas, none in the tri-town area now actively provide power for saw, grist, fulling and iron mills. Today power, planks, flour, clean wool yarn, and iron come from somewhere else. Why then go see their ruins? Most are on eroded stream banks overgrown with vines, bushes and trees. Go because they were important to our towns from the late 1600s to the mid 1800s.

There are a couple dozen sites here in the center of the Ipswich River basin, just short walks from a road. The other day Ipswich River Watershed Association naturalist Jim MacDougall and an old Stream Teamer visited a half-dozen in Middleton. There they tried hard to picture them alive, mill pond high, water wheel turning, with sawyers, drovers, playing kids, and farmers, horse, and ox teams bringing in logs or hauling away boards and timbers. Imagine a large mill pond surrounded by treeless pastures. It is spring; the water in the mill pond is high in potential energy being turned into kinetic at the large water wheel. Logs are piled around and even floating in the pond, awaiting transformation. Kids happily scamper over them. The sounds of the relatively quiet saw, no motors here, rotating wheel, falling water, and cutting saw provide background music for gees, haws, giddaps and whoas directing teams. Mud in the roads and between the piles is ankle deep. No matter to the children, this is an exciting place, an escape from home chores and school. Here too they can enjoy the workers' salty talk.

Topsfield's MacDougall, interested in the effects of dams, even those broken down, on fish movement, and Stream Teamer visited these sites armed with *Middleton, Massachusetts: A Cultural History* (1970) by the late historian Lura Woodside Watkins who in it provides information on about 12 in Middleton alone. She didn't speculate, but rather did much laborious research of old town records and Salem deeds. She found evidence in written words of their existence, and then with deeds in hand had old locals take her forth for more tangible signs. Thanks to Mrs. Watkins we can with little effort find the remains of dams, sluiceways and mill foundations on the banks of our streams and river, historic places we all should know about. Go find and listen.

December 2008

Improving Patient Care

On the last Sunday of each month about two score visiting nurses visit their 35-mile-long, 10,000-year-old patient to sample her fluids and to make measurements and observations. Instead of using syringes they cast buckets off bridges from Wilmington to Ipswich. These volunteers are in no hurry, after all their patient is old and only has medical records going back for less than two-thirds of a century. Last month two old Stream Teamers sampled from Thunder Bridge in Middleton, just upriver from Boxford. Volunteers have been testing for 11 years, rain or shine. The November Thunder Bridge results and judgments were: temperature 0.5 C, depth 5.8 feet, surface flow velocity 0.4-feet/second, dissolved oxygen 10.2 mg/l, clear, colorless and odorless. Information gathered at about 20 sites is sent to the Watershed Association's medical center where it is briefly reviewed and then stored for future diagnosis by river doctors. The visiting nurses, called "monitors," are gathering what scientists call baseline data for future comparisons.

If you stopped by Thunder Bridge while the monitors were testing and asked them about the health of their patient, they'd probably be hesitant to speculate. They, who often canoe the river, might simply lay the above numbers on you without comment. They've learned that rivers are alive and thus, complicated. There are scores of variables affecting their patient besides those measured. Monitors might be compared with 18th-century physicians who measured not much more than temperature and pulse; the rest was largely guesswork.

Not so long ago our patient was not seriously fretted over and was even used as a sewer when handy. Treeless flanking pastures, often overgrazed, sent manure and sediment down with runoff. Livestock daily visited to wade and drink. Factory wastes joined those more natural pollutants. Withdrawals for a dozen cities and towns were largely unregulated, even when flows were low. Thanks to watershed associations and the Massachusetts Wetlands Protection Act, which includes the River Protection Act, rivers, streams and wetlands now get much attention and abuses have largely been curtailed.

Our 18th-century physician-patient metaphor falls short for present monitor-river relationships. We know how to test live natural water bodies for as many variables as we do people. With increasing wisdom and necessity we'll realize water bodies and people are interrelated and equally important; at that point we'll put serious resources into tests, diagnosis, prevention and treatment when needed.

TWO WOMEN BY THE SEA

On a fine summer day in 1600, bhadbush blooming climbs up one of the picturesque ledges exposed above the low tide flats of Wingaersheek Beach. Her two young children play in a tide pool below. She looks northwest to a great arc of sand that stretches from Rockport to Rye. Parallel bands of color are peaceful to the soul: blue-green of the shallow sea, a gentle surf breaking on a continuous line of sunlit sand, dunes capped by trees. Beyond are blue hills. Above, a pale summer sky rises up over where she stands then falls behind the high granite ledge of Rockport.

As the old Closeteer imagines Shadbush Blooming he is sad because he can't use her names for the wonders he too has seen from the same rock. They are mostly gone except for the Annisquam River to her back. All he has for the beaches are Crane, Plum Island, Salisbury, Hampton, and Rye, all English names. These beaches, once offshore bars covered at high tide, rose to become barrier islands, gifts of sand down from the Ipswich, Parker, Merrimack and Hampton rivers. With each flood they provided beach-nourishing sand. Her people had long known that in winter, especially during great northeast storms, waves swept the beaches' berms out and deposited the sand just off shore. No great harm; in summer the sand, carried by gentle currents, creeps back and builds the beaches up again.

Recently Sarah, with a great deal of English DNA, stood on a Plum Island dune watching helplessly as the waves of a strong November nor'easter washed sand out from under her beachfront house. The porch fell to the surf and was soon followed by the whole house. Her beach may not be fully restored next summer. The nourishing sands from up the rivers dammed by her ancestors for water power no longer allow enough sediment to reach the alongshore currents that once restored that yearly lost.

Plum Islanders are begging that sand be brought in. Governments are sympathetic, but large amounts of sand are very expensive and who knows how much the ocean will rise and whether there will be even stronger storms, as many predict.

The superstitious might say the English and their descendants are being punished for building dams they knew blocked spawning fish. No fish. No sand.

FORGOTTEN CROP

The mid-December ice storm that so affected our neighbors to the west and northwest with loss of electricity reminded the old Closeteers of an industry some saw the tail end of in the 1940s. Recently, a friend loaned us a DVD made by a kindred soul who had collected 10 old film clips, 36 seconds to nine minutes in length, that were taken in Massachusetts and Maine in the 1930s and '40s. They are of men on ponds harvesting ice for summer cooling. Ice from our fresh water bodies was once shipped to the rich as far away as India. Households here had iceboxes that in function resembled little icehouses. Almost all our towns had at least one or two icehouses; large cities had dozens. Those were generally great, rough wooden warehouses with double walls insulated with sawdust.

Household iceboxes were wood cabinets with insulation around interior sheet metal boxes where perishables were kept. Delivery men carried ice, sometimes blocks of over 50 pounds on their shoulders, up several flights of stairs. The boxes were located in unheated entryways where perishables in the colder months could be kept without ice.

Those who lose electricity in the winter have no great problem in this regard if they have heating that doesn't require electricity. All they have to do is move the perishables to an unheated room. In the summer a cold cellar will do. Water coming up from the ground below four feet is about 55 degrees F. Up north, where there is permafrost, many folks simply dig holes for refrigeration.

The black-and-white clips of men, hard at work on the ice with large handsaws, pikes, chisels, horses, sleds and motorized contraptions with whirling saw blades, are fun to watch. A couple old Closeteers happily did so twice over cups of tea while swapping yarns of what they'd seen as boys. They chuckled at bygone phrases by the narrator such as "fine and dandy."

Now we give little thought to ice summer or winter unless, of course, the power goes off. It's the same with food and water; it comes from somewhere else without direct effort. We old-timers often wonder— the old have forever— if our marvelous machines haven't separated us too much from life's basics. We bet some of those folks shivering in candlelight after the storm had similar thoughts.

BEAVERS REVISITED

In northern Middleton there is a little-traveled wooded valley with a now-and-then brook the Stream Teamers, namers of brooks, have temporarily dubbed Cudhea's Crick. Six or so years ago Stream Teamers, while bushwhacking north up it toward Boxford, came upon a substantial beaver dam recently built. Eighty feet long and three-feet high, it backed the water up a quarter mile, flooding about 60 acres of a red maple swamp floor. Since then, there have been frequent visits to admire the beaver clan's works. Three more dams have been built downstream from the first for reasons we couldn't figure.* None have formed ponds deep enough to build lodges on. The first did, and there are now two lodges above it. In mid-December, after our first notable snowfall here, we went back again and found all four dams well maintained. The largest, now a foot higher than when first found, had two neat, one-foot-deep notches in its top. We guess that after over four inches of rain fell December 11 and 12 they cut them to lower the water below the floors of their lodges. The fourth dam, a fifth mile downstream, had also been raised and now has almost an acre pond, still not deep enough for a lodge. Water must be deep enough so cold periods don't freeze it all the way to the bottom, thus cutting off access to the lodge's entrances.

On our recent visit we returned with much new knowledge, thanks to the late Emil Liers' *A Beaver Story,* published in 1958. In this delightful book, he, naturalist and friend of trappers and hunters in Minnesota, tells of the adventures of Haloka and Akella, Ojibway names, and two generations of their offspring. He is unapologetically anthropomorphic and we readers are the better for it. Nothing of his family's actions contradict what we have observed or read about since the beavers' great increase here after Massachusetts banned the use of leghold traps in 1995.

Based on his and friends' observations, Liers gives his characters good human feelings and motives. These behaviors are very basic, such as raising offspring, caring for them and mate, constructing suitable habitats, and gathering food. We do the same and share well over 90 percent of their DNA. Liers reports no hint of war genes.

* Liers' book answered many questions. Can you guess uses for the lower dams?

2009

January 2009

Water on the Brain

Why are we so drawn to water waves? A simple pebble dropped sends out moving circles of them. Wind, even a gentle breeze, paints water surfaces. Tsunami waves travel thousands of miles; the wave does, not the water itself. On shores, their energy piles the water up and gives it horizontal movement that takes on an infinity of forms. Then there are the worldwide waves called tides. The earth's tides have essentially two moving crests and troughs stretching over 25,000 miles. Waves can be dangerous as well as beautiful. Perhaps that is why we are so attracted to them. One of the old Closeteers tried a poem about waves that he laid on us as we do here on you.

> Twice daily we are lifted by the moon
> Yet know it not with thought.
> It may be felt in alternating crest and trough,
> Perhaps distorts the brain just quite enough
> To cause the ebb and flow of moods.
> Such vertical fluctuations I can take,
> 'Tis all those horizontal pulls
> From hundred heads of neurons pulsing
> That have me in this state.
> Their tides in sync with mine,
> Reinforce my highs and lows at times,
> But when they don't sustain an interference
> Inversely rising with the space between.
> Go away! Leave me join the circling cycles,
> A part the very Moon and Sun and rippling Earth.
> I'll walk the inter-tidal sands,
> And let the static dampen with the swash.

He goes too far. The muddle in our minds is not due to water waves. And yet the stuff of brains is mostly water, and was much more so in our aquatic ancestors from which our nerves and brains evolved. How else might we explain the brain-water wave affinity?

Folks who can, travel over the world to watch and ride them. Our president-elect, recently vacationing in Hawaii, was seen happily

Winter calm. No waves. Photo, courtesy of Elaine Gauthier.

surfboarding. Let's hope the static so much around him is dampened on his get-away beaches. We would even approve a wave machine for the White House pool if it would help.

RIVERSIDE SASHIMI

In a section of the Ipswich River Valley in Topsfield, open fields, reminiscent of those along its length in the 19th century, descend to the floodplain. While walking there recently, Stream Teamer Judy Schneider spotted a large animal emerging from the river with something wriggling in its mouth. The channel was flanked by snow-covered fields and ice shelves floating out from each side across half its width, contrasting sharply with the water, making it appear black. The dark predator crawled upon the ice and ate. Judy, at a considerable distance, thinking it not too impolite, took a picture via telephoto lenses. The magnified results reveal a river otter enjoying a brown bullhead, sharp spines and all.

Now is the time to go and see these large members of the weasel family for yourself. They are not uncommon. If you don't happen upon one you are likely to find their signs near bodies of water, especially in snow. Their five-toed tracks, each nail showing, often include a dragging tail between. En route from stream to stream and river they often slide, leaving toboggan-like troughs eight to 12 feet long. They push themselves along with their short legs, run a bit and slide again. If you follow long enough, the trail will end in open water or a hole in the ice on its edge. They are much more aquatic than terrestrial. The water is where most of their food, such as fish, frogs, crayfish, water snakes and even turtles, is caught. We often see slides, entry holes, tracks and scat (largely of fish scales). Scat is found on scent mounds where they repeatedly return to defecate. We stumbled upon one near Pond Meadow Pond in the unspoiled country near where Boxford, Middleton and North Andover meet. It was an upturned root arising a foot above a huge beaver impoundment. The frequently used mound was coated with scales. They must have powerful digestive systems; there were no bones.

We'd like to go on about the sightings here these past few years of this playful mammal with the fine soft fur. Alas, the Closet has limited space. We urge you to research for yourselves, especially out there "where the wild things are." In evenings by the fire you might try Emil Liers' deservedly praised book *An Otter's Story* he gave the world over a half century ago.

New York City Waters

What a lesson in geography we were given of the New Your City area after the masterful emergency landing on the mighty Hudson between Manhattan and the high Palisades of New Jersey. There are photos, thousands, and three-dimensional computer diagrams showing Long Island and Staten Island Sounds and the East, Harlem and Hudson Rivers. Cold water from the Adirondacks and Catskills joined the brackish ebb and rafted the plane and rescue fleet downriver between thousands of spectators. Passengers and crew queuing on wings, only inches and minutes from hypothermia, were rescued.

Water, with its high heat capacity, receives lots of heat quickly from warmer objects in contact. The rate of heat transfer depends on surface area, temperature difference, and the conductivity of materials traveled through. The Hudson River water, near freezing, was only thin cloth and outer skin distance from hot blood. Had the people been immersed, the heat loss would have resulted in deadly body temperatures in a matter of minutes. Hard hat divers of old, before wet suits, wore leaky canvas suits and thick wool longjohns. One of the old Closeteers sometimes regales us with sea stories of his springtime at Navy and Salvage and diving school a half century ago on a Bayonne pier just down the Hudson near the Statue of Liberty. Lessons consisted of practicing underwater chores in murky water, 40 feet down. In about 20 minutes, despite woolen mittens and socks and heavy exercise, hands and feet became numb and students were mercifully hauled topside. Minds were affected also. Salty instructors above would listen closely on telephones. The object of those eavesdropped upon was to stay calm and cool under pressure. The latter was easy. We don't have to go in the Ipswich River in winter to experience this loss of heat. Most of us have but to wade in ocean water on our summer beaches to immediately feel the aching effects. This is why even fat L Street Brownies race in and out on their New Year's Day plunge, with no leisurely play between.

We belabor the obvious information the TV commentators on the emergency landing went over many times for a reason. Warning: even certain old-timers, who should know better, sometimes forget the dangers of cold water and, on explorations of frozen streams and swamps, now and then go through. BE CAREFUL.

FEBRUARY 2009

SEPARATION

"Article I. Congress shall make no law respecting the establishment of religion, or prohibiting the free exercise thereof; . . ." This is our famous separation of church and state clause. Since Roman times and before, we've seen the misery this lack of separation has caused, e.g., Crusades, Inquisition, and Middle East conflicts today. What does this have to do with water? Not much. It strangely came to mind when hearing of the cholera epidemic raging in Zimbabwe.

Here is a parallel example of separation, this one a pillar of public health policy. London physician John Snow was interested in the causes of disease. In 1855, when an outbreak of cholera killed 500 in Golden Square, he noticed many in the immediate area fetched their water from the square's public pump. The first cholera victim of the outbreak lived nearby. An investigation revealed that his building's cesspool had overflowed. Snow concluded the well had become contaminated and the cause was waterborne. He so reported to the neighborhood council and was asked what he recommended. After a pause he said, "Remove the handle from the pump." It was done and cholera subsided. Snow and others still didn't know the causes of such diseases, but were beginning to suspect there was something they couldn't see in water. Within the next few decades Pasteur and others proved that specific microorganisms were the culprits. A very successful separation policy followed; keep sewage away from potable water. Vast, expensive sewer and water systems were built, relieving cities of much misery.

We were reminded of Dr. Snow and separation upon hearing the sad stories out of once prosperous Zimbabwe, where an estimated 600,000 are suffering massive watery diarrhea attacks caused by the bacterium *Vibrio cholerae*. Its comma-shaped cells, only two microns long, are killed by stomach acids; however, when large numbers are ingested some get through to the pH-neutral intestine, where they thrive. There, billions secrete a toxin that causes the intestine lining to lose water at a rapid rate. The afflicteds' eyes turn gray; skin dries and wrinkles; blood thickens; coma and strokes follow. About 70 percent die if untreated. Treatment is easy and cheap, but not in a country where the infrastructure has collapsed due to more dangerous pathogens, corrupt politicians who exploit the people and their governments. Sewage and drinking water are no longer kept separate.

CONSTRICTIONS REVISITED

Light from the sky and off the snow entered the front window of our shack on the bank of the Ipswich River. We Closeteers had waded a fifth mile though snow a foot deep for lunch and talk around our old wood stove. There, we harkened back to canoe trips of past springs when the river ran high.

Somehow, the discussion got around to bridges and culverts and their effects on our river and its tributaries. Just downriver there are two roadways and their bridges, four lanes each, for I-95 built across wetland and floodplain in the 1950s. We guess the distance between bridge abutments to be 70 feet. Before I-95 the width of high water flow there had been close to 400 feet. "How about Maple Street, Route 62?" someone asked. "There since 1848, the Essex railway granite bridge abutments and roadbed have reduced high water flow from 300 to 30 feet." We went on like this for Route 1 in Topsfield, built early last century for cars, not horses, one that beelines from Everett to Newburyport, rivers and hills be damned. In the spring, on viewing flooding at the Topsfield Fairgrounds, you can appreciate how wide the river was before. We were reminded of the 19th-century empire builders who drew arbitrary boundary lines straight across continents without regard to tribes or topography. We all agreed that the Rowley Bridge Road crossing in Topsfield, built low on pilings to allow free flow underneath and above during floods, is the way bridges should be built.

Multiply these bad examples by millions to include all the too-narrow openings under bridges and through culverts. Countless ecosystems that once allowed free passage to native animals have been fragmented. You might think fish and other water animals are free to swim up even constricted channels; studies have shown many will not due to the closeness and faster currents. We now know the harm that reducing habitat area does to breeding populations.

Our watersheds, underlain with groundwater and laced with streams, are essential parts of the circulatory system that allows water back to its heart, the sea. In future planning we should do all we can to allow for free return flow and clean air for the passage back. In so doing we'll allow our fellow creatures to extend their courting ranges. Courting can be nice and leads to species preservation and diversity.

ISLAND MOTHER AND MIDWIFE

Shinobu Jen So Lai died earlier this month in Middleton at the age of 89. She was born in 1919 on the beautiful island of Taiwan. Taiwan, half the size of New England, is cradled in the arms of several seas, which provided water for her parent's orchard. To the west are the shallow Formosa Straits separating it from China, a separation the Chinese deny; to the north is the shallow East China Sea; to the east the very deep Philippine Sea, which blends with the Pacific; and to the south the South China Sea. The eastern half is a great mountain range running north to south with peaks rising over 10,000 feet; from its foothills, gently sloping west to the strait, is rich agricultural land.

Shinobu, a Japanese name meaning endure, spoke her native Taiwanese and then studied Japanese in school and later learned Mandarin and English. She went on to become a surgical nurse and then public health nurse out of a missionary hospital. She married and had two children. Later, she became a midwife and helped an estimated thousand babies enter the world, traveling by bicycle to attend their laboring mothers.

At 38, her husband died, leaving her with two teenage children. She took a second job so they could continue their education. Both went on to successful careers and raised families of their own here in the states. Thirty years ago Shinobu moved here to be with them. She helped with her grandchildren and worked part-time as a good chef.

An old Closeteer and wife, who have known Shinobu for the past decade, had grown to love this strong, talented, friendly and very generous woman from a culture half a world away. What has all this to do with water, our column's subject? Every time the old Closeteer thinks of her he remembers several visits his ship, courtesy of the Navy, made through Taiwanese salt waters, water quite like that of the amniotic fluid that accompanied the lucky babies competent Shinobu delivered.

Directly water related or not, we just want to wish a fond farewell to this little-known migrant to our area. The Closeteer, when he thinks of good Shinobu, imagines a young woman, one he never knew, in white nurse's uniform, pedaling countryside paths en route her patients.

IDEAS FROM DEEPER THAN THE SEA

This year we celebrate the 200th anniversary of Charles Darwin's birth. Biologists and geologists have been celebrating ever since his world-shaking book *On the Origin of Species* came out in 1858.

Darwin's ideas arose from the seas and marine fossils he observed in strata high above them during his five-year around-the-world voyage as naturalist aboard HMS *Beagle*. He returned at 27, married, settled down and never left England again. There, he intensely resumed his researches, mostly around his country estate.

The other day, while discussing Darwin, Emily Dickinson's name came up. We Closeteers noted things they had in common. Dickinson, born the year before young Darwin sailed, had also studied botany and geology in school. As a girl, she much enjoyed walks in the fields around Amherst. Many of her almost 1,800 poems show what an astute, original observer she was. Even in later life, when she retreated to her back yard garden and books, she still saw far more than most. He studied plants, animals and rocks in novel ways and learned much more than anybody else about what they had to tell us. His superb prose approached poetry at times in his efforts to explain a theory many didn't want to hear. Dickinson in her poems, most seen for the first time after her death in 1886, teases in a most puzzling way that is timeless and deep. Darwin's sense of time and change bothered many with his realization that creatures were here long, long before Genesis.

Then the fun began for us. We wondered if Dickinson, a voracious reader, had read *Origin of Species*. She, 28 when it was published, probably did. We imagined them, prodigious letter writers both, corresponding. Then our wonderings went too far. Darwin visits; he knows she won't sail to England or anywhere else. Gentle Darwin successfully negotiates a rare interview, face to face. Their animated genius talk leads to field trips armed with insect net and magnifying glass around her beloved girlhood meadows. After his return home we like to think she wrote poem 632; here is the second verse.

> The Brain is Deeper than the Sea -
> For - hold them - Blue to Blue
> The one the other will absorb -
> As Sponges - Buckets - do

MARCH 2009

DEEP, DARK AND DEADLY

This week's column is not about water. It is about weapons aboard Trident submarines hidden by water. Recently, an old Closeteer brought in an op-ed piece from the December third *Boston Globe*. He, who had seen the beginning and the so-called end of the cold war, has long tried to repress knowledge of American and Russian nuclear arsenals. In the article, Joseph Cirincione urges President-elect Obama to significantly reduce, from about 1,500 to 1,000, deployed nuclear missiles in order to save money. "The reduced arsenal of 1,000 weapons could be deployed on 10 safe and secure Trident submarines, each with enough weapons to devastate any nation. In total, the smaller, cheaper arsenal would still be sufficient to destroy the world 10 times over."

We guess for those in the know this is no news, and no new recommendation. However, being reminded again of what our species has the potential of doing overwhelms at times with a deep sense of horror and melancholy. In superbly built submarines manned by high-tech, well-trained crews, there are warheads on missiles that can kill us all, including other non-targeted animals and plants.

Beyond our beaches and rocky shores where many go for soul-regenerating walks, are lurking hidden monsters of our making. Their redundant communication systems await the awful code words we can only hope wise leaders will, at the last minute, not release and submarine skippers will not obey.

The authors and followers of this half-century-old policy of "deterrence," who proudly claim to be realists, have mocked those protesting against nuclear weapons with sentences like, "Stop the world, I want to get off." Remember that one? Is it any wonder that not dissimilar zealots in other nations want nuclear weapons and chide us, who have a vast monopoly on them, for our opposition to theirs? As you can see this is very complicated and well beyond us here in the Closet.

The height of irony would be if in our own defense or miscalculation we committed suicide, taking all with us, leaving no one to appreciate the irony.

We are left with depressing questions. Will we be able to walk our shores with any peace of mind, having been reminded again of what is out there where animals first evolved, waiting, waiting? We hope that nuclear disarmament will become a top priority for President Obama.

PROTECTION FROM THE SKY

On 2 March we received another nine or so inches of snow. Like tiny cereal flakes it accumulated loosely on the ground, leaving plenty of space for air in between. That was on Monday; later in the week an old Closeteer visited the site of soil testing for planned septic systems off Boston Street, Middleton. There he found the Middleton health agent and a civil engineer in a machine-dug hole doing perk tests. The dark topsoil and the red-yellow of the subsoil underneath contrasted sharply with the clean white snow above. The Closeteer asked, "How much frost?," meaning, how deep is the ground frozen? "None," the engineer replied. This surprised the visitor. The last week in February we'd had a cold snap with about six days of morning lows down under 10 degrees F and afternoons still below freezing. Upon further thought he remembered the insulating properties of trapped, still air and the constant movement of heat up from the bowels of the earth. On very cold winters with little snow the frost may penetrate down three or four feet, but not when there is snow cover.

We don't always think of cold snow as insulation. Small creatures such as the diminutive Ruby Crowned Kinglet have long known. At dusk in the sub-zero winters of northern Maine and Canada, kinglets burrow into clumps of snow on spruce branches and hunker down until the sun returns. Ruffed Grouse, rarely encountered here in the last decade, do the same; they descend from the air and land, usually leaving no tracks, and then burrow into snow on the ground, closing their entry behind them. A Laplander reindeer herdsman does the same by making a snow cave for sleeping bag and self. And we've long known of the igloos of the Inuit; within one, a tiny oil lamp will raise the temperature up to a snug 40 degrees.

Up in Caribou, Maine, friends of the Closet who have summer a home in nearby New Sweden, tell us of record snows last winter and record temperatures this. Last year snow was banked halfway to the eaves of some houses and must have been a great help to the inhabitants. The beauty of ice crystals and trapped air as insulation is that it leaves completely when no longer needed and becomes much-needed liquid.

POOLS OF ICE AND SUN

There is a lovely, scarcely known pool in southwest Middleton near the North Reading line where town bounds mean little. The rough wooded land there, no longer pasture, has never been developed. The nearest road is Old Hundred Lane, now just a woodland path. This relatively deep pool, without streams coming or going, is groundwater exposed between the rocky knolls of a mini-canyon. It is about 200 feet long, a fourth as wide. We like to visit and stand in the semi-shade of granite ledge and now naked hardwoods. As spring approaches, the daily higher sun provides warmth with much more meaning. Now the surface is still covered with white ice, only its edges show the blackening signs of melting. Most of that is due to ground water seeping in at a constant 55 or so degrees. When the snow is gone the darker duff and stones of the forest floor absorb more of the sun and thaw. Their heat will flow out to the edge. Soon, the remaining ice will be an unsafe raft detached from shore.

Then, on an early spring night, when the air is warm and saturated, wood frogs and salamanders will stir in the forest floor, creep forth and somehow head for the pool of their own hatching. After dangerous journeys of up to a quarter mile, they will frolic together in the shallow water; biologists use the words "congress" and "spawn." Sperm and eggs will be released, the latter fertilized and a new generation begun. All this may well take place in ice water. The race is then on for the developing embryos, later tadpoles. If this so-called "vernal pool" dries up before the gill-respiring tadpoles metamorphose into adults with lungs and legs, this year's generation is doomed. If there is too little spring rain many pools will dry up. Yet, drying is essential, at least in occasional years. Fish who would quickly gobble up the tadpoles cannot breed in such pools. Evolution has favored fast-developing vernal pool animals. The dark eggs and then embryos surrounded by spheres of transparent jelly absorb the light and warm up even in cold water. The unseen leaves above, not yet out, still enclosed in bud scales, allow light in. Timing, as we also learn in human courtship and reproduction, is everything.

DEATH JUST OFF THE HIGHWAY

Most of the people we know and those experts we see on TV and read in the newspapers seem not to understand our present economic woes. The fact that many folks are losing their jobs, houses and retirement investments is clear.

Last week in Middleton we had a seemingly simple situation that isn't clear. The fact is that several hundred fish corpses, large-mouthed bass, shiners, bluegills and perch, were found on the edge of Emerson Bog, a public water supply owned by Danvers. They are rotting within 25 feet of North Main Street, state Route 114. However, no dead fish were found a half mile northwest off the highway shoulder or a quarter mile southeast at the Lake Street Dam that forms the reservoir impoundment. All three sites are part of the same water body. The "fish kill" probably occurred in early March, judging by the stink and faded color of the victims. Now come hard questions, which remind us of our economic crisis. What killed the fish? Why are they all at a point where the highway runoff from half a mile of pavement pours directly into the bog? As with the financial troubles, many groups have become involved. They are the Middleton Stream Team, who received the kill report from passing fisherman Jack Gartside, the Middleton Conservation Commission; the Middleton DPW; the Massachusetts Highway Department (MHD); the Ipswich River Watershed Association; the Massachusetts Department of Environmental Protection and the Danvers Water Department. Jim MacDougall of the Watershed Association and Donald Bancroft of Danvers Water had done some water testing by the time of this writing. A representative of the Stream Team and Conservation Commission made the site observations noted above. There are hypotheses, but as yet no conclusions. MacDougall found dissolved the oxygen level at the kill site slightly higher than near the dam. Bancroft's consulting laboratory tested for many volatile organic compounds but found none at detectable levels. Like the economy, lots of variables. The Closet may be back on this matter after further research.

One old Closeteer guesses the cause was somehow due to a surge of road salts during a snowstorm when MHD trucks spread 100 percent salt for traffic safety. He and others wonder if such bushy reservoirs, also rich wildlife habitat, and highways shouldn't have wider buffers between them.

SURPRISE VISITOR

Last Saturday, a young beaver arrived unannounced and entered Skip and Stephanie Milotzky's garden pond off Forest Street in Middleton. Several children and parents who had gotten word were gathered around the small pond. The kids called the visitor "he" and an old Closeteer present asked them how they knew? Our quick-witted hostess responded, "It must be a she; it hasn't done anything dumb yet."

Closeteers, upon hearing the story, decided on a descriptive Algonquian name rather than the impolite and perhaps incorrect "he." Lonely-

One-From-Aunt Betts was chosen. We guessed Lonely-One was from a family at Aunt Betts Pond and swamp about a fifth mile south and had stopped at the pond to cool off on that unusual 60-degree day, one very hot for a beaver who had spent the winter in ice water.

Anyway, he, lets use the kids' pronoun, swam close to the dozen admiring humans seemingly as contented as could be. A neighbor had seen him walking toward the pond from the southeast, probably attracted by the Milotzkys' silent pump-produced waterfall that makes a lovely sound as the water tumbles over stones. A beaver family expecting two to three new kits, May to July, and needing room in the lodge, sends the offspring of two years before off to seek their fortunes. Perhaps this was one who, lonely, tolerated the gentle company around the pond.

Round and round he swam, long red-brown hair streaming, its color like the dyed hair popular among young Japanese. The fur-loving English and French of three centuries ago paid wampum and iron goods to the Indians for it. We don't think any of Saturday's spectators gave a thought to skinning this fine animal for his pelt.

About four that afternoon Lonely-One seemed to become fidgety. Soon after, he left the way he had come. Activity in the neighbor's yard spooked him and he quickly returned. Skip worried that Lonely-One, very vulnerable on land, might in his travels encounter dogs or cars. He gently caught him with a fish retrieving net and put him into a covered barrel and drove him to nearby Emerson Brook where he was last seen happily swimming downstream.

We, who received the gift of Lonely-One's visit, hope he'll meet a friendly "she" who will help him build a dam and lodge and use his proper beaver name.

APRIL 2009

RETURN OF THE BEAVERS AND COMPANIONS

North Andover, Boxford and Middleton seamlessly blend within Boxford State Forest. At the point where they meet on a hill of wooded ledge there is an ancient monument shaded by hemlocks. No path leads to this graceful slab of head-high local stone. The mature oak, pine and hemlock forest there is open and easily walked. The rough hill, shaped by continental glaciers, slopes southeast to wetland, now a decade-old beaver impoundment where over 100 acres of red maples, Atlantic white cedar, and a scattering of white pines have died. These species, especially the cedar and the maple, like lots of water but can't take inundation year round. Their roots need oxygen.

Near the turn of the millennium the beavers returned after a hiatus of three centuries. They built their dam on an eroded farmers' causeway that crossed Pond Meadow Brook between uplands. The dam closed a four-foot-deep gap where a stone culvert had washed out. A couple years after construction a farmhand, using a backhoe to remove invasive multiflora roses from a nearby cow pasture drove up to the downstream face of the dam and tore out a four-by-four-foot section. Three weeks later it was repaired and perhaps just for spite made a half foot higher.

This flooded area became a magical place as its trees slowly died. Within a year the pines' needles turned yellow. After two years the dark green cedar twigs were tinged with brown. All trees showed signs of stress, dead limbs and many fewer leaves. We visitors to this place, little haunted by other humans, fretted about the stands of Atlantic white cedars, which are the sole habitat of the Hessel's Hairstreak butterfly. We contemplated asking the Department of Fish and Game for a permit to take action against the beavers. We procrastinated and did nothing.

In time, we cheered up despite some lingering guilt about the cedars. Now, light pours in on shallow water. Fungus and insects that thrive in rotting trees attract woodpeckers and other birds. Ducks, geese, nesting herons and frogs at times fill the drowned valley with sound. Each summer billions of tiny duckweeds paint the surface emerald green. Dragonflies abound. Softer herbaceous plants move out from the edges. Another red maple swamp has become a water garden. We bet this was how the first English found them.

CREATURES UP FROM MARCH MUCK

There is a common swamp plant that is strange and deserving of recognition and wonder. Last month, a cold March, we saw them sending up spotted, wine colored minarets even through patches of lingering snow. No Muslim prayers were heard; they are the silent flowers of the skunk cabbage, *Symplocarpus foetidas*, which grow from frozen muck into even colder air. From cellular furnaces' burning sugars they emanate considerable heat of respiration. Within the flowers, temperatures rise at times 20 degrees C over that of the outside air.

On the Stream Team's vernal pool walk April fifth, we were reminded of skunk cabbage when one curious lad about six happened upon a few near a pool being searched for animals. He ripped off a minaret's fleshy roof; a modified leaf called a spathe, and found the yellow petalless flower parts within. What he noticed most was the strong odor from the broken spathe that forms a protective spiral around stamens and pistils, the essential reproductive parts. As kids will, he was dramatizing the skunk-like, some say rotting-flesh stink, with happy grimaces that attracted his companions. An old Stream Teamer's lecture on his discovery was not nearly as effective as the never-to-be-forgotten bouquet, which, with the heat, attracts pollinating scavenger insects.

Last week, in a wet section of the abandoned railroad bed in Topsfield, the Stream Teamer encountered large numbers of these wetland plants thriving in the sun. He is more familiar with those in the semi-shade of late winter and early spring woods. These, the earliest of blossoming plants, get a good jump on the tree leaf buds above. They rapidly put forth flowers and then great, soft watery leaves that grow on food stored last April to July in large underground stems called rhizomes. Blooming daffodils do the same. The Topsfield plants were already unfurling bright green leaves up next to their spathes. It won't be long before the enormous spreading leaves of each shade a square meter as cabbages do.

We who marvel at such seemingly simple organisms are sometimes asked what they do. What are they good for? We find such inquiries odd. And if in a philosophical mood, we ask the same questions about ourselves. Skunk cabbage is another species, one of millions with a tenure on earth much longer than ours.

Muskrat Meetings and Musings

On our first 2009 canoe trip, an old Closeteer and friend happened upon muskrats while quietly paddling the meanders in the Ipswich River's floodplain. At first they fooled us, our initial exclamations were "beaver." Small size and vertical tails soon led us to the proper conclusion. Swimming beavers' tails are parallel with the surface and not as clearly seen. Musquash, the Algonquian name, is easier on the ears and on *Odatra zibethicus'* reputation. These are not the much maligned Norway rats kids used to shoot in open dumps or the carriers of the flea in which the plague bacterium lurks. Musquash are very fast and graceful swimmers. We could not catch up with one that led us down river before it veered off into the buttonbushes. Maybe it was the 70-year age difference and lack of practice.

On a similar trip a couple years ago we saw ripples ahead crossing the river. Upon closing we could see a flexible green "V" of bent cattail leaves moving in the direction pointing; at its apex was a muskrat half the leaves' length. Upon reaching the west bank, animal and salad disappeared between submerged tree roots.

The Closeteer often harkens back to boyhood friends who made money trapping muskrats. He admired their knowledge of its habits and the gumption it took to faithfully tend trap lines in freezing weather. The working adventurers of American early history were trappers. French pelt hounds preceded Lewis and Clark up the Missouri to the Rockies. Many of us youngsters went through imagined voyages in birchbark canoes on distant rivers.

After our encounter we went to the books and learned many things. One is that muskrats have lips just in back of their incisors, which they can close to prevent gulping water when cutting herbaceous plants upon which they mostly live and when hauling them to feeding platforms. There is much more we'd like to share about these little seen aquatic rodents so common throughout much of North America. We may return and lay more on you. In the meantime, go to water bodies near your home at dawn or dusk and quietly sit on the bank and watch. Do the books or internet later, if at all. The famous 19th-century Harvard naturalist Louis Agassiz told his students to "Study nature not books." He studied both.

Water More or Less

An article by Elizabeth Kolbert entitled "Outlook: Extreme" in this

April's issue of the venerable *National Geographic* magazine caused a great deal of consternation and discussion among Closeteers. Computer models of climate change are displayed graphically on a handsome world map in a spectrum from dark brown to dark green, the shades representing percentages of change, drier to wetter than the 1971 to 2000 averages to predicted averages 2041 to 2070. The range goes from below 60 percent to above 60 percent change. According to the scientists' models, as the earth becomes warmer northern North America, Scandinavia, and northern Asia will receive more precipitation. A broader band of the middle latitudes will receive less. The Mediterranean area, much of South America and Africa, and Australia will become drier than now.

As the planet becomes warmer and evaporation increases the air will become more humid; however, that does not mean all areas will receive more precipitation. Rain, according to the models, will become more frequent and intense in cooler places where the air cannot hold as much moisture. Water vapor, moving from warmer places to cooler, condenses and falls as rain or snow. In warmer areas there will be less precipitation than previously. The water will stay in the hot air as vapor.

We gathered around the map and discussed what the changes, if they come to pass, might mean. Many questions arose during a lively discussion. Will the grain belts shift into the darker green areas of central Asia (Russia) and the Canadian and Siberian tundras? Will people move to the new agricultural areas or will the food raised there be exported to densely populated places? That is what we do now. Will we move water long distances as is being done from the Colorado River to southern California and the desert sprawl of Phoenix-Tucson? The Chinese have plans to do this on a massive scale.

The model makers also warn of greater floods and more severe droughts. The fact of continuous change on our planet is nothing new; what is new is the speed at which it is occurring. A couple of the old Closeteers who remember WWII idealistically wondered if the next great challenge, wisely adapting to environmental changes, might not be approached cooperatively on a worldwide scale. Dare we venture the old saw "swords to plowshares"? Are there alternatives?

MAY 2009

ICE TO POND TO BOG

Often in our local wanderings we try to imagine a half mile of ice burying us. At depths of more than 200 feet ice, due to pressure, assumes a plastic form that slowly flows. The great moving masses of glaciers carry rock debris collected from the earth and are then abrasive on it. As the retreating Wisconsin continental glacier turned to water it left thousands of ponds behind.

Last week in the waning 90-degree heat of a strange April afternoon, two old Closeteers and ornithologist Jim Berry climbed to a bog, once a glacier-left pond, perched above the floodplains of Pond Meadow Brook and Boston Brook in north Middleton, an area few people visit. After the livestock left about a half century ago the surrounding upland pasture gave way to trees. We were taking Jim to see this rare, saturated 13-acre sponge of past and present vegetation in hopes of finding birds that like bogs. Alas, none were seen or heard. A friend told of the trip said, "They were the smart ones on such a hot day." There are no streams flowing into or out of what we call Anne's Bog, named after Anne Cote who practically gave 30 acres here to Greenbelt; the parcel includes the bog and the surrounding knolls and high ledges that keep it full with runoff. Anne's Bog is on a divide. The bog's ends to west and east are the same elevation as its surface water and slope away to the brooks. Overflow from it spills almost imperceptibly down rough swales.

The first people on the scene, 10,000 or so years ago, probably knew it as a small lake. Through time, vegetation grew out from its edges. Runoff from rainstorms brought in sediment, which joined the layers of dying plants. Acid waters of the diminishing pond partially pickled the organic matter. The water has been slowly displaced by soil, the fate of all ponds. Jump up and down on such places and you'll bounce a bit; water is the matrix of bogs.

One of us waded calf-deep on the uneven surface of sphagnum, sedge, cranberries, bog cotton and pitcher plants; among low bushes: myrica gale, leatherleaf, swamp azalea and blueberry. The water was cool and invited a longer stay and look. We'll return some early morning when the birds are singing.

BRIDGE O'ER UNTROUBLED WATERS

Last week, a bridge of two steel spans was built in northern Middleton. The project, linking trails in Boxford State Forest and North Liberty Street, Middleton, over Pond Meadow Brook, was done by four guys and a gal whose average age is closing in on 80. The non-union steel workers spanned two eight-foot gaps in an ancient rock causeway with two steel, nine-foot I-beams, both with an eighth-inch of rust for foot traction. No surveying or planning preceded this feat. The noisy participants, their hearing not what it was, were not architects, bridge designers, lawyers, consultants or contractors. The whole important crossing was done without public hearings or a single sheet of paper. No permits had been sought or issued, yet now there are two eight-inch-wide spans not firmly seated on small, natural stone abutments. Such construction has its merits. If ice or flood topples, the beams, each only weighing about 200 pounds, can be easily hefted back into place if a few more codgers are added each succeeding year. A sound bridge would act as a dam in time of flood.

While there were no supervisors, there was a lot yelling. "Don't lift alone. All take your stations." "Watch it." "Be careful." Our transport man, with a pickup as rusty as its cargo, hauled the beams for a half-mile trip over a rough dirt road. He had wisely included a wooden toboggan slicked on the bottom for dragging them the last 200 yards over a rough woodland path. Two pulled; those observing hollered advice. At the site, rocks from the streambed were placed as abutments. The beams, which had been unceremoniously dumped in the riffles, were then hoisted into place. After each, a brave soul tottered across to test. All then precariously perched upon their creation for a photo. An observer watching from nearby bushes or listening from as far away as Boxford might have found the whole operation hilarious.

Nothing hilarious about it, the old-timers were just happily doing what they had done as kids when woodlots were wilderness, ponds great lakes, and brooks roaring rivers. Such places must have trails, rafts, dams and bridges. On the lively walk back to the truck one wag asked if anyone wanted to build a hut. "WHAT?" "BUILD A HUT." Laughter.

ESTUARIES: RICH RAGGED EDGES

Dark and light green grasses
In cowlicks swirl 'tween soft mud creeks.
Levied by dune and upland rock
Watering place for more than ducks,
Has depth and breadth
Beyond its bounds.
Where larval travelers get their start
And subtler cycles turn
To nourish out a thousand miles.

Water that falls upon our tri-town area as rain and snow eventually flows into the Ipswich River and then magnificent Plum Island Sound and surrounding salt marshes, a place of tides where the ocean rises and falls in a maze of creeks meandering through grass-capped strata of peat. During each twice-daily up-and-down cycle, dimensions of peat banks and mud flats are revealed. As kids lucky to live surrounded by estuaries, we saw the almost empty, low tide cricks as canyons. We climbed down in, then up and out those we couldn't leap. The other day a couple old Closeteers and friends visited the estuary that makes up much of northeastern Essex County to dig clams from a low tide flat. Crane, Plum Island and Salisbury Beaches, barrier islands, protect the vast "low green prairies of the sea," to borrow a line from the county's 19th-century bard John Greenleaf Whittier. The accumulated peat and sediment of 5,000 years, topped by fine salt grasses, is relatively soft. Direct contact with ocean waves would erode it away. Each layer, with different times of sun, moon, and spinning earth-allotted water, has its own animals, plants and microorganisms. Some plants and an algae listed from above, most highs to below most lows, are: blackgrass, salt meadow grass, cordgrass, Fucus and eelgrass. Mollusks over the same vertical range, high to low, are: salt marsh snails, ribbed mussels, periwinkles, razor clams and oysters. We can't do justice to a place so varied in words; in addition to viewing, smells, breezes and sounds must be felt.

We go there a couple dozen times a year, ostensibly for clams. We don't need to; they are not a source of needed food or income. Younger, stronger folks, who have commercial licenses, dig for the latter. For us, and them, we suspect the call is deep and ancient, something embedded in our DNA and brains. We share genes with our prey and ducks, fish, crabs, snails, worms, and on and on. They came before; we may be unconsciously visiting our ancestors.

LIVING FILTER

May is garden time, even here in the suburbs where farm fields have given way to pavement, lawns and woods. Folks flock to garden centers. Landscapers descend on lawns and shrubbery. Thousands of tons of loam, mulch and fertilizers are trucked here and there. Herbicides, pesticides and mowers follow. Much of all this attention is given the upper few inches of precious topsoil formed in the 12,000 years since the melting Wisconsin continental glacier washed most of the previous topsoil away.

When requisite test holes are dug for construction of septic systems the topsoils here are typically found to be only a half to a foot thick on upland surfaces. There are areas where loam has been stripped and sold, leaving only a couple inches or none. Some unscrupulous developers and contractors leave little behind for proper lawns. In southeast Middleton many acres of topsoil and thick deposits of underlying gravel were shipped out of town during the 1940s to 1960s, much of the latter to Logan for its runways. Holes dug there now reveal no true topsoil. It will take another 10,000 years to regain what was lost.

What does topsoil, tiny rocks darkened with organic matter inhabited by small organisms and roots, have to do with water, the subject of the Closet? Soil cleans up polluted water and does so effectively. Around the tri-towns there are perhaps 10,000 septic systems of soil, which daily receive our wastes. The sand particles provide enormous surface areas; interstitial labyrinths, walls coated with hungry bacteria, millions per cubic centimeter. These are alive so require food and water, which we provide. They digest our wastes and even our unnatural manmade organic compounds. The breakdown products are largely carbon dioxide and water. The cleansed water percolates down into the groundwater and makes its way to our streams.

Natural topsoils of sand, silt and clay, much more diverse in bacteria, fungi, plants, and animals, do the same. Each year dead and dying plant and animal debris falls upon them. Within just a year most is gone. Organic residues slowly build up, thus enlivening the matrix of mineral rock particles with worms, crustaceans and insects, which produce wastes more food for microorganisms. In 1972 the Massachusetts Great and General Court wisely passed the Wetlands Protection Act; perhaps it is time for a Soil Protection Act.

June 2009

Dams and Pens

Around the edges of the North Atlantic there are salmon "farms." People like cheap salmon even if its flesh is softer than native and dyed. Just four centuries ago salmon was very cheap here in the fall when beautiful silver adults, ranging in size from five to 100 pounds, entered our rivers and streams to spawn. Diverse native groups gathered at rapids such as those just up the road in the Merrimack to spend days happily catching thousands. Each spring they also gathered there, and hundreds of other places up and down the coast from northern Labrador to the Carolinas, for shad and alewife spawning runs.

French and English colonists came in the 1600s in great numbers. Gutsy fishermen from their countries and Portugal had preceded them by a century in tiny vessels on summer trips to this fishing wonderland. They concentrated on cod offshore. Early fishermen thought they had no effect on the abundance they found. Those who followed felt pretty much the same even as populations were decreasing and fish size getting smaller. One Closeteer's great-grandfather, a Salisbury farmer, left several sketchy diaries. In them he notes catching cod over 50 pounds for home salting and drying; now, most caught are less than 10.

For anadromous fish species—those that return yearly to fresh waters to spawn—decline was much more dramatic due to what seems in hindsight remarkably stupid behavior on the part of the colonists who, not long after arrival, dammed their life-giving streams. In a few years many realized the harm done as alewife and shad, and no doubt the salmon populations, precipitously declined. Dams built for water power by power, money and ambition, blocked the valiant would-be spawners.

Leaders in the name of progress, meaning wealth for a few and noisy factories for thousands, allowed even great rivers like the Merrimack to be dammed; it became a watery necklace of mill cities devoted to processing slave-grown cotton. The necklace became so rotten the Clean Water Act was passed in 1972 to clean up such rivers. Even after clean, the barriers, most no longer used for power, remain.

That brings us back to the questionable salmon farms. Are we making a dam-sized mistake all over again? These concentration camps have pollution and other problems much written about. Escapees hybridize with surviving native populations and affect their reproductive behavior. Thoughtful colonials knew what their dams were doing; now, in just a short time, we know what our numerous salmon pens might be doing. Isn't it high time to seize the reins of economic progress, "progress" so often in the saddle without reins, bridle or bit?

WHERE MEADOW BLENDS WITH MARSH

There are magic places of abundance and diversity not far from here where upland fields descend gently to salt marshes. The other evening family members five to 80 years leisurely walked along the edges of one on a winding narrow path cut through lush hay that will not be cut for cows. The Essex Country Greenbelt Association now owns this large Salisbury field that one human generation ago was the hayfield of a working farm. Before that livestock pastures and hayfields for 18 generations since distant King Charles granted the land, sight unseen, to an English colonist named French. And who knows how many centuries or millennia before livestock, when it was burned every year or two for deer browse, nut trees, and berries around cultivated patches of corn, beans and squash.

Open meadow habitat is much needed, so Greenbelt planted the fields in native plants and will mow each year after mice, rabbits, meadowlarks and bobolinks have finished nesting. We walked between waist-high walls of clover, red and white, supported by straight stems of timothy. Mixed in here and there were a dozen species of meadow flowers, dock and bladder campion the most plentiful. Beyond the undulating field is flat salt marsh stretching to the distant dunes of Salisbury and Hampton Beaches. An old Closeteer's uncle Karl Pettengill used to mow portions of it as well as the upland "English hay." To the south a stream, largely a wide swale, drains and filters runoff from the nearby town center through a thick maze of freshwater shrubs, grasses, sedges and wildflowers. Its water flows to tidal marsh ditches, making a rich, brackish water habitat where mosquitoes and minnows thrive. In awe we wandered slowly among evening birds through a great flower garden contained within a dark green wood of mature oaks, white pine and hickory. The old Closeteer, visiting sister, and cousin Karlene, daughter of Karl, happily remembered times there haying, blueberrying and collecting cows. In the backs of our minds was Karl, the last farmer here, one who envisioned the land one day as open wildlife sanctuary. A few years before, upon dedication of the land to Greenbelt, the old Closeteer tried to remember the late Karl with a poem, which ends:

> Look to the fields still open yet
> That roll to the woods and Sawmill Crick
> Cows, horse, and chickens all are gone.
> But look hard at Five Acre Field
> There riding a mower behind a horse
> You'll see a man with arms outstretched
> Holding reins, eyes on cutter bar
> He'll not see us wave or hear our calls
> And as we close upon the scene
> Will vanish as a gentle breeze.

PURITANS ALONG THE COAST

In today's column we are recommending a few books about this watery corner of world where Europeans in small ships unknowingly discovered a new continent. Along the estuaries and up the great rivers where fresh water off the land and salt water mingle the newcomers gained footholds, not in wilderness as is too often taught, but on land that had been well adapted to by people for 10,000 years. Most of the natives died within a century of contact. The newcomers, unknowingly carrying novel microorganisms for which they had immunity, thought God had blessed them. The coastal lands with only a handful of demoralized survivors were largely clear for settlement. The colonists in the early 1600s had only to cut weeds, bushes and small saplings that had sprung up since the annual Indian burns ceased about a decade before. Here in the Salem area the period of the "great dying" was 1617 to 1619. Leaders Roger Conant, John

Endicott and followers arrived in 1626. The following line, written by candid observer William Wood in his famous *New England's Prospect*, a book of unbiased observations 1629 to 1633, tells us a lot: "every (i.e. Salem English) household having a water horse or two." Such canoes of large pine logs weren't easy to make. The deceased left them behind.

The Puritans came to a land of great abundance where they squabbled among themselves and with people of the still somewhat intact native nations on the Cape, around Narragansett Bay, and in eastern Connecticut. Nathaniel Philbrick's *Mayflower* is a recent, very well-written account of that Machiavellian period.

Several years ago Charles Mann give us *1491*, a provocative book arguing that large established populations existed in the New World preceding the arrival of the deadly folks from the Old. His estimates of the numbers here are 10 times those of most.

One old Closeteer is now going on about recent *Paradise Found*, by Steve Nicholls, in which Nicholls writes of the abundance of fish, mammals and great trees in eastern North America before Europeans and their prolific hoofed livestock.

The last we'll recommend has caused much mirth. A Closeteer's visiting sister brought Sarah Vowell's delightful *The Wordy Shipmates*. Saucy, irreverent Sarah, lifelong fan of the Puritans and their shenanigans around Massachusetts and Narragansett Bays, tells of John Winthrop, Roger Williams, Anne Hutchinson, Endicott, and others. She goes back to the writings of her victims, whom she loves in her perverse ways, and then skewers them. She covers with much humor and sarcasm the same period the more sober Philbrick does. She reminds one of a brilliant smart-alecky aunt who relishes the beloved eccentricities of her strange family. We wish Sarah had been our history teacher. She has some of us anxious to seek out primary sources. In Winthrop's day her types were banished to Rhode Island.

JULY 2009

REPLENISH VERSUS DOMINATE

We were encouraged as youngsters to "aim high; shoot for the moon."
A modern cliché in government and business is "set the bar high."
Yet in our protection and restoration goals for species and habitats
we often aim low, not high enough to restore fish, turtle and whale
populations to even a fraction of their former glories. A few centuries
ago the ocean just to our east teemed with cod, haddock, halibut
and a dozen other species. In many places whales were common in
season. Large turtle populations astonished early Spanish sailors in
the Caribbean. Numbers rivaling those of the bison herds grazed the
extensive underwater prairies of sea grasses. At arribadas, arrivals,
millions of females invaded thousands of beaches around Mar Caribe.
Alas, sailors found big turtles easily caught, good to eat and to store
alive. They simply turned them on their backs in their ships. The
victims remained alive, fresh meat, for a couple months. Commercial
folks soon followed and took thousands for their flesh, shells and
leather. Estimates are that their populations over the last few centuries
have been reduced from hundreds of millions to tens of thousands.

We needn't repeat the whale and cod stories that have so long been
told. Despite precipitous declines restoration goals aim low. We
suppose this is political realism; something is better than nothing.

Those of us who were around at the creation of the United Nations
can still remember how exciting was the sense of hope, especially after
the terrible decade that encompassed WWII. Tourists and students
flocked to the UN's new headquarters in New York City. We walked
though the meeting halls with reverence. Perhaps it is high time for
a "United Oceans" organization without a security council with veto
power. Present schemes of conservation and restoration are hit or miss
by weak organizations and by individual countries claiming jurisdiction
for miles off their coasts. The oceans, seas and estuaries should be the
world's. They are where organisms arose and where most live. Their
waters flow from place to place and know no bounds below dams.
How obvious and trite, even embarrassing to write, are these truths
we've known for some time, yet deny. The planet's waters are more
important and essential than just one of millions of species. Yet, it is

our brainy species that now has the responsibility for all.

Let us embrace nature not "have dominion" (Genesis 1:28). Another phrase, much ignored, from verse 28 is "replenish the earth." Together, we'll build a fleet of great sailing ships that will house the meeting halls, offices and laboratories of United Oceans. The ships will be as white as those of Roosevelt's Great White Fleet, whose motto was "Speak softly and carry a big stick." Ours might be STUDY, LEARN, PERSUADE.

Source to Sea

The Ipswich River Watershed Association's (IWRA) annual paddle downriver is called Source to Sea. It is done each spring and summer in sections. Last Saturday morning 15 paddlers, Stream Teamers and friends, in four canoes and eight kayaks, did Middleton's eight miles from where North Reading, Lynnfield and Peabody join to the Peabody Street landing just upriver from Boxford and Topsfield. The goal is to paddle the river the Naumkeags and Agawams once did from its headwaters in Wilmington to Plum Island Sound. Some modern canoers have admitted hearing Algonquian songs emanating from riffles en route.

From the now Bostik dam's north abutment we marveled at the water tumbling down, as it has there for three centuries over a series of dams, and then descending over a hundred yards of gently descending rock bottom, producing some of the river's rare white water where, before dams, the natives caught alewives, shad and probably salmon. Don't you love the idea that this sky-given medium flows back to its giver, forever inviting us to ride?

Our 12 vessels, much lighter than dugout logs, quickly rode the rock-induced turbulence down under the Middleton to Peabody bridge without incident. We were now in a green tunnel. Tunnel is a poor word for such high, lacy, almost intertwining, arches, supported by trunks from both banks that provide the loveliest of dappled shade; soft canyon might be better. It reminds one of live oak-flanked drives leading to southern plantation mansions, only ours is more diverse and paved with cool reflecting water.

We meandered slowly east over a mile in perfect peace. On rounding each bend we were greeted with lush new scenes, many sprinkled with blossoms of wetland plants. Blooms of a dozen species were with us throughout the voyage. In stretches red maples, festooned with grapevines, were our walls. Now and then, trees that had fallen bank to bank, Peabody-Middleton, slowed us up and had us helping one another. Paddlers, strangers at the start, quickly became friendly; happy talk, much pointing things out, increased. One energetic fellow wanting more exercise flitted back and forth in his kayak, assisting at obstacles. IRWA naturalist Jim MacDougall helped us understand the wonders we were seeing.

We'll leave you here as we slowly move from the shade and turn north between Middleton and Danvers into a vast sunny floodplain where the channel becomes as sinuous as a writhing snake. The river keeps on going but the space in this column does not. Please return next week and we'll continue this vicarious tour for you as we paddle on into more water gardens graced with damsel and dragonflies. Better than wait, borrow a canoe and get out there on your own.

Meandering On

We left you last week on the Middleton section of the Watershed Association's paddle "Source to Sea" as we abruptly turned north and entered the wide floodplain between Middleton and Danvers. The loops of meandering 20- to 30-foot-wide channel in a floodplain a quarter mile wide are the towns' bounds. We were leaving the shade of mature hardwoods and white pines for a yearly more sunny stretch in transition. A decade ago the beavers returned after a hiatus of three centuries and started building dams across the channel that have each raised the water several inches to a foot. These obstructions keep the water higher and around longer in the whole flat scrub-shrub plain. There are now a series of low impoundments that stay flooded even in the usually dry months. Water-loving swamp white oaks, red maples, ashes, river birches, venerable old willows, swamp dogwood and buttonbushes along the channel banks and dotting the floodplain are dead, dying or showing signs of stress. They can only take so much water so long above their roots.

The floodplain with water year-round and unlimited sun is becoming a vast "beaver meadow," dominated by softer, shorter plants. Reedcanary grass, an invasive species, brought long ago by farmers to grow in their wet meadows, has taken over areas along the river in the past few years. We think it may be outcompeting the more famous invasive purple loosestrife here. The loosestrife is also being eaten by Galerucella beetles imported from Europe to do just that. The reedcanary leaves now rise three feet above the water, their yellow-brown inflorescences two feet higher. Interspersed with the lush grass and stressed loosestrife are swamp dogwoods and buttonbushes now coming into bloom. We could go on listing the many plants admired; alas, we are again running out of space.

Instead, we'll recommend a book happened upon this week in which two famous naturalists and writers had no such space constraints. In *A Conscious Silence* Edwin Way Teal and Ann Zwinger, from a canoe in rivers not far from ours, try their best to describe the Assabet, Sudbury and Concord Rivers made known worldwide by Henry David Thoreau through his voluminous journals. They try, as we have here, to describe the ever changing wild water gardens and rich animal habitats they paddled through. They quote from their hero and ours, Thoreau, from time to time. Here is one from an 1857 entry that relates to the above, "Thus in the course of ages the rivers wriggle in their beds till it feels comfortable under them." This doesn't explain the squiggly channel through our floodplain, but it sure is poetic. On the Ipswich over the years we've felt the poetry, often with breeze and bird song accompaniment.

AUGUST 2009

LILIES OF THE LAKE

In a bowl on the Closet table floats a water lily blossom open in the morning sun. Its many perfect petals ring a showy cluster of orange-yellow reproductive parts in a chaste white halo. In passing, we bend to smell one of the best of odors, one right up there with the bouquet of brief passing peonies.

The bowl is no substitute for Stearns Pond, North Andover, where the blossom was picked on Middleton's Friday morning COA/CC walk. That shallow 100-acre impoundment seems paved with leaves and a sprinkle of blossoms almost sparkling in the sun. If you didn't know they were anchored you might be surprised they weren't sailing before a breeze. When half opened each individual blossom with pointed overlapping petals brings to mind the water-surrounded Sydney Opera House. The blossom unlucky to be picked was being visited by pollinating insects as were its neighbors left behind. This seems an especially good water lily year; you needn't go to Stearns Pond in Harold Parker State Forest to see them, almost any shallow pond will do.

A couple mornings after the walk one old-timer went back alone to look more closely at *Nymphaea odorata*, fragrant white water lily. With an iron rake he dragged the shallows and pulled up several stout black rhizomes, perennial underwater stems, from which separate leaf and flower stems grow. Rhizomes, also anchors and food storage structures, are about an inch in diameter with lots of roots growing down and fewer stems growing upward. The stems each have four tubes that carry oxygen from photosynthesis in the leaves downward. Every few feet a rhizome gives rise to a stem that terminates in a floating flower. The leaves, often in thick patches, touch and almost completely cover the pond surface with round green solar panels that send their product sugars to the rhizomes where they are converted to starches and stored for next year's growth. Ducks, muskrats and beavers eat many. The amount of stored carbohydrates must be enormous on pond bottoms covered with webs of rhizomes. The nether surfaces of the leaves also provide substrate for a myriad of tiny creatures. Lilies function in their ecosystem as do seaweeds in our shallow coastal waters.

In the afternoon the blossoms of this lily close. Good thing, such beauty all the time might overwhelm and jade our senses as with some, perhaps biased by residues from Victorian poetry, who go on and on about roses now with us all year round. We'll soon forget the water lilies only to be happily surprised again next mid summer by their special white and fragrance.

BIRTHDAYS IN THE HUDSON BASIN

This month on our local public television station Pete Seeger's 90th birthday celebration at Madison Square Garden in May is being repeated for fundraising purposes. In addition to the famous birthday boy, who still stands straight and plays the banjo with gusto, were activists he has long inspired: Bruce Springsteen and Joan Baez, to name but a couple. All sang happily for Pete under strings of lights outlining the imaginary rigging of the sloop, *Clearwater*, he made famous. Just to the west of those famous minstrels the mighty Hudson River flowed between the ancient rock on which Manhattan perches and the Palisades of New Jersey. Seeger lives next to this ocean-drowned river, also a fjord, with tidewater 154 miles up to Troy. In the '60s, while still engaged in battles for civil rights and against the Viet Nam War, he lent his courageous voice to the cause of cleaning up his filthy river. The *Clearwater*, more than just a beautiful 106-foot-long replica of a 19th-century working sloop he helped build, became a worldwide symbol for the environmental movement. The Clearwater and champions of the Hudson, sailing gusty, ever changing political winds, have been successful; the longtime industrial sewer is, in the refrain of one of the celebrants' songs, "getting cleaner every day."

A week after enjoying the celebration shared above, an old Closeteer and wife just happened, through no plan of their own, to end up in a small house for another birthday—hers—between two clear mountain streams falling to the Hoosic River and then onto the Hudson. All the computer told her kids was that there was a place available not too far from Tanglewood and a concert they knew she'd like. Three generations gathered there to celebrate their matriarch's milestone birthday. The streams, not mentioned in the ad, were soon discovered. Sounds of water tumbling among diverse and interesting stones led them to explore. While fast-moving and cold they were shallow enough to be waded and led up and down through unspoiled forest. Granddaughters, 11 to 13, found in a stream bank a pure deposit of clay, and made dishes they dried in the sun. Later, they revisited and came back with ghastly green facials. On a family walk upstream toward unseen distant mountains they gave themselves Indian names. Now and then they dunked in pools where, no doubt, Mohawk children had played.

We don't think Seeger and watershed associations are asking too much when they plead for clean water. Star on a Moonless Night and Lady Hawk never gave Seeger, his fellow activists, or even the distant Hoosic and Hudson a thought; they just enjoyed what all should be born to.

Shared Visit to Waning Ice

We gather over the Closet's globe and search the seas, open and ice covered, around Svalbard in the Arctic Ocean from where Middleton friends Pam Hartman and Al Rosner recently returned. Out from Tromso, Norway, they cruised for 11 days on the Norwegian ship, *Prince Leopold II*. Photographer Pam, with excellent eyes, took over 2,000 photos. She later culled them to a striking 130, which she shared with us. Her fine images of places long only read about have us poring over the globe on a vicarious repeat of their trip. Some of us since childhood have been reading of Arctic explorers: Franklin, Barent, Amundsen and Nansen to mention but a few whose names are memorialized on our spherical smap.

Pam's lovely still shots convey moods movie and video do not. The cold mountainous isle of Spitsbergen is home to a handful of Russians and Norwegians; the latter "own" it, and the former stay, mining coal, in part to make a claim for Russia of continued use. The Svalbard islands, all well above the Arctic Circle, while very beautiful, have not been places for humans; her pictures clearly give one that feeling. From the ship the rugged land not covered by glaciers appears devoid of plants. Those there are ground-hugging flowering plants; our friend caught several in bloom, specks of warm colors among dark rocks and the varied blue-whites of ice above. Words just don't come close to doing her pictures justice. There is a special light coming in at a low slant through the October-like clear air that gives all a lonely, otherworldly look. Her photos of birds, walruses and polar bears make the atmosphere more inviting. Those natives on the ice seem perfectly at ease in their places, not ours. Soon the daylong dark, lit only by star, moon and reflections, will be upon the snow-covered land. The surrounding sea will freeze. Only ice breakers and perhaps planes may safely visit until next summer. *Prince Leopold II*, while double hulled, is not an icebreaker.

Buzzing in our heads while viewing her pictures are knowledge of global warming and reports of melting glaciers and ice caps. This bother adds another dimension, human time, to what we are seeing and have long admired from afar as true wildness. Thoreau somewhere wrote: "In wildness is the preservation of the world." Will its loss mean we lose the biosphere? Many, like Harvard's great biologist-author Edward O. Wilson in his writings on the accelerated rate of biodiversity loss, are sure worried. We had long thought that the cold and dark would keep folks, except for explorers and scientists, away from the arctics.

Now, even cruise ships with tourists venture beyond latitudes 80. How wise our friends to have visited before the ice is gone.

SOURCE TO SEA, ACT III

Saturday morning before last, the Watershed Association's "Source to Sea" paddle resumed from Route 97 in Topsfield. Over 20 vessels, most brightly colored plastic kayaks, joined the Ipswich River's easterly flow into the jungle that is Great Wenham Swamp. Old-timers imagined they were on the *African Queen* with Humphrey Bogart and Katherine Hepburn. Thanks to dragonflies and Tree Swallows there were few mosquitoes. The sinuous route, about two and a half miles as an earnest crow flies and seven as the channel meanders, is flanked by thick vegetation extending outward in places for over a mile. Much has an open aspect, more so every year due to beavers. Many of the water-loving trees that dot the savannah-like floodplain are dead or dying due to low beaver dams that keep the water high year round. A few woody bush species and a dozen herbaceous water plants thrive. The dominate grass is reedcanary grass an invasive gift of farmers who long ago planted it in their wet fields. It may be invasive but geese, ducks and water mammals thrive on and in it. In fall and spring flocks of ducks forage in these flat wet prairies. Along the edges of the channel thick swathes of floating smartweeds now bloom.

Hot muggy air was no problem; cool relief was just a few inches away. Many dunked themselves in the clear, tannin-tinted water. While global warming may eventually bring alligators, our swimmers had little but leeches to care about; we saw one attached to a basking painted turtle's shell.

We digress; let's get back to some of the many flowers admired. Delicate cardinal flowers, more than remembered in past years, grace the banks singly or in small groups with the brightest of nature's reds. Purple loosestrife patches, not as many as upriver, add more warm color. Buttonbushes drew passing eyes; their blossoms, vanilla-colored spheres, further soften the lush green scene. Then there are infrequent small patches of forget-me-nots; their tiny blossoms and color remind one of upland bluets. There seem more white water lilies this year; they, with blossoms open in the morning, were much admired and photographed.

In places tumbling out from the banks and seeming to lean on the river are venerable silver maples. We worry about them; the beaver-raised water is stressing many. Some of these lacy leafed maples, so common in the floodplain from Route I-95 on down, have been tipped by ice and wind. Roots are raised and exposed. Stems arise from the fallen trunks and become micro-groves perched on gnarled dark roots. We're told that such vast silver maple swamps are rare. Get out there and see for yourself before the beavers do ours in.

SEPTEMBER 2009

THE SOUNDS OF WATER

Naturalist-writer John Muir tried, upon hearing moving water in the high Sierras, to put rapture felt into words. One of his fans well over a century later went to the places described with a recorder and brought back the sounds he thought Muir had heard. We caught the end of a public radio interview with him recently. Sorry, we didn't get his name, just commentary and lovely sounds. He and the interviewer discussed background noises experienced. Their basic question was: Are there still places with just natural sounds, such as those of wind, birds and moving water without motor noises? We Closeteers asked ourselves the same question for the tri-town area. As this is being written the sound of traffic dominates if we shift our attention. We kind of knew the answer, but some went out to check. One favorite spot is along Boston Brook above Mundy Bridge in Middleton, the only natural white water here we know. There the water of this nine-mile-long tributary of the Ipswich River falls about 15 feet in just 500 over stones. Compare this with our quiet river that descends only about 20 feet in crossing all of Middleton and Topsfield where there is little sound except that from the trickles over beaver dams or murmurs around bridge abutments.

In the shade above Mundy Bridge water plays its stone-bank instrument nicely, sounds subtly different at each curve. Lying on the mossy bank we listen to the peaceful turbulence, an oxymoron if you think of the words and not the water dancing against and then joining in the lee of stones, the formation and breaking of bubbles plucking on the air and then our ears. However, we have but to search what seems the same air for sounds from somewhere else and the water songs disappear and are replaced by the never-ending chorus of motors from distant I-95. If we direct our minds and ears toward Route 114, buffered by a mile or more of lush summer vegetation, we hear another dull engine choir. And if we focus on the sky, there comes the drone of jet engines from miles above. All these machines have been around for more than a half century now, increasing all the while, ever added to by mowers, chainsaws, leaf blowers . . . Certain musicians might readily accept these sounds and see beauty in the mix.

Many leave our roads and seek out the sounds of moving water, whether it be by streams or ocean's edge. These sounds are the ones we knew long long before our ancient ancestors gave rise to us. Such sounds at times are probably why we built our shack close to the river. Water movement, except perhaps in great floods and storms, is comforting, and, during those, certainly exciting.

It starts to rain. Ahh, the welcome drumming on the roof . . .

WETLANDS PROTECTION ACT

In 1972 the Massachusetts Great and General Court in its collective wisdom gave us the Wetlands Protection Act, MGL Ch. 131, Section 40 (WPA, or simply, the Act). This enlightened law, to which the Rivers Protection Act was incorporated in 1997, protects swamps, marshes, bogs, wet meadows, ponds, lakes, streams, rivers, beaches and banks from alteration. We may not, with few exceptions, excavate, fill, dam, dredge, pollute or build in these wet areas. Entrepreneurs of earlier generations might have asked: "If alteration provides more useful land for building and agriculture, better access, flood control, water power for mills, convenient places to get rid of wastes, deeper ponds for storage, and deeper channels for navigation, why not?" These "why nots," after four decades since the Act was promulgated and has become generally understood, seem naïve, certainly uninformed and old-fashioned. From the 17th to mid-20th centuries here, movers and shakers asked, "Why not?" Early on, millions of beavers were trapped, their rich meadows drained for hay and pasture. Thousands of dams were built for power, thus changing vast areas above and below them and preventing the essential age-old movement of fish and other creatures. In the Midwest, our world-famous "Bread Basket," tens of thousands of ponds and swamps, feeding and resting way stations, bread baskets for billions of migrating birds, were filled to provide for more cultivation. Along our southern New England coasts Whittier's "low green prairies of the sea," salt marshes, were filled in many places. Much of greater Boston was built on such rich wet habitat. We are just beginning to understand the effects of these losses, some extending far out to sea.

The Act answers the "why not" questions by listing its "interests" or purposes. They are printed in each permit, called an Order of Conditions, issued by each of our 357 town and city conservation commissions for work to be done near or in wetlands. They are worth periodically reminding ourselves of. The purposes are: to protect the private or public water supply; to protect groundwater; to provide flood control; to prevent storm damage; to prevent pollution; to protect land containing shellfish; to protect wildlife habitat; and to protect fisheries.

One wag in the Closet likes to quote his physics professor's pronouncement after deriving a long, involved equation. He smiled while looking out over the heads of his mostly bewildered students and said, "Intuitively obvious to any rational being." We think many in 2009 are approaching this conclusion concerning the interests of the Act. The WPA is neither esoteric physics nor high math. We'll leave you with a final question: Isn't it sensible, even essential, to have clean, unimpeded water for all us animals?

SWAMP MAPLES

Acer rubrum, commonly "swamp" or "red maple," is now living up to its color name in and around our wetlands. Last week, Middleton's Friday morning COA/CC walkers hiked a beeline—more correctly a canal line—across the Great Wenham Swamp, and never got their feet wet, thanks to levees on either side dredged up in 1917 by the Salem-Beverly Water Commission to form a two-mile-long, 50-foot-wide, six-foot-deep canal that carries water from the Ipswich River in Topsfield across a portion of Danvers to a pump house in Wenham. From there it is sent over to Wenham Lake for storage and then on to Beverly and Salem as needed. The dominant tree in the great expanses of swamp on either side is red maple, its foliage now various colors, from royal purple to shabby yellow browns, with a spectrum of rich reds dominating. Many are dead or dying, probably due to the slightly higher year-round water, the result of beaver dams across the river.

You don't have to walk the canal edges to see red maples. They are everywhere throughout our towns where water tables are high, hence the common name "swamp maple." There are probably more now than ever. Before the English and the fur trade beaver impoundments no doubt reduced their numbers as they do now. In colonial times and right up into the mid-20th-century swamps were pastures, woodlots, or hayed wet meadows. In the 17th and 18th centuries charcoal makers clear-cut bushes and trees for fuel in local iron works. Red maples grow quickly from cut stumps. Jonathan Webber, a spunky Middleton lad and Masco student, cut many cords from his family's red maple swamp in the late 1970s, which he sold for firewood during the "oil crisis." Go there today and you'll find a fine stand of red maples almost ready for another harvest, were they not on what is now Middleton conservation/open space land.

"Red maple," a relatively soft "hardwood," doesn't have the density or BTUs of *Acer saccharum*, "sugar" or "rock maple." Twice a year, though, it does provide terrific shows, previews of coming attractions. We now admire their red leaves announcing the great October dying-leaf celebrations to follow. In the damp, cold days of early April they'll be the first to bloom and will, for a couple weeks, provide the only warm colors seen. Separate male and female flower clusters, both red, will burst forth from thousands of flower buds on red twigs long before the leaf buds give rise to three-lobed leaves. The twigs give the upper reaches of red maple groves in winter a pink tinge. Sugar maple twigs are the color of maple syrup.

Go forth and catch Mother Nature's red maple warm-up show before the more famous acts in October by sugar maples, hickories and oaks.

DAMS, LOTS OF THEM

We have among us large aquatic rodents who dam our waterways. They are especially active this time of year as they prepare for winter. This summer in the eight miles of the Ipswich River squiggling through Middleton we canoers/kayakers had to go over 10 of their dams while paddling from the North Reading line to Thunder Bridge, not far upriver from Boxford and Topsfield. Because of these dams, constructed from repeated applications of branches and mud, water is held back in watersheds and descends more slowly to the sea. It trickles over this leaky stairway of broad treads and short risers, which only drops about 10 feet in 40,000 in crossing town. The Indians in their dugout and birch bark canoes greatly valued these long impoundments that allowed navigation during times of otherwise shallow depths. Above the dams there is deeper water and little current. The disadvantages are short portages over and around dams. During times of high water most dams are well submerged. On a recent downriver trip after a September of little rain our canoes hung up repeatedly on exposed dams where we had to scoot forward in unison to slide down over.

Before the fur trade between French, English and natives, beavers held sway over our lowlands. In just the last decade or so, since a law banning easily used, cheap steel leghold traps, they are back in big way. A map kept in the Middleton Conservation Commission office shows over 30 dams in Middleton alone. Some are abandoned, not maintained; new ones are being built, so 30 is but a rough net total. Even if you don't see their many lodges and dams from our roads you can appreciate the changes while passing in the form of acres of stark, gray tree corpses, many still standing. Many of our swamp trees are dead or dying over a very rough estimate of a thousand acres in the tri-town area alone. In once shaded swamps "beaver meadows" are forming. Softer, shorter plants are replacing red maples, wetland ashes, and swamp white oaks, which are being drowned by beaver impoundments. These trees like water but can't take much above their roots year round.

Colonial farmers put a high value on the rich soils of beaver meadows. They took control after the beavers were trapped out and drained them for hay, pasture and cultivation. Parts were even excavated for their muck, which was dubbed "manure" and mixed with upland sandy soils.

Laws now protect these land-changers who alter wetlands humans may not. Permits may be obtained to trap, to raze dams and to install pipes called "beaver deceivers," but only for reasons of public health and safety. We've slowly become aware of what rich wildlife habitats and reservoirs of water these ancient fellow mammals provide.

OCTOBER 2009

THE FUTURE OF OUR DAMS

Last week in Middleton about a dozen people met to discuss the fates of the South Middleton dam across the Ipswich River at Bostik and the Curtis Pond Dam across Boston Brook. In attendance were five Stream Teamers and Closeteers, Beth Lambert of Massachusetts Division of Ecological Restoration, Eric Hutchins of National Oceanographic and Atmospheric Administration, Josh Ellsworth and Jim MacDougall of the Ipswich River Watershed Association, and Dan Welch, who is the Environmental Manager for Bostik, Inc. There were also two civilians who live near the water bodies involved. Ellsworth introduced fluvial geomorphologist Lambert who showed photographs and explained past, ongoing, and planned restoration projects, i.e. dam removals.

In the discussion period that followed an old Closeteer, hardwired on a Salisbury subsistence farm, asked, a little too loudly, why taxpayer money, experts' and officials' time were being spent on the partly-fallen Curtis Pond dam. Grumpily, he asked: "Why not let time and ice do their thing as they have since the Curtis brothers' sawmill, powered by the dam, was burned by vandals in the late '60s?" He must have missed his nap that afternoon for he knows full well how complicated the removal of dams is. Later, he admitted to having a vision of sneaking out there at night with dynamite and saving everyone trouble. One wag piped up, "I'll bet it was black powder, in your case." The curmudgeonly old Closeteer still has half the mindset of the Curtis brothers who built the sawmill in the 1930s and of the Peabodys who built a sawmill dam just upstream over two centuries ago. We bet they weren't involved with meetings, permits or environmental considerations. When the Closeteer was a boy his farmer kin just went ahead and did things to provide what they thought needed for themselves and fellow townspeople. For example, in the 1940s Breezy Page of East Street took the white pine logs he'd cut on his land to the Curtis mill. There, they were converted to lumber and trucked back to Breezy to build his house with. This was business on one's own land.

Later, he regretted his outspokenness. The earnest young people running the meeting were simply educating and seeking information before proceeding further. They are well aware of today's ecological, legal, political and regulatory complexities of removing dams. There are effects for miles up and downstream. Lambert showed us a map of Massachusetts seemingly with smallpox. Each red pustule represented one of several thousand known dams, well over 90 percent no longer functioning for power or flood control. Wouldn't it have been better if meetings such as this one had been conducted before each of the dams shown was built? "Progress" then didn't take other creatures and plants into account. We wonder if Mother Nature listening in wasn't pleased that her long-errant, strange species is finally catching on.

OUR WATERY NATIONAL PARKS

Ken Burns and team have done it again. This month they've given us, via public television, *The National Parks: America's Greatest Idea*. Sketches, paintings, old black-and-white photos and modern colored images are interwoven with historical narrative. Water flows through almost every minute of 600, because that is where plants, animals, and the minds of the park champions were and are. In the Everglades the water flows southward through vast flat prairies to the sea. In Alaska it descends quickly in rivers from high ice. In the now dry lands of the southwest water is very much felt upon viewing strata of ancient sea sediments in the Grand Canyon, the live Colorado River deep below. At Yellowstone it boils up through snow. In Redwood National Park it rises 300 feet in sapwood.

Public television stations will air this series again and again. Our grandchildren will watch as will some of theirs. The six long episodes cannot be fully appreciated in day-after-day showings. Now we should visit the parks ourselves. For people-persons there is much to admire. John Muir and Teddy Roosevelt, to mention only two of the dozens Burns features, were not only geniuses, but strong, fascinating characters to boot. We'd like to mention more here, but in a closet there isn't room for an assemblage of giants, champions who set aside thousands of square miles for all of us, including animals and plants.

Many after watching might say we can't afford or are no longer in shape to explore our national parks. A friend of the Closet said, "Watching the Burns series, I long to be young enough and free enough to climb to those remote places." Just up the road there is a small federal park, the Parker River Wildlife Refuge, that, if measured by its moving water, extends far out to sea. There fresh waters from the Merrimack, Parker, Rowley, Eagle and Ipswich Rivers join seawater from the Atlantic in marvelous mixing pans called estuaries. In the air above water comes in the form of clouds, mists, fog, rain, snow and the sounds of surf. And if it's wildlife you want, this refuge in major migratory flyways exceeds that found in more spectacular parks 100 times its size.

Federal Communications Commission chairman Newton Minnow in the 1960s famously called TV a "vast wasteland." TV, like all things human, is good, bad and all things in between. Burns' TV series, at times overly patriotic and sentimental, are well worth watching for their history. Yet better than watching, get the family up off the couch and visit Plum Island or other protected areas near home. We in Essex County have many thanks to our federal, state and town governments and to Greenbelt, Trustees of Reservations and Boxford Land Trust. Some are a walk away.

AMERICA'S LITTLE-KNOWN EXPLORER-TYRANT

A strange American from our history visited the Closet via Nathaniel Philbrick's book *Sea of Glory: U. S. Exploring Expedition 1838 to 1842.* Commodore, as naval Lt. Charles Wilkes chose to call himself, led sailing ships, six at start, finally four, zigzagging 87,000 miles around the world. Wilkes was the chief surveyor; other scientists, artists, officers and men returned with tons of specimens, voluminous journals, and hundreds of detailed charts. The latter made formerly dangerous areas of the oceans much safer for the world's ships. Wilke's charts were so good that some were used by the Navy a century later when planning attacks on the Japanese occupying South Pacific islands. The scientists' collections became the beginning of the Smithsonian Institution.

Why didn't we hear more of this explorer, world famous in maritime circles, in school? You'd think him right up there with Captain James Cook and Lewis and Clark. His prodigious accomplishments didn't end with the voyage; for years after he wrote, edited and published volumes of reports on the expedition's important findings. In the 19th century, when large parts of earth were still unknown, these were invaluable.

Alas, paranoiac, hard-driving Wilkes was a petty tyrant in his dealings with his capable officers. They, often victims of his capricious ways, hated him and filed charges upon return. Just when he expected to be feted and honored, he was defending himself in a court-martial at which he was convicted and for a time thereafter suspended from duty. Despite this, within a year he was promoted to commander, a rank he, as leader of an important expedition, should have had before departure. In the Civil War, two decades later, his audacious actions threatened relations with Great Britain. He was again court-martialed, despite Northern public opinion in his favor.

Philbrick's good account led to Closet discussions about Wilke's place in history and that of other leaders with conflicting reputations: Teddy Roosevelt, Patton, MacArthur, Churchill, and Clinton, to mention but a few. In considering historic figures shouldn't we judge ambitious men on the bases of accomplishments as well as conduct? Wilkes' good charts of places where none existed before no doubt prevented scores of shipwrecks. He and the officers and men who despised him went days with little sleep in dangerous conditions to ensure the surveys' completeness and accuracy.

In any event, we should be taught honestly so we can know them without the crippling biases of arrogant patriotism. We should learn of their shortcomings and failures as well as their successes. Philbrick so teaches in *Sea of Glory*, and in another book of his we strongly recommend, *Mayflower*, about Pilgrim, Puritan and Indian interactions here in the 17th century. If we are to navigate through future shoals we'll need accurate charts from the past.

WHEN THE MARSHES GO UNDER

During the nor'easter of October 18 we visited the drumlins of Great Neck, Ipswich, at midday high tide. From the heights of North Ridge we looked north across an inland sea behind the dunes of Plum Island. The salt marsh there was under a couple feet of ocean water that had entered the Merrimack between the wave-washed beaches of Salisbury and Newburyport and at the entrance of Plum Island Sound over the roiling bars off Crane Beach. Salisburyites used to call this combination of astronomically high tides and water-piling winds "high-runner tides." Plum Island, less than a mile away, was barely visible in the cold, hard rain off the ocean. We stepped out of the car to experience it face to face, but soon retreated. However, the old excitement accompanying such storms returned, and we felt wimpish back in our warm steel box. We then descended south to Pavilion Beach below Little Neck and parked just above the surf of the sound partially subdued in the lee of Plum Island. From there we could see the great waves sweeping across the treacherous bars between Plum Island and Crane.

Later, we worried again about the fate of our barrier beaches under the threat of ocean rise; Plum Islanders must fret much of the winter. New predictions received this month about the speed of arctic ice-cap melting are ominous. Some say it may be gone in a decade. And what about the high ice of Greenland? If its glacier cap melts the oceans will rise very significantly. From Antarctica, we hear similar concerns. Great chunks, the size of counties, are breaking off that continent's edges.

Maybe our trip gave the children with us a glimpse of the coastline they will know permanently, not just at high-runner tides. Salisbury Beach and Plum Island may then be submerged offshore bars. The salt marshes behind them, no longer protected by vegetated dunes, will erode away. The kids and theirs will be swimming off new beaches along what now are uplands. The drumlins along the coast will be islands. A trip to the Necks will be by boat.

November 2009

Wood Ducks Again

Over the past few decades the Wood Duck numbers here have been increasing. We have no good census, just observations from hikes along streams and swamps and paddles down the Ipswich River. They are gathering now to leave for winter in the Southwest and Mexico. Thoughts of them had us turning to a valuable gift from Middleton Stream Teamer Francis Masse. Edward Howe Forbush's three-tome *The Birds of Massachusetts and Other New England States* was published in 1925. We went to his half-dozen pages on our much-admired *Aix sponsa*.

"Loveliest of all the waterfowl the Wood Duck stands supreme. Deep, flooded swamps, where ancient mossy trees overhang the dark waters, secluded pools amid scattered pines where water-lilies lift their snowy heads and turtles bask in the sun, purling brooks flowing in dense woodlands where light and shade fleck the splashing waters, slow-flowing creeks and marshy ponds—these are the haunts of the Wood Duck. . . ."

He goes on in this grand Victorian style for another whole page before turning to data gathered by him and a dozen colleagues. We think something has been lost when picky ornithologists insist on just the facts without poetry.

These small ducks, on the brink of extinction here in Forbush's early years, have made a comeback since a devastating 19th century of intense hunting and habitat destruction by logging. These tree-cavity nesters became so scarce here preservationists imported many from Belgium where bird fanciers bred them. In Audubon's time, the mid-1800s, they were common throughout much of the country.

Our small column won't allow for more on these beauties. Google *Aix sponsa* or better still go out and see them for yourselves.

As this is being written a tiny male Wood Duck of white pine sits on an open page of Forbush's book. This beautifully carved and painted bird, by the late Salisbury cabinet maker, artist and naturalist Richard Currier, was given by him to a friend's Japanese wife soon after her arrival in America.

When the Wood Ducks return in early spring we will think of Dick. The paint on his lovely gift will slowly fade. The Wood Duck's striking colors and patterns, millions of years evolving, should last much longer now they are protected.

CLEAN, HARD, SANDY BEACHES

The low tide sandy beaches a half hour from the tri-towns by car seem the cleanest, barest places imaginable. Yet they, like grassy fields, are full of life, most tiny or microscopic. We human observers, our eyes five feet above the twice-daily washed sand floor, see only rock grains and a few well-scrubbed limestone shells. The sand fleas, crabs, mollusks and visiting plankton are mostly in interstitial passages awaiting another dose of ocean. The other day on the south end of Plum Island, it might just as well have been Crane or Wingaersheek beaches, an old Closeteer and wife happily walked the firm intertidal surface, their eyes on the relatively calm sea and blue-gray Cape Ann in the distance. The gentle sounds of surf helped clear their minds. Years ago, the old Closeteer tried a poem that might have arisen from such walks.

Waves
Twice daily we are lifted by the moon
Yet know it not with thought.
It may be felt in alternating crest and trough,
Perhaps distorts the brain just quite enough
To cause the ebb and flow of moods.
Such vertical fluctuations I can take,
'Tis all those horizontal pulls
From hundred heads of neurons pulsing
That have me in this state.
Their tides in sync with mine,
Reinforce my highs and lows at times,
And when they don't sustain an interference
Inversely rising with the space between.
Go away! Leave me join the circling cycles,
A part the very Moon and Sun and rippling Earth.
I'll walk the intertidal sands,
And let the static dampen with the swash.

Our distant fish ancestors, the first true vertebrates, and theirs without internal skeletons, came from tens of millions years of formation in the sea. Much of our bodies may still be attuned to those times, not yet out of mind. Fish evolved suspended in sea water; our brains are suspended in plasma, quite like that ancient mix of salts and water.

A Very Natural Greenhouse Gas

We Closeteers rarely think of our obsession in its gaseous form. Perhaps because water vapor cannot be seen; yet if water molecules in the air stopped dancing on our skins we'd quickly take notice. We remember well Sunday morning two weeks ago after Saturday's three inches of rain when we exited our stuffy houses into wonderful moist, clean air. No words can describe those first exhilarating breaths and the feeling on our skin. Water vapor makes up one to four percent of the air we feel and breathe.

Water molecules as gas are highly energetic and free compared with those of liquid water, which partially cohere and slip-slide over one another, or those of ice vibrating in place.

Water vapor is the most important of the so-called greenhouse gases. It is largely transparent to visible light, much less so to infrared or heat waves. Like all warm substances, soil and water radiate energy in the form of heat, some of which is absorbed by water molecules and other greenhouse gases and kept within the atmosphere, thus warming the air, rocks and water bodies. Increased temperatures result in further evaporation from ocean surfaces resulting in more water in the air and more heat absorption. If this positive feedback system wasn't balanced by the heat absorbed to evaporate liquid water the atmosphere would get hotter and hotter. Enter carbon dioxide, about .038 percent of the air, and methane, .0002 percent, also greenhouse gases that we are daily warned of. These gases, which are increasing due to people's activities, also absorb heat.

Recently recommended to us was Elizabeth Kolbert's book *Field Notes of a Catastrophe: Man, Nature and Climate Change*. Kolbert, a staff writer for the *New Yorker* magazine, visited scientists around the world who are doing basic climate research. She spent much time with them as they studied permafrost, ice core samples, animal population changes, and climate computer models. We'll not repeat the findings from 150 years of such research that is daily provided by our media, except to say that Kolbert and most scientists who study climate agree that man's activities are accelerating change; the many questions remaining have to do with details of how, and how fast. She left us with a new acronym her scientists use that bothers: DAI, for dangerous anthropogenic interference. We wonder if some wag didn't purposely create this one, which when pronounced sounds the same as die. DAI is defined as the point at which climate change feedback systems will rapidly continue even if our species stops its profligate warming ways.

While we enjoy and suffer our essential humidity at different times, we can't help wondering if its absorption of heat isn't helping to "Do Us In." Let's call this DUI, which might also stand for "Driving Under the Influence of fossil fuels."

DECEMBER 2009

BUFFLEHEADS PASSING BY

A favorite pond of Closeteers is Joan and son Peter Cudhea's called Prichards, her father's name. Her father's father bought land along Boston Brook and built a dam to provide for his family what an Essex County dam inspector called a "pleasure pond." Five generations have vacationed there. We non-Prichards also take pleasure in this artificial third-mile-long lake now surrounded by mature trees. We visit to see water birds, pickerel weeds, pond lilies, and cardinal flowers, to skate, and to fish from North Liberty Street at Mundy Bridge where Boston Brook enters the pond after being aerated by several hundred yards of descending white water.

This November we went several times to see ducks, especially Buffleheads, *Bucephela albelola*, the smallest of our ducks, also called "divers." They skim the surface quickly, lightly, and then disappear to arise seconds later. Even from a distance we know they are there because of the brightest of white patches on the sides and heads of the drakes that contrast sharply with the dark water and non-white feathers. Their head patches greatly expand as feathers are extended and become flashing flags. Only as we get closer do we notice the smaller, less colorful females. On our last visit 10 divers were dunking up and down in the shallow water that just a few weeks ago was covered with lily pads. We've noticed several times that upon approaching within a couple hundred feet, we spook them and are treated to a fine display of Blue Angel type, close-order flying, directly at us only to veer off sharply at about 100 feet. They fly low, wings so rapidly beating that they are scarcely seen. These little groups in flight are thrilling in their quick retreats.

You don't have to visit Prichards or Creighton ponds in Middleton to see them. We bet Topsfield's Hood and Boxford's Stiles and other ponds have Buffleheads and will until ice has them leaving for open coastal waters. They spend late springs and summers on lakes in the boreal forests of Canada from Hudson Bay on west where they raise families in tree nest cavities. We see them coming and going.

Upon return to the Closet we went to much-admired Edward Howe

Forbush's *Birds of Massachusetts* and were rewarded by his account of a sighting off Nahant after a winter storm a century or so ago.

". . . The sea still rages, and the white-topped surges pound and roar upon the sea-worn ledges, tossing the spouting, snow-white spray high in the sunlit air. A piercing northwest wind cuts the spindrift from the rollers and carries it seaward in sheets. The western sun lights up the heaving seas and the acres of foaming white water that now at low tide rush upon the shallows of the beach. Most of the ducks have flown to harbors or to creeks in the saltmarsh, but a few hardy, white-winged Scoters and Old-squaws lie out on the open sea; close in-shore, in shoal water and in the very boiling of the surface, groups of little Buffleheads ride easily, swimming and diving as unconcernedly as if on some calm, untroubled pool. Now and then the surf seems to break directly over a bird; but in an instant when the towering crest seems to fall on its uplifted head, the head is no longer there. . . .The Buffleheads play in the white-topped surf. They are perfectly at home and not the least inconvenienced by foaming surge, raging wind or stinging cold. . . ."

Forbush, contemporary of seascape painter Winslow Homer, does here with Victorian pen and ink what Homer famously did with brushes and paints in Maine only without warm-blooded, feisty swimmers.

Dam-made pond on Boston Brook. Photo, courtesy of Stream Team.

DARK WARNINGS FROM ONCE COVERED PEAKS

A Closeteer proudly tells us of his five-year-old grandson Django's drawings done with his father. After cars and trucks, their favorite subject is high mountains. Father and son consult, draw and then Django finishes with crayons. A mountain range shown us by grandpa shows the snow-capped peaks streaky white. Snow and glaciers are not completely covering. We wonder if the boy and dad aren't influenced by today's images from around the world of heights once snug beneath glaciers and layers of snow that are now less so.

On the back page of the "Ideas" section of the 29 November, Sunday *Boston Globe* is an eye-catching photograph of a U-shaped glacial valley, without glacier, in the high Himalayas. It reminded one old Closeteer of photos in books he pored over as a boy before the days of TV and limitless photographs. The black-and-white masterpieces of Ansel Adams drew us to our western mountains. Those mysterious all-year-white heights drew us in until the images were burned into our brains. We dreamed of visiting, climbing, someday. In the foreground of the *Globe* picture are two black-appearing yaks. The sun unseen is directly overhead. The animals and a man nearby are seen in silhouette. Great peaks, snow cover sparse, loom above the concave slopes of the valley. They lack the thick, white caps long seen even in summer at such high altitudes. Summer melting hasn't been replenished by winter snow accumulations in recent years. Mountain glaciers around the world are slowly disappearing. Most in the news are equatorial Kilimanjaro in Africa and other isolated peaks in the Andes. We've been following their retreat and that of glaciers in the Alps and Alaska for years.

Kumic, a village in northwest India, lies in the valley pictured. Last year, the villagers met and decided to move three kilometers down the valley, where there is a little more water for irrigation. The soil in the new location is not as good but they've concluded there is no other choice. The peaks are no longer supplying enough melt water for their short growing season. The Kumics, who have some contact with the outside world, surprisingly are not blaming the industrialized countries and global warming. They look to themselves and conclude that they have displeased the mountain spirits. The lesson they impart to us is that action is needed now. For most of us, global warming seems somewhere else. In Kumic the scarcity of water from above is readily seen and the results directly felt. They can't grow the barley, buckwheat and fodder needed.

We hope those meeting now in Denmark on climate change hear this story. In Kumic, a handful of farm families have recognized the problem, if not the cause, and are taking drastic, agonizing action. They and their ancestors have been living under the nourishing mountain glaciers in the high clear air forever.

Perhaps representatives at Copenhagen will take responsibility as the Kumics have and will agree to mutually developed solutions. We well realize that on a world scale solutions are infinitely more complicated than just moving down a valley; however, their lesson helps us understand who is responsible and who must make the moves.

Carbonic Acid: Carbon Dioxide and Water

We Closeteers who clam on the low tide flats of the estuaries where the waters of the Atlantic Ocean and the Parker, Rowley, Plum Island, Eagle and Ipswich rivers mingle have long wondered about the diversity of our prey populations. If, in our digging on the hundreds of acres of a flat, seemingly under similar conditions, we move but a few feet, we find more clams, fewer, or none at all. In some places they are small in size; others nearby are large. One might guess these differences are from gradations in the depths by which they are covered as the tides rise and fall twice each lunar day. However, this isn't supported. Large variations in densities and sizes are found at the same elevations. Soil properties certainly seem big factors. Yet the numbers found in high organic clay-silt-muck, boot-sucking ooze, and in coarse sand and gravel, and all mixes in between, vary also. One obvious factor is the significant digging by commercial clammers and the scratchings of us "mess diggers." The former move flat to flat, and pretty much clear out all the clams over two inches long; a couple seasons later they return for another round. The holidays left between diggings help explain some of the variations.

In this winter's issue of *The Working Waterfront*, published by the Island Institute of Maine, there is an article about Dr. Mark Green's work that provides another clue. Green is a professor at Saint Joseph's College of Maine. His research is on the effects of pH, which, too simply put, is how acidic or basic water solutions are. Seawater on average is pH 8.1. That is now. Prior the industrial revolution it was

8.2, slightly less acidic, or more basic. A tenth of one percent is no big deal, you say; however, these numbers are exponents of the reciprocal of the hydrogen ion (H+) concentration. A stream with water of pH 5.5, which won't support trout populations, is 10 times more acid than that of typical New England soil water at about pH 6.5. Our blood is maintained by the body at a constant 7.4, which like seawater is slightly basic. Citric acid at pH 4 is 100 times more acid than a soil water of 6. If you've forgotten your high school chemistry, no matter, the point here is that the pH of the biosphere's watery solutions is critically important to cells, organisms and ecosystems. Green's findings show that the pH of his sites, the surfaces of flats in Casco Bay near Portland and others in West Bath on the Kennebec, where he is trying to answer the question we only ponder, is more acidic at pH 7 to 7.5 than the seawater that washes over them each tide. Microscopic baby clams don't form shells of limestone as well, or at all, when the pH is too low. If they, who start their lives as plankton, land by chance in the wrong place, their developing shells erode and dissolve instead of adding necessary layers of protecting limestone.

Green has found that the pH, when carefully measured, place to place varies depending on the amount of organic matter decaying there. After dying, all organisms, zooplankton, algae, bacteria as well as humans break down to largely carbon dioxide and water. These compounds form a weak acid called carbonic acid, thus lowering the pH. Red tide organisms, microscopic algae blooms, and organic debris of all kind that settle in patches on the flats create different conditions. Some at slightly higher pHs promote shell growth; others, slightly lower, result in shell dissolution. (Obtain a pinch of garden limestone or a piece of clam shell and add vinegar or lemon juice to it and watch the reaction.) The ocean waters are not only slightly warming; they are becoming slightly more acidic due the natural intermingling of CO_2 and H_2O.

The world's representatives at Copenhagen, much worried about such changes, are wondering, along with Dr. Green and us curious clammers, what all this means. To water creatures, such as corals, clams and lobsters that make protective shells of limestone, the problem is much more immediate; their time may be only a few tenths of a pH change away.

Outdoor Rinks

Fenway Park now has an outdoor rink in the outfield where Dominic DiMaggio, Carl Yastrzemski and Ted Williams once famously chased fly balls. This past week we were treated with pictures of Bruins' great Bobby Orr and young hockey players skating hand-in-hand there on outdoor ice in clean cold air. It reminded us old Closeteers of our winter playgrounds as children. Wimpy indoor rinks were rare then. Most of us had never seen one. But before we go on with old-timer tales, lets review some cold facts.

Winter is the season of solid water. With lower temperatures water molecules slow down and at a point called freezing stick to one another to form rigid crystals of ice. These past two weeks have seen our ponds, swamps, and slow-moving streams ever more thickly paved by this phenomenon. When it occurs in clear, still water the result is transparent. At places and times when flow or breeze disturb it is translucent. Transparent or "black ice" isn't black at all; the light passes through and is absorbed. We call things not reflecting light as black. The wonder of ice, besides the beauty of its many forms, is that it can provide access to places only wondered about during the warmer months. On it we can explore woodland swamps. BE VERY CAREFUL when going forth upon ice. One old Closeteer reports almost departing this world of metamorphosing waters four winters ago. He foolishly went through to his chest while walking on the too-thin white ice of a beaver impoundment. As body heat was leaving, he thought about his folly and imminent end, more with disgust than fear. He was, however, able to move some by breaking a couple feet of ice he couldn't crawl out on, thus enabling him to just reach a sapling with his fingers. On it he climbed enough above unbroken two-inch-thick ice to distribute his weight on four points, hands and knees, where he crawled back to relative safety. There are a couple things he might have done rather than being so careless. In the past, he had carried a long, stout pole horizontally to the ice surface to act as a bridge if he went through. Another was to carry two tethered ice picks an ice fishing friend had given him. These hang around the neck and are used to pick your way out on the smooth ice without handles. It is, of course, as you've been warned by parents and others dozens of times, better to wait until the ice is thick and safe. Even thick ice during thaws and early spring may be rotten. Please heed these lessons learned through the unwise behavior of even old guys who should know better. Ice is irresistible to some.

There is no such danger at Fenway Park where the ice surface is just a few inches above dormant grass. All this digression has been leading to memories of the days when all ice skating was done outdoors on ponds, lakes and even groundwater puddles in fields. The latter, while often small, are perfect for children. Shallow, they freeze relatively quickly right to the ground below, as in the temporary Fenway rink. It was on such that many of us wee nippers learned to skate on clumsy "double runners" that were buckled onto regular shoes. Soon, we graduated to single runners firmly riveted to shoes. Upon becoming competent skaters we moved on to larger ponds where we played hockey. The older boys and young men would keep some areas free of snow all winter long. At each end of cleared rectangles pairs of boots served as goals. Our only equipment was usually a stick and puck. Sometimes goalies would have baseball catcher shin-guards. When the ice became battered from many games, the older boys, often in bitter cold, cut holes in the ice and flooded the rink. The following morning we'd have a fine new surface. On the banks above our favorite places log fires would burn late into the evenings and sometimes all day Saturday and Sunday and school vacations. After the last daylight we'd skate to the ends of the lake or ponds in the light of the moon and stars. White ice reflected and usually gave us plenty, but not enough to play hockey. In high school years those were courting times if we could find a warm and friendly hand to hold while gliding nervously yet happily under the sky. Back at the fire we might be jokingly asked, "Where have you been?"

Sixty years later one might answer, "I skated well with a friend on smooth ice, our faces tingling in the cold. The night was clear and we pointed out the Big Dipper, Orion and Cassiopeia to one another and struggled to say clever things, while wishing this evening on natural outdoor ice didn't have to end."

An Ipswich River Valley

Our Ipswich River flows over 40 miles to the sea, while descending only about 110 feet. As the Goldeneye duck flies source to sea the distance is only about 30 miles. Slow rivers in soft, flat terrain meander. We want to tell those who haven't noticed of a Topsfield valley, only a mile or so long, that contains the river from Rowley Bridge Road just east of Masconomet Regional School to Wheaton's Hill abutting Route 1. This beautiful valley, a phrase often associated with mountains and fast-flowing rivers, is of hills with many large, open fields that descend gently to a fairly straight stretch of river. In walks on four quiet back roads that encircle the valley, we are given a glimpse of what pastoral Essex County was like when there were still farms. The most famous, on the southern heights of our loop, was Meredith Farm, the home of champion Ayrshires, a once-popular breed of dairy cattle. The refrigerated semen of their bulls was mailed round the world. At Meredith there are no longer handsome cows and bulls with speckled maroon-and-white coats and impressive horns; however, the large fields mown for hay are still open. Across the river to the north the once Coolidge Estate's fields are also yearly mown or planted in corn. More fields continue on north above them. A leisurely one-and-one-half-hour walk, all within a few feet of old roadside farmers' stone walls, shaded in long sections by venerable hickories up to two feet in diameter and a few great ashes twice that, will have you on scenic heights and shady lows along the river. There is little traffic to worry about on the narrow roads that were a century ago dirt cart paths traveled by cattle, hogs, horses, oxen and children en route school or better still, a swim in the river or a sled ride on Wheaton's Hill.

And, like all New England roads, the scenery changes with the seasons. In late October we walked under the yellow-leaved hickories, fading, red-orange sugar maples, bare ashes and still dark green white pines, the latter loaded with cones in the best mast year most of us can remember. Then, last month, came the cold storm that left a half foot of dry, light snow; remnants, despite rain since, are still with us. Before that storm, air down off the Canadian Shield had come in brisk west winds for almost a week. Water surfaces froze; even the river's edges were paved. With the snow the countryside became white, decorated with patches of evergreen, gray groves of bare hardwoods, and a black line of open water. Last week the shelves of ice from the river banks were a faint yellowish shade of translucent gray. A year ago there, under similar very cold conditions, we walkers came upon an otter eating a fish on a shelf of ice, a couple feet from liquid water. He left its 32-degree warmth for the wind-chilled air of 10 to enjoy his or her sashimi. Even those of us who like raw fish shivered. The diner we were admiring was as black as the light-absorbing water, its wet fur glistening in the dim winter light.

Lack of development, open fields broken by patches of woods, a river fed by a half-dozen intermittent streams, and seasonal changes of clothes have this valley a lovely place for all us animals. It is looped and made accessible by Rowley Bridge Road, River Road, Salem Road, and Cross Street. There are miles of edge habitats outlining woods, bushes and bodies of water. On our visits we see hawks waiting in trees beside the fields where there is food for their prey. The pine cones mentioned have winged seeds, which sail great distances. On a walk in October we filled our jacket pockets with hickory nuts in no time. This past year the red oaks also had a bumper crop of acorns, rich food for squirrels, turkeys and deer. The grasses, even just stubble, are a great source of nourishment and shelter for smaller creatures, particularly when snow covered.

We tout this one-mile stretch of 40 of our favorite river and urge you to check it out. One of several places to park on the four roads mentioned is where the Rowley Bridge Road passes over the river. Better still go look for diverse habitats nearer home along sections of streams or up and down rivers. John Hanson Mitchell wrote his wonderful book *Ceremonial Time: 15,000 Years on One Square Mile* about the land around his home in Littleton. Perhaps inspired by Thoreau, he went out frequently in all seasons and conditions and watched what was happening. His observations were combined with geologic and social history about the area studied. We might not write voluminous notes as these naturalists did, but we can all explore and discover our own undeveloped parts of town. Many of us old-timers did this as children and wouldn't for anything give up those memories. Some of us have returned, at times wishing we had never left.

2010

January 2010

River Ice Cacophony

In northeast Middleton, not far from Boxford and Topsfield, the Ipswich River takes a great swing to the east. At the turn's start Peabody Street's farmed fields stretch out across the floodplain to the east and south as they may have for 4,000 years. A couple years ago Paul Richardson's cow corn there stood 10 or 12 feet tall. Four centuries ago, Indian corn, each plant several feet apart and probably shoulder high, was surrounded by beans and squash. The Indians too chose rich bottom land for cultivation. Many of their artifacts have been found here. Now the fields lie fallow; sleeping grasses, clover and alfalfa, await warmth. The river's winter-high water now half covers its floodplains. Its surface, due to the long, windy cold snap before Christmas, is covered by one to five inches of ice with sporadic openings over the channel. In the days leading up to New Year's Day the cold returned; the Closet's glass fluctuated between 10 and 20 degrees.

On a breezy frigid late afternoon an old Closeteer went out for his daily constitutional. From the Middleton-Boxford line where it climbs out of the river and crosses Endicott Street he headed north into Boxford among knolls of granite, covered and surrounded by mature hardwoods and pines. After a while he descended to a large beaver impoundment, which had drowned a red maple forest. The bleached limbless corpses of a few victims still stand, reminders to the encircling upland trees of the power of beavers. Despite these grim words the now open field of water has its beauty. Paved in snow-covered ice it is a place with much light. On clear, early morning and late afternoon visits all the trees around it are tinged for a while in subdued shades of red. In three or four months it will be a shallow liquid lake, absorbing rather than reflecting. While the ice looked safe, the Closeteer resisted its siren calls and turned west toward the setting sun into a good face-biting breeze. From the river some distance away came occasional loud sounds he has trouble describing. He knew they must be coming from expanding cracking ice, yet he imagined Paul Bunyan walking in fits and starts on the ice and now and then lifting great plates or logs and smashing them down on it. The peculiar noises had something of the long deep cracking sounds of growing lake ice, but were sharper and shorter in duration. The first few brought shotgun reports to mind. He crossed the impoundment on a manmade causeway, built from upland peninsula to peninsula, near the late Henry Sawyer's home where Henry's son Jonathan and wife live now. Henry was one of three founders of the Essex County Greenbelt Association a half century ago. Under the gravel causeway two large culverts allow water to pass into a swamp and then on slowly to the river. For over a decade beavers have been periodically blocking them.

On crossing, the Closeteer entered a large open field and turned south toward the noisy river. Fine pasture there is on what geologists might call a terrace. From its edge, 20 feet above the river, he admired the frozen floodplain among red and silver maples and swamp white oaks. Ice of varied shades of gray, from white to black, is decorated with concentric bands from uneven freezing and the straighter lines of cracks. He thought the latter, upon forming, must be the sources of the sounds. The noises, more frequent now, were much louder, an exciting show even tin ears could appreciate. In 70 years of winter walks he had never heard a river sounding off so. He wondered what the Indians had thought, not knowing the physics of growing ice. Was the river saying or singing something? We, his listeners, liked the idea. Maybe the cries are warnings to kids, "Keep off! Keep off!" This admonition reminds us of a story told us recently of a near tragedy downriver just up from Thunder Bridge. As young lads Leon Rubchinuk and two brothers ignored the nearby bridge and started crossing the river on snow-covered ice. His heavier older brothers crossed quite handily. Leon trailing behind did not. He broke through but was able to grab the ice edge just in time. The rest of his body was quickly pulled under by the current. His brothers turned and found he had gone through. The oldest got to him in time and pulled him out. He lived nearby and by running got home before freezing. Leon tells this tale very vividly, as if it happened yesterday, and adds that his late mother, as all mothers do, had repeatedly told her boys to stay off the ice. We bet squaws there had done the same for thousands of years.

The Closeteer while marveling at the swelling ice's complaints noticed where he was. A couple hundred feet from him, above the north bank of the river east of Thomas Road, on Christmas Eve 117 years ago a fire burned the huge J. B. Thomas box factory there to the ground. The next work day 40 men awoke, if they had slept at all, with no jobs to go to. The factory was never rebuilt. The ruins are gone; riding horse pasture has replaced them.

While listening to the river below he continued along the terrace edge to Thomas Road, also called Old Boxford Road on some deeds. There he again admired long lines of old sugar maples flanking the road. Despite the absence of Spanish moss and leaves they remind him of live oaks gracing southern plantation drives. They must have been tapped for sap in the past. Thomas Road took him to Peabody Street where he returned to the south side of the river via the bridge. He then continued easterly through floodplain fields and maples. There the ice on only knee-deep water, was safe although a little scary since his steps invoked more cracking music, only now too close. His new lower route took him by where good Leon almost left us five decades before. The sun had gone down; residual light guided him across Thunder Bridge back to where he had started this loop walk he'll not forget.

The stiff breeze on the return east from Thomas Road was on his back. Despite the cold his coat was open. His blood was flowing seemingly as fast as the dark ice water in the nearby current.

What would our world, one many fear is fast approaching, be without natural waxing and waning ice?

Ice Fishing

This time of year when the ice on our freshwater lakes and ponds and tidal rivers becomes safe fishermen go forth and cut holes, one-fourth to two feet deep, with augers and ice chisels, passages to their prey. Smelts from the brackish waters of rivers along the coast of Maine where friends go are favorites. Groups rent tiny shacks with leaky wood stoves, each shack straddling two long rectangular openings in the ice. Depending on conditions of tide, current, and population densities of smelt and prey, they catch many, few, or none. One Closeteer, a fisherman for seven decades, prides himself on multi-hook gear of his own design. He, who doesn't use the raggedy strings and rusty hooks provided by shack landlords, sometimes catches a couple dozen smelts in six or so hours and at others 10 times that many or more. A novice fisherman friend who sometimes goes along on his trips has returned from afternoons and evenings on the East Branch of the Kennebec with very few fish. At such times his good wife, Keeper of the Purse, can't resist some out-loud arithmetic. "Fifteen dollars for gas plus 15 for food and drink plus 20 for shack rent and bait equals 50. Ten fish at three ounces each equals 30 ounces or about two pounds. Fifty divided by two is 25 dollars per pound! We could have gone down the road to the Bluefin restaurant with a friend for sushi." He, who like most of the fish that passed under him unseen has learned not to take the bait, but rather smiles, knowing that non-outdoors-in-winter types just don't get it. The trip out on a Maine river under a pollution free night sky filled with stars was not for meals, although fresh smelt fried taste awfully good.

Several winters ago, although his bucket bottom was scarce covered with fish, the novice returned with a head full of memories and thoughts. He shares the following written soon after.

Ice Fishing
Up from the sea unsuspecting
In water that flows to and fro
To tunes of the moon and the sun
Smelts come or they don't in the darkness
To stalkers by holes in the ice.
We gather in stove-heated shacks
Long stare at the black depths below
Joke, gossip, spin yarns of past catches
'Til some lines start to slide to the side.
With no effort we hoist our small prey
And callously toss in a bucket
Ignore death slaps as lives fade away.
Now and then I stop to examine
Their streamlining and colors sublime,
As vitality's shine quickly dims.
We met at the river last night
On opposite sides of a good foot of ice
Violated with chain saw torn holes,
Above us the countless cold stars.
Is man too a snatcher of bait,
Hooked upon lines in his mind,

Seen draped from celestial heights
Just food for gods' feasts in the sky?

How good of fish, our most ancient of vertebrate kin, to sometimes take our half-dead sea worm bait and provide us with good protein, HDL fat, and bone minerals. With smelts the entire fish can be eaten. If we fell through our ice access hole they'd probably perceive us as food; older invertebrate ancestors like crabs and worms certainly would. As the pieces get smaller so do the eaters until bacteria, on earth three billion plus years, finish the recycling. How interrelated we all are even while separated by degrees of complexity and time beyond our ken. Such thoughts pop up as we are asked, "Cut up another worm or two and pass me a couple pieces. I have a feeling schools are coming our way."

CLAMMING IN ARCTIC AIR

Last week we three old men carefully descended to the Eagle Hill Cove clam flat in Ipswich on brittle cakes of salt water ice. The afternoon was rendered clear and cold by northwest winds. On the ice-free tidal flat, our backsides bent to windward, we planted our boots and clam forks in the muck. The six long tines sunk deep just inches beyond siphon holes kept open by soft-shelled clams, our prey. Pushing down on short handles and cleaving hunks of flat from the whole, we then pulled each up and over hoping clams would be revealed. We picked up those over two inches long, thus legal, and tossed them into our pails. Finding them lessened the discomfort of cold feet and well gloved hands. It would be a whole half hour of strenuous digging before the blood flowed freely and warmer, yet even then our extremities were becoming numb. The rest of our bodies felt revived upon filling buckets with good food and our spirits and lungs with the freshest of airs down off the Canadian Shield. By bucket-full time, despite the bitter cold, we were almost warm. We happily slogged off the flat as the low western sky glowed and the eastern sky above the ocean behind Plum Island darkened. We knew that squaws had dug on this same flat four centuries ago with forked sticks and we wondered if they had done so in winter.

In the waning minutes of sunlight and low tide two donned hip boots and waders and walked through salt water-ice slush along the edge of the Eagle River until thigh deep in the center. They, 81 and 87, dragged their rakes along the shell strewn bottom for oysters. (We bet you thought all oysters were from Chesapeake Bay and warmer waters south of Cape Cod.) In less than 15 minutes they waded out of the freezing water with their allowed 30 oysters, each over the required three inches long.

At the same time "commercial" clammers were returning in aluminum skiffs, singly or in pairs, from more distant Ipswich flats. One young clammer when greeted with a common Yankee question, "Cold enough for you?", answered happily, "Sure beats the office." The amateur called a "mess digger" responded with another old saw, "You can say that again." The man didn't, but we detected a smile. You can get away with such banal exchanges on the low tide flats. Language isn't important in such beautiful places where there is camaraderie in hard work done under what many would consider tough conditions. The recreational two hours of us amateurs are nothing compared with the four the commercial diggers do each daylight low and end up

Clammer on Ipswich flat. Photo, courtesy of Dorothy Monnelly.

with several times our allowed 10 quarts. We, however, like to think kindred feelings are shared.

The many Ipswich flats are well managed. The shellfish advisory board, shellfish constable, and selectmen rotate access to the flats and wholly ban digging and raking after substantial rains that result in bacteria-laden runoff and during periods of red tides. We hope there will be clams and oysters for as long as there are tides and even after human clammers. The mollusks in coastal waters have been there a half billion years, we only a few millenia.

Musings While Walking Mill to Mill

Last Friday morning in cold clear air the Middleton Council on Aging/ Conservation Commission (COA/CC) walking group hiked on ancient roads by the ruins of four once water-powered mills. Two, the Peabody and Curtis sawmills, used the power of Boston Brook in the 18th and mid-20th centuries respectively. The Boxford Iron Foundry, later replaced by a knife factory, and Nichols grist mill wheels were turned by water descending to the Ipswich River in Pout Pond Brook, which is now labeled on Stream Team sign posts as Emerson Brook because of an upstream name. John Nichols ground corn and other grains in the 18th century. The iron blooming mill was active 1708 to about 1780 and a knife factory at the same site in the latter half of the 19th century. All are easily visited and pondered in a leisurely two-hour hike.

As we walked and talked some of us tried to imagine the land once part of Topsfield, Boxford, and Salem, now Middleton, when it was largely pasture without trees. We wondered where the bog iron ore and charcoal for the iron foundry, probably modeled on the one preceding it in Saugus, had come from. We tried hard to imagine the paved back roads we walked as muddy cart paths two wagons wide. This was difficult even for a few of us old-timers brought up on farms who had known a few teams of working horses and oxen as children. Old photographs we remembered of bare rolling hills with only a few shade trees helped. The four mill ponds are easy; the foundry/knife factory dam is still pretty much intact; Mill Pond behind it is full. Beavers have built on the remains of Nichol's Mill dam off Liberty Street. Their impoundment, once the mill pond, stretches more than a mile up Emerson Brook to Lake Street. They've drowned the trees.

The impoundment probably resembles the pond there three centuries ago when Nichols ground corn.

The mills we tried to visualize didn't operate all year, but only when the water in their ponds was high enough in late winter, spring and late fall. We have to guess about all this because practical millers, sawyers and farmers didn't sit around the fire in late evenings writing journals. We have but their fallen sluiceways, mill building foundations, eroded dams and cryptic old deeds. The ruins remaining are fairly easy to interpret. The deeds, however, require tedious digging in the bowels of the Essex County registry, town records, and historical society libraries. We in Middleton are indebted to the late Lura Woodside Watkins, historian and author of *Middleton: A Cultural History*, who did much of the work for us. How we admire her dedication to revealing past truths. It isn't easy untangling the stories of four centuries from past deeds and wills written in bygone ways. Many town histories are little more than chronological lists of ministers and military actions. Wilkins tried her damnedest to tell us the true story of the lay of the land and the people who did the necessary work upon it: raised food, tanned leather, made shoes, forged iron, sawed boards, etc. We are lucky to have had her. Alas, her book is out of print. It is high time for a reprinting.

Some of us think local history should be taught in our schools. If some time could be spared from MCAS preparation students could enjoy field trips such as our COA/CC hikes. It is more important for them than for us to know from whence they came. Many don't understand where vegetables, grain, meat, lumber, iron, fuel and meal are truly from. If we answer Market Basket, Demoulas or Hannaford that just won't do.

FEBRUARY 2010

A NEW CONTINENT, TO THOSE NOT ALREADY HERE

There was a time not long ago in human history when Europeans only knew of three continents, Europe, Africa, and Asia together, and not the breadth of ocean beyond. Imagine it is 1400 and a Portuguese navigator looking west from a beach near Lisbon wonders how far to Cipangu and China. He knows of both because of Marco Polo's famous trek by land. On an eastern shore of Cipangu, correctly Nippon, Kenji looks east and has similar thoughts about what might be beyond the horizon. From an Oregon beach Tilamook Sharp Salmon Spear often stares west and wonders how far the gray whales go. On a shore of eastern Massachusetts an ancestor of Masconomo admires the rising sun and ponders other places it might shine on. He may have heard stories down from the north of Norsemen in huge sail-powered canoes who had long ago visited from somewhere east.

Recently from Middleton's Flint Public Library we Stream Teamers borrowed a remarkable new book entitled *The Fourth Quarter of the Earth* by Toby Lester. Good reviews had us seek it out. For 400 pages about maps, geography and exploration, we map lovers were not disappointed. Lester, who writes very well, had done an impressive amount of homework. He had heard of a famous world map made by Martin Waldseemuller in 1507 that had been lost for centuries. It inspired his research into the discoveries and lesser maps leading to it. In those early days of printing Waldseemuller made a huge four-foot by 12-foot map in sections. Woodblocks were carved for each and a few hundred very expensive copies were painstakingly printed. These were glued to cloth to make colorful rolled maps for use in university classrooms and rich men's homes. It wasn't long before they were worn out and none could be found. This loss resulted in a long search by scholars for survivors. In 1901 Father Joseph Fischer found an intact Waldseemuller still in sections in a pigskin-bound folio in the library of a remote German castle. He had been looking for years. After confirmation by colleagues news of the finding was made known. Why all the resulting excitement and fuss? It was because there between the "Indies," Cipangu and China, and Europe appears another continent running north-south almost pole to pole, flanked by two oceans. On what was later called Brazil is clearly printed AMERICA. Waldseemuller's is the first map known to include a fourth continent, a "New World." Lester tells us the fascinating history of map making and the thought that preceded this find from the time of the ancient Greeks, who had accurately calculated the earth's circumference.

Columbus, who made four trips to the "Indies" including his first in 1492, thought there was only one not-very-broad ocean between the Occident and the Orient. Amerigo Vespucci, part-time navigator on several explorations from Spain and Portugal soon after Columbus, ones he didn't lead, was given far more credit than some thought his due, perhaps because of reports he submitted upon return. Columbus's biographer Bartolome de las Casas and Columbus's son later petitioned one and all to no avail for a change in name for the new continent to Columbia or something similar in honor of Admiral Don Cristobal Colon. This dispute still lingers on in some quarters.

Now, as poor Haiti so severely suffers, we are reminded of a story in Lester's book about the first period of misery known to history in Haiti's long trials. It has been passed on to us by Las Casas. Columbus's log of his first voyage was lost. However, Las Casas is thought to have had it when writing his biography. The misery was brought ironically enough by Christians aboard the *Santa Maria* on Christmas Eve, 1492. That calm night Columbus's flagship scraped over coral and then went aground on the beautiful island soon to be arrogantly named Isla de España, later Hispaniola. The Admiral and crew awakened, and frantically, to no avail, tried to save her. At first light friendly natives in large canoes paddled out to help. All were saved including cargo and ship's timbers. Unfortunately for the handsome, admirable Taino, described so by Columbus himself, the admiral left a small murderous colony behind and kidnapped a couple dozen Taino for his triumphal return to Ferdinand and Isabella. Las Casas wrote two generations later, "Observe the humanity of the Indians toward the tyrants who have (since) exterminated them." And, we might add, most of the natives on Haiti and neighboring islands in the Caribbean. Those who didn't succumb to European diseases were murdered or worked to death as slaves. When they were gone African slaves were shipped in by the thousands to raise sugar cane. We'll not go on; Haiti's subsequent horrible history under the Spanish and later French planters is well known. At least the horror now comes from hurricanes and S and P waves, both natural phenomena. People from across the seas pour in not to exploit but to help. Haiti, originally Ayiti, has had its name back since independence in 1804. Let us hope the country will in time regain some pre-Columbian peace and happiness.

Maybe "America" for the new continent is the better name in the absence of a native one. There are too few native names remaining even here in New England. It is too bad they left no maps.

TRI-TOWN TRIBUTARIES

Down from the northwest in our towns two of the Ipswich River's largest tributaries flow. Together they collect the surface waters from 16 square miles and return them via the river to the sea. Boston and Fish Brooks, parallel and roughly the same length, receive the yields of hundreds of rivulets and lesser streams. When they are nearly dry, often in August and September, water from the ground provides some slow flow. On rare occasions the groundwater table sinks below the streams' bottoms in places. Creatures—there are millions in each curve—rest in the cool mud and under rocks, die except for their tough eggs or dormant forms, or gather where groundwater is exposed in low pools. With fall rains and waning water use by plants due to loss of leaves, the groundwater again rises, bringing the streams and river noticeably alive.

Great stretches, especially of Fish Brook, have beautiful stony bottoms resembling wet pebble driveways only with much more mystery and depth. There are places we could now visit between the old grist mill pond above Lockwood Lane and Howes Pond on Mill Road, Boxford, where water in the channel runs perfectly clear between borders of white ice. Several feet below are wondrous multi-colored pebbles paving a bottom much favored by many spawning fish. Upstream from the dark boulder-covered bottom of Boston Brook above Mundy Bridge that drops along several hundred feet to produce Middleton's only natural stretch of dynamic white water, are long stretches of more level channel whose firm floor is beige coarse sand. The interstices between all these rocks—sand grains, pebbles and boulders—provide hideaways and enormous substrate surfaces for insect larvae, crustaceans, tiny mollusks, algae and bacteria, the denizens of healthy streams.

In summer wetland bushes and trees shade more than three-fourths of these tributaries thus keeping their water cool. Colder water holds significantly more oxygen than warm. Yet even when the ice seals much surface bank to bank there is necessary warmth plus plenty of dissolved oxygen. February first at Thunder Bridge, Middleton, the water temperature was 30 degrees F beneath Arctic air whose temperature had averaged about 20 degrees F for the prior week. The dissolved oxygen in water coming out from under stretches of ice measured a fairly high 10 mg/l. While the water was colorless and transparent, we testers knew that a good microscope would reveal some plankton. The dark bottom below is loaded with life. Streams themselves don't hibernate in winter, they flow faster, their organisms slow a bit except for warm-blooded species like ducks, otters, muskrats and beavers. The fish despite blood temperatures close to their surroundings are somewhat active. We wonder if the otters find them easier prey in winter. Yesterday in a half inch of new snow on beaver impoundment ice extending outward from Pond Meadow Brook, an important tributary of Boston Brook that carries water from Boxford and North Andover, we admired otter trails consisting of a series of alternating slides and running tracks. Otters fish under the ice of ponds, streams and impoundments. We read they go from trapped air pocket to air pocket below the ice. Occasionally we find their entry holes kept open on the edges.

Fish and Boston Brooks squiggle around glacier-carved uplands about eight miles each not counting their unnamed tributaries. Fish Brook joins the river just east of Masconomet Regional School in Topsfield. Boston Brook converges with it just one half mile up from the Peabody Street Bridge, in Middleton. The flanking floodplain fields of the latter were faithfully mowed each year by the late Warren Evans and his teams of horses until the 1990s. About every five to 10 years the fields where the brooks enter the river host a foot or two of passing water. We have old newspaper photos of Warren and team towing the cars of foolish drivers who tried to ford inundated Peabody and East Streets. The tributary streams along their lengths also rose up over their floodplains. The last flood, Mother's Day, May 16, 2006, the river rose a record three feet over predicted 100-year flood highs. The prior record in March 2001 was close. Stop at the Stream Team's information kiosk at the Peabody Street landing and see the photo taken there at its crest.

The ice of this late January-early February cold period has allowed safe access to wetlands and the brooks' floodplains. (Don't go near their deeper parts and channels.) We'd like to explore them year round but bushes and fallen logs make tough going for wading and canoe paddling. The past couple weeks we've gone forth on a foot or more of ice covering beaver impoundments draining to Fish, Boston and Emerson Brooks. Emerson, another large tributary of the Ipswich, brings water down from Andover, North Andover and North Reading.

We could go on and on writing books about each of our brooks and river. Rounding each curve is like turning a page that brings new discoveries. This natural transport system of living habitats, known intimately by the natives before the English, has had a grid of unnatural roads superimposed upon it. We scarcely notice these natural wonders speeding on asphalt at right angles across them. That is one of the reasons the Middleton Stream Team has installed vertical green signposts at each crossing. We want you to stop and walk as best you can alongside them. In the summer you might wade, swim or paddle. For wildlife our paved roads are barriers and dangerous places. It is along our streams and rivers they hang out and thrive.

FIELDS OF ICE

This month we've been able to walk on level fields of ice in places not often accessible. In trees above Emerson Bog, Middleton, we were able, because of views from new angles, to see and count the herons' nests of a four-year-old rookery. We had long wondered how many nests were there; only 10 can be seen from distant Route 114. Our latest tally is 32, most high in spreading oaks and dead white pines. We saw no Great Blue Herons, builders of these haphazard but rugged stick nests at the complete mercy of snow-laden nor'easters. The herons have moved out to coastal salt waters that remain open for fishing. Ornithologist and friend Jim Berry of Ipswich tells us to keep our eyes out for Great Horned Owls that may be nesting now in some heron nests. They lay two eggs in February. Surviving young, often only one, may still be there with mother by the return in April and May of absentee landlords. The confrontation should be something to see as rent payment is demanded. We'll check nests for these feisty big owls; however, a thaw may render our access ice unsafe. In the absence of a Stream Team helicopter we'll have to use binoculars from knolls around the bog's perimeter.

Last week's much hyped blizzard, greatly affecting many of the mid-Atlantic states, left only a half inch of wet snow here. In the night it froze to the slick-thick ice, providing us with non-skid surfaces. We explored the next day and found fresh clear tracks of deer, otter, fisher, squirrels, mice, fox, coyote and several don't-knows among patches of emergent bushes—buttonbush, leatherleaf, myrica gale—and the standing corpses of dam-drowned Atlantic white cedars, red maples and swamp white oaks. Emerson Bog, inundated by a manmade dam across Emerson Brook near Lake Street, is a Danvers Water Supply reservoir. Our fellow mammals, those listed above, are attracted to this flat expanse surrounded by rocky knolls and broken by islands covered with mature oak and pine. Adding greatly to the varied habitats of this vast swamp/reservoir are two large circular bodies of deeper water called Knights Pond and Andover Meadow Pond. They may be glacial kettles where great blocks of residual ice slowly melted as sediments deposited around them. Fishermen and otters visit them; beavers have lodges on their edges. Soon footprints in the snow, ours included, will disappear as the ice melts from above and below. By the end of March most will be gone and sunlight will enter liquid water unimpeded. Soon after, the herons and the Red-winged Blackbirds will return. The male blackbirds who come first will, while singing lustily, establish territories in preparation for the arrival of the females. In the scores of acres of buttonbushes characterizing Emerson Bog, they'll build nests a couple feet above water level. With waning ice, turtles and frogs will awaken; thousands of fish will move more quickly. The denser water near the bottom at 39 degrees F will become equal in temperature and density to the warming surface water that was 32 degrees F while melting. The stability of the winter thermoclines will for a short time be gone and the nutrient-high bottom water will mix throughout. These nutrients and heat will result in blooms of plankton and population increases in the tiny creatures, fish food, who graze upon it. The pond will come alive as the buds of the trees and bushes above swell and we enjoy spring fever. A note may be needed here to explain the behavior of water as its temperature changes. Most substances upon cooling become ever more dense. Water does until 39 degrees F and then upon further cooling expands to become less dense. So ice at 32 degrees F and below floats, the denser liquid water beneath it is between 32 degrees F and 39 degrees F, with 39 degrees F the densest at the bottom. If water didn't behave this way skaters would have to don scuba gear and wet suits to access ice resting on the bottom. Each spring and fall when the water throughout the vertical water column is at the same temperature and density, the water in ponds and lakes top to bottom mixes. Plankton populations peak at these times.

The spring sun will daily climb higher across the sky; rays approaching perpendicular will give its warmth more meaning. But that is in the future; let's return to the safe ice of February 2010 with its thin layer of new snow showing the track patterns of many animals. We didn't see one track maker except ourselves in three two-hour visits. Animals lighter in weight have no doubt been coming forth since the first supporting thinner ice in December. The herbivores must be after the seeds of buttonbushes, swamp rose hips, and the numerous buds of anything they can reach. We recognized a dozen swamp plant species above the ice. No doubt white pine seeds have blown out there in abundance these past few months. 2009 produced a bumper crop of pine cones and seeds. It was also a banner mast year for oaks, their acorns cover the forest floors of the surrounding uplands. Many while falling must blow or roll out to the edges of the bog. The carnivores come down from the woods for the vegetarians. Dusk, dark, and dawn among the patches of wetland plants must be exciting. Some of us plan quiet visits alone soon at first light and last in hopes of seeing more than the patterns and criss-crossings of tracks we haven't been able to decipher. If we had the gumption we'd return with insulated pad and winter sleeping bag. We'd no doubt be rewarded with at least sounds, some horrible to contemplate. If really scientific we'd rent infrared detectors such as soldiers carry. In the meantime we will just have to imagine the interactions out there under the stars.

Fellow organisms who share much of our DNA are all around us in soils, trees, bushes, grasses, waters and even on ice yet most of us know them not. We wonder if school classes shouldn't be outdoors.

ANOTHER PERFECT STORM

At times people in the entertainment business and theatergoers rave about a terrific musical that happens when everything comes together just right and results in a show that may be repeated over and over for decades. *West Side Story* might be an example; choose your own. Writers, composers, actors, choreographers, costume designers, lighting crew and others work well together in magnificent synergy greater than the sum of its parts. On a less limited stage it happened here the afternoon and evening of Tuesday, February 16, in a vast theater-in-the-all-around. Damp snow came slowly out of the northeast on barely freezing air and fell on our trees and bushes making them wet and sticky. In the late afternoon and evening as the temperature slightly dropped, fluffy drier snow fell fast for a few hours and stuck. The night wind off the ocean was relatively gentle and didn't shake the heavily laden branches clean as so often happens. All we had to do was leave the snow scenes from the Vancouver mountains on the

Olympic TV station and go to any window for a wondrous preview of the next morning's show. Scenes from distant Whistler were rendered drab in comparison. At first light and before on Wednesday morning we knew we'd been blessed with a perfect storm. Snow, wet then dry, wind not too stormy, temperatures near and then freezing, and finally the sun all combined to dazzle a waking audience in Essex County and beyond.

Sugar maples and oaks, each branch and tiny twig thickly coated, stood relatively unbowed in the morning light. Birches, dark branches hidden, curled downward in obeisance, perhaps to the storm that had dressed them so, or to the lordly "white pines," then truly white, rising above in formal winter attire. The pines' trunks stood straight towering over even large hardwoods, their boughs drooping under heavy loads. We walked in groves of these noble trees correctly called *Pinus strobus* and found not the six-to-eight-inch accumulations of lawns and fields, but rather three or four, the balance captured on the branches above. The higher white branches, like still wave crests, alternated with dark caverns of green needles in the shade of the boughs above. The first pink-tinged light of sunrise made each pine top a frozen fountain with depth. Words just don't come close; clearly the pines dominated the overall wonderland from an unusually blue

White pines after snow storm. Photo, courtesy of Pam Hartman.

sky to hidden ground. We walked around Middleton Pond in awe of its perimeter of evergreens so enhanced, mature groves that are striking even in undress. The overall spectacle was too grand. When by noon a bright February sun had melted the face paint from these silent actors, we were almost glad. We can only take so much.

This is the second show in the last three seasons that Mother Nature has put on with white pines in leading roles. Late summer we noticed the same high boughs bending under the weight of masses of green cones. In fall, opening cones, by then brown, released billions of seeds. Most of us could never remember such a productive year for wildlife food, pine seeds and the acorns of oaks.

As we broke trail in a marvelous canyon of snow walls, our minds wandered and we exchanged information and stories about our native pine we'd so long admired. In the 17th century, British agents cruising New England forests marked the straightest giants, some six feet in diameter, 130 tall, with three axe marks making an upward-pointing arrow. These trees with the "king's arrow" were set aside for ship masts that were later felled by farmers and hauled by teams of oxen to the nearest coastal flowing river. Great pines of relatively strong wood—light colored, almost white—perhaps the source of the common name, were ideal for spars above the ship's center of gravity. The trunks were loaded on special mast ships and some even rafted across the Atlantic. We recalled a short article copied from an early 1700s Liverpool newspaper urging citizens to visit a certain dock to view the Yankee raft of mast logs rigged and sailed over from Newbury's port.

Stimulated by the surrounding beauty we imagined great men-o'-war and merchant ships, their masts billowing white sails, as we looked up at those spars' snow-covered descendants. The Indians here before the English painstakingly with fire and clamshells carved out canoes from white pine and chestnut logs. Colonists and those who followed sheathed their houses with boards sawn from them. Arthur "Breezy" Page's entire house on East Street, Middleton, was built in the late 1940s of white pine cut by him from his land and then converted to boards at the Curtis brothers' water-powered mill on Boston Brook. *Pinus strobus* may still be New England's most valuable commercial forest product.

As you can see, the storm's lovely handiwork is still with us as we wax on about only one of the many woody plants transformed for a few hours. The clinging snow, gone from the needles, twigs, branches and trunks, is still very much with those who gloried in its splendor. Two Yankee friends, one now in San Diego and the other in Myrtle Beach en route to Florida, bemoaned their absence upon hearing of the storm's creations. One friend here for the show fretted about plans she has to spend next winter in Florida. She says she knows what she'll be missing. As we've teased before this time of year in other Water Closet columns, Snowbirds eat your hearts out.

MARCH 2010

AQUATIC PRISON CELL

Orlando: On February 24th Dawn Brancheau, veteran animal trainer, was killed by her huge charge Tilikum, a "killer whale" (more formally *Orcinus orca*), who attacked her for reasons not understood. As the TV stations zoomed in and out from the Sea World pool where Brancheau breathed her last and Tilikum still swam, some of us were struck by the tiny volume of seawater in which captured killer whales spend their boring lives. These fast, over 30 knots, up to seven-ton mammals' natural 3D habitats are vast oceans. Cells in human aquariums can be measured in tens and hundreds of feet. Might these incarcerations without trial or conviction be likened to confining a captured wild horse of the high Wyoming plains in a small paddock a few times its length?

As we later zoomed away from a Google Earth check, the minuscule pool disappeared while the ocean and gulf flanking Florida came into view. It must have occurred to many others following the story that the restrictions put on these magnificent animals by another species verge on criminal behavior. Animal rights people internationally have said as much about these and other animals, especially the cute ones. Yet we allow what must be terrible confinements, for entertainment. Imagine yourself in a small room for years without the wonders of the larger world and without access to a diverse array of food, the equivalent of many fresh fishes and mammals in Orcas' case. We know what happens to many humans so locked away from normal society. Several confined whales sharing a pool hardly constitutes a roving pod.

Hell, an appropriate word here, we treat our food animals worse. Pigs concentrated in Midwest prisons, hardly farms, have scarcely room on wet concrete floors to lie down. They spend their short lives eating unnatural foods, and no time rooting around in soils and among plants for goodies. Then there are the infamous feedlots where beef cattle are gathered for a final few sick months to be practically force-fed cheap corn, which has little relationship to their ancestors' wild and varied diet. Most, before becoming too sick to remain standing, are mercifully slaughtered. From Maryland on south are enormous chicken buildings, notice we don't say "houses," without windows or open air. In each, thousands of birds are crowded almost wing to flightless wing, their diets devoid of grasses, weeds, insects and worms. Why all this crowding and poor diet? Agribusinessmen, hardly farmers, who run these operations would smile at such a naïve question from a fellow capitalist. It is to provide lots of cheap food high in tasty fat for Americans who worry about weight problems, or for money, a shorter more honest answer.

Tilikum and others so confined and fed thawed frozen fish will not be eaten for their steaks and deep-fried skin and blubber. They are animals for our entertainment. And, their "owners" and trainers might add, for our education. One old Closeteer tells of a zoo visit as a small boy. A kindly old uncle took him to one not too far from here hoping he would be entertained and educated. Stuck in his memory for life is that of an elephant shackled by short chains to a concrete floor. There it swayed back and forth going nowhere. A keeper came in with a crate of wilted lettuce and dumped it within trunk range. In Orcas' small pools they slowly circle round and round going nowhere while awaiting endless shows.

It isn't right to treat other species so. We know very well it isn't; now and then some brave people rise up to say so. We'd never treat our pets like this and when someone does we howl and condemn. Good farmers don't overcrowd their animals. The best include pastures and open ranges in the lives of their cows, hogs and birds. Agribusiness feeds cheaply and crowds for efficiency. We environmentalists, raised in a world where commerce is in the saddle, are well aware of the blasphemy of accusing those who quest for profits as anything but semi-sacred in our economic system. As we write we are thinking hard about how to dress up our pleas with economic arguments. We could;

many have. They'd argue that the less red meat and fat the less disease and medical costs. For Orcas and the oceans they'd argue that removal of top predators adversely affects the whole ecosystem and thus our important fisheries. We've learned over and over again the importance of predators such as wolves, cod, whales, seals and sharks.

Rather than these appeals to our short-term well-being and ease of living why not an honest moral declaration that it is wrong to treat our fellow creatures badly? What can be worse than overcrowding in grossly unnatural environments like minuscule pools and feedlots that completely separate animals from the ecosystems they evolved in?

The late President Reagan while at the Berlin Wall famously pleaded, "Mr. Gorbachev, tear down this wall." He wanted freedom for all to come and go east and west. Perhaps it is high time for us to ask aquarium folks, zookeepers, and agribusinessmen, "Tear down these walls and too-close fences. Treat animals in kinder and more responsible ways. Let them live as close as you can get to their natural environments. Let's rid ourselves of exhibition aquaria for whales and other sea mammals." We wonder what Dawn Brancheau, a dedicated friend and trainer of whales, deeply thought and felt about the artificial surroundings of her involuntary students.

WHERE SEA AND LAND ENTWINE

Henry Hudson cruised along our coasts four centuries ago searching for water gaps in an unknown continent that would allow shorter access to East Indian spices. *Fatal Journey*, a new book by Peter Mancall about Hudson's explorations that has received good reviews, is now being passed around and discussed in the Closet. He and small crews in small ships sought passages both northeast and northwest through Atlantic ice three times without the success he and well-heeled backers had hoped for. Mancall in his search for written records of those voyages beyond the well-known world, at least to those not living there, found disappointingly little. However, with imagination and information from other early daredevils seeking similar passages through the ice he fills in between scarce and sometimes cryptic journal and log entries.

While considering Mancall's patchwork of speculation and hard history we wondered about all the fishermen who we now know preceded Hudson and other big-named explorers along Maritime and Yankee coasts. They had been coming in the warmer months for decades throughout the 16th century. This is known from merchants' accounts of salt sales and dried and pickled product received. Mancall and his hero Hudson hardly mention those brave fishermen in tiny ships, who, probably illiterate, left few direct records. The early colonists in Plymouth, Salem and other places were surprised to find Indians who spoke a little Portuguese, French or English. A few had helped the early fishermen catch and cure cod. Entrepreneur as well as explorer John Smith had a fishing station 13 years before the Pilgrims at Plymouth on what were later, after Smythes Isles, called the Isles of Shoals.

Imagine an unknown new continent stretching west and north and who knew where beyond, a wonderful jagged coast of ins and outs, ups and downs, of great variety and beauty from Campobello, New Brunswick, to New York on the Hudson River. As a migrating bird flies, one not interested in estuaries, bays, rivers and capes, the distance is only 500 or so miles. Along her beeline route, within sight on a clear day, the tides lap against about 10 times that length of shore. Is it any wonder the Old World explorers came again and again to see what new marvels they would find around each cape and up each river? Over the distance mentioned there were a dozen Indian tribes in scores of villages, many seen from the sea. Smith counted 40 while coasting "downeast" from Cape Cod to Penobscot Bay. Let's list just the North Shore rivers north to south: Merrimack, Parker, Rowley, Eagle Hill, Ipswich, Essex, Annisquam, Danvers, Saugus, and Mystic. Omitted are perennial streams and salt marsh cricks that qualify as rivers under the Massachusetts Wetlands Protection Act. A child living near the coast has but to step from her back yard to find some watery connection with the sea. In estuaries saltwater comes and goes, rises and falls, and coincides with the life cycles of animals from tidal flats and pools to flyways above. In this great intermeshing of land and sea there were once fish in numbers scarcely believed by Old Worlders regaled with tales back home. The fishermen in little ships believed and returned each spring in numbers lost to time.

The Indians on the land side of this meeting of continent and ocean ventured forth in dugout canoes only a couple leagues. They didn't need to go farther; fish and fowl came to them. The intertidal flats, beaches and pools on rock ledges were populated with snails, clams, mussels, crabs and lobsters. Anadromous fish species came and went up streams and rivers in astronomical numbers leaving their next generations behind as eggs in clean bottom sands and gravel. We still have their names: alewives, shad, sturgeon, salmon, and lamprey eels. Yet we know them not compared with times past; just a few still trickle in and out past our dams.

Since Hudson and subsequent colonization, maps have gone from rough sketches with fairly accurate latitudes and way-off longitudes, the latter due to the inability to then accurately measure time, to those of live satellites that locate GPS users within a few feet. We are told that military posits are within inches. We bet the early explorers who used stars, lead line, surf sounds, and smells to feel their way along coasts without fog horns and lights might think the new technology has removed all the challenge and fun. One old Closeteer, who while in the navy just a half century ago much enjoyed using sextant, moon, sun and stars to determine approximate positions, grumbles about the instant new fixes without the variables of rolling deck and follow-up calculations with pencil on paper. We now have but to click Google Earth and see the passages Hudson and dozens of others sought through the ice that are now relatively open thanks to global warming and huge steel ships.

Before we leave thoughts of past explorations let's go to Google Earth and zoom in on the edges of land and sea at Ipswich. Coming into view are the salt marshes, barrier beaches, sound and rivers. Closing in further on a marsh many tiny cricks are seen. In all of these, seawater kisses the land twice daily; heat, nutrients and organisms are exchanged. There aren't just a few thousand miles of contact in New England, there are millions all told. The humble fishermen may have had a better understanding of the riches here than did the spice, fur and precious metal seekers. It is time for all of us to zoom in on and take care of micro-ecosystems on which all the others rest. The places on our planet where water and rocks touch are the bases of its vitality.

PLUM ISLAND ON EDGE

Many in Essex County and beyond are fans of the Parker River National Wildlife Refuge at Plum Island. There we might meet and speak with birders from around the world if they'd leave their scopes a bit. This winter an old Closeteer showed off North Shore coasts to a retired dairy farmer friend from Southampton, Massachusetts, on the Connecticut River. He, an amateur birder in his Berkshires, hadn't seen the ocean, only three hours away, for over five decades! Dairy farmers don't stray far from their herds. Cows have no weekends off and must be milked at least twice daily. Between milkings food must be raised, gathered, stored and fed. Excuse the agricultural digression; Plum Island, threatened by erosion, is our subject.

Last Saturday at the beginning of a now famous storm off the ocean the Closeteer and wife again visited Plum Island, a barrier beach so important in his three-quarters century. As a Salisbury boy he often rowed across the mouth of the Merrimack in his skiff or pedaled through Newburyport on his bike to get there. In the early 1940s the new refuge, as yet largely unprotected by the Feds, had far fewer plants. Great drifting dunes without stabilizing grass dominated. In walks down the center just out of sight, not sound, of ocean he imagined himself with French Legionnaires in the Sahara. Climbs up steep dunes to WWII concrete lookout buildings, protecting distant Portsmouth Navy Yard, in deep sand without camel feet were difficult. To the east the ocean stretched to the places of real battle. Frequent rumors were heard of unseen U-boats not far off shore. In those war years house windows and the upper halves of car headlights in coastal communities were blackened out by dark shades and black paint.

The day after a nor'easter the future Closeteer, then 15, was borrowed from his grandfather, farmer Will Pettengill, by Fred Brown, an old carpenter. They drove to Plum Island where the ocean was threatening to come through the barrier beach to the Basin, a southerly extension of the river, as it is again now. A seafront cottage's front porch had been badly damaged. A cottage next door had gone in and was somewhere out to sea. As they fixed the porch he remembers learning two things, one the hard way. Fred warned him at the start that shoveling beach sand was deceptively easy. Sinking the shovel involved no effort; however, lifting the heavy load was much harder than with less dense inland soils. Although in good shape he was soon tuckered out. The other lesson was neat, "cool," folks say today. Fred leveled some of the new porch timbers, window sills and rails by sighting on the Atlantic's horizon.

Closeteer and wife climbed a narrow path up a dune within a few

Cord grass at half tide, Parker River Estuary. Photo, courtesy of Dorothy Monnelly.

feet of the remembered work with Fred. He again told the story she had heard too many times. They were there to see where the ocean threatens to cut through yet again. Downslope a few feet away were the steel gray waves of the Atlantic just 10 or so feet below the bases of the cottages. Between high tide and them is a wall of man-placed sandbags the size of cars. The bags look pathetic when one considers what they are trying to hold back. The couple turned away from the sea and looked northwest to the Basin a few hundred yards away. A century and one half ago it was a part of another mouth of the mighty Merrimack River pouring out fresh water runoff with sediment from 4,700 square miles to the sea. A bar and dunes formed across its southern mouth, which then were built upon. The shallow tidal spur of river called the Basin, crowded with cottages above high tide, seems to await the ocean's return. Tens of thousands of dollars have been spent to replace the eroding beach to keep the Basin and ocean from joining. Millions more dollars are contemplated. In the meantime the ocean is very slowly rising; worsening storms are predicted. During the next couple days, the Sunday and Monday of hard rain riding in on gale force ENE winds, we worried for those worrying more, just a few feet above the waves. In our lifetimes we could be calling this barrier beach Plum Islands. The sediment sand no longer comes down the river past the dams in amounts enough to replace that eroded away. The jetties built to protect may do more harm than good. Maybe folks should heed Jesus' admonition not to build houses on sand (Matthew 7:26), especially near oceans.

FLOOD TIME AGAIN

We had been waiting a week for the predicted big rains and wind to arrive. Late Saturday afternoon on March 13 sprinkles came in on an easterly breeze; by late evening they were replaced by heavy rain on strong northeast winds. One Middleton Stream Team wag quoted Shakespeare's famous line from his play *Julius Caesar*, "Beware the Ides of March." As the night wore on gusty choruses of naked hardwoods and evergreens accompanied the more immediate sounds of house parts being played. Through rattling windows we watched water coming almost horizontal across the glowing sphere of a nearby street lamp. This storm's water and high winds seemed special. Perhaps the dire weeklong warnings affected our judgment. First light Sunday morning the rain continued unabated. Streams and river were already starting to rise. By the evening of the 15th, the day Brutus and others killed Caesar, we knew our friend's reference was appropriate. The Ides was a day of trouble. The soil was wet, as it usually is this time of year, and in some places still frozen. We harkened back to the wet May of 2006, when it rained for days. Then the unsaturated warm ground and fast-growing leaves took up the early offerings. After several days the soil was full and in the last few days of downpour water bodies receiving direct runoff quickly rose, and we were in the midst of a record flood. Almost 14 inches fell in two weeks. The floodwaters, as most of you well remember, closed our roads, filled cellars, and in Topsfield killed two people trying to cross flooded roads near the river in cars.

This time there was little lag. The near-saturated soil couldn't act the sponge. Eight inches of rain quickly ran to low areas and filled them. Internet pages for United States Geological Survey (USGS) gauge sites in south Middleton and Willowdale Dam in Ipswich show frequently measured depth in feet and rate of flow in cubic feet per second (CFS). Data appeared as steep climbing lines on logarithmic graphs. The depth at south Middleton started at 2.5 feet; by Monday morning the river at seven feet was well over its banks. It still rained hard; more was predicted. We knew then this flood would be another big one. Would it exceed past records? The Mother's Day Flood crest of May 2006 was 8.45 feet, 1,420 CFS, a record since measurements began at the gauge in 1938. That flood topped the previous record of March 22, 2001, 8.39 feet and 1,200 CFS. Monday evening, as the depth approached eight feet, we thought this one might top them all. About midnight the rain stopped. The upward curve started to level off and by first light Tuesday reached its peak of 8.43 feet, 1,320 CFS. In clear air and bright sun Middleton Stream Teamers and no doubt many others up and down the river, armed with cameras, took to our streets and drove around to see the sights. We didn't get far fast. Traffic was strange; there were too many cars in the wrong places. White water down from North Andover was sweeping a foot deep over North Liberty Street. Not daring to cross we stood on the south side of Boston Brook enjoying the spectacle of water four times its usual depth moguling over stone rapids. By midday kids in shorts were seen happily splashing in the flooded street. From there we went to where Peabody Street crosses the Ipswich River fed by raging Boston Brook and a dozen other swollen tributaries above in towns from Middleton to Burlington. From the 400-year-old Curtis Oak we could see that

Boston Brook had spread from a usual 10-foot-wide channel to a floodplain 100 times that, covering hayfields the late Warren Evans mowed with horses. That great shallow lake was a half foot over the road. Wanting to get closer to the river and not wanting to be seen as wimps, just fools, we forded the center line for 100 yards. Over the next dry rise we encountered the unruly Ipswich River gushing over a front 20 times wider than that normally seen within its banks. Wimpishness and wisdom ruled; we took photos and retreated. Back on Peabody and then on down Mill Street, paralleling the swollen river, we drove. Water was riding high over the old iron foundry/knife factory dam from Mill Pond. The road below was covered with a sheet of fast-flowing water. The Maple Street bridge was dry with water roaring just underneath against its ceiling and abutments. We turned onto East Street and headed back north. On approaching Thunder Bridge we slowed and then stopped at an expected Bridge Closed sign. Fast-running water two feet deep swept over the bridge pavement and low stretches leading to it. The water level at the bridge was about a half foot beneath the record May 15, 2006, Stream Team's crest mark. East Street at the river was flooded for a fifth or so mile.

From East Street we entered Peabody, the street we had retreated from on the other side of the river a half hour before. As expected we soon encountered floodwater covering the rich bottom land that has probably been cultivated for a thousand or more years. The Indians chose such fertilized-by-flood-silt places for their corn, beans and squash. Richardson Farms now rotates field corn, hay and cover crops on the same land where arrowheads and potsherds are found.

We were experiencing another major flood. A pattern seems evident in the records kept continuously since 1938. We'll list those floods in order of occurrence that have filled flood plains and closed roads. (USGS south Middleton gauge data)

March 1968, 7.09 feet, 833 CFS

January 1979, 7.12 feet, 839 CFS

April 1987, 7.51 feet, 1,010 CFS

April 1993, 7.05 feet, 690 CFS

October 1996, 7.88 feet, 896 CFS

March 2001, 8.39 feet, 1,200 CFS

April 2004, 7.06 feet, 783 CFS

May 2006, 8.46 feet, 1,420 CFS

March 2010, 8.43 feet, 1,320 CFS

As you can readily see, the floods are generally increasing in elevation and frequency. These floods have nothing to do with each other, or of course, the Ides. They come when there is lots of rain and conditions on the ground in the plants are right. However, this past week as the water subsided we were reminded of another historical flood of great fame in 1936, especially along the mighty Connecticut River where much damage was done. Whole bridges were carried away; the famous covered wooden bridge in Montague rode the torrent downriver many miles. What date did that happen? The river, after a winter with much ice and snow and a week of rain, started to ominously rise on March 15. At crest a couple days later it was flowing at 240,000 CFS, nearly 200 times the rate in the Ipswich from our recent Ides storm. We also harken back to mid-March 2001 (see data above). Maybe the seer that warned Caesar was on to something. We enlightened 21st-century folk rather look to frozen soils and the absence of active water-absorbing plants and fickle rains. Either way, "Beware the Ides of March."

APRIL 2010

VERNAL POOLS

Spring came on calendar time for a brief week. Five warm days followed three of cold rain. Just a few weeks before, northeast winds were laden with snow. Wet buds received bright light with swelling joy, or at least we walking in their midst so imagined. While we did not swell, something within us surely did. A woodland walk found pools full and without ice. Their dark bottoms absorbed light coming through clear watery lenses. Bird songs and wood frog choruses arose from around and within these warming sanctuaries, beckoning amphibians, crustaceans and insect larvae. Our pace around these temporary ponds slowed as we searched in their shallow margins for animals not seen since last year. Through a bottom paved with oak leaves a large yellow-spotted salamander gracefully escaped our admiring gaze. In a pool nearby we'd seen tiny gelatinous-white blobs stuck to leaves by male yellow-spots. On close examination we found them to be packets of sperm, called spermatophores, awaiting females to take them in where fertilization occurs. Fertilized eggs with males' DNA, laid in masses of clear jelly, are attached to submerged twigs. The dark egg centers absorb light and become much warmer than the surrounding water. An embryo rapidly grows from each. In a couple weeks, the time largely dependent on temperature, larvae with gills and tail swim from the protective jelly. Now begins a race with time. Will the pool without an incoming stream dry up before the tadpoles can develop legs and oxygen-absorbing skin, the requisites for land survival? Some years they dry too early and a generation is wiped out. Their parents, who may live up to 20 years, will likely return next year to the same trysting pool. Wood frogs, which usually precede salamanders to pools where they mate, have similar life cycles. Wood frog egg masses were found in pools in mid-March.

In the tri-town area are hundreds of these pools. Many dry up completely most summers. As a result, and the absence of streams flowing in and out, there are no fish populations. The absence of these voracious predators of amphibian eggs and larvae largely define vernal pools. The Massachusetts Wetlands Protection Act recognizes the environmental importance of vernal pools and prohibits their alteration.

In our post-equinoctial rounds we find some vernal pools not much larger than bathtubs, others several acres, and most in between. They must be of a depth that will have water into June when their tenants metamorphose into land-dwelling juveniles who then leave without guides for woodland soils up to one-third mile away. There is evidence that they go to the upland areas of their parents. Imagine a small salamander with new legs and no schooling trekking through bushes and forest detritus over ledges and down and up micro-valleys with no chance to view a destination it can scarcely know, except perhaps in some deep molecular way beyond consciousness. You can readily see that words about behavior fall short here. What can "view," "scarcely," "molecular" and "consciousness" mean in animals whose ancestors preceded ours by 200 million years? Let's just say the question of how offspring and parents know where to go is an excellent one worthy of the scientists who try to find out. These amphibians walk the walk and give no clues with talk, at least to our species far removed.

We've learned the necessity of these pools for reproduction by wood

Trees above flooded Ipswich salt marsh, drumlin. Choate Island looming in background.
Photo, courtesy of Dorothy Monnelly

frogs and certain salamanders where the bases of food chains are rich crops of leaves, twigs, small logs, blossom parts and acorns each year. Bacteria and fungi soften up the dead plant material; insect larvae, small crustaceans and worms further break it down to bite-sized pieces. Nutrients are released from the tiny grazers upon excretion and death. Algae, with more light from ever-higher sun, thrive, providing food for tadpoles and many others, and oxygen for all. Vernal pools might well be called vital pools, as are, of course, all natural bodies of water.

How lucky we are in the center of the Ipswich River Basin where large protected forests surround us thanks to the people who provided us with Harold Parker, Boxford, Willowdale and Bradley Palmer State forests; Essex County Greenbelt lands; and Boxford Land Trust's conservation areas and those of other towns. And even more fortunate are the organisms whose very lives depend on woods and their waters. We old Stream Teamers first heard about 40 years ago of "greenbelts" ideally designed to ring human population centers. The word "greenbelts" may be only a few generations old but Frederick Law Olmsted, famous for Boston's Emerald Necklace, and others envisioned them in the 19th century. Good wide ones such as we have allow for us and our fellow creatures to live in close proximity. They can't care for our part, but we can certainly value and care for theirs. The conservation concerns of the organizations mentioned are less than a century old yet look at the good they've done. If humans keep moving in such enlightened directions perhaps we'll see wider intermingling and habitat care replacing a half millennium of one-sided exploitation.

SLEEPING BEAUTY ON RIVERSIDE STONE

Like most folks, we Stream Teamers and Closeteers enjoy a stone seat alongside flowing water. In Middleton on the Ipswich River we have four places where we can sit on attractive boulders placed by man and think, or better still, not think. Vito Mortalo came to Middleton 45 years ago from Rome, a place world famous for stone structures. Over the last decade, despite a busy schedule, he has built fine stone steps we call works of art, at three long-neglected canoe landings. We often visit them for a break or to launch canoes and kayaks. Others are seen fishing from or relaxing on the beautifully placed flat rocks on the river's edge, especially those at the Peabody Street landing. It is a perfect place for young children to wade under the watchful eyes of papa or mama perched just above on the huge natural stones he has given us. We'll say no more of Vito's fine gifts; we do hope you'll visit the corners of South Main, Maple, Peabody streets and the river to see for yourself.

Some other stones on the river's edge were placed there long ago and recently moved around a bit and added to by contractor Tim Willey, who freely gave of his, helpers' and machinery's time to Xavier Chambers and the Stream Team. Xavier's Eagle project was the building of a park/landing where Logbridge Road had crossed the river for 300 years. Early on, this cart path connected Salem Village, now Danvers, to The Farms, now Middleton. The bridge was taken out in 1973, its great abutment stones left behind. Tim rearranged some on the river's west edge and added others along the road to keep vehicles off the lawn made to replace the shabby entrance to the former Logbridge crossing, long a victim of roadside dumping. Tim, his men, Xavier and other volunteers have given passersby a place to relax and picnic where flowing water washes stone. We hope someday while daydreaming there to be rewarded with the rumble of ox or horse-drawn carts and drovers' calls as they pass over the bridge's bygone logs. If we are lucky the drovers will stop to water their animals and gossip of seaport doings.

And then there are the substantial gifts from Leon Rubchinuk who quietly left fine granite blocks at the Peabody and Farnsworth's landings for people to while away their time on. These were painstakingly placed, one just two weeks ago, for fine views from the river's banks. Last Saturday, mid-morning, a pretty Irish woman and young son spread a tablecloth on the new rock at Farnsworth's and happily enjoyed brunch within 20 feet of river water passing quickly below, still high from March's floods. We Steam Teamers, there for spring cleanup, introduced ourselves and chatted in the warm sun. Mother and son were probably the first to use the rock as Leon intended. Since she, now 14 years a Middletonite, is Irish we dubbed Leon's one-ton gift the Blarney Stone.

Just a few days later, on a record-setting almost 90-degree April seventh, two Stream Teamers returned from a canoe paddle upriver to the Peabody pumping station and back and were greeted upon return to Farnsworth's Landing with an unforgettable sight. Curled up, sound asleep on the Blarney Stone was a beautiful young woman. The combination of cool water nearby, hot sun and spring air was perfect for such snoozes, so irresistible this time of year. We paused before hauling our canoe up Vito's steps so near her bed. We didn't want to disturb her. She continued sleeping as we quietly took the canoe out and loaded it in a pickup. Thoughts of Sleeping Beauty and the Prince entered at least one old paddler's mind. Our never-to-be-known princess seemed perfectly comfortable on Leon's bed of stone. We hoped her true love would come along soon and gently awaken her.

Thank you Vito, Tim, Leon, and other volunteers for the well-chosen rocks so carefully placed for us along the river. Stairs and seats of wood, even concrete, have to be replaced now and then; your rocks will be forever.

CHANGES AMONG RIVER MEANDERS

Danvers, Middleton and Peabody intermesh along the loopy lines of the Ipswich River's channel. The river changes character from more or less fast-flowing to lazy meanderings as it swings north from West Peabody. It is only two and one-half miles as an impatient duck might fly from the 90-degree turn in Peabody to the Maple Street bridge in Middleton. A channel-loving fish must travel twice that between the same points. Several great arcs cut by flowing water in ledgeless soils almost curve back upon themselves. Lewis, Clark, men and woman found such on the Missouri after they towed with ropes their heavy boat upriver against strong currents for whole days at a time. When climbing the bluffs above evening campsites they sometimes found that in laboring 10 miles they had made only one or two as a raven might fly. On the easy Ipswich we just get a little more exercise and greater opportunities to surprise wildlife as we round each bend.

Not long ago mature swamp white oaks, red maples, river birches, green ashes, willows, silky dogwoods and buttonbushes graced the river along these five miles. In warmer months they formed a shady green canyon our canoes glided through. In one wet savannah-like stretch upriver from Farnsworth Landing a dozen venerable willows, spaced over a mile, seemed to lean their gnarled trunks on the channel water passing underneath. Only a decade has passed and all the trees are dead or dying. Light now pours in by fewer trunks with broken branches, unimpeded by twigs and leaves. Each year more of these gray corpses fall. Bushes such as swamp dogwoods with slender branches that by August once almost arched across the channel, and shorter buttonbushes, spiky branches with bright green leaves and spherical vanilla-colored flowers, are now looking poorly. Even the once dominant purple loosestrife, an invasive species of great beauty and vigor, is on the wane due to Galerucella beetles imported from Europe to do it in and to competition from reed canary grass, another hardy invasive thriving in the increased light. Patches of loosestrife now appear scraggly. Reed canary, also an immigrant, which farmers have long planted for hay and forage, grows thickly and hides the floodplain's water with lush greenery. Cows, long gone, no longer graze on it; geese and ducks and other animals do to some extent. Environmentalists have put reed canary on the invasive species list because it forms dense stands that crowd out native plants which wildlife are best adapted to. In early summer their petalless beige inflorescences put forth large numbers of delicate seeds that blow with the wind or fall and float downriver. Reed canary now grows thickly in patches on both banks down almost to tidal water in Ipswich. Much of Great Wenham Swamp, also a place of impressive meanders, has been taken over by it. While passing through on fall canoe trips we've spooked large flocks of ducks hidden among browning stems and leaves.

How could a river floodplain here since the last continental glacier ice melted more than 10,000 years ago change from riverine forest to open shrub grass in just one thousandth of that time? The cause of this drastic change, in the short time Stream Teamers have been observing, is beaver activity. Beavers, the largest of North American rodents, were here in large numbers when the English and French came four centuries ago. The Indians used their fur and flesh in relative moderation. They also valued their dams, which kept more water in streams and rivers thus allowing for canoe navigation in dry months. The newcomers paid well for pelts and within a century the beavers here were gone. Naturalist Paul Rezendes in his chapter on beavers in *Tracking and the Art of Seeing* quotes from a journal of David Thompson's, an 18th century explorer in the Pacific Northwest.

The continent "may be said to be in the possession of two distinct races, man and the beaver" (Thompson), with man occupying the highlands and the beaver in solid possession of the lowlands (Rezendes).

From recorded early New England observations and from ours since the return of the beaver we are experiencing today, the same might be said for here now. The beavers since the mid-90s are back in force from a three-century hiatus. In the tri-town area alone they've killed hundreds of acres of trees. The area along the river's meanders described above has five of their dams, which have raised the year-round water levels one-half to one and one-half feet. The plants listed like lots of water, but can't take too much too long. Before beavers' recent inundations the water on a normal year was only well above their roots in winter and spring. We beaver watchers and readers of their history think their present effects may equal those of pre-colonial times. What were then open "beaver meadows" are becoming so again. The healthy trees on the edges of these impoundments must be shivering in their roots as they hear the beavers at work nearby happily humming "Times they are a-changin'."

Then, of course, times always are.

THE "GOOD OLE DAYS"

Ninety-eight right whales have recently been counted feeding off Cape Cod, significantly more than usually arrive for plankton blooms each spring. Marine biologists say this may be one-fourth the world's population of this species, which has been protected off our coasts for almost a century. This news came in early April as 40th Earth Day celebrations were being planned. In just two generations the EPA, DEP, hundreds of other governmental and thousands of non-governmental environmental organizations have come into being. The good whale news and thoughts of Earth Days and all that environmental movements have wrought precipitated a lively discussion among us Closeteers. Each month old-timers are bombarded with emails listing nostalgic memories of the "good ole days" from people who must have successfully repressed the bad. For whales the 19th and early 20th centuries were times of relentless slaughter with Nantucket, New Bedford and other Yankee ports, including Newburyport and Salem, leading the tormentors worldwide. Not only did many species of whales almost suffer extinction, the crews on whale ships were little more than slaves. Captains, ship owners and investors in that awful industry gave the sailors on those stinking blubber ships little more than bunk and board for two- to four-year cruises of dangerous work. The late Samuel Eliot Morison, our famous maritime historian, seems to completely lose the cool historians are supposed to have, in a chapter on whaling in his *Maritime History of Massachusetts*. He calls the leaders of the industry as many names as Goldman Sachs and other financial institutions are receiving now.

Our point here is that the good old days were not. Tom Brokaw in his much praised WWII book *The Greatest Generation* doesn't much mention the unforgivable actions and policies of our bold leaders who fought brilliantly yet often ruthlessly on a vast ocean and across a "civilized" continent. Then "Negro" servicemen were discriminated against. One old Closeteer remembers African Americans not being given equal access to all jobs aboard Navy ships right up into the late '50s. In WWII we fire-bombed and atomic-bombed cities of civilians. The "greatest generation" like most turned out to be both good and bad. The good news is we don't purposely blanket-bomb civilian populations anymore. We hesitate to remind ourselves of Viet Nam where we dropped thousands of tons of napalm and Agent Orange on lush jungles and fields. Those crimes were beyond the pale by any standards.

Here at home we had long used our rivers and lakes as depositories for wastes, many poisonous. In the '60s Rachel Carson pointed out what we were doing and successfully scolded. This led to Earth Day and the Environmental Protection Act, which was proposed and signed by President Nixon in 1970. Up until that point we routinely aerial-sprayed nearby salt marshes each summer so beachgoers wouldn't be discomforted by mosquitoes, food for birds and fish. We no longer do. The Merrimack and scores of other rivers, once stinking sewers, are now clean. We could go on and on listing improvements. The truth is that the old days were terrible in many ways. We should acquaint our young in history classes and in family discussions with how it truly was while emphasizing what needs doing now to make things better.

Masterpiece Theatre's present series *Small Island* ends with a black British grandfather showing his 10-year-old or so grandchildren a picture of their white grandmother. All the other photos in the collection are of dark-skinned family members. The dark grandchildren look with some interest but make no comment about grandmother Queenie being very white. Such healthy colorblindness isn't as it was.

Whales, now protected, may be on the way back; our rivers here are clean after three centuries as sewers; skin color is no longer a big deal, as our first family shows; and many pesticides and herbicides are now wisely feared and somewhat regulated. While much more is needed on the environmental front, compared with the bad old days these are "good new days" in many ways. When you hear old guys like us going on about the rosy past just put it down to lost or repressed memory and take it with a grain of salt. Be kind. Tackle present problems with eyes toward the future. We've had our turn.

MAY 2010

OIL, WATER AND ORGANISMS DON'T MIX

As this is being written crude oil on the loose continues to rise one mile up from the floor of the Gulf of Mexico southeast of Louisiana. At the surface over 5,000 barrels emerging each day form a very thin layer that spreads where the wind takes it. We marvel at the hubris of the brilliant doers of our species who prick holes in Mother Earth for oil even deep under the seas. This time her ancient black tears have gotten away from their pipes. This oil won't make it to our road-clogging vehicles.

In the Closet we fret about the contaminated water and all it might touch before microorganisms dispose of its poisons. We gather around our big atlas and look again at what we've known since fourth-grade geography. The coasts around the Gulf are more or less smooth lines, except between just east of Texas and west of Mississippi, where the delta land juts raggedly out into the shallow sea. There may be more miles of exposed sea/land interface in this section than around the rest of the Gulf Coast combined. One Closeteer pipes up, "The Mississippi delta reminds me of the continent's placenta." The word strikes us and we begin to see all kinds of things in this metaphor. We recall fluffy human placentas in pictures showing the tremendous surface area between the tissues of mother and fetus. Louisiana's ragged placenta intermeshes with the sea it feeds. The muddy Mississippi River is the umbilical cord carrying nourishing silt, clay and hundreds of other substances in solution and suspension. In school we were told this is the stuff that builds the rich delta marshes and provides for the plankton in the Gulf and beyond. Where plankton thrive, fish, shrimp, crabs, oysters and their human gatherers do too. The latter are very worried now. Where this fanciful comparison falls down a bit is that the

Gulf is not a baby within a mother continent. Its wastes don't diffuse into mother's system and get carried away. Such liquid water systems, and all they carry, are pretty much one-way due to gravity. However, the water does in time evaporate and return clean on winds to provide for erosion and runoff from nourishing land. It is as if Mother Earth were being continually washed in time beyond our ken to provide life-giving substances in usable form. As our eyes and imaginations wander north up the umbilical to the great tributaries, their lesser rivers and then streams from mountaintops, we are astounded at the grandeur of the system. Who in the world would even dream that it could be stopped or even changed by *Homo sapiens*?

Our species has done so without knowing the effects. We plowed and cultivated much of the Mississippi basin from Pennsylvania to Montana. After, off fallow fields, the water from rain and melting snows, instead of being slowed and absorbed by natural vegetation, flowed faster carrying soil down gullies to streams. Spring runoff came in bursts rather than gradually. Riverside towns and cities flooded. We Americans, used to thinking we could accomplish anything after the Erie Canal and the transcontinental railroads across mountain ranges, decided to build giant flood control dams and thousands of miles of levees. The latter in the lower Mississippi basin caused flood waters to rush by the floodplains that had slowed them and were nourished by them to enter the Gulf more quickly. Much of the former sediment was now trapped behind upriver dams. The faster, less heavily laden water eroded the soft delta land away. Climate folks point out that this is why hurricanes have more devastating effects on inland lowlands such as those around New Orleans and up and down the Gulf Coast. There is less marsh-bayou buffer now. After Katrina some engineers recommended that instead of spending so much on protective dikes around New Orleans, the enormous amounts of money be used to restore the living delta buffers. Attractive plans were put forth as to how this might be done. Dikes, the short-term solution, won out.

We half cease our placental dreaming and return our thoughts to the problem immediately at hand, the thin growing sheet of oil drifting toward enormously productive edges of land. Mother Nature's underground reservoirs of oil naturally leak from cracks in places around the world and no doubt have for millions of years. The amounts are relatively small. Bacteria eat most up before damage is done. Alas, people have accidents that release too much too quickly. Do you remember the EXXON Valdez and Prince William Sound? Organisms, even large ones like birds and sea otters, coated with oil succumb. The damage at Prince William has continued for two decades. We'll probably never know the total harm still being done. Observers there report that oil can be found by just digging a six-inch-deep hole in the beaches.

Last Friday, as the oil kept gushing from BP's leaks, environmentalist-writer Bill McKibben was Tom Ashbrook's guest on WBUR's popular morning radio show *On Point*. McKibben has warned long and hard about our wanton ways. He says that even if we mend them it is too late to have our planet as it once was a century ago or even as it is now. He points to our economic system's great god "Growth" and its faith "Consumerism" as the culprits. He, like Barbara Kingsolver and others, urges us to return home and make and raise what we truly need. McKibben's recommendations divert so from our present lifestyle that Ashbrook challenged him at every point. "Aren't you being downright un-American?" he asked. McKibben held his ground as he so long has and pointed out our over-the-top ways in which folks visit kin at a whim across the country and take vacations around the world and think nothing of it. We old Closeteers could relate to this. As children we might get to Boston a half hour away every few years. Vermont and New York were distant places on our fourth-grade maps. McKibben, Kingsolver and others have touted over and over the wisdom of pulling back, i.e. vacationing nearby (Why Acapulco when Plum Island is just a bicycle ride away?), manufacturing our own goods, raising food locally, and eating fruits and vegetables in season. Now, irrationally from an environmental point of view, we ship in greens from California, strawberries from Florida, and cut flowers from South America. These goodies don't get here without the use of lots of polluting fossil fuels.

You can see why anyone listening to *On Point*'s guest might wonder if he lives in the same NASCAR world we do where at the drop of a hat we drive 2,500 pounds of car five miles for an ice cream, for a half-dozen screws, or for no reason at all. Having just written that sentence and given it some thought, some of us conclude that McKibben is not the one who is nuts.

While radio host and famous guest spoke, the manmade holes in

Mother Earth under the sea continued leaking, and their iridescent product on the surface approached the coast. Who knows how many organisms, the bases of food chains, will be affected? Who knows what further crises worshipers of Growth and a selfish profligate lifestyle will precipitate? Rachel Carson, much maligned at the time, warned us of our poisons a half century ago. She was later heeded and now is thanked and praised. Perhaps we should listen to folks like maybe-not-so-crazy Bill and followers and try to live more lightly on land and sea. It may be too late for the world as we know it. If we don't it may be too late for any world with a rich diversity of life.

TUSSOCK SEDGE ISLANDS AND STEPPING STONES

A little-known yet common plant of our wetlands is now putting on quite a show especially in former red maple swamps inundated by beavers. The maples have drowned. High shade is gone and increased light has stimulated the growth of low herbaceous plants that also like water. The other day in a walk along the roadbed of the Essex railroad, 84 years without trains, we admired great clumps of what seems a grass in the flooded lowlands flanking the old line's shoulders. Between the knee-high two-foot-diameter tussocks are labyrinths of canals and patches of open water. If we imagine ourselves as whirligig beetles and water striders, movement there might be as on small boats flitting among lush tropical islands. To large animals like us, they, like stepping stones, invite a skip across the water's surface. Alas, these dense tufts of leaves, stems and roots are not stones; they sway and wobble when stepped upon. The lightest-footed contestants on *Dancing with the Stars*, tiny athletic leprechauns, and other small creatures might jump from one to another and never wet a toe. When ordinary folks try— even some old-timers can't resist — the passage is a clumsy show that usually ends calf deep in bottom mud and water.

These tiny islands, so common, yet so grass-like to the undiscerning eye and thus scarcely noticed, are passed by as are so many wild bushes and plants misnamed "weeds." Close examination would reveal attractive, novel features. A floral hunting hike along our swamps and meadows will in a short time result in a bouquet to rival any of the cultivated flowers. Grasses and sedges too have flowers, yet of a more modest nature. Grass stems are jointed; the usually triangular stems of sedges are not. Leave a patch of lawn alone and you'll soon see what you are missing by relentless low mowing. Why do we insist

Tussock Sedge. Photo, courtesy of Stream Team.

on lawns with crew cuts? There is something deep within us that likes to control. Pardon the digression, this essay is about the tussock sedge, *Carex stricta*, which no one mows. Now they are blooming and adding low-key color and beauty to our swamps. Crowning many of the numerous stems are grain-like inflorescences of rich browns and yellows that change each day during their short reproductive passage. Billions of seeds form and ripen within them, food for wildlife hiding in and all around. On our hike we spooked a half-dozen Wood Duck pairs swimming among the tussock islands where they hide and feed. The bright multicolored male Wood Duck contrasts sharply with the muted hues of sedges. Otters, muskrats, turtles, frogs, birds and other animals live among and rest on these green islands modestly covered below by a Hawaiian type skirt of last year's drooping brown leaves.

Later we returned with a hand saw and sacrificed one of these tussocks for the sake of science. We cut vertically from top to bottom down below the water and even into the supporting mud, on a line corresponding to the tussock's diameter. The halves were left more or less undisturbed; we think they will survive. We attempted to wrench one half from the water so we could study its internal longitudinal structure. The cut can be likened to splitting a log through its center. Pull as we might, the cables of entwined roots deep in the mud wouldn't allow even partial removal. At the bases of several hundred, tightly packed (the meaning of the Latin word "stricta"), are thousands of rootlets elaborately entwined in a cylindrical mass anchored by braided root cables unseen but felt in the muddy water below. In late summer when the swamp is dry we'll return with a long-handled shovel and do a proper excavation. What causes the stems to bunch together so? Did the entire clump of many stems rise from one seed? Why such a heavy structure? Has it evolved to provide a firm anchor during floods? Why don't the separate tussocks grow closer together as do grass clumps? We think our crude observations answer the last question. Such large plants require much from the soil below. If they were closer the competition for soil minerals would be too great. This is fortuitous for animals who like the airy sheltered passages between them. As usual with such research more questions were raised than answered.

Visit a beaver impoundment or swamp near you, roughly one-third of tri-towns' acres are wetland; the beavers are increasing that fraction each day. In Middleton just walk the old railroad bed from Essex Street and you'll soon find tussock sedges gracing the water below you. Go quietly; you are likely to see animals among them. Imagine swimming in or striding on the canals between them as do ducks and insects. The smelly canals of Venice have nothing on these rich passages between green-topped overhanging clumps. If daring you might even try them as stepping stones. If you are successful let us Stream Teamers know. We'll want a demonstration.

ESTUARIES: RICH RAGGED EDGES

Dark and light green grasses
In cowlicks swirl 'tween soft mud creeks.
Levied by dune and upland rock
Watering place for more than ducks,
Has depth and breadth
Beyond its bounds.
Where larval travelers get their start
And subtler cycles turn
To nourish out a thousand miles.

Water that falls upon our tri-town area as rain and snow eventually flows into the Ipswich River and then magnificent Plum Island Sound and surrounding salt marshes, a place of tides where the ocean rises and falls in a maze of creeks meandering through grass-capped strata of peat. During each twice-daily up and down cycle, dimensions of peat banks and mud flats are revealed. As kids lucky to live surrounded by estuaries we saw the almost empty low tide cricks as canyons. We

Parker River Estuary, Byfield. Photo, courtesy of Essex County Greenbelt.

climbed down in, then up and out those we couldn't leap. The other day a couple old Closeteers and friends visited the estuary that makes up much of northeastern Essex County to dig clams from a low tide flat. Crane, Plum Island, and Salisbury Beaches, barrier islands, protect the vast "low green prairies of the sea," to borrow a line from the county's 19th-century bard John Greenleaf Whittier. The accumulated peat and sediment of 5,000 years, topped by fine salt grasses, is relatively soft. Direct contact with ocean waves would erode it away. Each layer, with different times of Sun, Moon, and spinning earth allotted water, has its own animals, plants and microorganisms. Some plants and an alga listed from above most highs to below most lows are: blackgrass, salt meadow grass, cordgrass, Fucus, and eelgrass. Mollusks over the same vertical range, high to low, are: salt marsh snails, ribbed mussels, periwinkles, razor clams and oysters. We can't do justice to a place so varied in words; in addition to viewing, smells, breezes and sounds must be felt.

We go there a couple dozen times a year, ostensibly for clams. We don't need to; they are not a source of needed food or income. Younger stronger folks, who have commercial licenses, dig for the latter. For us, and them, we suspect the call is deep and ancient, something embedded in our DNA and brains. We share genes with our prey and ducks, fish, crabs, snails, worms, and on and on. They came before; we may be unconsciously visiting our ancestors.

Reservoirs Unseen

Just a few meters below our feet and sometimes no meters at all is a vast reservoir of water often mentioned in past Water Closet essays and much worried about by us Closeteers and boards of health. Groundwater is that found between clay, silt, sand and gravel particles, from microscopic clay micelles to boulders. The level of this so-called water table changes with the seasons and precipitation. There isn't much fresh water on our planet compared with salty seawater: only about two and a half percent. The ground is a great reservoir where it is stored for months to thousands of years in a cycle passing through sea, air and land. Our boards of health, conservation commissions, septic system contractors, civil engineers, and the Massachusetts Department of Environmental Protection go to considerable lengths to protect it. It wasn't always this way.

Old-timers with rural upbringings remember the septic systems of old. The worst were straight pipes from bathrooms or factories to the nearest stream or river. One Closeteer remembers a trip to Rumford, Maine, just 40 or so years ago. While waiting for his shopping wife he explored along the fast-flowing Androscoggin River where it tumbles over picturesque ledge and great boulders behind main street businesses. It was springtime, yet the water still cold off the White Mountains reeked of sewage. He saw pipes entering from the buildings. Here in our towns there were cesspools, most simple holes hand dug and filled with stones, in the rear of houses. As children we were well aware of their overflows, some merely open ditches or swales leading to lower land where sewage was absorbed into the topsoil. In the dim light of evenings we sometimes stepped into them while playing hide and seek or kick the can. While the wastewater stunk it may not have been as dangerous as present effluents with their scores of manmade chemicals. Don't get us wrong, today's elaborate and expensive septic systems required to be well above groundwater are probably much better than cesspools in filtering and cleansing, but there are many more compounds now to be broken down by soil microorganisms if they can. In colonial times they consisted largely of the wastes from chamber pots and kitchen, natural substances, which had evolved over millions of years. Microorganisms in the soil and bodies of water quickly broke most down to harmless carbon dioxide and water.

Then about two centuries ago brilliant men hypothesized atoms and molecules and soon proved them so. A new science called chemistry exploded, sometimes quite literally, in "civilized" parts of the world. Chemistry had been around long before in the form of largely trial and error alchemy where different natural substances were mixed to sometimes form novel ones. The purpose of those searches was largely the synthesis of precious metals. Once the bases of matter were discovered compounds and elements were combined or broken down in mathematical proportions under laboratory and industrial conditions. By the 20th century, hundreds of compounds, not just a few dozen, were being made that hadn't evolved over time with organisms, and by mid-century there were thousands. Now many tens of thousands, including those as elegant and elaborate as portions of genes, have been made. God-like, chemists and molecular biologists are creating more each day. In 1935 DuPont PR people coined the slogan "Better Things for Better Living Through Chemistry." Other chemical companies thought it clever and changed it a bit to "Better Living Through Chemistry." In 1999 DuPont replaced it with "Miracles of Science."* The miracle makers know the structural details of their synthesized molecules and narrowly what they do. Alas, they don't know their effects, especially those of small amounts, on us and other organisms. Traces of many are being found beyond septic systems in our precious groundwater.

Recently from the sandy land of Cape Cod, in which groundwater flows more quickly, come disturbing reports of contamination. A couple years ago similar findings were reported from Lake Mead near Las Vegas. Traces of the "miracles of science" now show up in our drinking and bathing water. Do they cause disease in people and other organisms? Cape Cod's Silent Spring Institute concerned with high incidence of breast and other cancers thinks they do, but such things are hard to pin down to cause and effect. Great expense is involved and most groups such as this one named after Rachel Carson's famous book don't have the wherewithal even on the relatively wealthy Cape. What recently precipitated all this worry in the Closet about groundwater pollution was a reminder this month of the events in Woburn, just beyond the Ipswich River watershed in the neighboring Mystic River basin, made famous by the book and movie *A Civil Action.* Dan Kennedy, later a reporter for *The Phoenix* newspaper, summarized that long and heroic, by some, saga in a 1998 article well worth Googling, entitled "Toxic Legacy, Behind—and beyond—the hype over *A Civil Action . . .*" Kennedy, a Danvers neighbor who appears on Emily Rooney's WGBH TV show *Beat the Press* each Friday, tells us of brave Anne Anderson who lost her boy Jimmy to cancer. Anderson, while knowing little of groundwater, had reasons to believe Woburn's water might contain carcinogens. She persisted with the help of Reverend Bruce Young, State Representative Nick Paleologos and others to require testing that found dangerous industrial contamination sources near her neighborhood and water supply. We'll not repeat that well-publicized story of trials, fines and cleanup. Our point is that stray manmade molecules, and there are countless zillions that didn't evolve with organisms, act as "wrenches in the works" in the enormously complex cellular machinery of organisms. So far people haven't often been able to prove specific causes. Rachel Carson gave us good reasons to suspect they did cause damage. Notice how that giant's name keeps coming to the fore when environmental concerns are being considered. She set the stage for Anderson and others. Earth Day and almost all subsequent environmental movements and legislation can he traced back to her. The outrages at Love Canal in Niagara Falls, New York, and Woburn have clearly shown that synthetic molecules do poison animals including us. We should shift priorities to testing, analysis and cleanup and away from further synthesis until we know what we are doing.

*Wikipedia

JUNE 2010

GREAT BLUE HERON

Just a couple hundred feet below Exeter, New Hampshire's busy center the Exeter River tumbles over two dams and rocky rapids to tidal water. The mills powered by this descent are gone. The same can be said for a hundred other New England towns so sited.

Several years ago a Closeteer and friend put a canoe in just below the flowing slope of white water and leisurely paddled seven miles on an ebb to Great Bay where the waters of the Lamprey, Exeter and Piscataqua mix with seawater. Twice daily a fast flood through Portsmouth Harbor fills the bay and enriches it. The mix then leaves as quickly as the cold seawater came.

On the edges of these dynamic movements the brackish marshes teem with life. On our paddle the most noticeable inhabitants were Great Blue Herons. We encountered these solitary giants on rounding every bend and passing each cove. They were wading in shallows stalking fish as they have done since the last continental glacier's ice a dozen millennia ago and who knows how many thousands before that.

On Father's Day, in drizzle riding in on cold nor'easter air, an old Closeteer, son-in-law and five-year-old grandson after lunch at Loaf and Ladle, perched above the upper dam, walked out on the bridge just down from the square to see the sights. The water in the wind blew around us as that collected from fourth a county descended underneath. Below, just downriver on a submerged boulder, stood a Great Blue Heron stalking fish we couldn't see. Every few minutes he leaned down from an upright stance, great beak pointing down. The legs slightly spread as the whole body and long neck cocked. Then faster than we could see, the skinny neck thrust its lance. As its head almost instantly arose we got a glimpse of a fish before it was swallowed. In two seconds he was erect again and waiting.

In 15 minutes four fish were caught. Our eyes were as intent upon the fisher as his upon the rapid flow. The last victim was alewife size; he shook it a few times while shifting its position in his beak. We wondered if it could be swallowed. It was; a bulge quickly rippled down his neck.

Great Blues are four feet tall with handsome wings spanning six feet and yet these athletes weigh in at less than eight pounds. We concluded that our subject was largely bone, cartilage, tendon, trim long muscle and feather perfected over countless generations. No wonder it held our eyes so long. We, hesitant to leave, suspect that despite acres of supermarkets just down the road, stalkers and fishers are still in us.

DEEP SADNESS AMIDST GREAT BEAUTY

In early June as the school year was winding down a group of seventh- and eighth-graders from the Merrimack River Valley Charter School gathered at the landing on the Parker River where English colonists came ashore in 1635 and established Newbury. The pupils and their science teacher Ellen had been invited to explore the Great Marsh in dories with a few members of the Rings Island Rowing Club. We went out on two beautiful consecutive mornings when the tides were at low ebb. Before getting underway groups gathered around a map to be briefed by an old Closeteer and marsh lover who had taken student groups on this famous estuary many times. He told how the salt marsh was formed behind an offshore bar, now Plum Island. The importance of estuaries where fresh and salt water mingle twice daily was explained, the word nursery used several times. During May's full moon, a few days before, horseshoe crabs had come in on the marshes from the ocean to mate. We hoped to see some stragglers.

Good teacher Ellen reminded her flock of another vast estuary 1,500 miles away that is receiving poisonous oil in amounts unknown. The Closeteer, who had also mentioned the leak without thinking, tried hard not to hear; the morning had started so well. It was as if a crude-smelly-dripping monster had walked among us. He hoped the kids didn't feel the awful thing, seemingly so far away, that made him so suddenly sad. He kept a poker face. He knew the clean water they were about to embark on is well connected over time to that fouling Louisiana's mangroves. There is a loop current around Florida feeding into the Gulf Stream that passes us not far to the east. The true effects of the Gulf disaster are far too large and widespread to comprehend. It reminded him of the times when Americans and Russians were conducting nuclear bomb tests in the '50s and '60s. The radioactive poisons from those explosive reactions rose into the jet streams and were carried quickly around the world. Now members of our species have done the unthinkable again. We are causing significant harm to our planet. The atomic and hydrogen bomb tests were irrationally purposeful; this oil leak was accidental. However, the decisions to drill under the seas were not accidental. The old Closeteer was personally involved by paying taxes for the American bomb tests and indirectly for the present leak by driving too much on cheap oil. In the 20th century we Americans morphed into a car country that now depends in too many ways on lots of oil. We've known the dangers to the world for half a century or more of what some politicians call our "addiction." The same people, those we hope will lead us, make little attempt to help us kick the habit. Though now, while escaping oil is daily in the headlines, is the time. The sun and wind and other alternative sources would supply plenty of energy if we'd settle for much less and crawl out from the coils of big oil.

The Closeteer's foul thoughts dissipated as the four dories loaded with jolly kids got underway on an ebb that took them easterly toward the Plum Island River. Steep banks of rich brown peat, the lowest strata 3,000 years old capped with new green salt grasses, flanked them. Some of the kids became quiet as the salty-smelling air and beauty overwhelmed. Others joked back and forth in happy gentle tones. The oil slicks on the old-timer's brain were almost gone. Stops were made to dig razor and soft-shelled clams by hand, to catch hermit crabs, to marvel at the millions of scavenger mud snails, to wade in the shallow water, and to run pond to pond, crick to crick, on the high marsh. We passed two Black-backed Gulls feasting on a large dead bluefish. Terns who don't like these predators of their eggs and chicks dove within inches of these gulls 10 times their size. The terns were taking breaks from acrobatically catching sand eels. We rowed past a Plum Island River flat where a score of clammers were spread out, bent to their digging. To list all the animals seen, from tiny sticklebacks to salt meadow prawns, would require another paragraph. Those caught were returned to their habitats after examination. Before noon the tide turned and we happily rowed back on the flood.

Back at home where TV continues after seven weeks of unending reports about the leaks, the oily monster far beyond our ken returns. We hope the kids are not watching. Let them remember the living marsh and return to it from time to time in all seasons. If we do this again next year perhaps we'll have them bicycle over to the landing from school. If we, their hosts, do the same on foot or bicycle a true lesson will have been taught. Perhaps when they grow up and take charge they'll not allow what we have.

UNEASY ON THE RIVER BANK

The mood in the usually tranquil Water Closet is somber. The WC is the Stream Team's imaginary shack on a bank of the Ipswich, our river which flows to the Atlantic where its fresh water mixes with salty warm water from the Gulf Stream. The Gulf Stream, if sailed against, will take us around Florida to the poisoned Mar Caribe, a more inclusive name than the Gulf of Mexico. For the past two months since the leak, unease has been the prevailing atmosphere among us Closeteers obsessed with water. We live hour to hour knowing the seas are being fouled on a vast scale by amounts of ancient oil inaccurately being estimated. The media, so often tired of a story after a few weeks, are staying with this oily gush up from the deep. The Closet, usually a pleasant hangout for old-timers, reminds us of what a cancer ward must be like where all the patients have metastasizing tumors. The frantic efforts of BP and others to stop the flow and the poison dispersants used to lessen effects might be compared with tumor and lymph node removals and chemotherapy. Even if the oil doctors' operations and chemo treatments are successful much of the oil, bad cells in our metaphor, will have spread far and wide and still be out there continuing to harm in ways and places we'll never know. Countless organisms in seas and estuaries will have been killed, weakened or changed. Here the analogy fails. The cancer cells will be gone in a few years upon our deaths. Oil residuals in oceans may be around for centuries.

Twice in our Closet column/blog since the oil got loose we've fretted about it. Some of us feel helpless sitting on the bank of our clean river knowing what it is doing and might continue to do in our grandchildren's lifetimes. If younger we might go to the beaches and mangroves, Texas to Florida, and join the good volunteers there washing pelicans and picking up tar balls from the beaches. Yet somehow their earnest efforts seem so futile, almost laughable, along hundreds of miles of once rich coast so damaged by careless behavior. Our tears are not those of laughter.

Champion of the Nashua River, 80-year-old Marion Stoddart, who is being honored now with a documentary film, would be disgusted by such despair. We are surprised she is not down there off Louisiana directing cleanup crews. Almost 50 years ago she found her river in a horrible state from industrial dyes and who knows what else and led a successful drive to clean it up. We hope to obtain the film *Marion Stoddart: The Work of 1000* soon for a Stream Team showing.

Jeff Jacoby's op-ed column in the *Boston Globe* last week waxes eloquently about the wonders of oil and our need for it. While we have trouble disagreeing with his points, we see a fatal flaw in his tribute. Mr. Jacoby ignores all except our species. The vast majority of animals affected are not *Homo sapiens*. If you consider the planktonic animals in addition to the birds, fish, shrimp and oysters affected, people are outnumbered many trillions to one. We thought Rachel Carson, often mentioned in Closet essays, had gotten us beyond ignoring them a half century ago.

Just the other day Rich Matthews, AP reporter, bravely, some say foolishly, joined Gulf water and oil in scuba gear and little else and soon became pelican-like. After only a few minutes and some dramatic photographs, he left the water he found so devoid of life. It took hours to thoroughly clean him. We come down on the brave side of this stunt. Mr. Matthews knows what it takes to get much-needed attention for his fellow creatures. Experts have been talking ever since on TV of the poisons in his greasy bath. Several are carcinogens. Like a war reporter he thought he must join the battle for a while to get a feeling for the conditions and our notice.

In our spartan WC we have no media at all, not even cell phones. We bring our tales of woe from home and TV. This is, of course, all dreaming; the WC is an imaginary refuge. However, if the leak continues and media remain saturated with oil we may build a real log cabin on the river and retreat more often. We hope our leaders and younger folks have more courage and will protest against risky drilling, not for the sakes of people alone, but for all evolution's creatures and their habitats. Perhaps the odious slogan "Drill baby drill!," part of the last presidential election, will be wisely replaced by "Stop the drilling!"

WINDOW ON WETLANDS

The finishing touches are now being done on a little-known woodland park with nature trail, which at times is within the floodplain of the Ipswich River. Under the sponsorship of the Middleton Stream Team, David Florance, Scout Troop 19, cleared the trail as an Eagle Scout project two years ago. The town land west of the river's channel is about 25 rods north of ancient Logbridge Road, as early drovers might have described its location, where there was a cart path connecting colonial Salem and Andover. Now this pleasant wood across the floodplain from Danvers conservation land is dominated by mature red oaks, some very large and impressive towering above witch hazel bushes with lovely ferns between. In March of this year and during the great floods of 2006 and 2001 most of these several acres of woods were covered for a few days with fast-flowing water. Between the floods of the last two decades, beavers, so often mentioned in the Water Closet, have, with a high dam a fourth mile downriver, kept the water high enough to drown the floodplain's trees. Green ash, black ash, swamp white oak, river birch and red maple like wet soils but can't take root inundation year round. These floodplain species between the river channel and the low upland oaks took several years after the dam was built to die. Window on Wetlands, the name the Stream Team has given the land, looks out on acres of standing tree corpses and a developing "beaver meadow" of shorter, softer plants such as pickerelweed, arrowhead, arrow arum, bur-reed, yellow iris, reed canary grass, and other sun-loving wetland plants. Visitors to the site may get a view quite like the Indians had for several thousand years before the English arrived. In just the past human generation beavers have come back in a big way. The Algonquian speakers, who took advantage of the year-round higher water due to beaver dams to navigate their canoes up and down the river, are gone forever.

These were thoughts that passed through the minds of some Stream Teamers as they worked at the site recently. We tried to picture birch bark and dugout canoes with painted paddlers going by. Stories of the great spring shad and alewife spawning runs only read about were remembered. Anadromous fish had been just out there by the millions each spring. People scooped them up to eat fresh, to preserve by drying and smoking, and to fertilize their patches of corn, beans and squash. It must have been an exciting time for kids who waded among them and helped tend the weirs. Squaws and girls in the flanking rich bottom lands planted, maybe right here where we paved a nature trail with wood chips. The Indians were a part of nature.

We hope to get our people, who have strayed so far, back for a feel and look. Now and then we'd take a break and walk down to visit the pickerelweed just starting to bluely blossom beneath the gray trunks of beaver-drowned trees. The rich muck and shallow water of the low floodplain, now that tree leaves are no more, receive much light and in a few years will be bursting forth with greenery and flowers. The change to a "beaver meadow," so coveted for rich deep soil by the early English farmers, is off to a good start. After their arrival they quickly did the beavers in. The Indians, who from 1616 to 1619 died of European diseases for which they had no immunity, were gone too. Historians guess that 80 to 90 percent might have succumbed in the two decades preceding the Puritans. When these foreigners first came to this area in the mid-1620s, the land, untended and no longer purposely burned since the "great dying," seemed free for the taking. Now and then the newcomers paid the few survivors, probably demoralized, a few pounds, iron tools, and trinkets for what later became entire towns. Some of us weep when we read the very legalistic deed signed by sachem Masconomo with his mark. He turned over the whole lower Ipswich basin and all rights thereon to deed author John Winthrop, Jr., for 20 pounds, a few acres to live on, and a gun. Many historians believe Masconomo had little understanding of what he was signing. If depressed, he may not have cared; most of his people were gone.

Our day-dreaming speculation probably goes too far. Historians say it isn't fair to judge from later times. Some of us are not so sure and suspect that the Enron, AIG, etc. types have always been among us.

But why spoil a beautiful Saturday morning fretting about past wrongs? The beavers are back and maybe someday after the English and American dams of the 17th to 20th centuries are gone the alewives, shad, salmon and sturgeon will be back too. The Curtis Pond sawmill dam off Peabody Street, Middleton, is scheduled to be razed next year. In the meantime it is our responsibility to keep windows on the wetlands open. Places for all, especially those who live there.

JULY 2010

POND LILY TIME

Check nearby ponds for *Nymphaea odorata*, "white water lilies." You can't miss them floating in the shallows. There seem to be more this year.

Some are reminded of Japanese Obon festivals where white paper lanterns each on a tiny wooden float are launched at twilight bearing a candle. These represent visiting spirits being sent gently back. As they sail before the breeze prayers are silently offered by kin and spectators. There is really little comparison. Lily blossoms open in the morning and close in early afternoon. Clusters of the finest white, often pinkish, petals, supported by a few green sepals, are moored by soft cables to large bottom stems called rhizomes, a favorite food of muskrats.

Join these aquatic rodents looking skyward as they munch. There, just a couple muskrat-lengths above, are circular islands: lily leaves and flowers, each a third-muskrat in diameter. Flat leaves, maroon beneath, appear as anchored clouds. The green upper surfaces are pocked with microscopic openings called stomates. Leaves surrounded by air have these gas-exchanging portals on their undersides. Let us leave the island analogy for a moment and think of these sun-facing surfaces as solar panels, which they truly are. The chloroplasts in their cells absorb light and convert it to electro-chemical energy. Carbon dioxide enters through the stomates and with water from surroundings and tissues below, reacts in the processes of photosynthesis to make sugars, which diffuse to stems and roots where they are used or converted to and stored as starch until the following spring.

Imagine thousands of creatures, scores of species, from otters to fish, from tiny crustaceans to insect larvae and even tinier protozoa, all in this shady dining hall. Pond lilies provide food, shade, protection, substrate for small creatures and perhaps even aesthetic delights as clouds above us do. Each leaf is a raft, smaller denizens clinging to the bottom.

Upon visiting such places reach or wade out and pluck a blossom leaving only a short piece of stem. Pop into a bowl of water so it floats. Bring home and observe your captive beauty's daily openings and closings. Play the visiting insect, lean down and sniff. The smell is as lovely as the look.

If you like the idea of Obon think of your stolen lily as some departed soul on an early summer visit. See it off with thankful thoughts. Leave the more tangible parts to the muskrats.

ACCUMULATIONS

It is hard to imagine a half mile of ice rising into the sky above the land, but that is what the glacial geologists estimate was here at the peak of the last glacier about 15,000 years ago. One half-mile is roughly the distance from Topsfield center to the fairgrounds. Before climax the ice accumulated from precipitation had exceeded summer melting for 15,000 or so years, thus forming a vast, slowly moving ice sheet. Then very slowly the reverse occurred and the ice gradually diminished here for four or five millennia until the land, sculpted by a series of continental glaciers, including the last called the Wisconsin, was open to the sky again. In its diminution, as in the presently melting glacier called Greenland, water poured out from underneath in great torrents. At the retreating front there was massive erosion and deposition. Upon the ice's passing the lay of the raw land roughly resembled what we see today, but without topsoil or plants.

Near what is now Middleton Center just north of Howe-Manning School a brook ran through a low area no doubt washed out by glacial runoff to a nearby river the Indians are said to have called Agawam, the "Ipswich" of the English. In its flanking wetlands and floodplain, as with all such waterways not confined by ledge, plants grew in abundance. Their leaves, fallen stems, and roots died with time and joined the water and wet soil. There they rotted very slowly because of low oxygen and acidic water, which like vinegar partially pickles. Each year a new layer accumulated. High in organic matter, largely carbon, the muck formed is very dark. It is happening now in all our swamps.

Somewhat the same occurs on drier upland soils but much more slowly. Most of the yearly plant detritus breaks down to CO_2 and H_2O and joins the air and groundwater. A little dark organic matter joins the sand, silt and clay left by the glacier to form what we call topsoil. Let's do some round-number arithmetic. If only about 10 inches of topsoil has formed in 10,000 years since the land has been free of ice, then on average about one-thousandth of an inch of dark topsoil formed each year. In the nearby wetlands the accumulated black muck of the same period is in places 100 inches thick. The dark accumulations of uplands and wetlands aren't at all the same. The upland soils are filled with active worms, insects and crustaceans, as well as efficient decay bacteria and fungi with oxygen. The surface accumulations of plant detritus are mixed over time with the tiny mineral particles that make up soil. In the swamps and lowlands there is little mixing with clay, silt and sand except that from windstorms off once fallow fields and from flood deposits. The muck building up is largely organic. In the 18th and 19th centuries when much- needed firewood became scarce here the muck called peat was dried and burned. Thoreau, just a couple watersheds west, tells of it being mined as "manure" and mixed with sandy upland soils as was no doubt done here.

In June an old Closeteer interested in land formation was tipped off by Middleton's Town Administrator about the stratum of peat exposed in the excavation for the footings of the new Howe-Manning School. He donned a hard hat—site rules, no danger from falling peat—and proceeded to what was until recently a town ball field. While he had never played center or right field there he knew from past hikes nearby the often squishy area well. Sometime early last century, well after the old Essex railroad bed was laid down, the swamp to the south of it was covered with fill to make a playground. As he descended into a 10-or-so-foot-deep hole, fond memories of the baseball twilight leagues up to and after WWII returned. Several evenings each week men gathered to play visiting town teams for seven innings until darkness blended with fly balls. Young boys tired of standing around watching took off after each foul ball into the surroundings. Here memorable home runs to right field no doubt ended up in the swamp. In the 20th century tens of thousands of Middleton folks' and visiting outfielders' feet have gotten wet on the saturated fill perched on buried peat. What will future archeologists think when they find the black peat mixed with glacial till down in back of Oakdale Cemetery where it is being trucked and stored? Footings can't be built upon it. The railroad contractors in the late 1840s must also have removed the layer of peat and replaced it with solid fill. Their firm bed doesn't slump even along its wetland passages.

The Closeteer took some photos, measurements and samples and wished the Closet had a proper lab for analysis of the micro-layers within the two-to-five-foot-thick jet black stratum. Microscopic pollen grains pickle well and last for ages. The pollen of each plant species is distinctive. In similar places studied, botanists have found within the lower layers spruce and birch pollen in abundance mixed with fibers of peat moss. These are plants of the cold millennia following the ice's demise. Up until 4,000 or so years ago the flora around here resembled that of northern New England today. After that oak, maple, hickory and chestnut pollen characterize the upper, younger layers. About 3,000 years ago in the muck calendars of southern New England, corn pollen has been found in places, the beginning of Indian agriculture. In areas around where studies have been done there was a dramatic change in pollen species found beginning about 350 years ago. We'll leave this puzzle with you dear readers. The old Closeteer scratches his peat sample and finds tiny remnants of plant fibers. He plans to dry a hunk and burn it as of old. When it's dry he'll weigh it before burning it in a pan in the Closet's woodstove. After, he'll weigh any mineral residue. The difference, the amount burned, divided by the dry weight before burning will tell the organic fraction. From its feel between thumb and forefinger he is guessing 90 percent.

There is 10,000 years of history in those exposed few feet behind the school, which can't be read online. Study will require a lab with good microscope, chemical analysis equipment and time. We hope some enterprising teachers at the new Howe-Manning and Masco schools will have their scholars leave classrooms and computers now and then to dig history holes.

Great Plastic Catching Gyres

North and Central America as all of us know, but Columbus didn't, are flanked by vast oceans with great water gyres that move clockwise between the Old and New Worlds. The Kuroshio and Humboldt Currents in the Pacific and the Gulf Stream in the Atlantic sweep along the continental shelves where they pick up floating debris from rivers.

For millions of years they've collected natural wood and corpses, which rot away in not much time to harmless CO_2 and H_2O. In the last .0001 million years manmade plastic has joined that biodegradable flotsam. Much of it also floats, yet breaks down very slowly. Two human generations ago Thor Heyerdahl and crew on their reed ship Ra II were dismayed as they sailed their seaworthy, yet rotting, vessel west among toys, Clorox jugs and other containers 2,000 miles out in the South Atlantic on the Gulf Stream. In the last decade Pacific researchers, fishermen and sailors have reported thousands of square miles littered with plastic flotsam in the vast interior eddies of the great currents. The trash accumulating within the encircling currents of the Pacific has been dubbed by horrified witnesses "The Great Pacific Garbage Patch."

Estimates are that worldwide less than five percent of plastic is recycled. Much of the remaining 95 percent makes its way to streams and rivers, thence the slow gyres of the oceans. There it will drift for years and perhaps decades more as microscopic particles and finally foreign molecules. Animals absorb or ingest the smaller forms. What happens to them then is not known. Scientific guesses as to their fate and that of the organisms entered greatly worry as amounts steadily increase. Is there no place left on earth where we can go without finding our cheap packaging? Even in places where we can't see it with our naked eyes we know now it is there throughout the water column.

We were reminded of ocean current collections this past week by reporter Marissa Lang's article in Wednesday, July 14's *Boston Globe*, entitled "Fishing for Pollution in the Atlantic," about Sea Education Association researchers' out of Woods Hole findings among natural Sargassum, a floating seaweed that characterizes the Sargasso Sea. They roughly estimate from net-catching counts half a million visible plastic pieces per square kilometer. This doesn't include the trillions of unseen particles from older broken-down containers. We don't have to list the specific items found, just go to any beach's high water line and you'll see samples of all the packaging we bring home daily from our stores. A few years ago during an Earth Day cleanup of island shores in the Merrimack River, Rings Island Rowing Club members filled dory after dory with plastic containers, toys and pieces of Styrofoam. In half a day the dozen or so volunteers hardly made a dent in the accumulations found. As light as plastics are they saw and left behind tons. Imagine all that rode the currents right by the four islands out to sea, much eventually joining the Gulf Stream. About 40 years ago David Taylor, a science teacher at Triton Regional School, had his students release a few dozen sealed Coke bottles containing addressed notes in the ocean off Newburyport. Within two years several were returned from people finding them on Portuguese and other Old World beaches. Those were but a few bottles of natural glass done for research. Daily from the Atlantic coast we send them countless pieces of our trash. We no doubt receive much from Europe in return. Now massive amounts of oil, the mother of plastics, have been added to a contiguous sea. Some oil companies threaten to leave the Gulf if the sensible moratorium on ocean drilling continues. They'll drill off other coasts where allowed. So we see again the need for an international organization like "United Oceans" proposed in a recent Water Closet essay. It is high time to respect the place we came from if we go back far enough. Our oceans shouldn't be dumps; they are the very life of the planet.

One Closeteer intrigued by the uncommon word gyre reminded us of Lewis Carroll's famous nonsense poem "Jabberwocky" in *Alice in Wonderland*. Here is both the first and last verse:

'Twas brillig, and the slithy toves

Did gyre and gimble in the wabe:

All mimsy were the borogoves

And the mome raths outgrabe.

We looked up the words in the Closet's old-fashioned dictionary. (For any young computer-savvy readers the dictionary referred to here is a paper book listing words and their meanings.) We wanted to see if these wonderful-sounding words that give rise to imagined scenes could be related to the ocean gyres we fret about. To our surprise we found that Carroll hadn't made them all up. Gyre is movement in a circular motion. Slithy is from two archaic words combined that translate slimy blend. Mome long ago meant blockhead. Since the others have no meaning we could find we gave them our own. Let Brillig be plastic; Wabe for water. Mimsy means sickly, Borogoves are the inhabitants of the water bodies. Outgrabe is our verb meaning to throw out, the opposite of grab. The others unassigned we leave to you. Now read the verse again and translate. Fiddlesticks and nonsense! you say. No sense, we quite agree, in throwing our wastes, much poisonous, into the once lovely sea.

AUGUST 2010

ROLL OUT THE BARRELS

Stream Teamers led by Joan Flynn want everyone in the tri-towns and beyond to roll out their barrels and install them under roof gutter downspouts. During droughts such as now rain catchers will have water for their gardens. It doesn't take much rain to fill them; a Closeteer and friend installed one this spring to collect runoff from only one-third of his garage roof. The area with a gutter below it is roughly 300 square feet. A half inch rain or 1/24 foot times 300 equals 13 cubic feet. Thirteen times 7.5 gallons per cubic foot equals 98 gallons or roughly two rain barrels full. If distributed properly that amount will provide a 300-square-foot garden the equivalent of a good half inch of water at a time when needed. Closeteers much interested in Joan's admirable effort discussed the units of measure involved and did some additional calculations. The Middleton Electric Department (MELD) has about a half acre of roof. Let's say an inch of rain falls upon it and is collected in cisterns. What volume container would hold it all? Twenty thousand square feet times 1/12 foot equals 1,667 cubic feet. This volume times 7.5 gallons per cubic foot equals 12,502 gallons or about 250 rain barrels worth. Let's fill a water-tight school bus (8 by 6 by 30 feet) just for fun. We'll let the kids out first. One thousand four hundred forty times 7.5 gallons per cubic foot equals 10,800 gallons or roughly one school bus overflowing. Please forgive all the numbers lain on you just to emphasize that a little roof runoff yields lots of valuable water. A few years ago the Middleton conservation agent asked MELD folks to collect for truck washing, toilet flushing, and perhaps even drinking after a little filtering. They didn't. We don't mean to pick on MELD; most owners of buildings, even large ones, make no effort to collect runoff even though they need water.

The lively discussion in the Closet went from arithmetic to language. We wondered how many different types of barrels there are. We looked up barrel and found 36 gallons the volume for a standard U.S. barrel. (Many visualize common 55-gallon drums when thinking of barrels. Most modern plastic rain barrels are of this size.) The dictionary further pointed us to archaic casts, pipes, hogsheads, butts and tuns. These were the containers of the wooden container ship era. Making these of oak and other hardwoods was the special task of coopers. Early farmers here in the long winters split out oak barrel staves for the coopers of Salem and other ports. Those old enough remember oak rain barrels, often retired whiskey barrels, with quite a different function. Many provided captured soft water for clothes washing and bathing. Do you remember the popular 1940 song by Saxie Dowell? The verse sung by us nippers with the greatest gusto was:

> Oh Playmate, come out and play with me
> And bring your dollies three.
> Climb up my apple tree,
> Look down my rain barrel
> Slide down my cellar door
> And we'll be jolly friends forever more.

After a couple rounds of that by us Closeteers we remembered another musical reference to barrels, a less innocent one of later years. Here is probably the most popular verse of the Andrew Sisters' "Beer Barrel Polka."

> Roll out the barrel, we'll have a barrel of fun
> Roll out the barrel, we've got the blues on the run
> Zing boom tararrel, ring out the song of good cheer
> Now's the time to roll the barrel, for the gang's all here

The barrel in the second song is now called a "beer keg." After the Closet rafters shook a couple times with off-key yowling, we took no further action. Any barrel rolling days for us are long over.

We ask those of you who remember these tunes to gather appropriate groups of young people around you and teach them these songs of your youth. Tell them about climbing trees and sliding down cellar doors in lieu of video games. If they are still awake and attentive and haven't disappeared, segue from the rain barrels of old to the plastic ones the Stream Teamers are hustling* and explain their virtues: free clean water from the sky, water for the garden available when needed, soft water for washing clothes if desired, bathing water as of yore, and water conservation.

* For info see nerainbarrel.com or call (877) 977-3135

ON PLEASURE POND

The usually white waters of Boston Brook up from Mundy Bridge level out into a pond created by Charles Pritchard Sr. almost a century ago. Now, after four months of little rain in Middleton, the waterless brook descending to the pond is a rough stairway of moss- and algae-stained black boulders. The brook trickles below unseen. Some say only gods can create ponds; not true, beavers do it all the time. Men used to do it here to power mills. Ruins of three mill dams can be found up and downstream all within a mile. Pritchard's lovely third-mile-long swelling of Boston Brook is not a mill pond. According to Essex County dam inspector B. B. Barker's report of 1932 it is a "pleasure pond" so aptly named on his inspection form.

The name conjures up Japanese teahouses on exquisite pine-shaded ponds where courtesans and guests pass their time, or Alpine hot spring lakes where wealthy tourists bathe away their woes and pains. Another body of water that comes to mind is the New Hampshire lake where a family spends its last days "On Golden Pond," the name given Henry Fonda's daughter Jane and Katherine Hepburn's last film together. They were there in the fall with all the joy and sadness of that season on New England lakes.

Middleton's pleasure pond is nothing like those. Pritchard from Salem bought a large area of woods and fields flanking one of the Ipswich River's largest tributaries. He erected an earthen dam topped with asphalt and, voilá, runoff from 10 square miles of north Middleton, Boxford and North Andover filled in behind to form a 10-acre pond for the vacationing pleasure of his family. On a rise gently sloping up from its north bank he built a modest one-story wood-shingled cottage, not one of the infamous Newport/Bar Harbor types. Pritchard built largely with white pine cut from the site and milled two-thirds mile downstream at the new water-powered Curtis sawmill. Three generations of Pritchards have skated, canoed, swum and explored its wooded surrounds since. Other folks passing by on North Liberty Street often stop to admire the shaded pond. Some fish, a few in winter skate. Many, like several Closeteers, frequently come to see seasonal changes and migrating visitors. Now water lily leaves pave much of the surface, green floating disks with every few feet blossoms of brilliant white. Here and there near the edges are patches of pickerel weed now in wonderful blue bloom. Just up from them are a few delicate brilliant red cardinal flowers.

In the last decade storms and beavers have changed the scene. During the famous Mother's Day Flood of 2006 a 30-by-2-by-2-foot chunk of concrete was torn from the north-south dam's southern top. The pond that summer dropped two feet. In the fall resident beavers built a new 35-foot section arcing just above the breach to get the water up where it ought to be. In spring they don't maintain their section and the pond falls again. The overall pond, a couple feet shallower, has become ideal for lilies, which catch sediment and each fall die above their bottom stems to fill the pond in a bit. As the cold of December approaches the beavers, anxious to get adequate liquid passage between soon downward-growing ice and the bottom, build yet again and so the pond yo-yos annually up and down. It isn't the pond of just a decade ago; however, it still gives pleasure to visiting otters that play and fish in its water and slide upon its ice, and to us who fish, skate, just look, or steal a water lily now and then. Bufflehead ducks grace the pond coming and going a couple weeks each spring and fall en route to and from nesting areas north of the Great Lakes. Northern water snakes sunbathe on the rusty steel culverts, once Mundy Bridge, entering from the west. Herons stalk the edges for frogs and fish.

Barker, followed by other county inspectors, visited the dam every few years from 1932 to 1960 and left each time urging Charles Pritchard Jr. to fix up the decaying dam as ordered. In the early 1960s he built a more substantial concrete dam upon the old. The inspectors were happy and there have been no inspectors since except beavers. They unlike the Pritchards take immediate remedial action for survival's sake. We wonder if they don't also think their lovely place, visited several times a year by friendly Pritchard descendants, a pleasure pond as did Mr. Barker. We observers certainly do without ever using the word.

WATERFRONT PROPERTY

We dug out the Closet's well-worn *Webster's Collegiate Dictionary* of the 1950s and looked up the word "lodge" after happening upon one we hadn't seen before built by beavers. Usually we keep a close eye out for development along our river and streams that might crowd the privacy of our weather-beaten shack dubbed the Water Closet. Waterfront people are protective that way: NOMS, Not On My Stream.

The lodge, near the arbitrary bounds of the tri-towns just upriver from their Masconomet Regional School, is only a swim and short hike for young beavers inclined to go to school. We think human students would get a kick out of their presence. Teachers and administrators would not. But kidding aside, we know beavers have more pressing needs than "book learning." (One Closet wag wondered if that old phrase has been replaced yet by "electronic media learning," EML.)

An archaic definition of the word "lodge" snooty beavers might not like is "hut or hovel." These better describe our shack, which can be anywhere where imagination might put it along the river. We doubt if such class consciousness has any place in their lives. Here is one of several definitions found that seems to suit their lodges: "The den or lair of a wild animal or gregarious group of animals, esp. one requiring constructive work; as, a beaver's lodge." Masonic lodges listed certainly have no relationship although the occupants of both are gregarious and known as practical creatures.

It is obvious that this essay should be composed by resident beavers. We humans can only admire their works done with teeth, paws, persistence and DNA codes from millions of years of evolution. The new lodge to us, found on Nichols Brook near where it converges with the Ipswich River and subject to the constant low roar of I-95 traffic, is now exposed to air three feet below its usual water line due to four months of low rainfall. Some of us viewed beaver lodge entrances, usually under a couple feet of water, for the first time. We didn't attempt to crawl up in; even if invited we couldn't. The diameters of both front and back entryways are little more than beaver shoulder width. A spunky kid might be able. There are many stories from the past about Indians entering lodges to escape gun-toting colonists and vice versa. A trapper in the Yellowstone area is said to have eluded angry Blackfeet within one and lived to tell the tale. We suspect, after our measurements, that he somehow burrowed into the side of his refuge. Did he huddle among friendly beavers? It certainly would have been warmer after a wet entrance. The surprised occupants no doubt fled. One old Closeteer too often tells the story of sneaking up, on a very cold day, from downwind in eight inches of new sound-muffling snow on a large lodge at Pond Meadow Pond near the juncture of Boxford, Middleton and North Andover. He lay on the lodge's lee side, with an ear buried in the fluffy snow, listening. After several minutes he became cramped and moved; a splashing sound from within was heard as the startled beavers no doubt dove off their platform just inches above the icy water and made for an exit.

Since the newly found lodge and dam 300 feet downstream is being maintained we gave no thought to disturbance although we'd like to know the details of its internal structure. On return visits measurements were made and photos taken of its exterior. From the bottom of the Nichols Brook floodplain it rises seven feet. Its elongated cone-like form has a base diameter averaging about 28 feet. There are two entrances approximately 120 degrees from one another on the floodplain side. The tops of these foot-or-so-in-diameter access tunnels are about two feet below the yearly average water level as seen from stains on the slopes of the lodge. There is a third, newer we think, entrance one foot below and six feet from the original rear entrance that may have been made to provide wet access as the water subsided. They've dug a two-foot-deep, 20-foot-long canal to it from the brook. As the water dropped further this entrance has also become half exposed. The beavers are thus vulnerable while entering and leaving. We don't know what they have to fear; perhaps fishers and coyotes. The main entrance also has a 30-foot-long, one-and-a-half-foot-deep dug canal, leading to it.

While we've not seen the interior of an active lodge we have come upon many rotting lodges that have caved into living apartments. These apartments are relatively small. Two to six occupants must cozily cuddle when all are present. A Pennsylvania teacher and his students dug into one and found the interior walls plastered smooth with mud and free of inward projecting sticks. The sticks and mud above the living quarters have small spaces for ventilation. In winter even after snowstorms the heat of respiration keeps them open. We've often sniffed the exiting air and detected no odor. They must urinate and defecate out in the water away from the lodge.

We could go on about the wonders of beaver engineering. The dams range from 400 to six feet long. Many of their lodges are as large as the one described above. In addition there are networks of paths and ditches, underwater food caches of branches, and adjacent woodlots partially cleared of useful saplings and trees. All this has been done in just the 15 years since their return. The most striking effects are on the landscape itself. In the tri-town area alone a thousand or more wooded acres have been flooded, their trees drowned. Water is held in watersheds longer by their dams. Wildlife thrives in the inundated "beaver meadows." While they live in lodges seen by the unwise as poor huts and hovels, we much admire them, especially the one recently found and described above at Walcott Island with its waterfront site; beautiful mature beech- and oak-covered protective knoll backing, northwest to northeast, access canals; ventilation system; thick insulating walls of mud and thousands of sticks from twigs to small logs 12 feet long and three inches in diameter; and stout, well-made, upstream curving dams. We never cease to marvel at these not often seen large rodents in our midst.

Ups and Downs of Great and Small Rivers

As the monsoons wash down over the Indus River basin, Pakistan, television images of the high waters and resulting wet misery flood our media. Again, as in Bangladesh and New Orleans in prior years, we watch and worry about the victims and shifting water patterns around the globe. The feeder streams of the five great rivers, the 2,000-mile-long Indus and four major tributaries (Punjab: pun from pan meaning five, jab from ab meaning waters), originate in high Tibet where the Himalayan glaciers have been diminishing at an alarming rate for some time. Those in the broad rich agricultural valleys worry about too little water in the future while trying to survive way too much now. Will the monsoons from the south, the cause of this summer's floods, increase while the life-giving waters from the high north continue to decline? Pakistan's future involves more than just survival from turbulent politics. As this is being written turbulent waters cover much of the land. Over twenty million people are estimated to have been displaced; their sugar, rice, wheat, cotton and other crops are under water. One guess is that 200,000 livestock have been swept away in just the past month. Few dare to predict the final human death toll, ironically much from a lack of potable water.

Last week here at home four Middleton Stream Teamers paddled kayaks down our Ipswich River, minuscule in comparison, from near the juncture of Lynnfield, North Reading, Peabody and Middleton to Logbridge Landing downriver from Route 114. In March our river was much flooded due to winter-spring nor'easters, not tropical monsoons. There was little damage, our bottom land farms are long gone and most people live well above flood waters. What do our floods covering a few streets every five years or so have to do with the mighty Indus where 20,000 miles of roads and bridges have gone under? Not much, but the drought we have been experiencing here may give hint on a micro scale of what highs and lows can do. The low river, after over four months of less than half normal monthly rainfall totals, is, in stretches, a series of puddles between exposed waterlogged tree trunks, sandbars and shallows. It took us four hours to do what usually takes a leisurely two. Our exercise wasn't paddling so much as raising ourselves in and out of low kayak seats to wrestle our vessels over logs, to wade in mud and sand, and to portage over beaver dams. Water in the river west to east along the rail trail path in Peabody, flanked by higher banks and uplands, is much lower than in most late summers. The channel's south to north meanderings through the flat wide floodplain between Danvers and Middleton is somewhat higher due to beaver dams. We had to drag our vessels over five of these dams in just a mile.

Anytime we humans try to describe annual, seasonal and daily undulations of water, things get enormously complicated. Our trip last week before the rain was an attempt to do just that. We took some temperature and dissolved oxygen measurements and photos of what we could see above the water surfaces. There were lots of intriguing ripples and splashes seen and heard that had us wondering. The water was murky with what we think were bacteria and algae in the beaver-inundated stretches. Turbidity allowed viewing down only a foot or so. Dying and dead water plants common in late summer made us suspect low dissolved oxygen. Tests confirmed this. The presence of four species of herons (Great Blue, Green, Black-crowned, and Great Egrets) and cormorants let us know there are probably plenty of pond fish, as opposed to riverine species, which like faster flows of cooler water. We won't even attempt to note all the water-loving plants seen except to mention very noticeable cardinal flowers, whitely blossoming arrowheads, purple loosestrife racemes buzzing with bumblebees, fading blue pickerel weed blossoms, ripening spherical red-brown fruits of buttonbushes and panicles of swamp dogwood's gunmetal- colored fruits. Clumps of cardinal flowers delighted in places we've never seen them before. We bet they've increased one hundred fold in just the past couple years. Reed canary grass seems to be replacing purple loosestrife over many flooded acres. The waterside trees — majestic swamp white oaks, venerable willows and pretty papery-barked river birches — are dead or dying due to prolonged root inundation from beaver dams. The point we are trying to make here is that teams of scientists would have to spend lifetimes on floating or riverside labs to get a handle on the dynamics of even this small river system. Alas, as they measure, things would be changing. Imagine the complexities along the mighty Indus basin rivers and their countless tributaries, from snow-capped peaks in the north to Indian Ocean estuaries in the south, many the works of man. We "Google-Earthed" the main Indus channel and floodplains and found scores of dams, offshoot canals, bridges and thousands of square miles of agricultural fields, many now destroyed.

While hard to get our heads around all the variables, we have learned that healthy river systems large and small need substantial buffers along them where natural life, however changing, is allowed to flourish. In Massachusetts, through the Rivers Protection Act, we are off to good start with 200-foot-wide bands with alteration restrictions on each side. These are measured out from the edge of mean annual high water, an elevation now about five feet above the water level we paddled and waded last Saturday. The record Mother's Day Flood of 2006 was eight and one-half feet higher over a half-mile fast-flowing front in some places. Multiply that width by a hundred to get some feel for what is happening in poor Pakistan.

SEPTEMBER 2010

TRUE VICTORIES AT SEA

For better or worse World War II hardwired many of us old-timers when we were boys. The *Victory at Sea* TV documentary series with Richard Rodgers' sound track in the '50s further impressed Pacific naval warfare on us. The other day a new form of warfare in the southern oceans around Antarctica was introduced to us by, of all people, the six-year-old grandson of an old Closeteer who bores us with sea stories from his postwar Navy days. Grandson Django's favorite battles are "Whale Wars" about an outfit called Sea Shepherd Conservation Society that harasses Japanese whalers. We don't have TV in the Closet so his grandfather watched a DVD at home of these recent "wars" and reported back. We told him we had already seen parts on the TV station Animal Planet.

Whale Wars struck a chord with us environmentalists, especially the ex-Navy grandfather. In Sasebo Harbor, Kyushu, Japan, a half century ago his ship docked alongside a large factory ship and her four black, much smaller, killer ships. A couple of the killers seen in the modern DVD may have been the same ships he'd seen long ago; they looked the same. Even then other countries were urging Japan and Norway to cease whaling. In subsequent decades Greenpeace and other groups have taken more direct action at sea, by going beyond the only partially successful meetings at negotiating tables. We Yankees, once world champion whalers on the Bering to Antarctic seas, no longer kill whales purposely for oil and baleen. The United States bans almost all whaling except for some done by Native Americans off Alaska. The Japanese, who love whale meat, continue whaling despite international pressures. Those who directly oppose whalers and harass them at sea reduce their take and no doubt increase the price.

Grandfather, enlightened by grandson, returned to the Closet and a lively discussion about whaling and war ensued. In these modern whale wars of harassment few are hurt other than economically. Their methods include daring maneuvers around and between mother factory ship, killer kids and their whale targets; shooting blood-red paint and butyric acid projectiles, the latter a very disgusting stinky chemical thought to contaminate whale flesh; squirting fire hoses called water cannons; sending forth ship-launched helicopters to pester; making loud noises to distract and bother; and constantly producing anti-whaling PR. The audacious saviors claim many fewer whales are being killed.

These ongoing sporadic battles to save whales have been publicized for decades, perhaps not enough. Magnificent species are still in danger of extinction.

A fanciful digression arose. We know well that folks never seem to tire of sports or war. We wondered if organized wars using stinky chemicals, biodegradable of course; loud sounds rivaling those coming from rock concert amplifiers; water cannons; risky maneuvers, as in team sports; and constant claims of victory might not replace traditional sea battles of the kind celebrated in *Victory at Sea*. If these were organized with rules like the Olympics there could be almost constant combat waged somewhere for those needing such vicarious action. One Closeteer cited a very readable recent history by journalist-historian Evan Thomas. *The War Lovers* is about the roles of Teddy Roosevelt, William Randolph Hearst and Henry Cabot Lodge in actively promoting the Spanish-American War, a particularly odious conflict most Americans at the time cheered on. Maybe war lovers would accept the substitute the boy introduced us to in *Whale Wars* where there is excitement yet few casualties. Viewers of the "whale stoppers," grandson's phrase, in pilot house and bridge scenes can feel the highs and lows the explosive-free warriors experience during and after battle.

We wondered if similar boats and ships harassing oil drilling rigs in the Gulf and elsewhere might not also be appropriate. It would certainly beat traditional expensive sea wars and would be popular on TV. Folks with war-lover genes could stay safely at home watching. Shipyards could shift to building "oil rig-whale stoppers" powered by non-polluting sails so the economy as well as the environment would not be affected. Conventional navy bases could be retired and replaced by United Nation bases for the war referees' fast-sailing ships. A thousand windjammers would be built for the cost of one deadly carrier. To spice things up crew members might wear buccaneer garb of old. After their battles the air would be much cleaner, the water less bloody and oily than in the past.

WILD RICE REVISITED

Wild rice, *Zazania aquatica**, is a handsome grass now gracing our river's edges. A decade ago, we Stream Teamers on canoe trips saw only an occasional plant along a stretch near where Middleton Brook converges with the Ipswich River below Richardson Farms' huge corn field. Two summers ago there were only a few dozen wild rice plants there. Last Friday Middleton's Council on Aging/ Conservation Commission walking group visited the area by land and found hundreds covering several wet acres. We were able to walk out among the head-high plants due to four months, April though mid-August, of less than half average rainfall. We found rice grains in some of the female florescences, quite different than the pollen-producing yellow male tassel just below each on the same stem. Many had already shed their husk-covered seeds into the water where they floated and eventually made it to muddy bottoms. These will give rise to next year's crop both here and downriver where many drifted with the slow current. A few petalless flowers, like all grass blossoms, were still somewhat green, their seeds unripe. A question naturally arises from the increasing numbers of plants. What has changed in the past few years? An obvious difference all along much of river is the increasing number of beavers. Their dams have made the river a series of lakes that are especially important in times of low precipitation. The leaky dams keep water around longer while not entirely stopping the flow, which we read is necessary for wild rice habitats. The famous watery fields where Indians have long harvested rice are the shallows of lakes in Minnesota, Wisconsin and southern Manitoba. All those lakes have outflowing streams; their waters are clean. Sections of the Ipswich with wide floodplains, meandering channels and slow flows are becoming more lake-like. Last summer downriver, we also found an increase in rice plants among the channel's great curves in Wenham Swamp in Topsfield and Ipswich. Ipswich River Watershed Association naturalist James MacDougall has wondered out loud in recent years if duck hunters aren't seeding to entice their prey. As we've often pointed out in Water Closet essays, the many interacting variables in nature are not easily understood. We can guess; it is quite another thing to prove. In the meantime we'll happily observe and ponder the never-ending changes.

As children we heard stories of the importance of wild rice to the Chippewa and Ojibwa nations of the Great Lakes region. Their people harvested it each late summer. Canoes, usually manned by two women, moved carefully among the vast watery fields. While one paddled, the other with a stick in each hand bent the stems with one so the ripe female flowers were above their vessel. With the other stick she tapped them with just the right force to release ripe grains and not disturb the others. The grains do not all ripen at the same time. Sometimes as many as eight trips were made in several weeks to get as much of the ripening fruit as possible. Estimates are that most grains, even in areas being harvested, end up in the water. Ceremonies were held and prayers said at stages in the harvest and subsequent processing. Rice committees determined the proper times. The husked fruits were danced upon in large smooth containers or pits and then scooped and winnowed in the breezes. An old Closeteer remembers his grandfather doing this with dried beans each fall. In his case the beans in dry pods were not only tramped on but beaten with a thail, a wooden club attached to a long handle by a leather thong. The results were cast upward in a good breeze, separating the heavy seeds from light chaff.

The same was done early on with most grains. Do you remember the wise old saying extended to our behavior? "Separate the wheat from the chaff."

Is it any wonder that wild rice now gathered by purists the old way costs 15 dollars per pound? Others have tried long and hard with only partial success to raise special hybrid varieties; those grains ripen simultaneously to be harvested by clever machines. Such commercial operations are usually in manmade paddies. The price was reduced. So was the quality according to those who gather wild rice from natural lakes. Health food stores want wild rice because of its nutritional and aesthetic values. The long dark grains are more wholesome than those of white rice. While both are grasses they are not related. The white rice we are familiar with has had the embryos, protein and fat parts removed leaving us with just starch.

It is exciting having this nutritious food for ducks and geese back along our river. If we are right about our beaver lake connection, wild rice must have been here before the English and French came four centuries ago with their yen for beaver fur. There were many beavers then, perhaps like now, before Indians were paid for pelts.

Try a stretch of river near you by canoe or on foot and look for a stately looking pale grass growing from the shallows with delicate flowers like clusters exploding from fireworks, the female top spreading upward like a green afro, the male's lower yellowish projections drooping. The leaf blades are wide and well spaced along the lower stem. Imagine a delicate corn plant, which is also a grass, with two tassels and no ears. In the case of wild rice the female tassel-like structure is just above the male tassel. No other of our many grasses is quite like it. Bend a few female florescences over a white bucket and gently shake. The old Closeteer will be trying this on Labor Day. Seeds, no doubt not enough to eat, will be passed around the Closet for planting. You can mix what little you've harvested, or obtained from a health food store, with commercial white rice to improve appearance and nutritive value. Check the label of any bought to see if it is "paddy" grown or truly wild. Better still, have females in the family go forth with sticks in a birch bark canoe. Bon appetit. Or perhaps more appropriately along the Ipswich: quack, quack.

---

* Identification and naming here is tricky. Are they from the seed of man-produced

hybrids or the natural varieties of old? We must do more research on the plants we've found along the Ipswich River.

TIDES

An old Closeteer told us of his lecture on tides given while going down Mud Creek in Rowley. He, grandson Django, six, and daughter Mika paddled their large canoe on a low ebb to the Plum Island Sound flats and back. His sons and their daughters in two other canoes completed the early August fleet. The temperature was near 90, the vertical distance between the low water and high tide salt marsh grasses seven feet. Crew members went in and out of the shallow water frequently to keep cool. Ojii, the Japanese word for grandfather used by the Closeteer's grandchildren, tried to explain the tides. Django's basic questions kept him going ever deeper into something that while truly wondrous, most take for granted. The exchange went something like this.

"We are on flowing water; that is why we are moving so easily and quickly."

"Where is the water going?"

"It is flowing out to the ocean." Ojii's unconvincing reply.

"Why?"

There is a long pause as thoughts of moon, sun, tidal waves with wave lengths half the circumference of the earth, and gravities churn in his head. Finally,

"Have you heard of gravity?"

"Yes."

"The moon and sun pull on the water making it deeper when the earth is in line with them than when at right angles to one another. So the water goes up in places and down in others."

Grandpa is becoming confused as he tries to visualize what he is saying through the eyes of a little boy, who, if worldly wise and cynical, might be saying, "Yah if he believes that he'll be telling me next that we are paddling through salty lemonade." Django, while sharp, like most children trusts grandpa and probably thinks what he is being told, whatever that is, is true.

The doubtful explainer proceeds.

"In a little over six hours the water will be up to here."

He raises his paddle skyward to the level of the grassy flat marsh.

"Why?" A question anticipated, but not looked forward to.

"Because the water will soon come in from the ocean. The wave crest, half the world's circumference between crests, moves under the moon as the earth spins east."

Silence. He is spared the "You've got to be kidding?" one might get from a teenager.

Fortunately about that moment a few sand eels flash into view under the portside's shadow. The crew concentrates on them as do some hungry terns above. Django with hand net tries unsuccessfully to catch the tiny transparent fish flickering by.

Grandpa reflects on what he is attempting so poorly to teach without models, globe, blackboard or mathematics. He is trying to explain what mankind's brightest had probably pondered forever until Isaac Newton came up with an explanation. And here he is laying on a six-year-old something he has spent a lifetime only half understanding. It is probably best for children to return again and again at highs and lows and all levels in between. Someday they'll notice, or understand if told, that the highest highs and lowest lows correspond to the phases of the distant moon. The concept of worldwide waves might have to wait until high school physics. The old man wonders, although he is afraid he knows the answer, how many adults watching the tides come and go on our beaches have some understanding of them. Ojii can tell from Django's questions that he is off to a pretty good start. Let the rest come naturally with time. There is no hurry. Let him observe what tides do, for as the old saw says, "They wait for no man."

Why?

Splashes From Below

On a recent Sunday morning a lone Closeteer walked the perimeter of the vast beaver impoundment that encloses remote Pond Meadow Pond, a favorite retreat for Stream Teamers, Closeteers, friends and no doubt kindred souls unknown. While doing so he spooked many groups of Mallards and Wood Ducks feeding in the shallow lily pad and duckweed covered water. There were few signs of other people except for the scarcely heard drone of distant Route 95 traffic and the now and then noise of planes passing high overhead unseen in the clouds. In his circumnavigation of 110 acres of flooded beaver meadow he passed over land that on maps is marked as Middleton, North Andover and Boxford although no lines were noticed except for some coinciding with stretches of 18th- and 19th-century stone walls. Only a few people have an interest in these woodland bounds, really no bounds at all. Now and then he passed Boxford Trails Association arrows, round Middleton hiking trail markers, and the diamond-shaped tags of Greenbelt and Boxford State Forest. Most of the leisurely two-hour hike in mature forest over rough and varied ground was off cleared trails.

It was cool and cloudy; the air had that might-rain-anytime feel. From a brushy path, within a few feet of the impounded water, the Closeteer heard splashes and looked out to see quick breaks in the otherwise calm surface. The many disturbances, seemingly at random like large raindrops, were in thin breaks between lily pads and duckweeds. He walked down and stood on a ledge just peeking above the water. All around splashes in the surface continued, some almost at his feet. He stared and stared yet saw no tangible cause. He held out bare forearms and hands for raindrops. None were felt. Some of the splashes were larger than others and appeared to have fleeting things in their falling wakes. After 10 minutes of maddening concentration that provided no good answers, he saw descending the familiar pale gray-green-white pattern on the belly of a bullfrog tadpole. A hundred close observations of water disturbances before had revealed no bodies or parts. It was as if tiny teasing ghosts quickly broke the surface and then retreated. For a time he thought the phenomenon some kind of insect hatch, yet none were seen. He concluded that tadpoles, as far out across the water as he could see, were coming to the surface for risky sips of air. The higher splashes in which things could almost be seen were probably tadpole tails on the way down. The water must have been very low in dissolved oxygen after a night of no oxygen-producing photosynthesis. Much of the oxygen gas produced by green plants and algae in the light is quickly used by microorganisms and animals respiring. They, like us, constantly take in oxygen and give off carbon dioxide. Photosynthesizing green plants in the dark do the same but there is usually a net plus in sunlight-produced oxygen over a 24-hour period. The Closeteer vowed to return with a dissolved oxygen measuring kit at the same time of morning to find out. Visits on bright afternoons would also be wise to see if the surface interruptions stopped. Amphibians like frogs and tadpoles can obtain dissolved oxygen from water through their skins. At this writing neither tests nor follow-up visits have been done so we are left with little more than a hypothesis by an old-timer whose eyes and ears aren't what they used to be.

Something further might be said about water conditions in these fascinating inundated places that have been with us since the beavers returned two decades ago and made them with their many dams. These evolving "beaver meadows" are places of enormous death as well as life, most of the lively latter microscopic. Looming over the scene described above are gray barkless corpses of Atlantic white cedars and white pines. The red maples that dominated much of these forested swamps just a decade ago are almost all gone from view. The higher water year round due to dams slowly killed them; their rotting roots could no longer hold heavy trunks and branches high in snow-laden winds. Most red maples fell in the first five years after dying. They were followed by the high white pines, which are probably 80 percent gone now. The dead cedars still stand in large numbers. Their bleached trunks and broken branches cast thin shadows. Just 11 years ago on visits into thick cedar stands, even midday one experienced semi-darkness. The point in mentioning this forest passing is to emphasize the massive amount of fallen biomass that now slowly rots beneath the still waters while life teems above.

Soon falling temperatures and waning light will cause photosynthesis to stop. The leaf factories will turn many colors then finally brown. Trillions of leaves from the surrounding upland trees will drift down upon the dying duckweed to sink and join the rotting logs. The tadpoles and myriad other aquatic creatures will slow down, some completely in the mud as ice forms above. We'll return on that new state of water to marvel at otter, fox, coyote, deer and smaller mammal tracks in the snow. Otters, mink and beavers will be active in the liquid layer between ice and slowly rotting muck. Birds, also warm-blooded, will search for dormant insects in dead tree trunks still in the air. We'll have trouble remembering what the beaver meadow was like just months before. Good thing, more to look forward to next spring and summer when green and all associated with it returns. And even if we do remember it won't be the same.

OCTOBER 2010

IPSWICH TIDAL WATERS

Down from a once working dam in the center of town we paddled among the houses oDown from a once working dam in the center of town we paddled among the houses of old Ipswich on a river by the same name, an English name brought almost four centuries ago after there were few natives to contest it. Some of us wonder what it will be called four centuries hence. Will its estuary be a bay due to global warming and rising waters that cover the labyrinth of marsh and cricks we see today? Will there be more rain running off and coming down from upper reaches above the tides? We all drove to the launching site carrying our 20 kayaks and one canoe on gas-burning vehicles thus adding to warming which results in less ice and higher water. We hope our addiction to oil passed down from parents will in some future generation wane and finally be kicked. While otherwise happily paddling some were uneasy about our hardwired hypocritical affliction, worldwide in its effects.

The natives used dugout and birch bark canoes on this river, some say they called Agawam. William Wood, a mysterious and candid visitor without Puritan hang-ups, 1629 to 1633, wrote in his famous book *New England's Prospect* about every household in Salem "having a water-horse or two." He was referring to dugout canoes of white pine "two foot and a half over and twenty foot long," the legacy of Naumkeags who were gone due to diseases and displacement. Their demise occurred a little over a decade before Wood's observations. Some have translated the survivors' oral description of that period as "the time of the great dying"; estimates are that 80 to 90 percent succumbed in just a couple years from Old World diseases, to which they had little resistance, thus leaving valuable fields and canoes behind.

The people took over amidst plenty and learned to farm and fish for themselves and an increasing stream of newcomers. Within a few generations there were more English than there had probably ever been Indians at any one time. The modern paddlers in plastic vessels left the river at one point and proceeded into the salt marsh up Labor in Vain Creek against a half-tide ebb. We pondered the name and wondered of the suffering implied. Had a farm family or families of the upland knolls surrounded by marsh failed in farming along its banks and in despair dubbed this rich tidal crick with such a mournful name? A visit to Ipswich's library and historical society might provide an answer; in the meantime we will, as Iris Dement sings in a line from her plaintive song "Our Town,"… "let the mystery be."

Odd thoughts such as these visited as we leisurely made our way under a beautiful September sky on clear water en route to Plum Island Sound, which is just in from the sea. At low tide 400 years ago, squaws and children would have been out on the flats, we glided over

Sandy Rubchinuk, Middleton Stream Team, and Kerry Mackin, Director Ipswich River Watershed Association, in forewater (Sandy left, Kerry right) with 20 or so other tiny vessels, most unseen in photo, on the tidal Ipswich River en route to Pavilion Beach, Plum Island Sound. Photo, courtesy of Katharine Brown.

in our kayaks, with clamming sticks. In spring they'd have been here in dugouts, Wood's water horses, tending weirs and seines. They had never seen horses so wouldn't have used his metaphor. We wondered if they visited Labor in Vain Creek and others in winter on tricky salt water ice to spear eels below in their muddy winter hideaways as did the colonists. The latter's long-handled spears, iron prongs rusting, can still be occasionally found in old barns and antique shops. A Middleton Stream Teamer's late friend used one spearing eels through holes cut in Salisbury's ice-covered cricks up until a couple decades ago.

Our fleet of tiny vessels turned north with the broadening river and headed toward Great and Little Necks, high drumlins of glacial debris tending southeastward toward another drumlin, Castle Hill, above Crane Beach across the river. Below them on the final great curve eastward, the flanking broad flat marshes of peat capped with salt grasses gradually gave way to sand dunes and bars. Century-old photos show these drumlins, now heavily forested and shrubby, without trees or bushes. They, like most of New England a century ago, were in pasture. In Indian times they were lush with strawberries and blueberries in season. Now without the Indians' annual fires or English and American livestock they have gone to trees, bushes and houses.

Upon rounding Little Neck into the sound we remembered accounts of the early Old World explorers from Samuel de Champlain to Captain John Smith who were here a whole generation before the Pilgrims at Plymouth and Puritans at Salem. They sailed by on fair summer winds and marveled at the beauties of hills, dunes, marshes of good grasses, and fine villages of neatly laid out wigwams and garden patches. On one coasting from Cape Cod down east to Penobscot Bay, Smith counted 40 such habitations.*

We rounded close to cottage-covered Little Neck on a strong ebb. The sand just below us was punctuated by glacier-strewn boulders washed twice daily for 10,000 years. Salty messages from the ocean out another half mile entered our noses. Plum Island stretched to the north and disappeared. To the southeast Steep and Castle Hills loom over the shifting bars that disturb the wide salt water entrance and fresh water exit connecting estuarine rivers to the world's oceans. Someone remembered Jack Nicholson in the movie *The Witches of Eastwick*, based on a weird novel by one-time Ipswichian the late John

Updike, which was partially filmed on the grounds of the Crane Estate on Castle Hill. One wag saw a connection between the great twice daily flushings of the estuaries and toilet fixtures, the source of Crane's fortunes. Brisk sea air must stimulate all kinds of far-out creativity. We wondered if the summering Cranes had ever seen such an analogy. We quickly pulled the chain on such thoughts as we turned northwest in the sound toward Pavilion Beach nestled between the Necks.

On beach cobbles our paddles stopped and vessels were soon loaded onto waiting cars. We reluctantly left the river we had traveled over spring and summer in stages of "Source to Sea," the Ipswich River Watershed Association's annual program to get members and friends out on its charge's waters. We did sections North Reading to Ipswich this year. We neither reaped, fished, nor gathered, nor sowed on our trips. All our stuff now comes from distant places: oil from the Gulf and Arabia; food from California, Florida and the Midwest; unnecessary fresh-cut flowers and mahogany and teak for our yachts and mansions from rain forest countries; labor from around the Caribbean; environmentally expensive beef and pork from stinking western feed lots; and eggs from rows of stainless steel cells in the South. Bad thoughts all around for some as we burned our way back home on imported asphalt roads with vessels on car roofs built from somewhere else's oil. It ain't easy in the mind being an American lukewarm environmentalist.

* Russell, Howard - *Indian New England Before the Mayflower* (Hanover and London, Univ. of New England Press) 1880

WINNIPESAUKEE AND BEYOND

Seemingly splashed across the center of New Hampshire is a great yet shallow lake. Winnipesaukee, some translate as "beautiful waters of the high place," is about 110,000 feet long, northwest to southeast, and averages less than 100 feet deep. This ratio of length to depth is 1,100 to 1. Upon reflection all bodies of water are shallow layers of the precious stuff. The Pacific, using very round numbers, is 40 million feet across and averages 10,000 deep for a ratio of 4,000 to 1. Lake Baikal in Russia, the world's deepest lake, averages 2,400 vertical feet and is about 2 million long for a ratio of 840 to 1, one not very different from Winnipesaukee's. The point of laying all these numbers on you is to emphasize how thin the layers of the Earth's waters are compared with the planet's overall volume. Above and below them are a few miles, let's say 10, of atmosphere containing some water; the ratio of the atmosphere's thickness to the Earth's radius is about 1 to 400. Above and below the atmosphere and hydrosphere are unimaginable distances of almost nothing or dense hot rock, certainly no places for life.

On a recent weekend an old Closeteer and wife with three generations of family gathered on Mark Island in the western reaches of Lake Winnipesaukee. A long-time Winnipesaukee waterman and friend of a son-in-law made his rustic palace available to us. We swam, paddled, rowed, hiked, or watched from the large camp's perimeter porch just off the water. Neighboring camps could barely be seen through the mature hardwood, hemlock and pine forests that cover most of the 250 or so islands' land area except for shaded lots on their edges. One morning a Pileated Woodpecker, not seen much down here, excited all by visiting nearby trees for an insect check. The following morning seven well-streamlined Common Loons graced our cove with their swimming and sudden scurries in unison across the surface for something we couldn't see. We saw nothing common about them and were disappointed when they finally swam away around the point. Now and then early and late we heard the wondrous cries of loons. They seemed to put us to sleep in the evening and to awaken us in the morning. Chatter, even the children's, stopped as we listened intently and wondered what was being sung. Alas, if we knew, the mystery might disappear. Some of us remember our disappointment upon hearing the scientific explanation given for seashore wave sounds from empty snail shells.

Farmers once ran livestock on these islands. Our host's boat picked us up at a place where Cattle Landing Road on the mainland of Meredith touches the water. The islands were once pasture, no fences needed. Moose and deer swim to and fro among them. We doubt if even adventuresome cattle would. We got another clue to former grazing on the island. Almost all of the large straight hardwoods on Mark Island rise up singly telling us they arose from seeds and not cut stumps or fire-killed trees, which send up clumps of shoots, many at first, called coppice. The growing saplings compete and most die leaving two to five mature trees in clumps, clones of the harvested parent. We saw very few such clumps on Mark indicating that it was probably pasture a century ago. We tried to imagine grass- and wildflower-covered islands without trees. Unlike the farmers, the present summer visitors, there for the water, stay on the perimeters. Inland on Mark we found many old beeches, oaks and birches topped by fewer white pines, many of the pines a 100 feet or so tall. The thick canopy makes for little undergrowth; walking, except for glacier-scattered boulders and fallen trees, is easy.

Let's leave the island and return to water generally. The other night famous PBS interviewer Charlie Rose had two athletic guests on his show. Susan Casey and Laird Hamilton are wave lovers. Tanned, blond and handsome they looked out of central casting. Hamilton is a professional surfer, Casey a swimmer and popular author. Hamilton helped with her recent book *The Wave* starring the medium they've loved all their lives. Rose, who must have liked the book, although he only held it up and mumbled "good" upon saying goodbye, was captivated by his guests' obsession with and Casey's dramatic descriptions of rogue waves, surfers, and sharks. He too seems to have done some surfing. The old Closeteer's thoughts, while telling us of this joint interview he caught the tail end of, turned to Closet hero scientist-author Rachel Carson who also loved the water and gave the world her lyrical masterpieces *Under the Sea-wind*, *The Sea Around Us* and *The Edge of the Sea*. Some say those books and her dedication to all of nature did more for the marine sciences than even the work of the late Jacques Cousteau that lives on through his offspring. Casey, from inland Texas, says she has had her love for the sea as long as she can remember and to paraphrase her words to Rose: Since three-fourths of our planet is covered with ocean and it is the place we came from such feelings seem natural to me.

Most of us love oceans, lakes and rivers. Look at these waters on weekends with people swarming on them and their edges; why go on about the obvious? What isn't so obvious is how we who love them treat them. We've long used them as sewers on massive scales. It wasn't so bad when the wastes came directly from us and not from our industries, farms, and mined or manufactured chemicals. Now to add injury to insult we puncture their bottoms with holes seeking poisonous cheap oil. On Winnipesaukee where the water appears clean, we cruise carelessly about in hundreds of speed boats just for kicks. Why can't we kick our yen for speed, or at least confine it to our millions of miles of paved roads? Our waters are far too valuable for huge polluting ships and toys. You'd think folks on recreational waters would be content with leisurely sailboats and body-friendly oars and paddles. They're on vacation, what's the hurry?

Last week TV news featured stories of Russian ships, not on vacation, rounding the edges of the Arctic Ocean where just a few decades ago mariners couldn't go even with icebreakers. Some scary estimates have all the arctic ice-free within this century. Drilling, mining and fishing there are already being planned. Undersea territory is being staked out. We may well have passed the "tipping point" that planet scientists have long warned us of. This is when the positive feedback systems of global warming accelerate beyond any hope of return no matter what we do. Why worry then, some might say, more water for people to play in and BP to tap; and anyway what can we do? It might be time to get our warships, tankers, oil wells, and salmon farms out of the water. Let's leave some parts of the planet for study, harmless play, and other creatures. And while we are at it let's leave buffers along their edges. We now realize that all life as we know it depends on healthy waters. We know, but do we have what it takes to protect them?

OLD TECH VERSUS NEW IN THE RIVER

The "south Middleton Ipswich River flow and depth gauge" in west Peabody, within a couple meters of the channel, the towns' boundary, is not reading as usual. Signals from its solar-powered transmitter travel via satellite to a United States Geological Survey (USGS) computer. Some of us go online daily and watch graphs of the river's flow rates and depths updated every three hours. The rates shown are those featured in the Water Closet each week. Records from the south Middleton gauge go all the way back to 1938, long before solar panels and satellites. A month ago the Middleton Stream Team via the Ipswich River Watershed Association received a message from USGS suggesting trouble downriver. Readings were staying high despite long periods of little rain. Several years ago John Bacon, Stream Team leader, calculated from gauge data during the months of active plant growth that after each rise following a significant rain the flow drops 13 percent of the previous day's rate for each succeeding rainless day. On an exponential graph this appears as a straight descending line. Now and since mid-September the readings have stayed more or less the same and show no such pattern.

From a decade of watching the data on our computer screens and occasional visits to the site we suspected there was blockage downriver. Large trees sometimes fall across the river, floating debris piles against them resulting in partial dams that affect the flow. However, from past experience we suspected the culprits were beavers. A walk or paddle along or in the river will usually find the problem, although hiking in the thickets along the banks or paddling the now low river isn't easy. A Stream Teamer went forth on September 13 and soon found a new dam, which coincides with the high voltage transmission lines above and a high pressure natural gas line a couple meters below, crossing the river from south Middleton into west Peabody. We don't think the gas and electricity crossings have anything to do with this 60-foot-long, two-foot-high dam started in early September that the beavers are still raising. Branches, some still with green leaves, are being daily added. We do know the high voltage lines produce an electric-magnetic field the dam builders work in. Does this excite and stimulate work production? We hope this isn't shown to be the case. Human overseers might install high voltage electric lines, more than there are now, around our workplaces. Workers would experience more than just caffeine buzzes. The dam probably has nothing to do with the gas just below coming down at 80 atmospheres pressure from the fishing banks off Sable Island, Nova Scotia. If an enterprising beaver with diamond incisors gnawed into the 30-inch diameter, one-half-inch-thick steel pipe and upon penetrating lit a cigarette to relax, those in the neighborhood out some distance might suddenly become very aware of the breach. Anyway, some foolish things to ponder while standing in the electro-magnetic field admiring the dam so quickly and effectively put together. The visiting Stream Teamer reported no smell of gas.

At the new dam we can easily see what happened. The water behind it rose up a couple feet and backed to the gauge depth sensor a half mile upriver rendering derived flow rates invalid. Here in the Closet we don't fret. With late summer's and early fall's low depths the beavers may be programmed to worry about having enough water under the ice in the winter for passage to and from their lodges. In the fall there is a flurry of renewed dam building and maintenance. With the loss of green leaves that no longer pull water from the ground, the water table will rise and our streams and river will fill again and well override the river's many beaver dams. Maybe the beavers don't remember year to year. When the water is low, the dam builders go.

So here we have a dam of branches and mud gathered and formed by mammals a quarter our weight, without permits, affecting a high-tech measuring system in and on a tiny green building that looks like an old outhouse. The obvious differences are antennae and solar panels on the roof and measuring instruments and recorders within. Young readers, please ask old-timers from the country what outhouses are. A moment's digression here might be enlightening. Outhouses were simple toilets placed above shallow holes, septic systems of native wood and soil. A board seat with one or two holes, the smaller for kids, to support the buttocks of defecators and urinators was perched above a hole in the ground. Toilet papers were often pieces of old newspapers and magazines, sometimes read before use to pass the time. In some outhouses there may have been candles. There was usually enough moon and starlight coming through small holes, some in the form of new moons, cut in the upper rough board walls for light and ventilation. The composted wastes of some were mined every couple years and spread on gardens for fertilizer. When the earthen holes of others were filled they were simply moved to new locations nearby. These systems without the input of manufactured chemicals (soaps, cleansers, medicines, hormones, etc.) were light upon the land and groundwater. Our natural organic wastes are fairly quickly broken down in the soil to CO_2 and H_2O. When an outhouse was abandoned its boards also rotted and joined the enriched soil below. There was no corroding chrome-plated or copper plumbing to contaminate the soil. In a few decades the only sign there had been an outhouse might be a ring of lilacs, a favorite shrub for privacy and delightful spring odors, around where it had been. Trips to these usually crude buildings, also called privies and even more direct names, on early winter mornings while carrying a chamber pot of wastes collected through the night, must have been character-building experiences. Imagine blue buttocks exposed and hanging in stinky zero degree air. While harkening back to those bygone places some of us old-timers fondly remember, the cold and odors long forgotten, we wonder if higher tech doesn't sometimes cause problems to our environment and fellow creatures. Now we pour wastes, natural and artificial, some poisonous, of all kinds down our sink drains and toilets. Out of sight, out of mind, some might say. We might do well to think harder about "out of mind." Too many times our wastes have come back to haunt us and do direct harm to other organisms.

What does this all have to do with water, beaver dams and gauges? A great deal, if rational thinking considers them all together. High tech in the form of solar-powered instruments will help us learn what is happening in our water, air and soil. Will we use the knowledge wisely and proceed with caution where there is doubt, and boldness where there is not?

Beavers, despite much complaining by those humans who don't go out and marvel at their works, are holding water in stream and river basins longer, thus keeping groundwater levels higher. The beaver meadows formed by their inundations are rich diverse habitats. Let's install more clever light-powered sensors, not traps, in each to learn more.

HEADWATERS OF STREAMS AND RIVERS

Have you ever wondered where a river or stream begins? "What's so difficult?" some might say. "Just go against the flow until you can see no further movement." However, more often than such obvious exploring, we consult an atlas; one old Closeteer remembers as a boy looking for headwaters of the great rivers on maps by going up them only to become frustrated as the tributaries got smaller and the names ran out. It might be likened to climbing a spreading tree to its highest point while not being able to see the top during the ascent. The challenge becomes which branch to take. Near the summit the twigs are so small further climbing becomes impossible; so too with ever smaller tributary streams and streamlets grading into intermittently flowing swales scarcely seen.

In their shack along the Ipswich River, Closeteers, who sometimes entertain such idle thoughts, get out maps and follow, for example, Fish Brook from the river at Masco to Stiles Pond, Boxford. They know it doesn't end there but the only way to find out for sure would be tough hikes in dry late summers or very cold winters on not always trustworthy ice. Then of course the question arises, which obscure swale or icy path to take?

Last week the Middleton Council on Aging/Conservation Commission Friday morning walking group hiked around the lovely headwaters of Boston Brook, one of the Ipswich River's largest tributaries, in

Ward Reservation, North Andover. Looming above them yet out of sight due to mature forest were Boston and Holt Hills, the latter the highest point at 410 feet in Essex County. Runoff from these drumlins descends in now dry wooded swales to Rubbish Meadow and Mars Swamp, which just a decade ago were wetlands shaded by red maples before beavers raised their waters and drowned the trees. The names intrigued us. Did a traveler once ask a farmer working along Boston Brook in Middleton, "Is this brook's water flowing from Boston?" The farmer, smiling derisively and shaking his head, asks in return, "Can't you see it's flowing southeast toward Boston?" The stranger, not intimidated by the rude rustic, asks, "Why then the name Boston?" That causes the farmer to pause and scratch his head before replying, "They say you can see Boston easily from the top of Boston Hill where the brook comes from. So Boston Brook must have gotten its name from the hill. By the way, on old deeds and maps this brook is called Beechey Brook." He hopes there won't be more questions, so quickly adds, "Maybe there were once groves of beech trees along it." If you visit Henry and Mary Tragert's old place on Essex Street, Middleton, today, just to the southeast near the brook you'll find a fine stand of beeches.

The names that really got us going were Rubbish Meadow and Mars Swamp. We know early farmers often saw wetlands as wasteland to be drained or filled for cultivation, grazing or haying, which might explain the harsh "Rubbish" for swamp maple land not tamed. Maybe another colonial farmer teasing a passing stranger might have answered his, "Where is Boston Brook's water coming from?" with, "From Mars for all I know." Some North Andoverite amused upon hearing of the exchange may have then dubbed the swamp, the brook flows out of Mars. Fun perhaps, but most would say foolish speculation. Why not just ask the North Andover Historical Society? Alas, scholarly replies might disappoint.

The answer of course to the question beginning this meandering flow of nonsense is that the water comes from the sky as rain and snow falling over an area called the headwater's watershed. This wise yet obvious explanation gives us incentive to explore even higher streamlets to their sources. There are wonders to be found up each.

Many Friday morning walking group participants, Stream Teamers and Closeteers, while living just downstream, have only recently discovered Ward Reservation, 15 minutes away by car. We strongly recommend its 30 or so miles of well-kept trails and two high hills with views to you. If you'd like a challenge go to Rubbish Meadow (elevation about 230 feet) in the spring and follow Boston Brook as close as you can until you reach the Ipswich River (elevation about 40 feet). This will give you an Indian's and colonist's view of the land before straight rail lines, mid-1800s, and roads, mid-1900s, twisted viewpoints so that streams were no longer noticed. Streams were the lifeblood of our early predecessors. For our unfortunately not widely known or appreciated fellow creatures, they still are.

VITO'S LANDINGS

Men for four centuries here have built wooden structures, often on unsubstantial stone foundations along the Ipswich River. You'll not see any now we know of. Rot and floods have taken them away or broken them down. If you visit Rome along the Tiber River you'll see, we're told, stone access steps and foundations going back two millennia. In lucky Middleton, Rome came to us about a half century ago in the person of Vito Mortalo. Since 2002 he has built the town far more than just access steps to the river at Farnsworth Landing off South Main Street, at Peabody Street, and most recently at Maple Street. We of the Stream Team who asked him for help have slowly learned his methods. He visits the sites usually alone and unbeknown to us and makes a plan in his head. That was about five years ago in the case of the one at Maple Street. Then occasionally we'll see some signs of his activity around our preparatory clearing and cleanup at a site. He might have left some selected stones or removed a previous rotting old landing. At Stream Team meetings we wonder aloud how Vito is doing. One of us then may contact this busy man with a large family and many projects of his own. Always friendly, he will smile and may even visit the site with us and reveal pieces of his plan with no mention of time. We've learned from him to apply the wise old saying "Rome wasn't built in a day." After a while at Farnsworth, on Route 114, and Peabody Street the stone accesses just suddenly appeared and much pleased us. Unlike others who use steel and wood for such projects, Vito builds his landings of forever stones, beautifully arranged.

For the steps at Maple Street we learned he had been picking out large flat stones for years he happened upon in his work. One time a couple Stream Teamers saw them laid out waiting in his back yard. And then last year there they were, some weighing a ton, artistically placed where once rotting steps made of old railroad ties had been. Visit the landing there and descend on a half-dozen great native rocks to the river. One is seven feet across. To their sides are inviting higher stones to sit on after a canoe trip or when just passing the time, perhaps with a snack from Farmer Brown's across the river. It is pleasing to imagine generations hence sitting there letting the passing water sweep their troubles away.

Let's go with that flow of diluted washed-away worries two miles downriver. Upon rounding a great curve in the shade of silver maples off the Greenbelt's field just up from Peabody Street we are greeted with great stones stacked in a most attractive way, not steps at all, rather a sculpture to sit on. One Stream Teamer yearly visits there with his young grandson. The old man sits on one of the stones and watches as the boy 70 years younger wades below him in the gravel and sand shallows. Before Vito's gift there was an eroding bank of briars. Please visit the Peabody Street site, you'll find it as pleasing to the eye from above in the park as it is from an approaching canoe or kayak. A

Vito Mortalo's resting rocks, Peabody Street landing. Photo, courtesy of Stream Team.

couple years ago a Stream Teamer on passing one fine early morning saw a man sitting at the picnic table above the stones smoking. His motorcycle was parked nearby. The strangers chatted quietly for a bit. The cyclist said he stopped each day to clear his mind en route home from the graveyard shift at his workplace. He was obviously content and so was his new acquaintance upon hearing the simple story. Such places are needed round and about any town. Before Vito's steps the land along the river there had been a rubbish-strewn parking area with wheel rut puddles inside a moldering roadside safety barrier.

The other evening the Stream Team met, appropriately in the Historical Society museum, and agreed to name the Maple Street access park Vito's Landing. There were no dissenting voices, all were happy with the choice. The selectmen will be asked for their approval. We know that long after this generation of Stream Teamers and Vito have been forgotten the inviting stones will be there. Maybe some intrepid historian will learn that 400 years after the Indians and 200 after the colonists, a stone-loving man from distant Rome had placed stones not for his own castle or mill, but for people he didn't even know.

November 2010

An Awful Arrogance Resumed

On October 12, 2010, Secretary of the Interior Ken Salazar lifted the offshore drilling moratorium. The government of the United States of America under pressure from suicidal Gulf States and the oil industry allowed the resumption of drilling for oil in the ocean; this arrogance is being resumed in one of the world's richest wildlife habitats and sources of seafood. The Gulf States' political leaders, after understandably crying for help this past spring and summer while loose oil was gushing forth, have dried their tears and urged that this terrible gamble continue. Surprisingly even the fishermen are not complaining, at least not loudly at barricades. Madness. Big Oil is back in its greasy saddle assuring us that everything is alright and that accidents won't happen again. The dismaying thing is that our governments, media and people generally seem to be naïvely listening and passively going along.

Many of us think ocean drilling, although legal, is criminal and the height of irresponsibility. Others say calm down; we've got to have cheap oil to keep our addiction going, withdrawal would be too painful. That word addiction is President Bush's, former oilman, not ours. To his credit he told it like it was and is. Oil is one dangerous legal drug we allow to flow into our country with a vengeance. It supports our over-the-top standard of living, which includes tooling around, often alone and going nowhere, in heavy vehicles doing less than 25 miles per gallon. We environmentalists are also addicted after five generations of oil-powered vehicles and ever more convenient roads. Without alternatives, we know no other ways or at least ones we have the gumption to take. Some of us can vividly remember the guilt experienced while watching the popular 1973 movie *American Graffiti* in which boys and girls, from the 1950s on, nightly paraded in huge cars with finned fenders on the main streets of our towns looking for one another. Not surprisingly, our children and grandchildren probably drive and ride more than we did. Legs are for getting between computer/TV screens and cars.

Let's return to the long-suffering Gulf and Caribbean, parts of the Atlantic Ocean, Columbus and followers came to five centuries ago and killed directly or by enslaving those Indians who had survived their Old World diseases. In a few generations the once friendly natives of the islands and mainland coasts were pretty much gone. The newcomers had found land good for valuable sugar cane so they shipped in Africans to replace the lost natives in the fields. They quickly worked these new slaves to death and kept bringing in more. The natural vegetation was decimated. Erosion runoff swept topsoils into the sea. Once idyllic Haiti was the saddest victim. The situation was repeated with cotton in our southern states. That diabolical system was aided and abetted by northern textile mills along the Merrimack just up the street. We'll not dwell further on the history of this rich, much exploited corner of the world for which its European discoverer was celebrated last month. Columbus was bold and brutal as were his colleagues who expediently proclaimed Christianity. Many of us are glad the hemisphere wasn't named Columbia.

The pollution and exploitation there goes on. Down the great rivers come soils from the continent laced with contamination while on the Gulf's coastal shelves oil drilling resumes. There are reported to be 27,000 abandoned wells out there becoming reefs. We Stream Teamers are now trying to find out how many are actively pumping and the number planned. The industry had also done a number, even before this spring's disastrous leak, on the coastal marshes and mangroves. Pipes and roads to and from the water form a labyrinth of disturbances in once unspoiled habitats.

Life on our planet is worth far more than the ease and comfort of a few generations.

We need new systems of government and business that will not embrace the ideals of "rapid growth" and lifestyles in which "children are better off than their parents." The latter certainly can be an admirable goal if the lifestyle is of a less materialistic nature and allows for our fellow creatures. As to the former one might argue we have grown to the point of becoming highly toxic. It is high time, and we hope in time, to pull back, or change direction toward true green technologies.

Also in 1973, the year of *American Graffiti*, a much proclaimed economics book was published. In *Small Is Beautiful* respected economist E. F. Schumacher, friend of Keynes and Galbraith, urged a Buddhist style economics that takes the environment and lower-key local lifestyles into account. Perhaps he had anticipated the movie. In his reportedly widely-read-by-hippies book he gives specific examples of manufacturing done locally on smaller scales. We bet Barbara Kingsolver, author of *Animal, Vegetable, Miracle*, read Schumacher. Most hippies probably did not and only waved his book above their heads. We wonder where they have gone. They, like Schumacher, were overwhelmed by the gospel of growth and have disappeared with their regrets. They rightfully and noisily for a while pointed to our problems and then were themselves absorbed. As Kermit, of Muppets fame, sang, "It's not easy being green."

Fall Watercolors

Canoes and kayaks are gone from the river. They hibernate upside down in back yards, collecting fallen leaves on their bottoms. The rising river also collects leaves. Those of oaks now descend on breezes and join the soggy sinking leaves of maples that fell in October. Thanks to many beaver dams the flow is slow. The colorful dead flakes, green photosynthetic factories not long ago, drift slowly down, gathering against snags and curves. Two- and three-year-old pine needles that turned yellow and fell this fall join them. This year's needles still on their branches will ride out this winter and maybe next, green and functioning. Those fallen appear to stitch the gathering flotsam together into light rafts. Floating patches of parallel needles remind one of spring log rafts in Maine lakes as seen from surrounding hills before water transport of timber was banned in the early 1970s.

We wonder in passing how long the leaves will float before becoming waterlogged and sinking to the bottom among waiting animals. Tiny crustacea, insect larvae and worms will shred, chew, ingest, digest and defecate. As the water warms in spring bacteria and fungi will make short work of the remains of autumn's bounty that comes each year forever. If we fall through ice and are not found, a similar fate will release our substances for renewal.

Now many leaves float in great fading rafts. It is as if a Jackson Pollock masterpiece, which these accumulations remind us of, were left in the rain by some scared museum thief on the run. The colors fade as does memory of them. Only in this case we know the seemingly random painter will return again next year about this time. New masterpieces from airborne palettes and breeze brushes on water canvases will form. In the dry Southwest some Indian tribes make beautiful paintings using dry sands of a half-dozen colors. After the ceremony for which they are so reverently done, the artists sweep them away. An artist called Sidewalk Sam on the plaza around Faneuil Hall did somewhat the same with chalk. He created; rain and the soles of passersby erased. Then there was the famous Harvard naturalist Louis Agassiz who drew multicolored wonders with chalk on a portable blackboard of rolled cloth during spell-binding lectures. Now and then, while still talking, he'd whip forth a pocket rag and erase, causing his audience to gasp at the sudden loss.

There may also be mathematics involved here in what we think are nature's chance patterns. Benoit Mandelbrot, the genius who gave us fractal geometry, died last month. He used numbers to describe natural processes and structures such as plant growth and circulatory systems with branching, ever smaller, repeating patterns. We old-timers who had trouble with Euclidian geometry as sophomores haven't even tried to decipher his elegant equations, but by looking at illustrative photos and natural phenomena we know there may be something more than just randomness in what we see. While admiring collages of floating leaves, we wonder what the disciples of Mandelbrot might derive.

In six years of Water Closet essays beavers have often risen to the fore, some, not beaver fans, might say too often. Anyway, here they come again as unknowing leaf raft painters. A couple weeks ago behind one of their new dams across the Ipswich River and the south Middleton-west Peabody bound, we were impressed by a hundred-yard-long new leaf raft, which was there before last week's almost two inches of rain. South Middleton gauge's depth readings as daily checked on the United States Geological Survey website suddenly dropped just after the rain. We suspect the leaf painting was swept away along with the dam by a storm-produced crest. Perhaps it is best that all works of art be ephemeral to make way for the new. "How long?" you say, shocked. In return we ask, "On whose time scale?"

NOR'EASTERS BUTT QUODDY HEAD

Now and then one of the many photographs we receive through cyberspace stands out and is branded on the brain. The Closet got one this past week of Quoddy Head sticking out as easterly as the United States goes into the Bay of Fundy off the Gulf of Maine. On clear mornings the rising sun shines a country first on its high rocky spruce-fringed brow. During great counterclockwise swirling storms it receives hard rain and high waves. This gift photo is of the latter during a recent fall nor'easter. Filling the right side of a cove is high granite ledge with a few feisty clinging spruces. Dominating the left and foreground are the silhouettes of larger spruce. Between these dark frames, filling the center out to sea is a white mix of air and water. The swells after long trips over vast reaches are lifted by the bottom to break and churn. In the distance are gray sea and sky. These dramatic contrasts of black, white, black and gray remind us of the power where continents meet the oceans and vice versa. The rock stands firm; the ocean keeps coming in wild visits. The tough spruces literally hang on for a while. We visit at times of calm and turmoil to ooo and aah as folks do in the glow of fireworks. Some, like Winslow Homer and thousands of other seascape painters, show their awe in pigment on canvas. They share with us as naturalist Fred Gralenski has done with his Quoddy Head photo.

Inherent in such striking images are the excitement and fear, perhaps lingering from sailing days, they arouse. We coastal Yankees are brought up with stories of disasters on our lee shores. Maps showing shipwrecks from Labrador down the coast to Hatteras and on southward are sprinkled with the symbols of thousands. These do not include boats. If they did, each a line with shorter lines across like keel and ribs, would merge and blacken out the continental shelf. Walks along our beaches in the winter, after the sand that is returned each summer has been washed back out, reveal the ribs of 18th- and 19th-century brigs and schooners. There are several skeletal remains visible some years protruding from Salisbury and Plum Island beaches.

We humans fret about the inconveniences to us from these great storms that smash ships and erode beaches, toppling houses. For the natural life in these dynamic places where sea and land go head to head there are great influxes of oxygen when water and air mix. Many seabirds, such as Bufflehead and Oldsquaw ducks, to mention but a couple, seem to delight in surf almost as rough as that seen in Fred's photo. We'd like to know the dynamics during storms in the less turbulent waters beneath. Certainly invertebrates such as crabs, barnacles, mussels, snails, sea stars, anemones and urchins thrive in battered tidal pools and stirred bottoms. Tide and storm surges flush

Nor'easter off Quoddy Head, Maine. Photo, courtesy of Fred Gralenski.

clean the rocky edges, beaches, estuarine marshes and flats and bring in plankton as well as essential dissolved oxygen. Warm water, with heat accumulated throughout hot days, is replaced. And if we think in the long term about evolution, those animals listed and seaweeds that don't have what it takes to hold on in such a wild habitat are culled. Their populations' less adaptable DNA is reduced. These edges of land are also great nurseries and food sources for life extending out hundreds of miles to sea.

Here in Massachusetts and other coastal states wise heads have recognized the importance of protected edges. The Massachusetts Wetlands Protection Act has restrictions even on uplands within 100 feet from almost all water bodies and swamps and 200 feet from perennial flowing streams and rivers. Naturalists and environmentalists would have these buffers many times wider. These compromised widths came from hard-fought negotiations. We are reminded of the sea butting its soft heads on the rocky heads of commerce. In the last three centuries, during the industrial revolution, people and their activities called business seem to have had the upper hand. Some animal populations in and on the edges, from estuaries across continental shelves, are declining at alarming rates. If again, we look long ahead, we can envision the oceans rising with ever more miles of land contact after we are gone. We bet, never to collect, the scenes caught so well by Gralenski and Homer will millennia hence be similar, but without *Homo sapiens* to record. We will have had our turn. Let us hope we don't leave too many more innocent species without theirs during our tenure. Let's take a look at that Quoddy Head scene again. In a way it comforts. Regardless of what we do the waves will keep on coming; with them are possibilities of renewal on a time scale we don't understand.

Muskrats Along the River

In mid-November as a brisk west wind cleared air and minds a small group of Stream Teamers and friend got underway in kayaks and canoe from Farnsworth Landing where the Ipswich River passes under State Highway 114, South Main Street to us Middletonites. The road was busy; the river was not. For the next three hours we passed no other vessels except those resting upside down on banks for the winter, some partly under leaves. Almost all deciduous leaves have left their trees and bushes. Evergreens in the floodplain are few and far between.

The lush verdant corridor we experienced during an August paddle in lower water is gone. How lucky to live at a latitude that gives us four worlds each year with gradations between.

This section of the river is very familiar to us. We have paddled its length several times a year for decades. Soon ice will prevent us. We must walk along its banks to get a feel for it in winter. We'd walk on its ice but the flow makes the ice unsafe even when apparently frozen hard bank to bank.

Fifteen minutes downriver brought us to Logbridge Road, the ancient cart path between colonial Salem and Andover on the Merrimack, which since the early 1970s has been without a bridge crossing the Ipswich. The old abutments of large stones are still there. Under the sponsorship of the Stream Team, aspiring Eagle Scout Xavier Chambers, with the help of volunteers, made a welcoming park above the abutment on the Middleton side.

We passed between these venerable stones and entered an ash-red maple forest killed by beavers, who, a half mile further downriver, have had for almost a decade a substantial dam that drowned the trees. The inundated river here is wide. The stark branchless trunks of deceased trees produce little shade. The whole area has become a "beaver meadow" now dominated by lush lower herbaceous plants that muskrats like. On rounding the next great meander we passed a newly built muskrat lodge and soon another and another; about six were spotted spaced out not far from the channel in just a quarter mile. We'd never seen them there before. Unfortunately we paddlers that day did not include our muskrat expert. Stalwart Stream Teamer and outdoorsman extraordinaire Frank Masse, muskrat trapper as a boy, was up country hunting deer. We had to go to a couple of our favorite mammal books upon returning home. As on most of our trips, despite their being common near water, we saw neither hide nor hair of them. On such trips we happily call to one another pointing things out. We no doubt spooked many more animals than we saw. One old-timer plans to return alone in early morning or evening before the ice. He says this every year, yet somehow never gets around to it. The floodplain is an active place in winter despite the bitter winds and ice. When we older Stream Teamers were lads we knew it as a place for trappers, hunters and ice fishermen. Now we can walk alongside its length December through March and see nary a soul. The denizens may think this is just fine or perhaps they have forgotten or never heard grandparents' tales of steel leghold traps, bullets and bait minnows on lines. "Young Perchy if you see a tasty fish squirming in place, look to see if it is attached to a line from above. If 'tis, don't touch! I got pulled up once and shook myself free just before reaching the deadly air. See this scar." Then there was ancient Uncle Musky who was missing a front leg. He liked to show youngsters the scar where he'd bravely chewed his leg off before the trapper made his rounds. And we won't say much about old Malcolm Mallard who claimed to be carrying lead pellets in both legs.

Enough anthropomorphic nonsense, back to the books. They tell us that muskrats born in spring leave their parents' lodges, usually through tunnels in the banks, to build floodplain lodges of their own in late summer and fall. Those we admired looked fresh. Several had still-green cattail leaves entwined with mud and other debris as sheathing. They were all built on homemade mud islands, bars, or upturned tree root masses. We didn't cruelly dissect the three- to four-foot-diameter, two- to three-feet-high mounds, to see their passageways and apartments. One reference said each has a chamber about one foot in diameter lined with shredded plant parts. Muskrats, like beavers, often very close neighbors, don't hibernate. Some are known to burrow tunnels in the walls of much larger beaver lodges while the owners are within.

We don't see women wearing muskrat coats any longer as some did when Frank and fellow trappers got a dollar or so a pelt. A dollar then was like 10 or 20 now. By way of comparison, in the '40s, we boys could earn two dollars setting up candlepins for a two-hour bowling match. We earned less working all day on the farm. Automatic pin setters put thousands of us out of that lucrative work done while breathing lots of secondhand smoke. Changes in fashion and sensitivities did in the fur industry. We are glad the trapping of fellow mammals has been greatly curtailed. Beavers, otters, muskrats and mink are welcome sights along our streams and rivers. Soon we'll see their signs in the snow. May they and we live to see another spring.

December 2010

Embracing Everything and an Ocean

Many years ago an old Closeteer came upon a quote attributed to Blaise Pascal, 17th-century French mathematician, physicist and philosopher. He hasn't been able to find it again but remembers its essence. "The mind of man is but a speck in space, yet with it he can contemplate the universe." We might add the verb "study" to contemplate; Pascal certainly studied. His quote was recalled in the Closet upon reading two books recently loaned us, Bill Bryson's *A Short History of Nearly Everything* and Simon Winchester's *Atlantic*, the latter just off the press. Two mere mortals, experienced and popular writers both, take on broad subjects that are a million subjects. Bryson researched the history of science and tries to explain the great advances in contemplating and studying the universe and the particles and energy that make it up. You can readily see he has bitten off more than he or anyone can chew and regurgitate. Valiantly, he does very well and thanks to his fascination with the eccentricities of many of our pioneer scientists makes partially digested knowledge more than palatable. Bryson, an eccentric of sorts himself, is a funny man deeply interested in all things. Chuckles often bubble forth upon encountering some novel turn of phrase. His chapter, one of thirty, entitled "The Bounding Main" is about water from molecules to oceans.

Winchester, author of a score of books, immersed himself in our whole ocean and remarkably didn't drown. In half a thousand pages he attempts to describe the things on and under 32 million square miles of water and beyond to its continental divides. What hubris Bryson and Winchester have in tackling these enormous swaths of matter, space and time. They are bold enough to take Pascal at his word. Not only are they ambitious, as good writers they are also good leaders, urging us to follow and to learn. Winchester looks beyond the Ipswich River's waters flowing to the Atlantic and does his damnedest to appreciate the whole ocean over time. He starts with a geological overview of its formation starting about 150 million years ago and carries us on into the human history of exploration in three dimensions, especially the activity on its surface and edges. For only one immodest volume, he could include but little from mountains of information. He chooses fairly well and certainly gets an A for effort. If we have a criticism, it is that his enthusiasm too often results in hyperbole.

Bryson writes in his introduction to "The Bounding Main" chapter, "We love to be near water," an underlying theme of our Water Closet column over the years. He and Winchester do far more than just dip their toes in. They wade, sometimes deeply, into fathoms of material and write of what they learn and bid us share. We do so comfortably by the Closet stove while envying them the travel done in their extensive researches. It is obvious that their explorations in literature, in museums, and on trips to historical sites have been labors of love. Neither are worried about political correctness; both are not hesitant to challenge myths, too often carried forth by textbooks. Bryson often gives credit to minor scientists whose work was co-opted by those better known. In his searches he goes deep.

How fortunate we are to have such intrepid intermediaries interested in the large subjects of cosmology, astronomy, geology, evolution, history and oceanography. We learn from these books that despite two centuries of underwater research only a tiny fraction of one percent of the oceans' vast volumes has been explored. More is known, but alas is classified by the navies of the world. They are the only organizations with enough money to go way down for extended periods. We know from the few deep visits made by civilians that there is much life in the lowest depths. A flounder type fish was spooked by a bathysphere seven miles down in the Marianas Trench. Blue whales, the largest animals ever on the planet, are still a great mystery. Scientists don't know where most are or where they breed. We are more aware of the surface topography of Mars and the moon than we are of the submerged three-fourths of earth. Bryson gives an example of what we humans do when ignorant. From 1946 until 1990 the United States yearly dumped thousands of 55-gallon drums of radioactive wastes into the oceans. Other industrialized "civilized" countries did the same. What have and will be the effects? We don't know.

Vastly more of our treasure is being bled in surface wars than in basic research. Our expensive war subs cruise the dark depths, their logs sealed. Pascal shared his knowledge of our Earth with its finite lawyer of water. Such writers as Bryson and Winchester pass on his baton.

THE UPS AND DOWNS OF ICE, LAND AND SEA

We in the Ipswich River watershed live near the edge of land. A brisk three-hour walk from the center will have us at the quay in Salem Harbor. Fifteen millennia ago, a short time to geologists, we'd have had to walk on the half-mile-thick ice of the Wisconsin continental glacier to reach the ocean. Such a hike from the same latitude and longitude, if at all possible skirting crevasses, would have involved several hard days to reach seawater. The edge of the sunken ocean was roughly out where Georges Bank is now. Much of the world's water was locked up in ice; ocean levels dropped several hundred feet. The earth's crust sunk under the great weight of tens of thousands of years of accumulated snows. Two hundred feet down, ice under pressure turns plastic and flows slowly outward from mountains. In the Wisconsin's case its area and depth grew for an estimated 50,000 years. A series of other continental glaciers had preceded it.

Almost 15,000 years ago the ice began to melt in summers faster than it accumulated from precipitation in winters. The cause was probably due to a minor change in mean world temperature. A "tipping point" temperature, an ever more common phrase among climatologists, had been reached. The vast lobes of ice terminating at Georges Bank, Cape Cod, Martha's Vineyard, Nantucket and Long Island melted away and by 13,000 years ago the ice front had receded to our area. Glacial ice doesn't flow back whence it came. Its front and top melt away. As the weight of the ice diminished the land rebounded upward while the oceans, retrieving long locked-in-as-ice melt water, rose. Over time, the water rose faster so the coast moved west and north. Early on, land extended out to banks where the edge of the continental shelf is now. Mastodon and mammoth bones are occasionally brought up by fishermen in their trawler nets. What is now Jeffreys Ledge was well above water. There is evidence that when the land here was tundra, for a period after the ice had retreated, the Indians were there hunting caribou.

The land is still rebounding slowly. The ocean rises slightly faster. It is estimated that over the past 3,000 to 4,000 years, the differential has been four to eight inches per 100 years. Sediment carried down by rivers and creeks has filled in the bays behind the offshore bars fast enough to keep up and support vegetated salt marshes. Our beloved "low green prairies of the sea," so called by John Greenleaf Whittier in his famous poem *Snow Bound*, are only 3,000 or so years old. The other day several of us were admiring a watercolor of the Plum Island marsh by the 19th-century Newburyport painter Frank Thurlo. It shows dozens of large salt hay stacks awaiting shallow draft gundalows, one is shown, to collect them on flood tides. It is during those monthly highs that sediment is caught by salt marsh plants and becomes part of the thickening marsh. The dance between water and marsh rise rates over time is tricky. If sea level rise is too fast, sedimentation can't keep up and the plants are drowned. With stabilizing plants gone, much marsh peat erodes away on ebb tides. If water rise is too slow or less than rebound, the soft marsh, not constantly repaired and built up, erodes away. Now with accelerating ocean rise— estimates range from 20 to 80 inches this century— the salt marshes will go under and be no more. The protective barrier islands are already being relentlessly battered and carried away in places each winter. We've all watched and read about the drama being played out at Plum Island. Way down the coast the Outer Banks are in jeopardy. We heard a report last week that Charlestown, South Carolina's city street drainage system backs up at high tides. Low Miami worries many who study climate change. They wish city and state officials would worry with them. Norfolk, Virginia, does have plans and is now razing buildings that are being threatened.

In a few generations folks here may have shorter walks to the coasts. They will be able to go to what is now Danversport or downtown Peabody and sit on the levees. The sea is coming to us. It has been doing so slowly for millennia; now it is coming faster.

The global climate change deniers won't worry, since they already have their heads in the soon-to-be-wet sand. Some are still buying waterfront property.

Natural Ice Has Returned

Ice is back on our ponds, lakes and slower streams, certainly not surprising this time of year. Yet freezing is a phenomenon that never ceases to amaze many of us. Last week we went forth one cold morning and found the surfaces of ponds glazed with black ice. Closer examination of the transparent glass-like ice found no black at all; light enters the pond and is absorbed by the water and dark bottom with a result we call black. Before freezing, breezy caresses made ripples on the surface, the morning after none. Mother Nature's glazier had changed the surface liquid to a solid by cooling, simply taking away some heat. (The verb "to glaze" and the noun "glazier" used to be common. You old-timers who had to fix windows you broke as children please define these words for the young.) The water molecules slowed until they could no longer overcome their attractions to each other. At zero degrees Celsius, 32 Fahrenheit, they bonded to become the crystalline solid we call ice. The water body, whose surface was so quickly frozen, became a different place, one wave-proof and separated from the atmosphere. Smooth surfaces of ice are irresistible to young humans, and childish older folks, who venture forth upon them. Some might say in imitation of Christ on the Sea of Galilee; we suspect the exciting, sometimes fatal urge goes back much, much further. Anyway, such strange thoughts came to mind while testing Prichards Pond's edge to see if the ice thickness had reached the requisite two to three inches that allows somewhat safe passage. Many learn early on that you can't trust that the thicknesses will be uniform. One Closeteer, in almost eight decades, has foolishly gone through a half-dozen times. Not many years ago his soul almost departed this marvelous water world of summer liquids and wondrous winter solids as he struggled, chest deep in ice water, until he was able to reach a savior sapling and climb it to safety.

Ice thoughts continued as we discussed the recent cold snap that gave us such gifts, though some rather inconvenient. Our clamming leader and friends had just returned from the Ipswich flats and reported that there was frost in the top couple inches of mud despite twice daily immersions in liquid seawater. We were surprised; usually the flats don't freeze until January and then not often deep enough to impede digging.

Another old-timer went on about the bygone days when every puddle and pond was a natural rink. Even running brooks presented opportunities. Middleton Brook just down from the town center was dammed in winter at the Mount Vernon Street culvert to form "King Street Pond" in "Sheldon's Meadow," both bygone names. The result was a nice acre or more of good ice. In farm fields there are often puddles, shallow safe places for little kids, even toddlers, which freeze down to the ground. We remember happy nippers flopping around on double runners or running and then sliding on shoe soles or sleds. On the banks of certain larger, more popular ponds, smoldering fires burned all day Saturday and Sunday on into the evenings. One old Closeteer has bored us with his skating yarns as a boy in Salisbury many times. Young people would walk a mile or more to Great Brook, no brook at all, just a low couple acres on the edge of farm fields. Hockey matches started right after school and continued on until the black puck blended with the dark. Girls and smaller kids skated safely outside the imagined and agreed upon rinks without lines and boards, only pairs of boots, one at each end, serving as goals. In front of each an unprotected goalie, usually not the best skater, would stand and await his fate. Would he be hero or goat after the next attack? Sometimes the goalies wore baseball catchers' shin guards. Someone recalled goalies with football helmets. Older boys, some much admired hockey players, would, prior a cold night, cut holes with axes and flood the ice with water. The next morning the rink had a smooth new surface. We didn't have Zambonis or indoor rinks then. Most of us had never seen or even heard of them.

In the evening after supper, especially on Friday nights and weekends, we'd return to find someone had perked the fire up and added new logs. There would be no hockey; we had only moon, stars and a fire for illumination. The cold crisp darkness brought on other possibilities for excitement. We'd race around until our eyes became adapted to the dim light. We'd lose it on each visit back to the fire. We hoped others would come and when older that they were of the opposite gender. Gender and sex were not words used easily then. If lucky we'd find a girl who would skate back and forth with us. The route took us by the fire and back into darkness at the ends of the long pond. If the skating in tandem went well, talk would become less awkward, or sometimes there was no talk at all, just gentle squeezes between warm hands. If all went even better we'd dare a kiss at the dark ends among overhanging clumps of alders. Some of those tentative first kisses lingered days after in our minds. We are reminded of Robert Frost's famous poem "Fire and Ice." It was ice that brought us together. We didn't yet understand the fire. If we weren't lucky enough to meet someone or hadn't arranged a rendezvous we'd skate recklessly in the dark until tired and then sit around the fire jealously teasing those who had, or maybe plan for hockey matches the next day when pickup teams from Seabrook or Amesbury might hitchhike the three miles to our pond or us to theirs.

We old-timers don't at all envy modern kids on tightly scheduled indoor rinks, transported to them by parents. Our remembered natural rinks were of a hundred shapes and sizes. We walked, bicycled or depended upon friendly motorists to get to them. Sometimes older boys, some acting as ad hoc coaches, would give us rides in borrowed family cars.

How we do go on! The aches and cold of too tight skates, the bruises from flailing hockey sticks, the pant legs frozen like stovepipes after immersions, and the rejections from admired would-be skating partners are forgotten or no long bother us. Memories of the good times are as strong as ever. We harken back and tell of them, as old guys do, over and over or each year in a Water Closet essay. Be kind, forgive. We promise not to next winter at ice time.

BEAVERS AGAIN

We humans spend our time on and along a web of asphalt roads. Another mammal population lives in and along our swamps, brooks and rivers. Most humans rarely see beavers although they have become common here in the last 15 years. So here we have two populations within the same area on what town officials might call overlay zoning districts. Humans not long ago clearly had the upper hand in all things. They could even trap and kill members of the minority population, one that preceded ours by hundreds of thousands of years. Now we wisely protect them. Despite this new status our two populations don't freely intermingle. Some beavers flee to our upland asphalt grid at flood times and then return to their lowlands when the water subsides. Often on off-road hikes we visit their wetlands that are expanding due to their dams.

We, Closeteers, Stream Teamers and other outdoor folks, never tire of the beaver works we find. There are 40 dams we know of in Middleton alone and at least that many lodges. These might seem but few compared with our 2,000 or so houses, yet beavers have dramatically changed 500 to 1,000 of the town's approximately 10,000 acres. We don't know how many beavers there are in Middleton; let's multiply an estimated 50 lodges by six for a total of 300. The ratio of humans to beavers here is then 10,000 to 300 while the land affected by this small minority may be 10 percent of the town's area or 33 acres per beaver. Of the remaining 9,000 acres in town potentially available to people, the ratio is 9,000 acres to 10,000 or 0.9 acres per human. These ratios might be roughly repeated throughout the tri-town area.

Isn't it strange to have an active population of fairly large mammals in our midst so little known? Some of us who look for them see fewer than three or four a year not counting road kills after floods. However, evidences of their works are common, some even vast and spectacular such as dead red maple swamps of over half a hundred acres. One impoundment we often visit is that around Pond Meadow Pond in the wilds near where North Andover, Boxford and Middleton join. The bleached corpses of still standing red maples, Atlantic white cedars and perimeter upland oaks and white pines stretch a mile east and west and southwest to northeast from North Liberty Street almost to Middleton Road in Boxford. These roughly 300 contiguous acres are inundated by only three dams that were built by animals a third our size without axes, chainsaws or dozers. The quiet tools of each are two incisors, strong jaws, forelegs and paws, persistence and engineering skills evolved over time beyond our ken. One dam we marvel at is 200 feet long with a four-foot head; head is the vertical distance between the water level above the dam to that just downstream below. Another lower dam of softer plants and mud stretches from Middleton to Topsfield 400 feet across the Nichols Brook floodplain. In the nine miles of Boston Brook from Boston Hill, North Andover, to the Ipswich River there are 10 dams. Above the river in Emerson Brook and its tributaries there are seven. Nichols Brook has five from Danvers to the river. In the Ipswich River from North Reading to Topsfield there were nine at last count this fall. These tallies do not include lesser dams across small tributary streams. Cudhea's Crick, tributary of Boston Brook, has four in less than a quarter mile.

Last Friday morning on our Council on Aging/Conservation Commission weekly hike we found new beaver work on a significant scale. In the upland woods above the Pond Meadow Pond impoundment are scores of arm-diameter saplings, many white oaks, recently cut neatly about two feet above the frozen ground. There were no signs of the 20 or so foot-long trunks or their branches, which must have been dragged into the water before ice sealed it off. Were they adding to their underwater larders? We know they gather lots of branches in the fall and stick them into the bottom for under ice winter food. We again marveled at the toughness of their incisors and jaws; the fourth-inch-wide marks of the former are clearly seen on pointed stumps and on stripped logs where the underside of the bark had been eaten. Ship builders of old, for whom white oak was a preferred wood because of its decay resistance, strength and weight, complained it more quickly dulled hand tools. An old Closeteer once found a quarter-acre stand of white oak felled by beavers; the average trunk diameter was a foot, one in the group close to two. Imagine taking those down with your two front teeth.

However, what struck our fancy more than all the freshly cut sapling stumps were two busts, perhaps of beaver heroes, done in white ash by beaver sculptors. They may have been works in progress; we saw no eyes, nostrils or mouth. Or perhaps the artists have evolved beyond realism to an impressionistic stage. We paused for some time to admire each of two found. Tree trunks about 10 inches in diameter had been gnawed round about a foot off the ground to form a neck. Sometime later another encirclement was made about beaver-head high above the first. The second went all the way through and felled the tree. One tree trunk got hung up and still rests tipped upon the head. What was left on each stump is what we imagined as a head with a samurai-like top knot. If the unseen sculptors overheard us they are probably still chuckling at our interpretation of their Russian-church-like steeples.

You can see again, if you've read our Water Closet essays on beavers over the years, that many more questions are raised than answered. The list grows longer and ever more interesting. Go see for yourselves their flooded meadows, lodges, dams, paths, tunnels, canals, girdled trees, underwater caches, scent mounds, and sculptures. One of Friday's walkers spoke of setting up an observation blind for a camera near their outdoor studio. That's a proper way to study them. Perhaps during a break they, using pantomime, might explain their works.

LONG, LARGE VIEWS

Three big thinkers about our world crossed the Closet's threshold in the last months of 2010. If we can imagine a crude yet snug shack that relocates almost monthly along the Ipswich River we can certainly imagine visits by noted authors. They didn't of course come in person but their mind-expanding books did, which may be even better. How could we ordinary folks comfortably converse with brilliant researchers and writers? We read their important tomes at our leisure and then discuss what we have learned. One Closeteer was so impressed by *Smithsonian Ocean* recommended to us by Kerry Mackin, director of the Ipswich River Watershed Association, that he bought three copies of Gloucester resident Deborah Cramer and Smithsonian team's handsome book for his sons and daughter and their families. He is still happily reading a copy borrowed from the library.

Another work that looks large at the universe, especially the world over time, is Bill Bryson's *The History of Nearly Everything*, a beautifully and profusely illustrated volume loaned us by David Shaw, a friend of the Middleton Stream Team. Dave generously told us to take our time with this gift from his son. When studying the history of everything you certainly must take your time because there is so much that even while delightfully written requires considerable thought. Bryson has thought deeply and urges us to do the same. This successful author of a dozen popular books looked long and deep before giving the world this gift. Bryson is very smart; who else could seriously delve into cosmology, geology and evolution and then brilliantly translate for mere mortals? He is also very funny, especially when telling of great characters like Newton and Darwin, to mention just two of scores he includes who discovered basic truths. Bryson writes smoothly with low-key humor. Gems unearthed cause quiet chuckling throughout. His eccentric, competitive scientists certainly help in this regard. While we've read of them before, he with new-found facts about their lives surprises. For instance, did you know that Newton was an ardent alchemist as well as "given over to a wayward religious sect called Arianism"? Bryson's book is full of such interesting asides. What has this got to do with water, the Closet's subject and obsession? A great deal as you will find if read. Ours is a water world and Bryson dives in deeply.

And while speaking of diving, and flying over and sailing on, we recommend Simon Winchester's recent favorably reviewed book *Atlantic*, which attempts to tell our ocean's stories interwoven with related ones from the continents around it. Prolific author Winchester has obviously spent much of his life thinking about this impossibly large subject. In his final well-researched chapters he worries about the effects of intense exploitation, of massive pollution and of the melting of ice on his vast subject. These contentious subjects are well handled in a balanced way with up to date information.

On a more positive note let's return to Cramer's lovely and what looks like a showy coffee table book, before pages are opened, marvelous photographs admired, and fine prose read. How we wish Stream Team and Closet hero Rachel Carson had lived to learn what Cramer has about findings by Alvin and crews along the deep water trenches described in the first part of her book. It is the best overview we've read of these strange Edens. We bet Cramer and Carson, both lovers of the sea, would have been bosom buddies had the latter been with us longer. Cramer wisely begins her book with Carson's words.

> *To stand on the edge of the sea, to sense the ebb and flow of the tides,*
> *to feel the breath of mist moving over a great salt marsh,*
> *to watch the flight of birds that swept up and down the surf lines of the*
> *continents for untold thousands of years, to see the running of the eels and*
> *young shad to the sea, is to have knowledge of things that are as nearly*
> *eternal as any earthly life can be.*

The prose that follows does not let these introductory lines down.

Bryson too can be eloquent about the sea as seen in his Section Five, "Life Itself," chapters 16 through 26. He speaks to the thoughtful layman with fewer undefined scientific terms and names then does Cramer and less hyperbole than Winchester. He thinks it important we all understand and does his best to explain clearly.

The rare people who tackle huge subjects in an effort to have us understand are far more than just good authors and literary entertainers. They are teachers in the finest sense, in classrooms without walls. Their students are all who will turn a page and enter their voluntary schools. Good teacher-writers such as Bryson, Cramer and Winchester make school enjoyable; readers are not thinking about vacations, credits or grades. And it requires considerable courage to approach such vast subjects. What is to be included? What is to be left out? Winchester in researching the Atlantic must have left out 99 percent of all he had learned. This persistence so admired is of years of study on subjects that never end. Such generous people want to share what they have learned in a way we'll understand. We recommend *The History of Nearly Everything* (Special Illustrated Edition), *Smithsonian Ocean*, and *Atlantic* to you. Take your time, enjoy. We in the Closet are still slowly finishing two of the three.

2011

JANUARY 2011

LEST WE FORGET

Who remembers Ixtoc I? Certainly we remember Deepwater Horizon and *Exxon Valdez* even while memories of those accidents too quickly fade. In all three oil was released into the sea in massive amounts; Deepwater Horizon leaked 18 times more crude into the Gulf of Mexico than did *Exxon Valdez* into Prince William Sound. In 1979 Ixtoc I, a well off the state of Compeche, Mexico, lost roughly three-fourths of BP's record 200 million gallons. Some estimates are that 75 percent of BP's oil is still out there in forms and whereabouts not fully known.

We were reminded of these environmental disasters this past week on hearing from Pamela Beaubien, longtime friend of the Water Closet who is excited about an upcoming ecotourism trip to Costa Rica. We old Closeteers about Pamela's age are excited for her. Can you believe that this grandmother who has been to Pakistan and most of South Asia is as worried as a schoolgirl about whom her as yet unknown roommate will be? Her Road Scholar tour group and many others go to beautiful Costa Rica because much of the country's area is wildlife preserve. There is no standing army. Upon hearing about her planned

River otters playing above and below thin ice, Willowdale State Park, Ipswich, MA., courtesy of Winston Ajce.

trip we got out the Closet atlas as we argued about whether Costa Rica is on the Gulf of Mexico or the Caribbean Sea. Fourth-grade geography was over six decades ago. We thought it ironic that Costa Rica, Mecca for environmentalists and naturalists around the world, might be on a body of water where two of mankind's most careless accidents had occurred. The evening after Pamela's email we watched Ray Suarez of PBS *NewsHour* interview Dr. Jane Lubchenco, director of the National Oceanic and Atmospheric Administration, about Deepwater Horizon, the story of the year.

Before we continue, let's review the geography of the area. Costa Rica isn't on the Gulf of Mexico. Its eastern shore abuts the Caribbean Sea; on the west coast, over high mountains, twice that length is washed by the Pacific. Is the Gulf part of the Caribbean Sea? The Mexican name has both connecting bodies of water in "Mar Caribe." Suarez asked Lubchenco if the oil still lingering in the Gulf would eventually get flushed out into the Atlantic. She said there is a loop current coming in and going out so there is some exchange. Back to the atlas we went to look for current arrows on the maps. Sweeping west across the Atlantic from Africa come the warm surface waters of the North Equatorial Currents, which flow between the many islands of the Lesser Antilles on into the Caribbean Sea. The broad current continues west under Puerto Rico, Dominican Republic-Haiti, Jamaica and then Cuba, the longest of the Greater Antilles. The Antilles swing north then westward in a 1,600 mile arc from Trinidad just off South America to the tip of Cuba which points toward the Yucatan Peninsula. Upon passing northward between the Yucatan and Cuba the current enters the Gulf of Mexico. It then turns easterly north of Cuba and south of Florida on to the Bahamas where it merges with the Gulf Stream, which flows on north to us warming and bringing weather.

How long will any residual oil remain in the Gulf? Lubchenco didn't know but guesses "years or decades." One big concern is the oil on the bottom of the Gulf around the capped well and beyond. One estimate has a "kill zone" there of 80 square miles of bottom thickly covered with oil, about a third the area of Essex County. In late November 4,200 square miles of the Gulf were closed to shrimping because of tar balls found in nets and on the surface. Some of this information is from a December draft of Wikipedia on the subject. All these estimates are very approximate. It will be years, if ever, before all the areas affected and the long-term effects are known.

We have an idealistic scheme for civilian Pamela and North and South American and UN officials visiting Costa Rica. Cultivate contacts and then urge Costa Rica to serve as environmental consultant and perhaps even cop for the Caribbean and its western extension the Gulf of Mexico. The deal might be: we warriors will protect you from foreign bother if you with our monetary help act as park ranger to the Caribbean's ecosystems. Think of what might be done with such aid to governments in the West Indies in amounts spent each week in Afghanistan and Iraq. With that money the islands with Costa Rican and Cuban help could protect the environment while promoting ecotourism. Transport for tourists would be by sail and solar-powered vessels. A Euro type confederation might be formed called the United Islands of the West Indies (UIWI). Coral reefs, turtles, bird migration flyways and fisheries would be protected by UIWI swat teams in fast catamarans, their base in Port-au-Prince, Haiti. The western world brutally exploited the Caribbean, Haiti perhaps the most, for five centuries. Now it is time for reparations that benefit all from booming Brazil and Venezuela in the south to our Gulf States in the north. We would all help the islands for our mutual benefit. Crazy dreams you might say, but how else are we to solve global environmental problems without bold moves? Rio, Kyoto and Copenhagen gatherings haven't worked. We have past examples of great accomplishments. Look what Mandela peacefully did for South Africa, Gandhi for India, Roosevelt with war on two fronts, and Truman and Acheson with the Marshall Plan after WWII. Oscar Arias, President of Costa Rica from 1986 to 1990 and 2006 to 2010, won the Nobel Prize in 1987 for successfully negotiating peace among neighboring countries. Humans are capable of doing big and wondrous things. It takes inspired leadership and responsible people.

We old-timers can remember the hope felt by much of the world back in 1945 when the United Nations was formed. It is high time for another idealistic move outside the bag of traditional "self interest," the mantra of state departments and foreign ministries around the world. We have long known that the interests of all are intertwined, especially in the case of environmental problems that should have no national bounds. Let's look at these arcs of islands and seas ringed by continents not as arbitrary political entities but rather as migration flyways, nursery beaches for turtles, continental shelves, deep ocean trenches, tidal flats, mangrove swamps, marshes, enriching currents, fisheries, land areas providing nourishing runoff, rookeries, coral keys and reefs, paths of hurricanes, sources of our weather; the list is endless. All these things are ours collectively; in the long run our lives depend on them. For half a millennium we've taken from them mindlessly; now we need to come together and nurture, to give back. Far out you say, we answer, yea. We want healthy birds, coral, fish, and the thousands of other organisms including us that need clean water. Let's have an annual "Remember Ixtoc and Deepwater Horizon Day" until the dangerous oil wells are gone and cruise behemoths are replaced by smaller ships under sail and solar. And while we are at it let's ground polluting planes and leave the skies over the migration flyways to birds.

Your travel plans Pamela will be alright, this won't start for awhile. You and other Road Scholars must return and lobby for a UIWI.

CRANE BEACH

On a recent late afternoon air off the Canadian Shield flowed easterly between Castle Hill and Little Neck, sentinel drumlins guarding the mouth of the Ipswich River. A lone Stream Teamer walking on the firm low tide sand of Crane Beach leaned into its face-tingling cold. The brisk wind straight out of the west dried surface grains of sand and lifted many less than calf high. These wisps of sand made wind gusts visible. It reminded the hiker of an enormous field being plowed in a strong breeze by invisible ploughmen and oxen. The wisps like low smoke off imagined furrows were semi-transparent, yet there were no furrows visible below them, just ripples in the wet sand from last tide's waves. Above the beach beyond a thin line of debris left by the twice daily highs, dune grass played by pulsing air sang songs we call rustling. Their beige stems, blades and flower heads nodded above a layer of late December snow. Up beyond these grassy low dunes are larger ones where sea-wind-stunted pitch pines hold sand that not too many human generations ago shifted place to place. For three centuries livestock had yearly eaten and stamped the vegetation low. Now without the many sharp-hoofed grazers, just relatively few deer, dune grass, false heather, beach plum bushes and trees are coming back, their roots sewing dune surfaces in place and slowly blanketing them with thin topsoil. Animals, whose tracks are numerous in the sand and snow, thrive among the plants. All hail industrialist Richard T. Crane's family and The Trustees of Reservations (TTOR), who indirectly kicked the descendants of Old World cattle and hogs off and now ban motorized vehicles except those used by reservation personnel.

The same huzzahs might be given federal and state governments who protect Plum Island, an even longer barrier beach clearly seen by Crane Beach walkers, a mile northwest across shifting bars, changing channel, and the daily up and down mix of fresh and sea water that enters and exits Plum Island Sound. The water draining from our tri-town yards will eventually join them. Some of the water now rounding the Azores will visit the Parker and Ipswich Rivers and several in between. Plum Island and Cape Cod were also once open range and share much the same history, including early logging, as the Crane Estate reservation.

Let's return to the lone Closeteer exulting in these scenes as he followed in the snowy sandy tracks of hikers on a New Year's Day hike sponsored by the Ipswich River Watershed Association (IRWA). Ryan O'Donnell, Programs Coordinator of IRWA, led and ecologist Franz Ingelfinger, formerly with TTOR, explained. On that balmy first day of 2011 18 participants, some in shirtsleeves, were led up and down twisting dune trails. The participants apparently returned speechless, or out of breath, with only two adjectives, "great" and "awesome," the latter describing Mr. Ingelfinger. (We guess these too common words, which have obliterated dozens, are embraced by more than one generation.) See Middleton Stream Team photographer Judy Schneider's link http://www.judithschneider.com/Stream-Team/Crane-Beach-Dunes/15289970 for fine photos taken on that hike.

Stream Teamers and thousands of others will visit Crane's half-dozen or so miles of trails this winter despite the cold, we hope many for the first time. The beautiful stands of hardy pitch pines covering much of many dunes are alone worth the trip. In open areas between them are rich browns of ankle-high false heather interspersed with patches of pale reindeer lichen and all around healthy stands of dune grass that were sparser half a century ago. These vegetated areas are pocked with small blowouts that remind the Closeteer of the dunes at Plum Island remembered from boyhood explorations. Then much of the dune areas were bare sand vulnerable to the whims of wind. While walking down the center among the dunes, out of sight of flanking unseen salt marsh to the west and ocean to the east, he imagined he was on camel caravans in the Sahara.

Please visit these marvelous rare places. Your taxes pay for the Parker River National Wildlife Refuge and state park at Plum Island. Join TTOR and help it nurture the Crane Estate at the mouth of the Ipswich River; and Ward Reservation protecting Boston Brook's headwaters, to mention just two of its many well-managed reservations open to all. If you have money left join the IRWA and Essex County Greenbelt Association if you haven't already. How lucky we, especially wildlife, are to have these organizations.

WATERMEN WHO COULDN'T SWIM

The comics are full of supermen and women who get far too much attention. We had a real superman in America who could neither fly nor swim. In his early fifties he sailed alone around the world in his good sloop the 36-foot *Spray*. Upon return self-educated Joshua Slocum wrote a terrific book entitled *Sailing Alone Around the World*. Arthur Ransome, British children's writer, wrote after reading it, those "who do not like this book ought to be drowned at once.*"An old Closeteer read it 30 or so years ago and liked every paragraph and page. After three years and 44,000 miles with Slocum, he didn't want the book to end. Slocum was not only a crackerjack sailor and navigator, he was a natural writer, some would say right up there with Herman Melville and Robert Louis Stevenson, his hero.

The other day in the Middleton library while checking new books just in, the Closeteer happened upon Geoffrey Wolff's new biography of Slocum entitled *The Hard Way Around*.* It kept him in his reading chair for four days, feet close to the fire. It isn't a long biography; the Closeteer is a slow reader. Anyway, he went back to sea with Slocum and Wolff this time on the former's other much larger vessels, over a decade with a spunky wife. Captain of several trading ships, he took his family along as skippers could. Aussie first wife, bright Virginia Walker, deserves a book of her own after 13 years mostly at sea with her ambitious husband. She bore seven children while sailing port to distant port; four survived and were ship-schooled well by their parents. She died at 34. Their quarters aboard several ships contained a library of classics. Both Virginia and the captain were serious readers.

Wolff does a fine job telling of his hero's many adventures; he wisely leaves those of the great lonely voyage to Slocum's own famous account. Lonely might not be the word, he had his books and made leisurely stops at many ports. The well-balanced *Spray*, with sails properly trimmed and helm lashed down, was capable of steering herself. This allowed builder and master to commune with the many authors he'd brought along as undemanding passengers. Wolff has Slocum's wry sense of humor. Surprise zingers delight the reader throughout both their books. At one point he declares his "love" for his subject; you might think this a dangerous thing for a biographer to do. Slocum had a short fuse that got him into scrapes in his 65 years. Wolff relates both sides of those confrontations fairly. On return from his famous voyage, the first around the world alone, Slocum wasn't comfortable ashore. He set sail in the somewhat neglected *Spray* again and again, the last time in 1909, and was never heard from after. He evidently died where he had lived. We wonder if he wished he'd learned to swim on the way down. We recommend Wolff's lively account of this seaman, mate, captain, superb navigator, trader, fisherman, writer, boat builder, arresting speaker, and charmer to you.

While discussing Slocum in the Closet the Closeteer harkened back to a hero of his Salisbury childhood. Sherb Eaton was a talented jack of many trades who like Slocum couldn't swim despite being a fisherman on the cold ocean waters off the Merrimack. We boys thought this rugged boat builder, grave digger, naturalist, water diviner, fisherman, clammer, and part-time farmer was the pinnacle of success, an inspiration to us all. The Closeteer's mother attended grammar school with Sherb who left about fourth grade. The rumor was he didn't do well there. He could certainly build good boats; the last of his four motor fishing vessels built stuck out both ends of his fair-sized barn. Alas, Sherb stayed close to home and never even ghost-wrote a book, so few will ever know him. Betsy Woodman, Newburyport historian, did write a good booklet about him from interviews with Sherb and friends.**

In Captain Slocum and Eaton, captain of his own fishing boats, we have men who were brought up in what today might be called poverty; both worked from an early age. Slocum on a hardscrabble farm in Nova Scotia, Eaton under somewhat similar circumstances in Salisbury; both not far from the sea. They did what a New Hampshire friend building a retirement house in Washington County, Maine, when asked what his down east neighbors did for a living, said simply, "Scratch." On further probing he went on to explain that they do what comes their way or what they can go out and get in season. Our subjects were scratchers at different levels. Sherb had a dozen jobs in town; ambitious brilliant Joshua strove mightily and by age 25 was the skipper of a large windjammer in the days when commercial sail was fast becoming obscured by the dirty coal smoke of steam power. Slocum failed again and again yet continued to scratch at commercial ventures on the world's oceans. Eaton stayed close to home and, as far as us boys could see, scratched successfully within a 15-mile radius. He used to take out fishing parties from his mooring up Black Rocks Crick. In between he'd clam, fish on his own, farm a bit, divine for wells, and dig graves without a backhoe.

Why do these men attract us so? In Slocum's case it is obvious. He was the first to sail around the world alone and return to write a masterpiece. Scores of sailors since, male and female from 15 on up, inspired by his feat, have followed in his wake. Eaton on the other hand lived at home with friends and family and did things well that we could readily understand, except, of course, divining for water. We think these men would have liked and understood each other; both were good story tellers. Both had tough fathers; Sherb who admired his is quoted by Woodman as saying, "He was as tough as a boiled owl." Joshua's was physically abusive. We boys who knew one and idolized the other admired them because they were doers. We couldn't understand why Sherb wasn't given higher status by all adults. We learned later that wealth and formal education are rewarded by many above all else. On farms, in shops, at sea, and in the woods men were largely judged by their abilities. Joshua and Sherb would have been in full agreement on this. Their lives overlapped a bit. Sherb was born in 1900 two years after the *Spray* and Joshua had returned. If you haven't read Slocum's book please do so before you read Wolff's revealing biography highlighting his adventures on other ships including the fast clipper *Northern Light*. For Woodman's out-of-print account of Sherb contact the Stream Team and we'll loan you ours after a generous deposit as collateral. You'll recognize able Sherb; each community up and down the Yankee coast, no doubt everywhere, has a few such characters.

* Wolff, Geoffrey, *The Hardway Around* (Knopf, 2010)

** Woodman, Betsy, "The Life of Sherb Eaton: Salt Haying, and Fishing in Salisbury, Massachusetts" (Essex Institute, Salem, 1983)

DOROTHY OF GREAT MARSH

Westerly beyond the arc of barrier beaches from Rye, New Hampshire, to Rockport, Massachusetts, are 25,000 or more acres of flat soft land interlaced with tidal creeks. These are our salt marshes that Whittier famously called "low green prairies of the sea" in his poem *Snow-Bound*. We old-timers who grew up near salt marshes played upon and in them. In summer as children we'd visit several times a day at all tides to swim. The most popular places on the Salisbury salt marshes were meanders of increasing size in Pettengill's Crick off the Merrimack River called Little Dock, Middle Dock and Big Dock. Young kids who couldn't swim learned in the shallower, narrower Little Dock. Those who could only dog paddle short distances graduated to the Middle Dock a hundred yards down crick. The Big Dock, significantly deeper and wider, just around another meander, was the place all aspired to. The name dock no doubt came from their use in earlier times when shallow draft scows called gundalows came in at high tide to off-load salt hay. There is a rectangular cut in a bank off the Big Dock about 36 by 12 feet, just the size of a gundalow. Imagine the pool patio of soft grasses around our docks stretching from upland woods out more than a mile to the river and distant sand dunes, barriers to the sea beyond. The once "docks," our swimming holes, are still there. Swimmers are not, even on hot days. Boring chlorinated pools have taken their place. Pettengill's Crick is contiguous with the ocean, which twice daily flushes it clean.

The salt marshes of Massachusetts in the arc described above were dubbed the "Great Marsh." Much of it was officially designated an Area of Critical Environmental Concern by the state in 1979. Salt marshes were certainly thought "great" by those who swam, duck hunted, clammed, sailed, rowed, fished, hayed, bird-watched, photographed, painted, ice cake jumped or simply hiked there. One old-timer used to visit at all times of the year often on brittle ice when low tide cricks were more easily crossed. He would walk away his worries or sneak up for closer looks at ducks and shorebirds sheltered in the lee of banks. In summer he moored his skiff across a tight loop in Pettengill's Crick called the Ox Bow. He and friend would row out and back on the tides to clam and fish on and above the Merrimack River flats. He too often tells us of those times. We stopped listening long ago.

Perhaps if he had had a camera like Dorothy Kerper Monnelly, just up the road in Ipswich from the Great Marsh, his stories would receive more attention. She too visits the salt marsh cricks, flats, and bars, punctuated by drumlins and dunes, with her large camera in all seasons. She returns with images needing no words. Thirty of her fine black-and-white photos and all shades in between now grace the foyer of the Performing Arts Center at The Governor's Academy, once Governor Dummer, not far from the salt marshes of Byfield. In them she has captured many of the moods of our estuaries as they change daily with light, tide and season. We will not attempt to describe them in mere phrases; you must go and see for yourself. We'll simply list some elements on her palette, ones she didn't even have to brush, just choose: soft once salt hay grasses in wind- and wave-combed cowlicks, expanses of soft mud flats, wave ripples in firm sand, exposed crick banks of two-millennia-thick peat, cordgrass or thatch between high and half tide levels, glacier-left drumlins, sand dunes and dune grasses, spongy sea ice, clouds, sun, moon, mists, forested upland knolls, pools of calm reflecting water, waves, snow streaks on ice, and more. We are sorely tempted to try and tell you more as glib art critics might. Some of us are irritated by such pretentious blather; we too have eyes and feelings. She and film have left room for any color we might want to add or not. Do we admire Chaplin, Bogart and Davis movies any less because they are in so-called black-and-white? Those films leave us with something to do. Dorothy and Ansel Adam's photographs do too; on viewing we like what arises from their minds and souls and mingles with our own.

Note: Dorothy Kerper Monnelly published a handsome book of her photographs in 2006 entitled Between Land and Sea: THE GREAT MARSH, with forward by Jeanne Falk Adams and essay by Doug Stewart.

FEBRUARY 2011

WAVE OF DEATH FLOWED EAST TO WEST

In school we learned of the fur trade in a most romantic way. Bold Frenchmen mingled with Indian friends and penetrated deep into the unknown expanses of a new continent. In 1609 a Dutch crew and ship captained by Henry Hudson sailed up the river later given his name until their ship the *Half Moon* ran out of deep water. En route and upon return they met Iroquois hustling furs. Giovanni da Verrazzano had traded metal objects for fur with the Abenaki in Casco Bay 85 years earlier. Cash-strapped Pilgrims from Plymouth established fur trading posts early on up the Kennebec and Connecticut rivers. By the early 17th century the fur trade was on a roll from Quebec on south and west among the Great Lakes. The Indians did the catching, the newcomers the trading and water transport. Catchers and traders used large birch bark canoes on a vast network of waterways. Beavers, otters, anything with fur beware. Old World folks lusted after furs for status and fashion. Their wild fur bearers had become scarce.

First the Europeans came tentatively exploring for land and cod. Some of the more entrepreneurial fishermen, after meeting the Indians, realized that fur might be even more lucrative than salt-cured fish. To make a long but fast-moving story short, the fur traders in just over two centuries had swept across the continent. Lewis and Clark on their Corps of Discovery, 1802-1804, found French traders all the way to the headwaters of the Missouri.

Please permit a cranky digression from pelts. Have you heard of Alexander Mackenzie? He and his men had crossed the continent, also largely by water, in Canada, 13 years before Lewis and Clark. One old Closeteer only learned of this a few years ago and has been grousing about it ever since. He'd gone through almost six decades thinking gutsy Americans under Jefferson were the first. It was not being later that bothers, it was not having been told the whole truth. The president and Lewis knew about Mackenzie, they'd read his book. Would telling all in school history make the Corps of Discovery less heroic? Did Ken Burns in his fine PBS account of the great adventure a few years ago mention Mackenzie? Did the late Stephen Ambrose in his dramatic gung-ho fashion mention him in his popular book *Undaunted Courage: Meriwether Lewis, Thomas Jefferson, and the Opening of the American West*? We are checking now in hopes of calming the Closeteer down. We'll only tell him if they had. He has a point though. We should teach history straight for better or worse. One-sided patriotism, whether old or new, will not do. Whew! Now that's over, back to aquatic mammals and the waterways they traveled alive, their skins later dead.

What brought fur bearers to mind in the Closet were the receipt this week of a new much acclaimed book entitled *Fur, Fortune, and Empire: The Epic History of the Fur Trade in America* by Marbleheader Eric Jay Dolin, and Winston Ajce's wonderful photos of river otters recently playing and fishing in the ice water of Rockery Pond, Ipswich River Wildlife Refuge. Here is photographer Ajce's account of the encounter.

"I got those pictures on January 22 at around 9 am . . . I had just finished setting up my camera equipment on a very cold morning when I heard the sound of ice cracking behind me. When I turned to look, I noticed an otter had climbed out of the hole it had just created with a good size fish. I missed the shot because as soon as it saw me it jumped back into the hole. About 10 minutes later, I noticed it was back and just watching me. I got a few shots . . . and it took off again. I was about to move to another location, when I noticed it was back . . . with friends! They were very curious about me and gave me a good opportunity to take pictures . . ."

Ajce captured and shared with us several otter that we won't wear. They are probably none the worse for meeting a fellow mammal with strange traps. Not so a couple centuries ago, after beavers and bison, river otters and later Pacific sea otters were favorite victims of the fur trade. Animal rehabilitator and natural history teacher extraordinaire David Taylor brought a young otter into Triton Regional School several decades ago. He let us pet it after warning of a pair of hind teeth that curved inward and didn't easily let go. We were all startled at the softness and other indescribable qualities of its thick fur. Since then the Closeteer has found freshly killed voles in his wife's mouse traps. Voles, only three inches long, that are almost as svelte. We can understand the attraction of those needing or wanting to wear furs. The otter petted was also cute. We couldn't imagine trapping one of these truly playful, graceful fish eaters for their wonderful waterproof pelts. Of course, unlike the fur traders and trappers of old, we have social security.

The early fur trade was intense. Countries, plantations, colonies, companies and individuals were competing for a rapidly dwindling resource. Their highways into the interior and to the catchers were rivers and streams. There weren't even cart paths then except along the coasts and those were impassible much of the year. Can you imagine going town to town in snows like this winter's without plowed roads? The colonists didn't. A trading trip from Salem or Ipswich to Newburyport or Andover would be by sea and river under sail. After the snow was gone the roads were axle-deep mud. Ships, even small ones of the French, English and Dutch, drew enough water to stop them at upriver shallows where they set up ramshackle trading posts. The Indians brought furs, thousands upon thousands, down by canoes. They were paid well or so they thought with knives, iron pots, axes, guns, trinkets, liquor and wampum. Dolin writes that both sides were usually satisfied. Competition between traders drove the prices up for the Indians; profit margins for the traders were high. Alas, the boom here in the Northeast was over in a few decades. The animals were gone. Doesn't this sound all too familiar in our history? Forests, even those away from the coasts, were replaced by fields; 80 percent of Massachusetts was cleared of trees even in the Berkshires. Michigan lost its hardwood forests in a few decades in the 19th century at the same time billions of Passenger Pigeons were killed for meat and millions of bison for robes; the former disappeared forever. The fur bearers to the west were decimated in a few decades after Lewis and Clark's explorations. Before railroads the highways allowing this carnage were rivers. Once they'd served their transportation functions many rivers were dammed for industry. We understand the harm done now. It is high time to set them free for beavers, otters and fish. Maybe someday bison will again be fording western rivers. Beaver and otter populations are on the rise.

Waves, death waves mentioned above, are followed by others; let us hope new ones are waves of life.

SNOWBOUND

Confined in the Closet during recent storms some of us old-timers harkened back to John Greenleaf Whittier's long poem *Snow-Bound* that many of us Yankees had to read in school. Whittier lived two centuries ago just up the road on a Haverhill farm.

Snow-Bound's first four lines are perfect:

> The sun that brief December day
> Rose cheerless over hills of gray,
> And darkly circled, gave at noon
> A sadder light than waning moon.

An old Closeteer, who was made to read all 30 or so pages of rhyme, some bordering on doggerel, lays the above lines on us every December. We decided to find our copy of *Snow-Bound* to help relieve this winter's periods of cabin fever. As the snow appropriately piled up around our drafty riverside shack, its wood stove hot, we went back with Whittier to his farm and a remembered boyhood storm. It may have been like those blizzards we had in 1978 and 1996 that went on for days leaving two to three feet of new snow and higher drifts in their wakes.

A couple pages into the poem after the storm forecast above, Whittier continues:

> And, when the second morning shone,
> We looked upon a world unknown,
> On nothing we could call our own
> Around the glistening wonder bent
> The blue wall of the firmament,
> No cloud above, no earth below,
> A universe of sky and snow!

In the past two months we've wakened several times to such transformed worlds. One storm has piled upon another with no thaws in between. So far, two months of winter to go, two yards have fallen; to date one still covers unfrozen ground. Without truck-powered plows we would be truly snowbound.

John Greenleaf and brother while admiring the new world are ordered to action:

> A prompt, decisive man, no breath
> Our father wasted: "Boys, a path!"
> Well pleased, (for when did a farm boy
> count such a summons less than joy?)
> Our bushkins on our feet we drew;
> Our mittened hands and caps drawn low,
> To guard our necks and ears from snow
> We cut the solid whiteness through;
> And, where the drift was deepest, made
> A tunnel walled and overlaid.

We boys over a century later reveled in the mornings after. Our snow shovels like Whittier's were of wood. So armed we went forth and cut narrow canyons in cold drifts. When done with paths to cow barn and chicken pens we sought out neighbors who paid us well for clearing their walks and driveways. We could earn what seemed a fortune in a morning. Our parents blessed such enterprise. One storm remembered in the mid-'40s blocked back country roads for several days. Even the largest town plows couldn't get through. Gangs of men and boys living along the roads went with shovels and broke through. Deep snow was not only exciting and beautiful, it left us with lifetime memories of working well with neighbors and kin.

Such storms don't just end; afterwards, arctic winds shift the hoary dunes around to fill in cleared paths and roads. Whittier remembers well those post-storm winds down from Canadian highs:

> All day the gusty north-wind bore
> The loosening drift its breath before
> Low circling round its southern zone,
> The sun through dazzling snow-mist shone.

Then back we'd go with shovels, tired and even a little bored like our round-the-clock, day after day, modern plow crews must be. We wish that our grandchildren on no-school days would venture out in face-tingling cold with shovels. Alas, now snowblowers exhale the "breath."

Young Whittier, chores over, explores the novel scenes just beyond his snowbound farm:

> We minded that the sharpest ear
> The buried brooklet could not hear,
> The music of whose liquid lip
> Had been to us companionship,
> And, in our lonely life, had grown
> To have an almost human tone.

Here he misses the sound of a deep buried brook. He knows it flows below but cannot see or hear it. Miles of brooks around our towns are now so hidden. Above fast-flowing riffles where the snow has melted are holes revealing fast clean flow, yet not well heard due sound-absorbing snow. Beware of passage over, upstream and below, these unseen tunnels. We'd hate to find you missing 'til spring thaw.

One old Closeteer is struck by the word "lonely" in a line above. His school vacations and weekends were spent with self and grandfather hoeing and weeding; picking sweet corn and other crops; mowing and haying; and doing endless farm chores. He says his patient kindly grandfather must have suffered from his endless chatter when they were together. Quiet grandpa gently acknowledged him with low grunts, perhaps sighs now and then, and every couple days wise comments that weren't soon forgotten.

We'll leave Whittier now, man of a million lines, who last lived in Danvers. His famous *Snow-Bound* goes on and on about other joys experienced over the years by farm boys near the coast. He, like other Victorian poets, mixes all kinds of classical analogies with local history. Our favorite lines from *Snow-Bound* quoted every few years here are of his thoughts during winter chores of summertimes with father just down the Merrimack by the sea:

Boston Brook almost buried after storm. Photo, courtesy of Pamela Hartman.

Or nearer home our steps he led
Where Salisbury's level marshes spread
Mile wide as flies the laden bee;
Where merry mowers, hale and strong,
Swept, scythe on scythe, their swaths along
The low green prairies of the sea.

Those salt marshes are now white with brittle salt water ice and snow. More is on its way.

MUSINGS ALONG POND MEADOW BROOK

The snow in woods and fields off our roads has been deep for two months. We've needed snowshoes or skis to explore places easily visited scores of times before. They, so thickly carpeted, are as different as can be. On sunny days even in the shade of white pines there is lots of light, almost too much beneath leafless hardwoods. Fields in midday hurt the eyes. Woods where boulders, twigs, fallen logs and low bushes are hidden invite even the less spry.

On Super Bowl Sunday afternoon, while the country was napping or doing other pre-bowl things, a Stream Team family and few friends from Middleton hiked from snow-blocked North Liberty Street to fields and forest carrying picnic stuff on snowshoes. Three generations, ages five to 60, entered a now rare pasture surrounded by undeveloped woods. A century ago most of our towns' terrain was open grazing land. It was afternoon; the harsh glare off the largely unmarked snow was gone. Pond Meadow Brook was open and running free in its snow-walled mini-canyon along the east side of Second Pasture. Water sang in welcome to the trekkers as it flowed o'er gravelly bottom.

The clear water stunk of hydrogen sulfide gas, a common phenomenon this time of year. Microorganisms under vast impoundments, a fifth mile up behind a beaver dam in this case, are sealed by ice from oxygen for energy-producing respiration. Many bacteria and fungi can respire anaerobically, meaning without air. A product of anaerobic respiration is hydrogen sulfide that smells like "sewer gas," many say rotten eggs. This collects and concentrates under the ice until exposed to air at openings downstream. The picnic group laid their blue tarp picnic blanket on the snow alongside the brook and soon became less aware of the odor.

A week after that unusual mid-winter picnic an old Stream Teamer, inspired upon receiving a photo of the picnickers, decided to brave the treacherous off-road snow with snowshoes older than he. The shoes looked pretty good, but leather binders and rawhide mesh hadn't been oiled in a decade since last use. He, although a frequent hiker, wondered if his snowshoe muscles were up to the strange step that hickory-rawhide shoes with tails require. He'd learned the hard way on past trips that if the binders go awry getting back to solid walking is a great challenge in deep snow such as we've experienced this winter. Only a fraction of a mile of ups and downs, breaking through each step, or worst still every other, quickly exhausts.

With four-foot-long platforms finally attached to boots, the Stream Teamer ventured into First Pasture on almost completely unmarked snow. The going, due to a long period without practice, was slow. There is a special step to snowshoeing quite unlike walking or skiing. The trick is not to allow the front tips to go under the snow. Soon dormant muscles coming into play began to mildly ache. Walking on even somewhat firm snow is slow business. After a while he caught on and enjoyed the leisurely pace that allowed plenty of time to enjoy the lovely winter scene. He came upon Pond Meadow Brook running darkly yet cheerfully singing below two-foot snow cliffs. For the next five minutes while following the brook north he tried to find words to describe its sounds. They certainly weren't babbling, tinkling, gurgling or sloshing. On return to fellow Stream Teamers he proposed a contest with a prize for the best description of a running brook's sound. They agreed to accept words standing alone or in prose, poetry or song. Instruments could also be used. The winner would be given a guided tour of our several brooks with singing riffles. People's tastes in music differ wildly, but have you known anyone who doesn't like that from water flowing over uneven stream and river bottoms? Many folks travel miles to hear.

As the snowshoeing got easier, newly used muscles became even more apparent. After a half hour passing through field and woods the Stream Teamer came upon the tracks of the Super Bowl Sunday picnickers. If he didn't know of them and snowshoes he would have guessed giants had tramped on the snow of Second Pasture. It was obvious where they had laid their plastic blanket. The Stream Teamer continued on north until he was back on scarcely marked snow. There were only a few tracks on the surface crust made by lighter animals. He looked back at his own tracks only an inch deep, perfect imprints of the leather and graceful hickory bows of his light shoes. They looked like Escher fish following in side by side rows, alternating tail to head, tail to head, the gaps between the rawhide, scales. The tracks were perfect records of his passing in such a pristine setting. The sun going down in the west behind mature woods sent gray-blue shadows half across the field. He was on the bright white side beyond them near the transparent water of the black-appearing brook. Across the brook, all along its east side, a fine stand of white pines rose 70 or so feet, their needles the only green in sight. Overarching all was a light blue February sky. A soft westerly breeze barely got a whisper out of the pine boughs. The song of the stream gently dominated.

At the north end of Second Pasture the brook channel disappears at a head-high dam spanning 150 feet between uplands of ledge. About 12 years ago beavers started this dam on an old farm causeway that crossed Pond Meadow Brook's channel and narrow floodplain. They've added yearly since. Above it is a huge impoundment stretching a half mile up into Boxford and North Andover now characterized by still-standing dead Atlantic white cedars and a few rotting white pine and red maple trunks. A few large pines supported high Great Blue Herons' nests. Five years ago we counted 26 nests, last summer eight, and last week the Stream Teamer found only six. The pines they prefer will soon all be gone to winter winds and sticky snow. The place we call "The Rookery" and have visited several times each year may soon be that no longer. The Stream Teamer stood in the 10-acre man-cleared field below the dam and looked across the 150-acre beaver-made meadow in all its desolate beauty. The red maple swamp and interesting heron nests, that drew us before the noisy young had fledged, are largely gone. Forest has been replaced by rich new habitats with low aquatic plants and much more light. We visit to see amphibians, birds, mammals and other aquatic creatures who have moved in or are passing by. A large year-old beaver lodge, a fifth mile up from the dam, stands, a striking cone above the snow. Snow-covered flat "beaver meadows" lie quiet. However, we know from peering through "black ice," more correctly transparent ice, over the years in midday that much is happening even in the 32 degree F water underneath. The lodge occupants who visit the deeply impounded water daily well know what happens there. If younger we might exchange our bulky clothes for flippers, wetsuit and scuba and join them. Much light must penetrate even the thick ice covering.

The air that balmy afternoon was far too nice to consider dives with beavers under ice. The Stream Teamer well knew, as he turned south toward home, that life for humans is better in the air above especially when a three-quarter moon is one-third up in the east reflecting the sun at the same angle in the west. Snowshoe aches were gone, as was any bother from the stream's bouquet. All was well with the world. The Stream Teamer correctly felt that he was walking on water.

WATERSHEDS VERSUS BOXES

This past month the eyes and ears of the world have been on what we usually think of as dry Tunisia, southern Sudan, and Egypt where springs of liberty are bubbling forth and flowing outward, who knows where they may go. There has been little blood tainting these springs gushing with young people.

Here in the Closet we got out our well-worn atlas to review the lay of the land and scarce water bodies in these countries and those of their neighbors. We were immediately struck by the long straight boundary lines that were lain out in royal drawing rooms in London, Paris, Lisbon and Berlin. These cruel lines drawn by distant foreigners were and are unnatural. However, there is no sense crying over such poisonously applied ink. Perhaps the young faces so hopeful in Tunis, southern Sudanese villages, and Cairo will someday look for new bounds, or better still no bounds, that make sense to Mother Nature.

The next thing to catch our eyes was the mighty Nile River we usually associate with Egypt due to the ruins of ancient pharaohs, the modern Aswan Dam, and now the political revolution near its banks. Most of its vast watershed continues on and on southerly deep into eastern Africa. In Sudan the Nile branches into the Blue Nile and White Nile, which branch into great tributaries for another 3,000 miles in the uplands of Ethiopia, Uganda and Zaire. A large part of the Nile's drainage is in the soon-to-be new country of southern Sudan. In Egypt it runs through just 800 of 4,000 or so miles within narrow fertile floodplains without tributaries. There are light blue lines on the map in the Sahara called wadis, which are shallow river beds, dry much of the time, that carry rare water to ephemeral desert lakes. Wadis and salt lakes are largely surface features unassociated with the Nile. The water providing Egypt via the Nile comes from greener highlands to the south and east.

For the next hour we Stream Teamers and Closeteers gathered around our map of Africa and western parts of the Middle East discussing the geography we had learned in the fourth grade and had largely forgotten despite unending reports since from those long-troubled areas. Someone, perhaps inspired by recent political events, suggested we look to the future and think outside boxes with straight line dimensions. We'd done this before for areas nearer home. How might a stricter Mother Nature have allocated land as people populations increased and societies evolved? We see the world through hopeful green lenses even in brown and yellow deserts and those of white ice. Did you know Antarctica and the Arctic have very little precipitation? Most people live in the lower parts of watersheds whether in the draws and runs of Appalachia, the high valleys of the Himalayas or in the great cities on rivers near the seas. We have to because that is where the water is that makes agriculture and transport possible. Perhaps basin divides should be the natural borders between populations. Instead of countries, states, counties and towns we'd have major river watersheds, large tributary watersheds, within them smaller river watersheds and so on down to those of streams. Let's do the Merrimack as an example; forget Massachusetts and New Hampshire. The elected chief watershedder and legislature would have jurisdiction over the entire Merrimack River basin. Subdivisions (how naturally this word from divide fits) would be the Pemigewasset, Nashua and Concord rivers to mention just three. There would be elected groups responsible for the welfare of each. The numbers of representatives might be based on basin area. Then there would be stream groups, one for each tributary. The smaller subdivisions would work with and report to the river groups who'd be under the major river government. In our smaller Ipswich River the hierarchy would go down from the river to its several tributary streams. We already have the non-governmental Ipswich River Watershed Association and several stream teams. For smaller tributary brooks of each stream there would be volunteer neighborhood groups called "Brook Bunches" reporting to elected larger stream groups. We would of course need new constitutions whose main goals would be the health and welfare of watersheds and all the creatures and plants living within them. Passage between watersheds would be easy, no passports required at divides. We could go west from Ipswich's, to Shawsheen's, to Concord's and on to Nashua's without stopping except to read signs and view watershed maps. Rivers without dams would flow freely to the oceans.

And how about the oceans? Who would oversee them? How about a group like the United Nations called United Basins (UB)? Representatives from the large rivers would meet on large sailing ships, constantly traveling between ports, to do what is needed for the health of their huge charge. There would be subgroups representing each ocean. Here we have a difference; there are no divides. The ocean groups would include research centers and "watch humans"; there are no watchdogs at sea. They would report to the UB, which would have legislative and enforcement authority. By the way, representatives of these watershed and ocean groups by constitution would be required to have some background in science and history. These were some of the ideas enthusiastically argued for and against around the atlas. We old-timers were inspired by the thousands of upturned young faces and excited voices in Tahrir (liberation) Square. They reminded us of similar faces in Tiananmen Square two decades ago and in the streets of Tehran in 2009 that sadly ended covered with tears and blood. The watersheds of freedom are flowing now again.

Wild! Far out, you scoff! Have you alternatives? Let's hear them. The basis of life on the planet is water, what could be more important than its proper care? It is high time to think outside our rigid boxes. Some of us hope the gutsy people, especially the young, we've seen in Tunisia, south Sudan, Egypt, and we wish someday to see again in China and Iran, with their new forms of instant communication so difficult to effectively jam, will break out of the containers they were born into. We hope the freedom to which we think they aspire will not be as destructive as ours has often been. We want them to don Mother Nature's green lenses in order to truly see and to seriously study other organisms living in her watersheds and seas. They must if our species is to be around much longer.

March 2011

Atlantic White Cedars

Once upon a time dense groves of Atlantic white cedar darkened swamps from Maine to Mississippi. Right up until the beginning of this millennium there were two stands totaling 13 acres in Middleton and certainly others around the county. *Chamaecyparis thyoides*, actually a cypress not a cedar, grows slowly in peaty acid soils largely devoid of silt or clay. Our trees reach 60 or so feet, one and a half in diameter; southern trees may get up over 100 feet, three or more in diameter, if allowed by beavers, fires and loggers. Some of the most venerable may have experienced a thousand years. In the Closet we have a three-inch-diameter section of white cedar from Aunt Bett's Pond swamp near Middleton center that is 45 years old as determined by counting its thin annual rings. A red maple, another swamp tree, of similar diameter is only 25 years old. Forty-five-year-old upland trees in well-drained soils might be a foot or more in diameter.

As we've mentioned so many times before in the Closet, in the 1990s the beavers returned, some might say with a justified vengeance. Protected since 1996 in Massachusetts from cheap efficient steel-jaw leghold traps by law, they've thrived. Now there are scores in each town; in the previous three centuries beavers were rare or nonexistent here. In just a decade the prolific beavers have killed 18 or so acres of white cedars in the two groves mentioned above and in sparse stands other places around Middleton. Beavers don't girdle or fell them; they drown them with their dams. Some wag, opposed to the Massachusetts leghold trap bill, may have said to voters, "You vote for such a law, cedars and other swamp trees be damned!" We Stream Teamers like beavers and applaud the law. White cedars thrive in very wet soils, but can't take water in depth year round as do some cypresses. The beavers raised the water just a foot or two and did them in. Where swamp forests once stood there are now large sunny areas of shallow water called "beaver meadows." The Atlantic white cedar groves are dead but we can visit and marvel in the scarce shade of their still standing trunks and leafless branches. Their trunks, branches and pickled roots decay very slowly. Red maples so inundated will last but six to 10 years before they fall; it is pretty much the same for white pines growing in swamps. Drive northwest on Route 114 out of Middleton center.

After about a mile pull over at Meritor Academy and look west at the pale corpses of a white cedar grove still standing. They were drowned by man 50 or so years ago when the Emerson Bog dam at Lake Street was raised by the Danvers Water Department. The year-round higher water slowly killed the cedars and quickly drowned cranberries and other wet meadow plants. Stream Teamer Frank Masse remembers picking cranberries there in what is now a reservoir.

About 12 years ago on a winter hike, Masse, outdoorsman extraordinaire here for three-quarters of a century, and the then Middleton conservation agent walked south out of Boxford into Middleton on a trail just west of the swamp surrounding Pond Meadow Pond, a glacial kettle. To their surprise the old logging road was flooded in places. They hadn't seen it covered before even in wet times of the year. They guessed there must be a beaver dam down drainage. Another half mile and their conclusion was confirmed. They found a new dam on a farmer's ancient causeway crossing Pond Meadow Brook and its floodplain between two points of upland. About nine months later in November a worker with backhoe was removing invasive multiflora roses from a cow pasture just below the dam. Tire tracks showed that at one point he drove to the dam and breached its center with a seven foot wide, four foot down from top, hole. The water from 70 acres above flowed quickly down lowering the impoundment a couple feet. The agent discovered the breach soon thereafter. By mid-December, a few weeks later, the dam had been patched and raised almost a foot over its 100-foot length by the beavers. The bases of the white cedar groves, red maples and scattered white pines were again inundated. The farmer passed, the beavers raised him one. More upland above the dam became wetland.

We fretted for the uncommon white cedars. The following summer there was good reason to do so. The usually dark green scales, which are their tiny leaves, had a yellowish-brown tint to them. The agent voiced his concern to the conservation commission. Beaver dams, then, with permission of the Massachusetts Division of Fisheries and Wildlife, now by town boards of health and conservation commissions, may be breached or modified with large pipes called beaver deceivers. The builders themselves may be trapped and killed. Permits, however, can only be issued for reasons of public health and safety. Alas, Atlantic white cedars and the creatures that live among them aren't considered members of the public. The commissioners wondered what could be done especially after learning the trees are the habitat of the rare Hessel's Hairstreak butterfly, the only one it has. Their larvae feed exclusively on its live leaf scales. The commissioners and agent had never seen the small mint-green beauty called Hessel's Hairstreak except online. Another winter and spring passed; the cedars were looking progressively browner and more sickly. Time was running out, perhaps already had. Nothing was attempted or done. Three years from the time the impounding dam was first noticed all of the several thousand trees and no doubt any Hessel's streaks and who knows what else that depend on white cedars for food and shelter were dead or gone. There are several warbler species that are said to prefer nesting in white cedars; they must have looked elsewhere for sites.

Several times each year we visit these changing places becoming ever more rich beaver meadows. The Atlantic white cedar trunks and naked branches still stand; we harken back to when the stands were so thick that in midday the gloom within them was even thicker. In dense groves upper branches touch to form effective canopies. One old Stream Teamer used to visit them when possible on winter ice or in late summer when the swamps were somewhat dry. His favorite for midday semi-darkness was the grove around another glacial kettle called Aunt Bett's Pond. Inspired by Teddy Roosevelt he used to beeline across them and other places. TR was famous for challenging straight-line hikes with his children and anyone else around with "spunk." One trek in Washington is said to have caught up a visiting ambassador who didn't want to appear wimpish, then "sissy," and ended up with TR and kids wading waist deep in the Reflecting Pool between the Lincoln and Washington memorials. On a beeline through a white cedar swamp back when the cedars were still healthy, the Stream Teamer started too late one afternoon. The USGS map showed less than a half mile, nothing to it he thought. In dwindling afternoon light after what seemed an hour, climbing over and around fallen trunks (swamp cedars have shallow roots and are vulnerable to storms) and up and down peat hummocks, there seemed no end in sight. He was doing 50 feet for every 10 along his planned line. His respect for cedar swamps grew fast as light diminished. He worried about getting out; he'd brought neither compass nor matches to read one by. He did get out and tells this tale too often.

After we who hiked among them are gone there will still be a record of their time here sheltering animals we didn't know. In a 1991 state flyover photographers using infrared film took pictures of the land below. Their remarkably sharp aerial photos are at conservation commission offices if you'd like to see them, most towns have a set. We borrowed Middleton's to measure the acreage of pre-beaver Atlantic white cedars. Even without double photographs and stereoscopic viewers as foresters have, we with knowledge of what's on the ground can pick out tree species.

If you want to see a small healthy grove of white cedars go north on Route 114 as directed above. Before you get to Meritor Academy stop and park on the northeast side of the highway under the NEPC electric lines. Walk east under the wires for a few yards and there in the wetland below you'll see a grove of evergreens very different from the common white pines in the uplands behind them. Last Sunday morning the two old walkers mentioned above visited the grove in a gentle snowfall, which since midnight had added two inches of cold frosting. Each of the few dozen trees will shed millions of tiny winged seeds next fall. They'll ride the wind; perhaps a few will fall in proper places. Cedars do not reproduce asexually by shoots from stumps and dying trees as do many hardwoods.

Atlantic white cedars were here and now are largely gone; it is the beavers' ecosystem and community's turn. People for over four centuries have cut them for their light, easily worked and relatively decay-resistant wood. The two groves we knew probably arose from the seeds of parent groves clear-cut about a century ago. This may have happened several times since the arrival of the English. Any such passing is sad and mingled with a tinge of guilt. Could these last groves have been saved if people had acted more quickly and decisively? What then of the beavers? Perhaps caught up in human time we care too little about other organisms in theirs. This swamp cedar may come back in places now that we know enough to protect wetlands and some of their surrounds. Many people in Atlantic and Gulf coastal plains are now dedicated to their restoration. We won't see many, our grandchildren might.

Whale Stories

We don't have much contact with whales in the Closet even though the

Ipswich River flowing by our shack connects to their ocean habitats. The early whalers thought their prey were big fish. Four centuries ago very large fish did come up our river to spawn. Atlantic sturgeons were reported to reach 14 feet in length. When the Sylvania, Willowdale and Bostik dams are gone perhaps they'll try the Ipswich River again. This time we'll greet them with measuring tapes and cameras not with lances as the Indians did. Their "birchen"* and dugout canoes were not much longer than their prey. We'd like to say more of this magnificent, now threatened true fish, but must return because our subjects are false ones with warm blood and milk hence mammals.

Recently a Closeteer borrowed Eric Jay Dolin's much acclaimed 2007 book *Leviathan: The History of Whaling in America* from the library and followed the author around the world mainly with Yankees after their mighty prey. Here long before the name "New World" the whale fishery started on our beaches. Dead whales would wash ashore and live whales, especially pilots, would sometimes swim in on the tides and go aground. Researchers still don't understand the cause of the latter's behavior; whales don't lack sonar. The Indians and later the colonists put high value on these gifts from the sea. Lookouts were posted on dunes and headlands in season. They, often boys, upon sighting a whale would raise a flag and then run to spread the word.

We know that whales were tossed up and stranded on what we call Crane, Plum Island, Salisbury and other beaches and no doubt have been forever. The last we remember locally was a humpback on Seabrook Beach. It was buried in the sand where it rotted and emanated such a stink it was dug up and hauled away. One Closeteer helped biologists and students cut up a 65-foot-long fin whale on a winter beach at Brewster, Cape Cod. That was 25 years ago; he claims to still smell it when harkening back to that very cold day with a brisk west wind you'd think would have swept any odors quickly away. Researchers and helpers removed masses of semi-frozen putrefying flesh from the great skeleton, which was destined to be displayed at Northeastern University. American seagoing whalers were mainly after whale oil and baleen. Tons of meat from each blubber-peeled whale were left to ocean creatures.

As the population of English grew here the demand for whale products increased apace. Gutsy colonials along the coast started to go out after them in shallops. There is some evidence Indians had done so in dugout canoes. Sloop-rigged open shallops, the coastal equivalent of trucks in the 17th century, were framed and planked with white oak. Here we have an Ipswich River connection; many of the logs for shipyards, just gently sloping banks above high tide, were floated down rivers to our ports. White oak and logs from other trees were a winter source of cash or trade goods for farmers. The Indians had spared huge white oaks for their acorns and shade, and perhaps because they lacked tools to fell and cut them up. If you want to see a survivor of the shipwright's lust visit the Curtis Oak on Peabody Street in Middleton. Not far from the river it must have shaded both Indians and colonists and the latter's livestock. This venerable white oak, circumference 17 feet, is thought to be over 400 years old. We stray again from whales, but certainly you can see how oak for hulls, white pines for masts, rivers for transport, ships, oceans and whales were all connected. The newcomers here early on, for example Bray Wilkins and family in Salem Farms, later Middleton, spent long winters carving out oak barrel staves for coopers in Salem, Ipswich and other ports.** Some of their barrels may have ended up full of whale oil.

We have no intention of repeating much from good writer and researcher Dolin's lively account of three centuries of whaling that expanded from here outward to the ice of both poles. He does it well; we can but recommend his *Leviathan* and last year's *Fur, Fortune, and Empire*. Both industries' sagas were largely played out on the seas where the furs also ended up en route somewhere else in ships. We Stream Teamers innocent of the rough playing fields of high finance and business (our shack's assets have never exceeded a dozen beaver pelts or a barrel of whale oil) were struck upon reading and discussing both histories how similar in ways are the shenanigans of the movers and shakers on Wall Street and those of the fur traders and whaling leaders of old. Competition was often fierce in undulating markets. Fortunes were quickly made and lost, but not by the guys actually catching beavers and killing whales. The great differences in tough businesses over time seem largely those of speed. Whaling voyages in slow sailing ships, as prey got ever scarcer, stretched to four years. Mail was months and years going ship to ship. The British-built Rebel raider *Shenandoah* was still rounding up Yankee whale ships weeks after Appomattox. Now communication between traders is instant round the world. However, the people who wrote log entries and letters with quills on wooden ships and in counting houses would well recognize kindred souls in our modern businesses, banks and investment firms. To the Nantucket and New Bedford owners and captains the foc'sle hands in their servitude hardly counted, so low was their pay.*** The same might be said in those days of the textile mill owners and stockholders in Lowell, Newport or Bar Harbor compared with their factory hands whom they never knew or even saw.

The great difference might be in the sensibilities toward wild animals in the 19th century and now. Even sensitive Herman Melville in *Moby Dick*, the best of whaling books, rarely took pity on his prey while serving on the whaler *Acushnet* or writing of the fictional *Pequod*. Today many of us wouldn't think of chasing and killing noble whales. Would we if whale oil was valuable? As we discuss the subject of perceived evolved sympathies toward whales, seals, beavers and buffalo we are reminded of the way we treat domestic hogs, cattle and chickens in their small pens, feedlots and cages. We'd better leave the subject. We humans are sympathetic or cruel depending. These are our speculations. Dolin wisely avoids the subject and just tells us what happened.

We'll end with another local tale that took place on the Merrimack about 70 years ago. After school an old Closeteer, then a young lad, and friend were searching the debris strewn on the salt marsh along the edge of the river's mouth in search of treasure such as duck decoys, useful planks, and ornithologists' tracking bands on the legs of dead ducks. Once they had found a loose skiff following a storm. After a three-day ad in the *Newburyport News* no one claimed it so they kept it. That afternoon on Morrill's Rock, a large protruding cone of ledge, they found a mass of ambergris sticking to the rock. They'd just read of this very valuable product from sick sperm whales' guts, used as a perfume base. It smelled and had the consistency their source seemed to describe. Several pounds of the dirty smelly tan wax-like substance were gathered up in a high state of excitement. "We're rich! We're rich!" They lugged their treasure the mile home, its value increasing with each step. They ran into the future Closeteer's kitchen and showed his mother who barely gave it a glance. She said it was probably tallow from upriver tanneries. "Take it outside."

Would-be whalers had similar high expectations during the boom days when ships laden with oil, baleen and even some ambergris returned to port. Many jumped into the business only to be eventually told by the market, not mothers, although we bet a few did, they had failed. Whaling was a rough business dependent upon skill of catchers, whereabouts of whales, storms, shoals, ice, competition, availability of crew, capital, demand for product, war, and luck.

Petroleum and later electricity quickly did the industry in.

Maybe global warming and sea level rise will bring whales up a westward expanding Ipswich River bay long after the Closet's shack and members have joined the soil and future sea bottom. Enlightened humans will stand on islands, once hills called Castle, Great Neck, Will's, Bald, and Boston, watching. Posted lookouts will tweet the words "Thar she blows!" and boats powered by sails and oars, quite like the beautiful whaleboats of yore, will be womanned and manned. Boat steerers, the mates of whale ships, in charge will whisper to crews upon approaching their great prey, "Belay the chatter. Steady, lads and lassies. Steady on." The harpoonless technician in the bow will make a final check of recording devices and then shift places with the lanceless steerer. Others ashore will safely watch on television.

* Wood, William New England Prospects, Chapter 16

** Watkins, Lura Woodside. Middleton, Massachusetts: A Cultural History, p.16

*** Note: Yankee whaling is usually and rightfully associated with Nantucket and New Bedford. The following however is from J.W. Barber's Historical Collections of Massachusetts, 1837, Newburyport Chapter: "Four vessels were engaged in the whale fishery; tonnage, 1,440; sperm oil, 148,480 gallons; whale oil, 80,650 gallons; hands employed, 120." (one year's tally). A search in the records of other New England ports with two fathoms of water at low tide would no doubt include similar lists.

TSUNAMI

We have long known the Pacific is not peaceful. Perhaps the ocean was so named in contrast to the "Ring of Fire" surrounding it. Last Friday afternoon, Japan time, there was a jerking upward by its bottom that sent energy in the form of waves out in all directions and over the continental shelf and then upon the land where seawater is not supposed to be. We watched in fascinated horror as moving waterfalls on wide fronts poured over fallow fields and plastic-covered gardens and towns taking all in their paths. That was not flooding, rather a giant wave finding a broad opening where people lived and planted.

How vulnerable tiny Japan looks on geologic maps. How very dangerous is her largely mountainous land, the meeting place of several moving plates of the Earth's crust. The Eurasian Plate is said to have moved west four meters of longitude during the quake.

Let's leave the terrible devastation so thoroughly documented by hundreds of people from the air and streets. Tens of thousands now carry digital "movie" cameras. We'll take our minds home and then return traveling from our coastal plain here around Massachusetts Bay west toward Sendai at a speed of 15 longitude degrees per hour. We'll keep the sun at noon above our heads as if in a jet doing 1,000 miles per hour. A half hour or so off the Miyagi Prefecture coast we'll pass over the Kuroshio Current as it flows northeast somewhat like our Gulf Stream. If we soar low we might feel its warmth. In 10 hours, 150 degrees, we'll be among the debris volunteering to help. Our Cape Cod is about the same latitude as that other coast on another ocean so cruelly afflicted. The Japanese east coast can well be compared with ours in many ways. From east to west: deep ocean, continental shelf, beaches and rocky headlands, coastal plain, and then mountains run side by side in great bands southwest to northeast. The latitudes of warm Georgia and Kyushu, of Tokyo and Washington, and of Maine and cold Hokkaido closely coincide. It is easy to explain the geography and climate of eastern Japan, which is quite like that of our original 13 colonies and now. The enormous difference lies unseen, yet for the last half century known, beneath the surface. The Japanese are perched on the Eurasian crustal plate riding upon the Pacific Plate, which is diving underneath. We here are ever farther from the edge of our plate, a line down the mid-Atlantic oozing magma.

All these thoughts flood over us as we gather around the Closet table looking down on our large well-worn National Geographic atlas, away from the sad TV images at home. Our old minds have trouble getting around Google Earth's marvelous views. The names on familiar paper maps stay in place and don't keep shifting or fluctuating in size. What we really want to do is go and help in a place where the water that so obsesses us has gone astray through no fault of its own. We on a coastal plain protected by low vulnerable barrier beaches can well imagine what has happened there, and could even if we hadn't seen it. It may happen here over time from quite another source if Greenland melts and northeast storms increase in intensity. We could even have a tsunami-producing earthquake; there was a large quake off Cape Ann in 1755, no time ago at all to geologists. After, people of the Leeward Islands, 1,000 miles south, reported a strange wave. The Puritans thought God was punishing them for their sins. We are glad the victims of this one know about plate tectonics. But back to our imagined visit; what would the busy Japanese do with a couple dozen old Closeteers who arrive without equipment or much strength, not speaking the language? We would just be in the way.

One old Closeteer visited a couple of the places so much in the news the past few days. In 1959 he took a train from Tokyo to Niigata on the west coast of Japan, west across the country from Sendai. That large city was much rocked by last week's quake. Ten years ago, while visiting kin with his Japanese wife*, he, traveling alone, took a train from Tokyo north along the eastern coast. His navy ships over a half century ago hadn't visited the ports or waters of northern Japan. That last trip was like taking a train from New York City to Boston along the Connecticut coast. The track is never far from the sea and sometimes in sight. The land in Miyagi is relatively low as the world now knows. Much of the rugged Japanese coastline falls steeply to the sea. The calm Pacific he saw from his train window last week rose seven meters as it approached the beaches and then flowed over land. Passing trains despite great weight were swept along with it.

We are at loss for further words. As the old Closeteer's son wrote in an email the day after the Sendai tsunami, "There is a Water Closet story somewhere in those images." He is right, there are thousands that will be told for generations. Closeteers and Stream Teamers, awestruck and distant, are not the ones to tell them. We'll leave that to the survivors who daily live so dangerously on the edge.

* She called her elder sister 50-miles south of Tokyo late Friday; early Saturday there. Kikuno Yamaguchi, 83, like all Japanese is used to earthquakes. Normally the Japanese just stop and silently wait until the tremors pass. Kikuno-san said this was by far the most frightening and longest she had ever experienced. She and kin suffered no physical damage. Mind scars must be deep. The American sister who called didn't shed tears for her countrymen until the second morning when a mini-mini tsunami of salty water came.

VERNAL POOL TIME AGAIN

Last week's warmth shooed away most of the remaining snow except for some on shaded north slopes and in dirty piles around parking lots. The ground long unfrozen because of thick snow insulation now warms under a daily higher sun. The water table, always there but little realized, which rises each fall, peeps above the ground in low places. From our air perspective the table appears as ponds. Rain and runoff from saturated soil keep them topped off this time of year. Many ponds and lakes still have ice floating in their centers. All around their edges the groundwater seeping in at 55 degrees F has them open; the ice is circled by widening black rings. A closer look at the latter reveals clear water waiting.

In the surrounding woods beneath the duff amphibians stir and think, in whatever ways they do, about rising from their dark winter bedchambers into the air. This stirring is due to their chemistry now receiving requisite heat. When the temperature and humidity are right they will go forth and head for the birthing pools from whence they came. We know from blue-spotted salamander studies that some will travel up to a quarter mile without paths. Each twig and hummock to them is like a log and hill. Roughly one-fourth foot long they travel up to 5,000 times their own body length. This does not include all the zigs and zags. That's as if we who have the advantage of warm blood crawled for six miles over rough ground. Some fraction of the tiny travelers, under the spell of sexual urges, if that is an appropriate phrase for salamanders and wood frogs, will make it to their pools. Many of us can remember long trips to dances as teenagers and even longer ones when seriously courting, hardly the same but . . .

Yearly in the Closet and local newspapers there have been articles about vernal pools so we will not say more of their biology here now. We do recommend you obtain the vernal pooler's bible by gurus Leo Kenney and Matthew Burne, northeastern Massachusetts neighbors. All families should have *A Field Guide to the Animals of Vernal Pools*, less than ten dollars, readily at hand.* Keep it beside your Sibley bird guide or better still in a pocket. It was written and includes many photos with amateurs in mind.

There are some interesting historical questions having to do with the species that depend on vernal pools to breed. How did they survive almost three centuries of agriculture? Old Closeteers can remember when wet areas were routinely filled in and even used as dumps. In the Midwest tens of thousands of swales, ponds and wet meadows were filled to obtain more crop acreage. Tens of millions of water birds migrating to and from summer nesting and feeding areas in the tundra and winter hangouts around the Gulf lost their en route fueling and resting stations. Here we filled red maple swamps and hundreds of depressions, many vernal pools. Then in the early 1970s came the Massachusetts Wetlands Protection Act and its regulations that provided protections to almost all wetlands, even often dry vernal pools. Scores of building projects in just the tri-town area have been affected. Our conservation commissions under the act are not allowing wetland alterations; in addition they are protecting uplands around them to some degree so wet habitats aren't adversely changed. We've seen major development plans stopped or severely modified by the existence of vernal pools, some smaller than our living rooms. We find this great change in just the past two human generations enormously encouraging. *Homo sapiens* have clearly recognized the right of other species to exist. Now back to the question raised at the beginning of this celebratory paragraph.

When hoofed animals and plows yearly tore up much of the land including many wet areas, how did small animals survive? Thoreau, naturalist and ecologist before the word, who roamed west of us in the Concord River basin wasn't surrounded by woods as we are now,

Beaver drowned trees, Ipswich River. Photo, courtesy of Judy Schneider.

rather by grazing and croplands. The same was true here and most of the rest of southern New England, even the Berkshires. Forested areas were few and far between compared with now. In the century prior to Thoreau, before railroads and coal, even wetlands were clear-cut at times by the charcoal makers. Open range livestock often allowed to overgraze left a mess of valuable topsoil, which was then carried by runoff to our wetlands. Erosion in grazing areas and from fallow cropland was a major problem. We can show you plenty of upland places around our towns where the topsoil the English found upon arrival is a fraction of the foot it was before. The Indians had a rotating agriculture without devastating livestock. To summarize: agriculture, especially when done poorly, renders terrain a very unnatural place for the creatures who evolved here over time beyond our ken.

We'll leave our two questions above largely unanswered and resort to speculation. There must have been wood frog and salamander populations that survived in the few pools left in farmers' woodlots, especially those farmers who didn't fill in all seemingly unproductive wet areas. There may have been a few places on the North Shore where wealthy landowners kept small wooded areas more or less intact. People were so short of fuel here in the 18th and 19th centuries that peat was mined from swamps and firewood shipped down from Maine and the Maritimes. Organizations like The Trustees of Reservations, Essex County Greenbelt Association, and town and state parks that protect woods didn't exist before the 20th century.

While the Passenger Pigeons were famously exterminated and the buffalo nearly so in the terrible 19th century, the vernal pool animals were not. They survived somehow in tiny forested and wet meadow islands among fields yearly scarred by hooves, plows, harrows, and in the 20th century poisoned by manmade chemicals. Their descendants sexually celebrate each early spring in thousands of now protected pools in Massachusetts and beyond. This Sunday Middleton Stream Teamers and friends, all folks are invited, will go forth on foot looking for adult animals and egg masses in still very cold water. Check the wet areas in your neighborhood. Vernal pools, pools not on a stream and those that dry up most years, range in size from bathtubs to several acres; some are within a few yards of houses. All are protected by law if we see to it.

---

* Available from the Massachusetts Division of Fisheries and Wildlife. natural. heritage@state.ma.us or call 1 (508) 389-6360.

APRIL 2011

RADIOACTIVE WATER

Trinity Test, Hiroshima, Nagasaki, American and Russian nuclear bomb tests, Three Mile Island, and Chernobyl are events burned in old memories of when radioactive elements resulting from man's activities got out of control purposely or otherwise. Now we add Fukushima. The poisons rose and are rising with water into the air to become part of the clouds. Water is a neutral carrier of life's good stuff like salts in the sea and sugars, salts, amino acids, and hormones in the blood to mention but a few of thousands of natural solutes. It also carries radioactive isotopes, pesticides and herbicides in air and flowing water beyond where they ought to be. Quiet Rachel Carson, very loudly in writing, warned us a half century ago in *Silent Spring* of agricultural chemicals on the loose in our waters. This past week in the *Boston Globe* we were reminded of another outspoken woman, pediatrician Helen Caldicott, who spoke, many thought unpleasantly, against the dangers of radiation. She started a decade after Carson bothered us and has gone on ever since. She opposes all nuclear weapons and power plants. One old Closeteer remembers attending a meeting where she in quiet fury told the group what we people were doing. Sometimes the truth it is very uncomfortable. Now politicians are warned over and over, often by timid advisors, about keeping their cool. Some of us old folks are nostalgic for the rare times when our leaders let us know how they truly felt. Caldicott continues to speak out from her home and medical practice in Newton. She is now watching the out of control events at Fukushima's power plants very carefully. She hasn't and doesn't need to say "I told you so." The media are making that point very loudly, albeit not always clearly. They remind us daily of past events and doubts; leaders and their advisors around the world are listening.

Man, and woman, such as Marie Curie, brilliantly learned to separate radioactive elements from natural rock, not always for the right reasons. We saw that at Hiroshima and Nagasaki. Many survivors there still suffer 65 years later. *Homo sapiens* then decided to "harness" these elements' tremendous power and release it slowly as is happening in several hundred power plants around the world. The nearest to us is just a half hour up the road at Seabrook. At Chernobyl and Fukushima the faulty harnesses broke. The wind- and water-borne radiation from Chernobyl fell even farther away than distant Wales where 25 years later the soils in certain pastures still grow grass that taints the milk of grazing livestock. Centuries-lasting poisons descended with the rain. The measurable, but not dangerous we are told, plumes from Fukushima passed over the United States last week; more may be still coming. Two generations have passed since the nuclear bomb tests of the 1950s when radioactive elements in jet stream droplets circled the world. The tests in northwestern Russia resulted in strontium-90 contaminated milk being dumped in New York State 20,000 plus jet stream miles down wind. We could go on about the contamination from U.S. tests and others far away. We needn't; past and present escapes are now being recalled daily on BBC, CNN, PBS and other media. Have you noticed how many times even the experts are saying "We don't know" when asked questions? That was a main point of Caldicott's. She told us as a medical doctor who studied radiation on the side what was known and warned again and again about what wasn't. As we have, and are again learning, even very small doses may cause harm. That is why they put a lead apron over your lap when x-raying in the dentist's office. They don't want sperm, eggs and vital organs too much affected. In Tokyo as of this writing milk and certain other foods are being banned for babies due to low-level contamination.

President Obama, who is about as well-read as any leader we've had since perhaps Teddy Roosevelt, knows all the above and more. Last year he announced his administration's energy plans; nuclear power despite daily vulnerability and the potential dangers from long-lived wastes, was an important part of his plans. He and others the world over, stimulated by communications from Japan, not yet physically by abnormally high levels of radiation, are giving the whole subject further thought. We hope he and his advisors will speak with firebrands like Caldicott. It will provide balance for the cool rational assurances they are receiving from engineers who say water will cool reactors down and keep their operations safe if systems are designed and built right. Alas, we've seen with the BP's Deepwater Horizon disaster in the Gulf and now in Japan that the engineers don't and can't know so aren't fully prepared. Who would have predicted a nine-point quake and the resulting tsunami? We do know that when fuel rods, active and spent, are not surrounded by water things spin out of control. The results end up in the natural water of the sky, ground and seas and there do we know not what.

We need lots of energy that doesn't produce greenhouse gases say the president and other movers and shakers for environmentally responsible progress. In the Closet we naively ask, why not put much more money into wind and solar, but most of all settle for less of everything? That's just not human nature you scoff. We counter: human nature much needs changing. Edward O. Wilson brilliantly argues that some of our behavior can be traced to evolution and is in our DNA; however, by no means all. We are not fully hardwired. Our advances in science and Wilson's, Carson's and Caldicott's ideas strongly support this statement.

We end with the old saw "moderation in all things." Radioisotopes and cosmic rays are natural constituents of our habitats. It is the excesses which we have some control over we should worry about. Lifestyles of too many are examples of excess. Huge houses with few people; multiple houses per some families; several large vehicles per household; no good public transport systems in too many places, and none even seriously asked for; thousands of acres of huge shopping centers at a distance, many like those in Danvers and Peabody covering once good agricultural land; common foods and flowers shipped thousands of miles instead of being raised here, etc., etc., etc. . . . Our English teachers warned us repeatedly against the use of etc., its use likened to "whatever." Et cetera sure does apply to lifestyles in many countries, especially ours, styles that are poisoning the planet.

Let's cool it. We can see what excess heat is doing at Fukushima. Excessive mutations and radiation sicknesses are far too high a price to pay for the lifestyles of a fraction of the world's human population. Let us start by keeping wastes from water.

EARLY WATERFOLKS

In our jaunts and paddles around the watershed we often wonder about the people here for 10,000 years before the newcomers from the "Old World." The explorers and colonists in the 16th and 17th centuries didn't write much about the natives who didn't write at all. However, a very few of thousands did and have left us their observations. We find them quoted, usually just a sentence or two, in later histories by others. We Closeteers are not professional historians; we have not gone back to original logs, diaries and books. The other day one of us stumbled upon a useful book in Middleton's Flint Public Library. Ronald Dale Karr did what we might have done if not so lazy. He read the writings of 22 famous sources and organized extracts from them into chapters about the Indians here. He entitled his 160-page book *Indian New England 1524 to 1674**. After reading these observations by famous explorers like Verrazzano and Champlain, businessmen and adventurers like John Smith, candid amateurs like William Wood, wise tolerant leaders like Thomas Morton and Roger Williams, and rough ship captains like Christopher Levett, we have a better handle on those people who populated our coast before European plagues killed most. A few survived and lived not always comfortably alongside the English who rapidly moved in on their land. At Patuxet, later Plymouth, the once populous land there had only a half-dozen survivors who had left for somewhere else by the time the Pilgrims arrived.

What do Indians have to do with water, our subject? Almost all people, Indians, and for a century early colonists, lived well within a day's walk of salt water. Both the Indians and many of the new people were water folks extraordinary. The former went several leagues to sea in canoes that foreign sailors admitted they had trouble to keep from tipping. The latter sailed a thousand leagues across the ocean in small ships to get here. The colonists, until the end of the French and Indian War, stuck close to the coast and on navigable sections of the larger rivers where many natives had lived and had kept open with yearly fires. Travel overland hauling any load was difficult most of the year. A trip to Falmouth, Maine, a day's sail from Salem, took over a week by land even when cart paths were passable in dry seasons and ferries across creeks and rivers were operating. Children, both Indian and English, were near the waters of our estuaries and played in and upon them. The Indians learned early in life to catch fish cleverly in a dozen ways based on their prey's calendars and behaviors. In frequent contact with sailors many colonists knew more of London, Lisbon and Liverpool than frontier towns just a few miles inland. Several of the early observers noted what good swimmers the Indians were. When their canoes capsized miles at sea, they'd right them and then bail out, or drag them ashore swimming in cold water. No doubt colonial kids played on the beaches, on clam flats, and in tidal creeks as the Indian children had. The Indian children caught fish and lobsters with lines, lances, nets, baskets and hands as did their fathers. The women clammed, often in winter, and gathered lobsters at low tides. The colonists too became adept fishermen.

Perhaps the natives' frequent exposure to water had something to do with their appearance and longevity. One old Closeteer says his mother often hailed the healthy virtues of bathing in salt water. He agrees. Here is what John Brereton wrote in 1602, "These people . . . are exceedingly courteous, gentle of disposition, and well conditioned, excelling all others that we have seen, so for the shape of body and lovely favor, . . . of stature much higher than we [Englishmen] . . ." Over and over we read similar praise of their "well proportioned" and "strong limbed" bodies, which were decorated with paint, fancy hairdos, and hung with belts and necklaces of shells. We think some of our modern youth with purple Mohawks, beads and tattoos would feel comfortable among them. They dressed lightly in elaborately decorated skin clothing, very skillfully made.

Their "birchen" canoes, framed with white cedar, were also works of art much admired by the newcomers. A couple canoes described were 17 feet long, three wide, capable of holding a half-dozen men and gear, yet so light a lone man could carry one on long portages. In warmer months they might venture in them several leagues to sea. Other canoes were laboriously burned and carved from large pine and chestnut logs. William Wood, here 1629 to 1633, tells of many dugout canoes left by the Naumkeags in now Salem after the time of the plagues, 1617 to 1619; "every [English] household having a water horse or two,**" no doubt from the many left behind.

The "great dying" from European diseases to which they had little resistance took 80 to 90 percent plus of some tribes. The colonists entered on coastal land largely clear of forests and the people who had cleared them. Some marveled at the "plantation"-like nature of the land due to yearly burning and agriculture. Groves of trees were largely restricted to wetlands. The uplands were savannah-like with large nut trees, oak, hickories and chestnuts much valued for food. The mature trees have thick fire-resistant bark. Around them were meadows lush with berries in season. Strawberries and blueberries were raved about by the English first arriving here in June and July after a month or more at sea eating salted, often rancid, meat and hard biscuit. Berries of a half-dozen species were an important source of food for the Indians. Imported livestock no doubt quickly reduced the berry patches.

Corn, bean and squash fields were extensive. Recent estimates of the number of people in the Massachusetts and Narragansett Bay areas are much higher than those of the early observers.*** There were many villages; all had large gardens. Observers tell of natives fertilizing them with an abundance of fish that came to spawn each spring at planting time. The kids must have had a fine time catching shad and alewives for food and perfect fertilizer. The English marveled at great Atlantic sturgeon up to 16 feet long that the Indians attracted with torch light and killed with lances. Wouldn't you love to see anadromous fish return to our Ipswich, their Agawam, River?

We'd like to share more of what we learned from editor Karr's collection and other histories we have.**** Check his long-dead writers' words for yourself and the next time you walk along our estuaries, streams and rivers, beaches and bays imagine their clean waters abounding in fish, lobsters, clams, waterfowl and handsome healthy people. Sounds like paradise to us, alas paradise lost. Such visions may be the unspoken reasons some Closeteers often visit the flats to dig clams. We sense squaws among us gossiping and laughing as they dig with forked sticks. Men, also unseen, are hunting waterfowl or fishing nearby.

As you read carefully between the lines of the Puritans, Pilgrims, Catholics (Verrazzano, Champlain), and maybe agnostic Wood you might, despite their "civilized" biases, catch as we did a faint whiff of envy of the "savages."

* Indian History of New England 1524-1674: A Compendium of Eyewitness Accounts of Native American Life, edited by Ronald Dale Karr (Branch Line Press. Pepperell, MA) 1999

** Wood, William. New England Prospects, (London) 1634. (later Univ. of Mass. Press) 1977

*** Mann, Charles. 1491. Mann's bold theories have stimulated much debate since his book was published in 2005.

****Our favorite history of New England Indians and early colonists is Nathaniel Philbrick's highly acclaimed Mayflower published in 2006. We recommend it be read before all others. He tells of Indians' and colonists' shifting politics and in so doing brings both alive and all-to-human in their intertwining and shifting alliances. The far too general word "Indian" fails us as it did Columbus. There were several native "nations" and many subgroups in just the area the newcomers called New England.

Another valuable reference for those interested in the daily lives of Indians here is Howard Russell's Indian New England Before the Mayflower published in 1980. Both Russell and Philbrick relied heavily on the early observers Karr quotes. Their eyewitness accounts are interwoven with much that has been learned since.

HEALING WATER

Strip mines usually conjure up visions of truncated mountains in West Virginia and eastern Kentucky and great open pits in Montana. In the 1940s, '50s, and '60s a big chunk of southeastern Middleton was stripped of thin topsoil and then the thick layers of gravel and sand underneath. We don't know where the dark topsoil that took ten millennia to form went. While excavating and for a while after, the hundred or so acres resembled raw moonscape. One old-timer told us that on some days 500 truckloads left town. We are reminded of the archaic name "borrow" for the pits where soil was borrowed for fill somewhere else. Modern contractors use the words "cut" and "fill." After examining pre-mining topographic maps we estimate as much as a couple million cubic yards were "borrowed" and trucked south to East Boston for Logan's runways. However, that was not a loan. No interest was ever paid. Ironically as the millennium began lots of fill came the opposite way from Boston's "Big Dig" and was deposited on and close to the same site to cap Middleton's landfill. Logan bought gravel, sand and silt; we were given glacial marine clay a half century later.

Enough of this word play, some of us often hike around the score or more pits that pockmark the land roughly circumscribed by South Main Street, River Street, Hilldale Avenue and the Ipswich River floodplain.* If you count all those who visit the transfer station, industrial park and soccer fields on the old strip mine site they number thousands per week. We Closeteers explore off the paved and developed areas and find the once bare pits now heavily vegetated with a rich diversity of weeds, bushes and trees. From old maps and surviving grades east of Hilldale Avenue we can see where 10 to 40 vertical feet of low hills were removed and the land lowered to elevations near that of the river. Animals returned with the vegetation. The area without any topsoil to speak of is one of our favorite wildlife habitats. Plants don't need topsoil to grow. Water is what they need and have plenty of. The water table, thanks to the miners, is near the surface and often above in the low areas, and eastern Massachusetts averages about 45 inches of precipitation each year. Water slowly dissolves the small amount of minerals from soil particles that plants need. Green plants make their own food from light, carbon dioxide and water in the processes of photosynthesis. Plants have grown quickly in and around the pits. Many of the post-mining trees are 30 to 40 feet high. There are a few large oaks and pines 60 or more years of age that are growing up from pre-mining surface elevations in places near the river floodplain.

We may be belaboring the obvious here. Almost everyone around here must have noticed how quickly places with water revive after catastrophes. We only have to look at the subdivisions of the booming '90s and early years of the millennium. One old Closeteer had the position of conservation agent in Middleton during that time. He had the unenviable job of checking forested areas, subdivision plan in hand, before permits were issued and clearing work began. He tells of beautiful spring mornings with clear water running in intermittent streams, birds singing and buds bursting. Two months later there were no trees or even weeds** on the upland there; knolls had been flattened, low areas filled. Loam saved and not sold was set aside in huge piles. In the first month of the summer when most plant growth occurs there were no plants except in the wetlands and narrow buffers around them. The exposed subsoils and boulders were shades of yellow, rust colors, and grays. Chainsaws followed by great earth-moving machines had returned the land to post-continental glacial status of 11,000 years ago in just days. Yet in a couple years the greens were back in the form of chemically treated lawns. Water and heat did their seeming magic, only this time with unneeded additives. However, the places cleared but not used, around the edges of those areas covered with buildings, asphalt and lawn, were also green again with natural pioneering weeds and bush and tree seedlings, signs of healing in just a short time. We marveled at the speed these plants appeared from raw rocks sprinkled with wind and animal-borne seeds.

People everywhere have looked to water for symbolic and actual cleansing and healing. One Closeteer's sister-in-law visited from Japan. Upon being shown his parents' grave, a natural uncut foundation stone, Buddhist Kikuno, without saying a word, filled a bucket with water from a graveyard tap and with great vigor splashed it on the stone. In a somewhat similar vein, since the time of John the Baptist Christian baptisms are performed with water perhaps symbolically preparing and healing the soul. Water helps heal wounds of flesh, mind and land. No one washes wounds with dirty or poisoned water, no one visits polluted rivers for peace of mind, and no animals except humans add poisoned water to damaged land. As we've so often pleaded here in the Water Closet, let's keep the water in air, soil, rivers and seas free of our manmade chemicals and those, such as oil, sealed in the earth. They slow its healing properties.

* If you'd like to visit this interesting place go to the parking lot on the left side of Natsue Way off River Street, Middleton. The lot is just to the left of the transfer station entrance. There you will see a sign and map attached to the cyclone fence inviting you to follow the "Lonergan Road along Ipswich River Trail".

** Weed is a pejorative we in the Closet don't like, but we have no other good general synonym for lovely plants too many people have prejudices against. Let's make up a word. Send your suggestions to the Middleton Stream Team.

WOOD DUCKS

The other morning Middleton Stream Teamers while spring cleaning at the park at Farnsworth Landing on the Ipswich River compared notes on *Aix sponsa*, Wood Ducks, recently seen. We agreed that there has been an increase of this species in the last couple decades. Sometimes on a paddle downriver we'll scare up several as each of its many meanders is rounded.

This discussion led one member to the Closet's treasured volumes by ornithologist extraordinaire Edward Howe Forbush; for such a giant we feel we must use all three names and should have the letters all in capitals. A century ago he gave us three volumes, 400 to 500 pages each, entitled *Birds of Massachusetts and Other New England States*. This monumental work was published by the Commonwealth of Massachusetts in 1925 and issued by authority of the legislature in 1929. We have a set in the Closet thanks to Francis Masse who passed on this gift from father Chester Masse who served as a state game warden.

We can't resist starting with an old-fashioned bit of what some would call Victorian purple prose. We much like Forbush's found throughout his pages between more objective passages and anecdotes. Authors didn't have the flashy media we have then; illustrations in books at the time were black-and-white ink sketches and a few expensive colored plates of paintings, hence the need for word pictures. Here is Forbush peeking from a riverside hiding place:

> *See the mating pair on the dark and shaded flood of a little woodland river; they seem to float as lightly as the drifting leaves. The male glides along proudly, his head ruffled and his crest distended, his scapular feathers raised and lowered at will, while his plumes flash with metallic luster whenever the sun's rays sifting through the foliage intercept his course. She coyly retires; he daintily follows, exhibiting all his graces, the darkling colors of his plumage relieved by the pure white markings of head and breast and the bright red of feet and bill and large lustrous eye. What a picture they make, as, intent on one another, they glide along close together, she clothed in modest hues, he glowing and resplendent. He nods and calls in low sweet tender tones and thus, she leading, he pursuing, they disappear into the shadows where the stream turns upon another course.*

Wow! Maybe we should end here and leave them to imagined bliss.

The courting Forbush so delightfully and anthropomorphically describes may lead to a snug high-rise apartment with the female sitting on up to 15 eggs. Wood Ducks along with a half-dozen other duck species are cavity nesters. We wonder if the increase in Wood Ducks isn't due to an increase in holes in trees. In the last half century there has been a significant increase in protected forests and less cutting in others. The trees are getting old hence more holes. People have put up Wood Duck boxes. Along our rivers and streams the beavers are drowning many acres of trees. The upright corpses attract woodpeckers, insects and fungi hence in time more hideaways. Then there is the change in people's behavior so vividly remembered by old-timers who lived in the country. Just 60 years ago there were shotguns, 22-caliber and air rifles often loaded in every barn, workshop and farmhouse. To some any wild thing that moved was fair game. All hawks and owls were deemed chicken killers. Ducks were shot and eaten. Other animals, even small birds, were targets for practice. Sixty years before those waning agrarian years the hunting of birds was done on a massive scale by market hunters. The "good ole days," so nostalgically remembered by many humans, were very bad ones for many creatures. Wood Ducks that in the mid-19th century darkened the skies in places at times, according to Forbush's research, became by the turn of the century almost extinct. European poultry fanciers were sending Wood Ducks raised there back to the states from whence their ancestors came. Anyway the good news is they are back in more ways than just guessed at from our casual observations. Jim Berry, Ipswich ornithologist, who is working with colleagues throughout the state on the Mass Audubon *Breeding Bird Atlas* (atlas edition 1, 1974 to 1979; atlas 2, 2007 to present) reports that Wood Ducks were reported in 377 of 1,077 area blocks inventoried three decades ago. Atlas 2, one year short of completion, has them in 664 of the 1,077 blocks. Jim warns us to take these numbers with a grain of salt. The inventories for atlas 2 have been more intensive, the areas better covered. However, he a life-long North Shore birder agrees with us Stream Teamers that there are more of these very beautiful dabbler ducks that are roughly half the weight of common Mallards. One old Stream Teamer reports seeing more of the former this spring.

We digressed above and left the developing embryos in the tree cavity under mum where they will be for four weeks until hatch. They'll then hang out in the protective apartment fasting for a day before venturing forth in the open air dressed in light down. Now observations become dicey. John James Audubon, all three names again with bigger caps than Forbush's, observed a brood jumping from an exit hole to water several human stories below. Their mother gathered them up and then led them on a much longer more dangerous adventure through to fledging. Others have them with their sharp claws and a bill tip, called a nail, climbing down to ground and water. Still others say they've seen mothers carrying them to the water where they'll feed for life if the snapping turtles, large fish and snakes don't feed on them first. Life for young ducklings and goslings is precarious.

The Closet's small reproduction of Audubon's famous elephant-size portfolio is open now to his Wood Duck painting. He without camera shot his subjects and then wired them into dramatic poses. Here before us are two "glowing and resplendent" males and two females "clothed in modest hues" so necessary as camouflage. One of the females is looking out from a hollow tree.

A couple weekends ago Stream Teamer Glenice Kelley, while spring cleaning at one of the team's parks along the river, touched with rake a hidden Mallard, distant relative of the Wood Duck, incubating a dozen or so eggs in a ground nest. Mother Mallard moved, hence was revealed. We've returned several times since to peer in at her among the leaves at the base of a red cedar just twenty feet from major highway Route 114. She sometimes has her wings half spread over the sides of her nest, feathers somewhat extended, almost a perfect match for the brown oak leaves. May her brood and those of all ducks survive to be led by mothers to water and then on to fledging and flight. We can only wish for this unnatural situation; predators will determine.

TURTLES EN ROUTE THROUGH TIME

We, a couple Stream Teamers, walked the old Essex rail bed on a recent cold and breezy April morning. A spotted turtle, *Clemmys guttata*, with faded yellow spots was found crossing our path slowly from east to west sides of the Boston Brook floodplain, now beaver impoundments. Its battered black carapace absorbed the bright sun's rays to warm the blood below. We, well fueled, temperatures independent of those without intrinsic warm blood, stood and watched it stop as it sensed our presence and pulled in head, legs and tail. We gently picked up the hand-sized animal so like its ancestors well over 100 million years before. We counted the annual growth lines of a plastron's scute and found the number approximately a third of our old ages. We gently spoke to its almost completely hidden face and got no response. We wanted to linger since we hadn't seen a not common yellow spot in six years. By the way, the last spotted turtle seen by one of us was found very close to this place, perhaps the very same. David Carroll, turtle man extraordinaire, of Warner, New Hampshire, would have sketched its shell scutes for spots and marks the first time and would, soon after checking his records, have known if this was the same turtle.* The Stream Teamer hadn't been so diligent.

We also saw several lively warbler species and a male bluebird on that turtle passing morning. Despite the very special blue of bluebirds, which have become ever more common this past decade, it was the turtle representing something timeless and relatively unchanging that excited and left us pondering many things. On Patriot's Day a few days before on a canoe paddle down the river we'd seen several common painted turtles, *Chrysemys picta picta*, basking on Ipswich River logs under similar brisk cool breezes. They were recharging their fluid electrolytic batteries. And a few days before that paddle Edward "Butch" Cameron from his home perched above the river called and reported a baby painted turtle in his yard en route the river from a south sloping lawn, the place where mother had left its DNA and perhaps that of a dozen others in eggs in a shallow cavity the summer before. Butch kept it overnight so we could see, which we did on a visit the next morning before release to resume its journey. He had seen them many times before. As viewed from above it is circular about the size of a half dollar and the only word that suits is cute. Its underside and shell margin are graced by the bright yellow and red marks of an adult. Later we did some rough arithmetic and figured it had to go 2,000 times its length to reach the relative safety of the river water 200 feet away downhill. An old question that has bothered again and again over the years arose. How does it know which way to go? Mother's trail marks and any odor must have been washed away dozens of times since her climb up late last summer. Perhaps it smells the river. Turtle experts tell us turtle egg and young survival is a very chancy thing. Skunks, raccoons, possums, and who knows what else who like fresh eggs get most soon after they are laid. At least at Butch's there is little worry about road traffic, which is a great cause of death to mothers going and little ones returning near well-traveled pavement. A very small percent of many successfully make the round trip from sun-warmed nesting soils and in the vulnerable periods of being tiny. Painted turtles are relatively common due to many reproductive years.

Environmentalist David Carroll who has devoted much of his life to studying these creatures he unabashedly loves is greatly encouraged by their continued presence after 200 million years on an ever-changing planet. Turtles have survived the passing of dinosaurs and hundreds of thousands of other organisms. They'll no doubt surpass us unless on the way out we take all else with us. Some distant day we hope another creature will pause upon finding a turtle passing. Will it wonder as we are doing here?

* Carroll, David M., *The Year of the Turtle* (St. Martin's Griffin, New York) 1996. The pages of this beautiful book, illustrated by the author, appear in the form of prose. Upon reading they emerge as scientific poetry available to almost all. Carroll narrates of his wanderings and tells us of the myriad plants and animals and conditions he and they experience. The same can be said of his Swampwalkers Journal, winner of the John Burroughs Medal for the Best Natural History of the Year (1996) award. Swampwalkers Journal is a former Middleton Conservation agent's favorite. The plants and animals the agent daily walked among on his rounds are put in context in their habitats in a most inspiring way. Leisurely reading is like taking an intensive course in wetland ecology while enjoying every sentence and illustration. Since giving us these marvelous gifts, Carroll won a MacArthur genius award in 2006.

MAY 2011

OBSERVATIONS FROM A NEW HILL

In the past two decades an old Closeteer has become obsessed with manmade changes along the Ipswich River. Others scoff and say "Let sleeping fills lie"; he does so himself at times. Yet he could not and probably would not reverse them even if he was watershed dictator. On a recent warm afternoon in light rain he hiked to the summit of a manmade mountain midway source to sea of his beloved river in a town appropriately called Middleton, probably named without a thought to location in the watershed. The glacier-left rise had been a low hill greatly added to in the latter third of last century, first with cleanup trash from burnt cities in northeastern Massachusetts and then by state officials who took it over and covered the illegal landfill. The upland was expanded by urban debris upward and five or so acres easterly over wetland. A state-ordered cap using earth from the bowels of Boston's "Big Dig" raised the area another 40 or so feet. A grassy hill mowed yearly and pleasing to the eye now rises 80 feet above the surrounding floodplains of the Ipswich River and its tributary Nichols Brook. From the top one can look down on where Middleton merges with nearby Boxford, Topsfield and Danvers; no bounds are seen. The new hill has become one of our favorite places to view wildlife and glacier-sculpted topography as far away as Holt and Boston Hills in distant North Andover.

In the mid-20th century an even greater change in the watershed was wrought just a half mile to the east. From the landfill hill (we must find a proper name) we look east to mighty Interstate 95 providing fast straight transport from Florida to Maine and connecting to a marvelous highway system that links us with the rest of the country. In hindsight this was probably the worse human project ever inflicted on a country. Our interstate highway system so highly touted has made us a CAR country "addicted to oil," the words in quotes from one-time oil man and President George W. Bush. But, good heavens, this is all too much for us provincials to contemplate. From our pretty-new hill let's look closer to home and see what the massive interstate filling to cross the watershed here did to our river. We urge you to walk to where they intersect near Masconomet Regional School and see for yourselves. I-95 bridge builders made a shelf-like walkway under their two bridges that hangs from the south side abutments. You can safely stroll under ceaseless traffic for 250 feet on it. The north and south abutments flanking the river channel are only 60 feet apart. Before the bridges (north and south lanes) the floodplain there allowed about a 400-foot width of free flow. Without much thought the engineers reduced flood flow passage six to seven fold. Not only that, a wide wildlife corridor was eliminated. We've never seen animals walking the shelf's walkway as we do. Two very dangerous four lane highways block almost all east-west migration for those without wings or fins. Multiply this filled wildlife corridor by thousands as the great road passes from Houlton to Miami.

Let's climb back up on the now protected hill and look for the interesting and good. It seems that people will do nothing serious about most blocked wildlife corridors until the oil runs out. That may be a while, deep drilling has resumed in the Gulf. How depressing, let's hurry up the hill out of the traffic's roar.

From back on top the broad floodplain stretches before us from Ferncroft heights on the Danvers line on into Topsfield. It isn't the same as just a decade ago. From the freshly capped hill at the beginning of the millennium we looked down upon red maple forest. This time, thanks to a mammal without dozers or trucks, the trees are showing signs of stress and the floodplain-red maple swamp is becoming a "beaver meadow." The red maples, which love water but "can't take too much year round," are dying. We've said this over and over before in the Closet when describing the formation of beaver meadows. With increased light due an absence of tree shade and increased water, lush low tussock sedges now dominate watery scenes here and around the county. They remind us of thousands of tiny islands with mazes of channels between. Other changes we know of here, ones not readily seen, are legal protections now afforded the low land and its higher buffers. Much of the terrain to the south and east is protected by the Wetlands Protection Act, the Essex County Greenbelt Association and the Town of Middleton. As long as their restrictions last there will be no highway projects, landfills or farming. Much in view has gone back from agriculture to wild animals and plants. We have in us the power to taketh away and giveth. Let's stay up here in the clean air of the now green summit and wait until the 24/7 drone of traffic from I-95 wanes and then disappears. We, the addicted, will not know it; we must soon descend to get our periodic gasoline fixes. We can, however, hope our descendants will experience such a passing. These surrounds will change again and again; let our species consider others as the changes flow on.

SPRING HIKE IN FILTERED SUNLIGHT

Each year in late April and May a wondrous change is ours thanks to water and warmth. Cold and the absence of transpiration (water loss) from dormant plants had saved much of winter's precipitation in the soil. Groundwater is high; streams and ponds are full. As the soil warms under ever higher sun, buds take up water and grow. In mid-April although the buds are swelling we don't give them much attention; a week later red maple flower buds seem to explode and hover over swamps in what seem at a distance low red clouds. Gray-barked red maples live up to their name. Earlier willow flowers called pussies had given us a preview of this coming.

On May 6, the Middleton Council on Aging/Conservation Commission Friday morning walkers entered "The Lost 50" conservation land off North Liberty Street en route to other protected lands that stretch deep into Boxford State Forest. How lucky we in the tri-town area and North Andover are to have several square miles of forests with ponds and hills set aside for plants and animals including us. We can hike the many trails for miles without ever encountering houses or even a bit of pavement. On that Friday morning in new spring shade the trails were wet but easily passable. We did have to cross Pond Meadow Brook on a few old logs and stepping stones someone had lain down.

The winding up and down paths were pleasant open tunnels of light green. The bright sunlight from the east at a slant was softened by the rapidly growing but still tiny leaves above. Yellowish birch catkins and maple samaras subdued the light even more. It was as if an army of pointillist painters with green, red and yellow pigments had been given three-dimensional canvases of twigs and told to use small dots. Along the trail wood anemones delighted with their beginning pinks opening to chaste white blossoms. We found three-lobed purple leaves of ground-hugging hepatica that had blossomed weeks before. Ferns of a half-dozen species were putting up fiddleheads. We picked a handful of bracken fern tops to eat later at home. Walker Joan Cudhea identified one evergreen fern as a Christmas fern. She showed us how each side leaflet resembles a Christmas stocking hence the name. Last year's still green fronds lay flat in a rosette against the brown duff. Seemingly exploding from its center were pale fuzzy fiddleheads, this year's fronds yet to fully unroll. In puddles along the way we spooked wood frogs. Photographers among us recorded two, who posed scarcely seen on last year's leaves. In one heavily wooded new beaver impoundment flooding a mini-valley an American toad was admired. In an oak above a Baltimore Oriole sang lustily and then revealed himself.

Our trail gradually sloped to our destination, the Pond Meadow Pond beaver impoundment. We won't call it "beaver meadow," a phrase we often use for beaver-changed areas, because the beavers' almost yearly additions since 1999 to their now huge dam have turned more than a hundred acres into what appears a shallow lake, hardly a meadow.

Full morning light poured down on us from the east as we walked out of the woods and then along the west bank of the new lake, oaks just leafing out above high granite ledge on our right, shining water to our left. Rising gray out of the water are the trunks of drowned Atlantic white cedars. Swooping in graceful flashes were many Tree Swallows picking off insects we couldn't see; maybe some were black flies that bothered a bit but did not bite. We were forced half up the ledge onto the rough ground above the stone wall because the beavers have flooded the ancient trail below it. We soon happened upon a room-sized glacial erratic, the substrate of rock ferns and columbine in bloom along with poison ivy, red and shiny now, just leafing out and warning us to beware; "Our garden is beautiful but dangerous." Remember the Sirens who tempted Odysseus and sailors when passing their rocky isle? We dared not pick the lovely columbines.

Finally we rounded the 170-foot-long, five-foot-high beaver dam built on a long ago farmer's causeway to make the lake. We crossed its outlet stream, Pond Meadow Brook, and turned northeast up a knoll to look down upon the well-made dam. From there we could see seven Great Blue Heron nests high above the impounded water in dead white pines. Parents were at each, incubating two or three eggs or standing sentinel on a limb nearby. Old now, we did not swim out and shimmy up 60 feet to check. We had visited this rookery in previous years when there were 26 nests and had seen one or two young almost as big as parents on each large nest. Most of the rotting nest pines have fallen.

What a marvelous place the beavers have made for herons they don't even know. We wonder if young raised in such high wild beauty are affected by it; we periodic voyeurs certainly are.

PRIVATE WATER

A lively debate, the only one during a sparsely attended Middleton Town Meeting last week, went back and forth during the discussion about Middleton's water conservation bylaw. The petitioners' Article 32 was for an amendment that would exclude private well owners from the bylaw restricting irrigation. The dominant word by far that echoed off the walls of the hall was PRIVATE, which was repeated loudly and emphatically about a dozen times. "I drilled a well at considerable expense for my large house and expensively landscaped lawn. It is PRIVATE. I can do what I want with the water." This was the gist of several speakers' remarks supporting Article 32. That basic strongly felt feeling by the proponents carried the night 78 to 71. Many on both sides or without an opinion were not present. Opponents were not well prepared. There had been no campaign against the important amendment. Only about 160 citizens of 10,000 attended the town's once a year legislative session.

Sandy Rubchinuk, stalwart of the Middleton Stream Team and a well owner, spoke clearly and strongly against the amendment. Gaylen Kelley, another Stream Teamer, likened the water in the basin to a jug of sangria in which well owners were dipping their expensive straws. The highlight of the exchanges was Town Administrator Ira Singer's 10-minute history without notes about the last few decades of water issues in the Ipswich River basin. Regulations, permits, 14 water departments, court cases, watering bans, DEP, bylaws, and upriver drilling were events and subjects reviewed clearly and chronologically. One old Closeteer and Stream Teamer who had been tangentially involved in the history said he finally half understood it all for the first time after Mr. Singer's summary. Twenty years of bits and pieces fell into place. Board of Selectmen Chairman Christine Lindberg told us why, according to DEP permit language and the ruling in a court case in which Middleton was involved, private well owners must be included in any conservation laws by the town. Since bylaws need the blessing of the state attorney general's office we'll see what happens.

Time, so often mentioned in the Water Closet, was the hippopotamus lurking in the room during the discussion. Deep aquifers contain ancient water unseen for tens of thousands of years. Deep wells draw it up into the light and pass it through showers, sinks, toilets, septic systems, shops, factories, gardens and lawns laced with additives. Much water evaporates into the air when used for irrigation. The rest joins the soils and surface waters and slowly percolates to surface water bodies. In both air as vapor and the ground as liquid it migrates across PRIVATE lot lines. Imagine someone claiming exclusive ownership to 50,000-year-old water that she borrows for a while. Under our system of land ownership it is easy for some to claim ownership of our natural resources. They are deemed by law PRIVATE and not necessarily to be shared with neighbors, other animals and plants. One old Middleton surveyor told us that such rights in places and times have extended from surface bounds down to the center of the Earth. The landowners might have a point if the water was confined in isolated pockets like copper ore, unconnected over time to the whole.

The opponents of the amendment, who knew deep aquifers and groundwater are connected, left the meeting realizing their loss may have been due to their failure to explain in terms all might understand. In the days since the meeting the Closeteer mentioned above has gone to geology books and to a 1998 report* of water resources in Middleton and west Danvers. *Roadside Geology of Massachusetts* * * and the report show our area resting on Bloody Bluff Fault. The rocks and fossils of the Avalon terrane to the southeast of this southwest to northeast running complex of cracks and formations are similar to those found in northwest Africa. The rocks to the northwest across the fault are those of the Laurentian terrane. Those ancient continents were once part of supercontinents Gondwana and later Pangaea, 600 to 300 million years ago. About 200 million years ago the part of Pangaea now to the northwest and old Gondwana to the southeast parted and an ocean we now call the Atlantic started to form between. It is still widening. The great Bloody Bluff line of disturbances from the crashing and parting of continents was right here. The rock formations found with the help of I-95 road cuts show that the now tri-towns were in the middle of the slow-moving action. In the fault area are many different rock formations with billions of fissures, joints and faults. It will take a year of study before we laypeople half understand. Then we will try to show there are connections without all the geologic names and jargon. We wanted a simple explanation of deep aquifers, and if tapped, their recharge from surface waters. While researching we soon found ourselves over our heads in geologic time and complexity.

In the meantime we will place our faith in what geologists tell us. There are connections, and pumping from deep aquifers does affect the surface waters that replenish them. If the amendment withstands attorney general and Department of Environmental Protection scrutiny we may resume the debate next May at town meeting in the new Howe-Manning school gym. This time we hope to be prepared. A town whose people use 65 gallons of water per day per person (13 five-gallon pails!) more water than many folks in the world use in a week or month should conserve. Even when there is plenty just passing it though our systems does harm to a precious finite resource.

* Emery & Garrett Groundwater, Inc., Exploration of Groundwater Resources in Bedrock Aquifers Phase I: Towns of Middleton, with portions of Danvers, North Reading, & North Andover (Meridith, NH 1998)

** Skenan, James W., Roadside Geology of Massachusetts (Mountain Press Publishing Company, 2001)

FLOODS AGAIN

It has been misting and drizzling all week yet the Closet's rain gauge Saturday morning showed only 1.4 inches of precipitation over five wet days. The Ipswich River at the south Middleton gauge had risen only a foot; flow rate is back up to average for this time of year. In May of 2006 we got 10 times 1.4 inches in two weeks. The Ipswich River collected and rose to record levels.

This spring television news daily features the mighty Mississippi receiving distant snowmelt and too much precipitation simultaneously. It and its great tributaries are overflowing natural banks and levees. The vast floodplains where people raise crops and have built towns are under, as is periodically expected. Sediment from far away will settle on destroyed spring crops and fields, enriching the soil once again as the water slows and then recedes. We feel for the folks whose houses and businesses are flooded. They purposely planted and built there knowing collectively what would be coming every few years. The good land was there and that is where they earned their livings. When people settled in the 19th century there was little choice. You couldn't then load the truck with family and livestock and escape to higher ground. By the 20th century towns were well established, and after the great flood of 1927 more and higher levees were built to protect civilization in the floodplains. This sequence of events was and is not peculiar to the Mississippi basin. One old Closeteer vividly remembers as a little boy his parents every few years bemoaning the poor victims of the Yangtze and Yellow Rivers in China. The death tolls were astounding. His family and others had no TV; the great rivers, their widths swollen many miles, had to be imagined.

Let's leave the grim realities of the effects of these natural phenomena on people and escape to the high mountains from whence much of the flood water comes. There is grandeur in the magnificent process. Warm moisture-laden air comes in off the vast Pacific and climbs into the cold of the Sierras, Cascades and Rockies where its water freezes and falls as snow to pile up and up. The peaks, no places for people in winter, become striking as seen from the valleys especially during sunrises and sunsets when the snow glows shades of red. In spring the sun rising daily higher, giving its warmth more meaning, begins to melt the accumulations, some many meters deep. Again metamorphosed water descends in trillions of rivulets, which braid into billions of small streams, which join into larger ones, some even given names. These converge into small rivers, which do the same forming larger ones like the Jefferson, Yellowstone and Madison that with others form the fast-flowing Missouri, the wet highway of Lewis, Clark, their men, a woman and babe. The clear rivulets carry wee bits of unseen sediment downward; in the ever widening surge more and more is added at each tributary. The transparent water becomes translucent then opaque with natural fertilizer: fine sand, silt and clay, to be deposited far downriver. We are going to ignore the reality of the enormous cockily placed flood control dams across the Missouri and levees along the Mississippi. In our minds we'll let the river run free, loud and wild as it did before the Army Corps of Engineers. Its increasingly heavy burden becomes much more than nutrients and new layers of substrate for crops. What flows past the cultivated floodplains is the stuff that formed the vast Mississippi delta lands once projecting far out into the Gulf. Now the flood waters are constrained by levees resulting in high-speed transport of sediments out into the sea's deep water. There it finally settles out, no longer building protective marshes that protect New Orleans. The existing marshes, unfed, erode away. The deltas are retreating.

During this spring's floods officials have been opening floodgates and breaching levees to spread the front thus slowing the flow and lowering its level. Farms and towns in the floodplains are being further flooded in order to save the cities.

Maybe in addition to the levees we should do as the mound builder Indians along the Mississippi did before the European newcomers. With modern equipment even larger mounds could be made and towns relocated upon them. Floodplains would be left to agriculture and at times flood waters. People in the horse and wagon days needed to live near their cultivated land. With "agribusiness" in the tractor-saddle many of the great fields are now visited by only a few vehicle drivers and their machines at planting and harvesting time. Alas, folks no longer need to live on farms. Those who like waterfront property might buy lots atop the levees and build small houses on stilts for just-in-case. Water access gaps would be cut through the levees resulting, during spring highs, in a series of long narrow islands. Floods might become times of greatly anticipated entertainment viewed safely from above. Crazy you say? Think what folks must have said when the dikes in Holland and the mammoth levees were first proposed. Perhaps it is high time to think outside the floodplains and to let them perform their ancient functions.

JUNE 2011

CLIMBING UP THE PARKER RIVER

Folks along West Coast rivers who know stories of salmon yearn for their return in former numbers. Also, we on the East Coast want the shad, alewives, sturgeon, lamprey eel and Atlantic salmon back in the multitudes earlier generations observed. The other afternoon two old Stream Teamers happened upon a father and daughter who may have never heard or read those yarns, yet there they were at the easternmost Parker River fish ladder in Byfield staring intently at swimming alewives* in the stone and concrete watery rungs while waiting for glimpses of them airborne as they leapt upward to the next.

The line-drive leaps are almost too fast to be seen with old eyes and processed by declining optic lobes. We wondered if the father half our age and his young daughter saw more. The friendly dad upon our arrival was bubbling over with enthusiasm about what they were seeing. The intent kneeling girl never glanced up. She reminded us of Narcissus staring at his reflection. Yet we sensed her focus not so shallow. Did the girl feel an ancient kinship with the fish? We, burdened with knowledge not of our own gleaning, became immersed in admiration for these

Climbing up the Parker River. Photo, courtesy of Stream Team.

beauties on their migration from sea and salt water up over stone steps against fast flow. Even the dozen rectangular pools of the ascending ladder don't make for easy passage. The climbers with thrusting tails had energy enough to accelerate against adversely flowing water, exit the surface upward a body length and shoot horizontally several more. Unlike runners over hurdles they didn't quickly leap one after another, but lingered off to the side of each water-filled pool catching their watery breaths while building up strength and perhaps courage. There were many more waiting than jumping at any given moment. These less than one-foot-long athletes had been fasting, or so we read, since the beginning of their spawning runs. Studies of migrating salmon in Europe's Rhine River have shown they digest their muscles en route. They arrive at spawning ponds upriver loaded with sperm and eggs, little muscle tissue left.

Drastic physiological changes, which we couldn't see and wondered if they felt, happen internally when going from seawater to fresh in a short period of time. Most species of fish can't do it even over time and die if they are made to do so in the lab. Fish that go from salt water to fresh to spawn, or vice versa like the American eel, can. How much damage, if any, is done in the process may not be known. Bony fishes' body fluids are about one percent solutes (salts and other substances in solution) and 99 percent water. Do you remember osmosis from your high school biology? Osmosis is the diffusion of water from higher to lower water concentrations through differentially permeable membranes. In the ocean, water constantly osmoses out through the skin from 99 percent to 96.5 percent, the concentration of seawater, yet blood concentration doesn't change because bony fish at sea swallow salt water as fast as the body fluid's water is lost through osmosis. Alas, the 3.5 percent salts swallowed along with the water will quickly poison if not constantly excreted in highly concentrated salty urine. We'll not go into how the cells actively transport salts from gut to urine, it is beyond the scope of this essay. Now let's consider what happens when the beautifully balanced creatures enter fresh water, essentially 100 percent water. Water osmoses in from 100 to 99 percent. Essential salts diffuse out from one to zero percent. Wonder of wonders, again the body fluid concentrations don't change from the essential 99/1 percent concentration equilibrium.** By the way, these concentrations and substances are quite the same as in our blood. Is there anything in all this that has us visiting the ladder and the girl so intent on fellow vertebrates? Something in us likes to think so.

We digress, let's save those alewives who find themselves in fresh water in the fish ladder. We don't need to. They save themselves by excreting lots of water as very dilute urine. Their gills actively absorb tiny amounts of salts even from fresh water to keep the one percent. All these numbers laid on you are actually fractions. Fresh water for instance may be 99.99 percent water, 0.01 percent salts. The gill cells using energy in a process called "active transport" pull salt ions in against the concentration gradient, the opposite of diffusion. Forgive us for all this physiology, we only know because we read it; many others over the decades did the experiments and tests to figure this out. Evolution has seemingly wrought miracles to allow the eggs of anadromous fish to be deposited upstream in fresh water shallows, perhaps where there is less danger. Most herring species spawn at sea.

We were reluctant to leave the fish ladder where something marvelous and admirable was happening. We wondered if the Indians from far and wide who peacefully gathered in Pennacook territory at Pawtucket Falls in what is now Lowell on the Merrimack felt the same during spawning migrations, which they took advantage of each year.*** Smaller groups were congregating at riffles and falls simultaneously on the lesser rivers like our Ipswich. Early colonial reports indicate considerable protein, our word not theirs, was caught during those weeks of fishing and celebration. We fervently want the girl and her generation to reduce herring exploitation at sea and to provide damfree passages to their spawning places. Perhaps the anadromous fish will then return in seemingly stream-clogging numbers as before. We hope future admirers along rivers of both west and east coasts will have joyous yearly parties with modest sustainable catches the rule.

It is Memorial Day weekend. One of the old Stream Teamers mentioned above plans to take his grandson to the Byfield ladder to see if stragglers are still coming. He will tell stories of old only touched on here. Memorial Day might someday be one for all species.

* The fish we saw may have been blue-backed herring, *Alosa aestivalis*, alewives, *Alosa pseudoharengus*, or both. It isn't easy to tell the difference and their life styles are similar, so we use the old name "alewives" for both here. Many folks now combine both as "river herring".

** If you want a more thorough explanation of the physiological changes look up osmoregulation in anadromous fish (fish that go from sea water to fresh to spawn).

*** Meader, J. W., *The Merrimack River: Its Sources and Tributaries*, (B. B. Russell, Boston) 1869

Water and Whirling Wind From Unruly Skies

Wednesday, June 1, 2011, on what turned out to be a historic day, we had a substantial morning thundershower here that lasted less than half an hour. Precipitation came as mostly liquid water mixed with a little ice. Warm moist air rose high to where the rumbles came thus producing more thundering. Cooled, it returned as raindrops and hail. Afterwards the air felt good as the old Closeteer walked across a grateful lawn to a rain gauge in his vegetable garden. The storm had left 0.35 inches. A good rain, no hail harm done, a young zucchini leaf was bent a bit.

We didn't know it at the time, but that morning rain with impressive thunder from a dark sky was but a preview for serious disturbances later brewing above warming ground to the southwest in a part of our state we barely know. There from West Springfield, Monson, Brimfield to Sturbridge air masses rushing and rising to fill voids high above set up whirlwinds that danced like prancing ballerinas upside down with inverted gowns, their stage a darkening sky. Counterclockwise they pirouetted dipping in places, their swirling arms touching the ground with which they plucked tree-tops, roofs and cars. Fortunately folks' ubiquitous TVs, radios, and handheld electronic devices as well as dark clouds gave warning. While much was damaged, amazingly few people were physically hurt during the several tornadoes' very brief but violent passages.

People in the tornadoes' paths interviewed soon after were excited; few were seen crying despite their losses or at least those the TV reporters picked out. Wet warm air misbehaving isn't something we whine much about. Abruptly called to action we help each other out. We've seen such spunk repeatedly this spring in the Midwest, places we since Dorothy and Toto's sudden rise in Kansas have associated, unlike here, with tornadoes.

Though surprised, those affected were mentally somewhat ready. Joplin far away had given fair warning of what might happen elsewhere. Many of the survivors there and in south central Massachusetts thanked God perhaps meaning luck. At least some observers find little or no little difference. Gods and luck operate in mysterious ways. Operate may be the wrong word. Gods and luck probably don't operate at all. There is no plan or strange conspiracy between them. Wind, warmth and water dance dangerously or they don't. At times in some places they destroy our houses of cards. The best we might say is: "He was lucky, she was not." To say God killed her and spared him would be the height of blasphemy. We know in listening to the good folks interviewed they don't really blame or not blame God when they say "Thank God!" They simply like most of us don't understand, and chance for some is hard to buy. Most clear debris and carry on.

It's a watery world and sometimes as with hurricanes like Katrina, tornadoes, tsunamis at Aceh and Miyagi, vast floods in Bangladesh and along the Mississippi, lots of wind and water arrive quite uncontrolled. Perhaps it is time to analyze the risks and build accordingly, or even continue as we have been, boldly building anew and gambling. Gods and Mother Nature are not vindictive, although they might well have reasons to be. They are creations of our minds, which is not to denigrate either. We can be prepared or not. Whatever its sources, faith, scientific knowledge or both, human spirit is impressive. Survivors rebuild after wars and natural disasters. It is too bad we can't eliminate the former and with the money and energy saved wisely prepare for the latter.

Wood and Water

At first the Old Worlders came in tiny wooden ships across the sea for fish. Almost a century later they came for new lives on land. Once precariously settled on the coast the newcomers, connected to other countries and colonies by sea and to the largely unknown interior by rivers, were much in need of boats and ships. Oak for keels, frames and planks was here in abundance. Straight white pines for masts and spars, some six feet in diameter towering well over 100 feet, were available along river bottoms. Alas, the talents and tools to turn this abundance into vessels were scarce. Amateurs driven by need did the best they could with axes, adzes, saws, augers and planes all powered by muscle. After a couple decades leaders here put out the word for skilled shipwrights from home. Incentives were offered. By the early 1640s a serious industry had begun and small ships were being built on gentle slopes in the open just above high water in estuaries all along the coast.

The other afternoon while passing through Essex an old Closeteer interested in local history was reminded of the small town's famous past. From the mid-1600s to the mid-1900s, 3,000 plus ships, not including boats, were built on a quarter mile of Chebacco River bank where restaurants and antique shops now dominate. After the Civil War there were as many as 15 active yards at times building schooners for the Gloucester fishing fleet. Essex is down to one on-and-off-again yard, building in the old way. A pinky schooner is now being built there by Harold Burnham and his crew.* The Burnham and Story**names have been prominently intertwined with shipbuilding and town affairs since the first colonists in the 1630s.

Just up the coast, a couple hours' sail on a fair wind, is the once famous port of Newbury, which became Newbury's port. There along two miles of the Merrimack's bank another 3,000 plus wooden ships were built including a dozen huge fast vessels known as clippers, which became well known around the oceans of the world. During the Revolution, Newburyport, small in area, exceeded Boston in population largely because of its shipbuilding industry.***

Up until rail in the mid-1800s almost all serious transport was by water. Timber came to the Essex, East Boston, Newburyport and Portsmouth yards floating down the rivers, and when local trees were gone, by ship from as far away as the Carolinas and Canada. Good roads were rare, many of those barely passable in winter and early spring. The equivalent of rail cars and trailer trucks here in the 17th, 18th and early 19th centuries were ships of ever increasing size built locally. In the early days when we still had timber and Europe didn't, we built ships for sale overseas. In the early 1700s a few gutsy entrepreneurs from Newbury lashed great white pines together into rafts. They rigged them with spars and canvas and in summer sailed across the Atlantic on the Gulf Stream. In timber-hungry British ports the raft logs commanded top prices for use as masts. Most mast trees were shipped across in safer, much more expensive mast ships.

These stories all flooded back to the Middletonite. His town, once a part of Salem, had provided oak and pine for Ipswich and Salem yards. He has no records but guesses many timbers were rough cut here and laboriously hauled to the yards or to streams and the Ipswich River by oxen and horses and along with logs floated down on spring highs. This happened in streams and rivers all along the coast from Newfoundland to Georgia until the 19th century dams. In Newburyport great logs down from New Hampshire were corralled into saltwater basins near the yards where they awaited the shipwrights' needs. Water, especially seawater, preserves and keeps wood from checking. We were reminded of those maritimes by a front page story in the June 9 *Boston Globe* by Peter Schworm. "Buried in the briny mud at the Charlestown Navy Yard was a cache of pristine antique oak, hand-hewn specifically for ships in the great tall ship era." Restorers of the famous 19th-century whale ship *Charles W. Morgan* docked in Mystic, Connecticut, serendipitously discovered the badly needed timber for their project as the "live oaks" salvaged from Katrina they had been using were running out. This treasure trove found is estimated to be over a century old. The timbers had been set aside in the yard's timber basin and never used. The wood will be used in the *Morgan* at great savings to the 20 million dollar project.

Let's return to Burnham and his lovely pinky in Essex. He has built several of these forerunners to the beautiful schooners his ancestors were famous for. Bicycle, sail or hike over to the Essex Shipbuilding Museum. It is on the Essex River and a trunnel's throw from the three-quarters-built pinky. Trunnels are what Burnham, faithful to family's history, is using to fasten planks to frames. They are dowels turned from our common black locust. Tough decay-resistant locust doesn't shrink in their holes. "Tree-nails," the origin of trunnels, are put in at slight angles thus locking plank to frame. Even the great clippers built by the famous designer Donald McKay in Newburyport and later East Boston were so fastened. Iron was an expensive commodity then. Trunnels were turned out in 19th-century Newburyport yards by kids lined up to pedal-power the lathes at a penny for 15 minutes. Trunnels were cheap. We suspect they still are. Locusts are common here. We wish kids working for low pay were.

And speaking of kids, Triton Regional School (Rowley, Newbury and Salisbury) used to have courses entitled New England and the Sea. Ours was a seafaring place before rails and motor highways. Local resources were used to build grand non-polluting ships navigated around the world by men using Salem mathematician-astronomer Nathaniel Bowditch's methods. When the old Closeteer was navigator on Navy ships in the 1950s the great man's tome, *The American Practical Navigator*, revised and amended for two centuries, was simply called "Bowditch." Now GPS has taken all the challenge and fun out of navigating by the stars. We wonder if ships still carry sextants and Bowditch.

There are some things we should hold on to where wood, water, sails, and people like Burnham, McKay, Bowditch and scores of notable North Shore folks unnamed here were interdependent. They constitute a rich history our young should hear of and perhaps take lessons from. Might not hauling halyards to raise sails, shooting stars, and shaping locally grown timbers be better for the environment, body and soul? Let's at least teach kids of those times when our waterfronts were not just collections of boutiques and restaurants for those passing through. Perhaps when the oil runs out sails pulling vessels of wood will return. Dream on old Closeteers . . .

*Google Harold Burnham ship builder to see photo of his schooner presently being build in Essex.

** Story, Dana Frame-Up! The Story of Essex, Its Shipyards and Its People (Barre Publishers Barre, MA) 1964   This delightful read by a man who watched his family build ships, some famous, is one of the Closet's favorites.

*** Cheney, Robert K.   Maritime History of the Merrimack: Shipbuilding (Newburyport Press, Inc.) 1964.   This is a remarkably comprehensive work by an amateur Salisbury historian and Boston theatre light operator.   As a boy the "old Closeteer' sold Mr. Cheney eggs.

July 2011

Reed Canary grass Now, What Next?

In the first decade of the new millennium reed canary grass, *Phalaris arundinacea*, has gradually replaced purple loosestrife, *Lythrum salicaria*, above some beaver dams. Both these beauties are featured prominently in the Massachusetts invasive species booklet we used to read and fret about in the Closet. Here is what it says about reed canary, a valuable hay and grazing grass in the days when we had lots of livestock. "Threat: This species forms dense colonies that can overwhelm native plants or forage crops. It is of little food value to wildlife, and its dense vegetative cover may be poor habitat for many indigenous animals." The first of these sentences is certainly true. We wonder about the second. In some farmers' fields it provides three to four tons of hay an acre. We suspect there may be much more biomass per acre in thick high stands in floodplains along the Ipswich River and Boston Brook. We expected to find even more this summer; populations have been increasing each year. Yesterday, a fine day near the end of June, an old Closeteer who has been watching our wetlands closely for 16 years went by foot and canoe to see how the large grass was doing.

The Essex railway of old, up from Old Essex Street, Middleton, provides easy access into the floodplain of Boston Brook, a major tributary of the Ipswich River. The rails and ties are long gone. A nice path of cinders remains. Flanking the forested, still in good shape rail bed, the brook down from Boston Hill in North Andover, divided by the railroad engineers in 1848, flows south. Head-high jungles, if one were to walk in waders, are now lush greens. The inflorescences of reed canary, purple to tan stages, and the more modest flowers of tussock sedge are now putting on a quiet show. Sprinkled around these knee- to waist-deep beaver impoundments are highbush blueberry, arrowwood, rushes, and lots of an unidentified sedge. Floating in open patches of water are white pond lilies; around them pickerel weed pokes forth. Both lilies and weed are now in bloom. It is worth a trip to wetlands now just to see the distinctive pure blue of pickerel

Spiky waist to shoulder high buttonbushes, Cephalanthus occidentalis. *While paddling along the Ipswich River we pass acres of these beauties. They can also be seen from North Main Street, Middleton, across from Meritor Academy, covering much of Emerson Bog. Photo, courtesy Judy Schneider.*

weed flowers, their color quite like that of roadside chicory. This lovely walk that never disappoints and usually surprises at all times of the year is one the Closeteer often takes and has for two decades. In 2000, and before the wetland, there was nothing at all like today. It was a typical red maple swamp, always shaded when trees were in leaf, wet most of the year but often somewhat dry in late summer and early fall. Thanks to a series of beaver dams built starting around the turn of the millennium across Boston Brook the maples are dead; the naked trunks of many still stand, casting no shade. The sun pours in upon these low jungles called beaver meadows. The other day's observations in no way resemble those of just a decade ago; just the latitude and longitude are the same. When the trains, 1849 to 1926, passed along this line the scene was pastoral. Passengers looked out on treeless meadows with cows and in late summer haymakers. We might expect change in a century, but in just a tenth? Had there been a botanist with the old Closeteer they might have found two score of plant species that hadn't been in the floodplain since before the Indians and colonists trapped out the beavers over three centuries ago. The Closeteer's expectations for much more reed canary and tussock sedge along Boston Brook were dashed. While there are still plenty, other water-loving species are increasing.

On the same afternoon the Closeteer in canoe paddled from Farnsworth Landing, Middleton's park on Route 114, south on the Ipswich River two meandering miles to the Peabody water supply pump house and back. The previous four wet cold days' three inches of rain had raised the low water two feet at the south Middleton gauge. The wide floodplain where Middleton, Danvers and Peabody join has also lost most of its trees and bushes due to beaver dams and year-round higher water. The paddler spent almost the whole two hours in beaver-flooded marsh of reed canary, water smartweed, pickerel weed, arrow arum, dying buttonbushes and silky dogwoods. As in other impoundments the red maples, willows, swamp white oaks, river birches and ashes are largely gone. The same trip just 10 years ago would have been in semi-shade and in stretches full shade. In open areas purple loosestrife dominated. The buttonbushes and dogwoods were then vigorous, the latter almost overarching the narrow winding channel. It is still a wondrous place, but very very different. In the last few years reed canary has replaced much of the more notorious invader purple loosestrife. This could be due to imported *Galerucella sp.* beetles brought in to eat the loosestrife rather than competition from the grass. The beetles may have given reed canary an advantage. No living plants of the once lovely purple menace were seen. Sparsely scattered dead stems from last year were. How quickly the mighty fall, even those with purple crowns. The Closeteer was again surprised, having expected the reed canary, increasing yearly in the previous four to five years, to have completely taken over. There is still plenty however, in large areas, but seemingly much less. Smartweed, *Polygonum sp.*, is taking the upper hand. There are thick stands with little else where loosestrife and reed canary once held sway. We must now paddle downriver to the Great Wenham Swamp, a similar place of great meanders, and check there.

Essays about change and beavers have been frequent exports from our six-year-old Water Closet. We, who have gone out repeatedly and taken notes and photos, had no realization of how fast Mother Nature rotates her crops and livestock. Within these vibrant beaver meadows along our waterways, dedicated teams of biologists and chemists might spend lifetimes studying just a few cubic meters of these rich habitats so filled with animals, plants, fungi, algae and microorganisms. We now know that surprises would never end for them. Their papers one, 10, and 100 years from now wouldn't be the same. It is frustrating for us who like our predictions to come out somewhat as expected. We should make our observations while singing along with Dylan, "Times they are a changing." Alas, there is something deep in us old-timers that wishes it wasn't all so fast. We wonder if the water smartweed will take over for a while now that reed canary grass seems in decline; and after that . . .

Wetland Bushes Blooming

July Fourth weekend is upon us. This year colorful sprays of fire in the skies above some cities around the country are being banned because of the dangers of fires on the ground. In lieu of fireworks we in the Closet recommend you visit our wetlands to see bushes blooming. Many are putting on explosive floral shows in silence.

The half-foot diameter flat white flower clusters of elderberry (*Sambucus canadensis*) are now at peak. The weight of hundreds of tiny flowers in each have them slightly bowing. They'll give us more displays later as each tiny blossom produces a shiny berry, green to red to purple, as summer progresses. Wine makers will be out picking them for their fermentation jugs. As children we ate the distinctive-tasting BB-sized fruit. The other day on a canoe trip along the Ipswich River elderberry bushes at intervals were very noticeable among the dominant silky dogwoods (*Cornus amomum*) also now blooming smaller more dainty clusters. The dogwoods may whisper to the elderberry and to the swamp azalea (*Rhododendron viscosum*), which have scores of small Easter lily-like blossoms: "You don't need to show off, see what more modest and delicate off-white displays can do. We commoners are prolific."

Among the dogwoods, in stretches dominant as seen in a recent paddle up and down from the Ipswich River Park in North Reading, are invasive buckthorn bushes (*Rhamnus frangula*), almost small trees, long a worry to those who don't like fertile foreigners taking over from so-called native species.

Excuse the temptation to bring in people and farfetched comparisons that are probably nonsense. We can't resist. The Indians, once they learned colonists here from the Old World wanted land and took it, may have seen them as an invasive species. Alas, it was too late. When the Yankees, largely of English stock, two centuries later and after brought in Irish, Italians and other Europeans to do the work, they fretted about the newcomers' growing numbers and fearfully saw them as prolific invaders. Again, it was way too late. Now Spanish speakers are among us working hard and well. Friendly Israel from Guatemala pumps gas in Middleton Square; down the street near the river at Blue Fin, a Japanese restaurant, young Sandra, also from Guatemala, serves customers with good cheer. We dare someone to call them undesirable invasives or to pass rules against their being here. We liken them to the new invasive exotic plants in that it would serve us well to learn their names and language in order to enrich our lives as the previously mentioned alleged invaders in the 19th century did.

What strange thoughts flit through our minds after paddles and walks through our wetlands. Forgive our swerving off from plants to people.

Back to the buckthorn that produces tiny hard-to-see green flowers that bloom July to October, each becoming a spherical shiny black fruit. In the last two decades they've spread like Topsy in disturbed upland and wet places where they can get a seed hold. Their numerous fruits, which attract birds, are cathartic. An old Closeteer tried half a small blueberry-sized fruit and within 10 minutes was looking for a bush to hide behind. Birds spread their seeds far and wide along with deposits of rich fertilizer. We've tried cutting buckthorn down where not wanted to give what we call "natives" a chance. Cut one and a half-dozen sprouts spring from it. Because they are so prolific the ground everywhere must be filled with dormant seeds awaiting the right conditions. Buckthorn also does well in wetlands so we include them in our list.

Arrowwood (*Viburnum recognitum*) is often found on our walks and paddles. This basketball-player-high viburnum also has flat-topped flower clusters this time of year. The name no doubt comes from its new shoots, which are as straight and smooth as arrow shafts. We wonder if the Indians so used them. The dark green leaves of arrowwood are serrated and prominently veined.

There are flowers of other bushes we admired earlier or missed this year and those that will bloom later. Highbush blueberries (*Vaccinium corymbosum*) in May have clusters of small bell-shaped white flowers that some of us eat in passing. The blossoms taste pleasingly tart, yet nothing like the familiar fruit each flower will produce.

Another bush about the same size as highbush blueberry is spicebush (*Lindera benzoin*) found in shady wet woodlands. While still leafless in April and early May spicebushes put out tiny yellow flowers scarce seen along their twigs. Each produces a small shiny fruit that will turn a brilliant red in the fall. Scratch any part of a spicebush and sniff to enjoy a pleasant reminder of its name.

The last we'll mention, not yet in bloom, is buttonbush (*Cephalanthus occidentalis*). Its head-high spiky-branched bushes dominate shallows of Emerson Bog, many vernal pools and flooded patches of our river floodplain. Now their flower buds are but little green spheres. In early August they'll become compound flowers almost the size of golf balls. These flowers, light beige in color, have at one stage a fine vanilla smell.

Words do none of these plants justice. They are out there for all to see, feel and smell. If you like vicarious sensations from computer screens Google their scientific names. You'll find many good photos without odors or the richness of their surrounds. We'll give the computer wizards another decade or two to obtain these dimensions while hoping that they fail. We spend too much time before electronic screens. There is a wealth of three- dimensional plus life just outside our doors year round.

Go to any swamp or wet meadow from early April to October and you'll get a show looking more or less horizontally at bushes, or down at grasses and falsely named "weeds," or up at trees, all flowering plants. And don't forget ferns and mosses, which, while not flowering plants, have been on Earth much longer.

If you like your July Fourth floral fireworks in red, white and blue we've got that too. The pale red blossoms of swamp rose (*Rosa palustris*) while not found in ostentatious bunches are lightly sprinkled throughout our wetlands; they along with the whites mentioned make up our flag's stripes, the original 13 now 50. And if we look lower to the water's edges pickerel weed (*Pondeteria cordata*) is just now blooming a wonderful blue representing, if you want, our republic.

These bloomers, of course, are best seen in all their rich diversity along with the many other plants not mentioned here. Some of our meadows and swamps have half a hundred species painted by Mother Nature on a grand ever changing canvas. If this abundance continued all year we couldn't take it. She gives us winter and another kind beauty in which to rest our senses while we await next year's new shows. Trust us, they won't be the same.

SOFT-SHELLED CLAMS

Just down the Ipswich River is a valuable animal that does not run or swim away when sought for food. Its vertical journeys, up and down a few inches with twice daily tides, are in a hole of its own making. It does not leave on highs for new sites or to explore. We might think this a dull life. Even as drifting larvae, part of the plankton for several weeks, it simply goes with the flow. Those conceived in the Merrimack's mouth don't head for Plum Island Sound, Hampton River or Chelsea flats, but there is a chance they might wind up there on fickle currents.

Actually we who visit the Ipswich flats often and have done so for decades know little about the biology of soft-shelled clams (*Mya arenaria*), commonly called "steamers" or "fried clams" by their eaters. We mechanically invade their space with steel clam forks and if two inches or over long chuck them into our buckets. Indian women and girls dug the same flats with sticks. The clams found have no last-minute words for us about their lives or ancestors. We read what the biologists who have painstakingly studied them have to tell us. We do know a bit first-hand about their immediate ecosystems. They seem at home in salt marsh peat; in oozy black mud high in organic matter and low in oxygen; in clean sand, course and fine; and in gravel including that with boulders. Yesterday in the midday heat a Stream Teamer and amateur clammer found them four feet above the low tide water elevation in salt marsh peat several hundred years old. With water over them less than half a day they looked healthy and who knows, perhaps as "happy as a clam." The tide with planktonic food comes to them, so why worry. Those higher up in the vertical tidal range must get less food from the water they pump through their guts during the fewer hours available, or maybe they just pump harder than their kin at lower elevations. Reports have single large clams filtering up to 13 gallons of seawater a day.

From the water pumped in and out in separate tubes called siphons, that clam eaters mistakenly call the head, they filter out suspended microscopic plankton and organic debris daily for as much as 20 years. From this nourishment they may grow a half foot long. The largest we dig from the Ipswich flats are about four to five inches. The other day we overheard one professional clammer nearby say "slim pickings." They certainly were on the much-dug "Jennings" flat; it took us twice our usual time to dig the 10 quarts allowed amateurs. The good news is we found lots of young clams less than an inch long. They may be ready a year or so from now. Ipswich has many flats, which the town regulates well by rotating openings and closings.

Even if we dug them all year after year new clams would come because soft-shelled clams live out to depths of several hundred feet in the ocean where we can't get them. They spawn for a couple periods each year when optimum water temperatures are roughly 50 to 60 degrees F. A female will release one to five million eggs in her lifetime. Fertilization is external followed by two to five weeks, depending on temperature, of embryo and larval development while drifting. The microscopic larval stages are neither clam-shaped nor similar physiologically.

Google trochophore and veliger larvae or go to a zoology text to view their interesting forms. Finally the veliger larva forms a foot and the beginnings of two calcium carbonate shells. The latter, of limestone, cause the semi-microscopic clam to descend while metamorphosing into what we would recognize as a clam. On the bottom it uses its new foot to burrow its home for life. As you can readily imagine much luck is involved. One of thousands will survive the larval drifting among hungry fish. And then what fraction land on suitable substrate?

The other day we worked hard in the heat for a couple hundred clams so valued in restaurants from Paris to Boston. Even if we hadn't come back with one clam the trip was worth the scene among the soft green marshes between Ipswich and Essex. Hog Island, a glacial drumlin, and the high dunes of Crane Beach, now forested, rose up between us and the sea. While we could not see the ocean its bouquet was strong. After digging we washed our clams in the cool flood tide waters. Had we not been so tired and old we'd have immersed ourselves. As a child growing up on a Salisbury estuary the old Stream Teamer visited the salt marsh cricks, the kind we were digging in at Jennings, with other kids several times a day in all tides to swim. At lows we wallowed in the mud, on highs in cold seawater we almost siphoned it as do clams, it was so refreshing. If we had had gills like clams we would have. Maybe that is where the old saw, not much heard now, "happy as a clam" came from. As kids we may have deeply sensed while playing in salt water that was where we came from too.

RETURN TO THE ROOKERY

The afternoon heat was oppressive. No air stirred among the napping leaves. We slowly walked from North Liberty Street across Second Pasture en route to a decade-old heron rookery to see how any families there were faring. We hadn't visited this flooded corner of north Middleton near its intersection with Boxford and North Andover since mid-spring. A few years ago there were hundreds of beaver-drowned trees including a few score of white pines (*Pinus strobus*), the trees Great Blue Herons (*Ardea herodias*) prefer for their large nests. At the rookery's peak there were 26 high up on dead branches. We have for years visited after hatching to watch parents feed voracious young. As the adults approach the nest, usually coming in low, they make raucous calls. The hungry chicks join in with cackles. These words don't adequately describe the guttural exchanges. Raised on partially digested protein and fat regurgitated into them, it isn't long before the rapidly growing offspring, one or two per nest, are of parental stature.

Only a dozen or so standing pines remain. The rest have succumbed to wet snow carried in on northeast winds. Eight of the still-standing corpses have a nest, some two. We, moving slowly in the heat, approached along the top of what we think is an esker. It cooled us to imagine a river carrying melt water and debris gushing through an ice tunnel at the base of the Wisconsin glacier 12,000 years ago. In time these rivers became clogged with sand, gravel and boulders and ceased to flow. The walls and roof melted away leaving an often serpentine levee-like knoll behind; some, despite ten millennia of erosion, are still quite long. There is one in Parker River National Wildlife Refuge almost a half mile long; our high path to the rookery is only a couple hundred yards. Its northern end slopes bleacher-like to the once red maple (*Acer rubrum*) swamp, now a beaver impoundment. Seated in the shade beneath oaks we have fine views of the nests and families. We often return in spring and summer to watch and hear the show. Bullfrogs (*Rana catesbeiana*) provide background music. Tree Swallows (*Tachycineta bicolor*) swoop for unseen insects above the shallow hundred or more acre year-round lake. Two-thirds of the surface is now paved with a thin layer of duckweed (*Lemna sp.*) and watermeal (*Wolffia sp.*), shining green in the bright sun. Approach any of the edges of this impoundment, kept high by the beaver dam on Pond Meadow Brook just down drainage, and you'll spook many frogs. The herons who are strictly carnivorous and eat almost any small animal from fish to mice have not far to go for snacks. If food is scarce near their rookeries they are reported to search up to four miles for prey. We usually stay a half hour or so, but often think of staying the day with intermittent naps upon the duff and moss. Somehow, you know how it is, restless we return to chores and miss what might be learned with more patient study. We should bring waders and wander out under the nests.

On a lovely morning four days after the recent hot afternoon visit described above, the Middleton Council on Aging/Conservation Commission Friday morning hiking group visited the rookery in hopes the young herons soon to fledge were still there. They were; only one nest of nine was completely empty. Most of the young, almost as big as their up to four-foot-tall, six-foot wingspan, and eight-pound parents, were standing erect on their nests awaiting food. Nine of us sat happily for a half hour on the esker slope quietly talking of heron behavior and listening to the frog chorus which filled the air. This time we saw no swallows; maybe they take mornings off or had found an insect hatch elsewhere. Smaller predators were busy over the water. Dragonflies, some quite large, kept the air insect-free. No one complained of mosquitoes, even those without repellent, yet there was water all around us. The frogs and dragonfly larvae must eat the mosquito wigglers.

On the way in to our esker-end perch we rounded a shaded cove covered with a millimeter-thick mat of watermeal and duckweed, the smallest of our flowering plants, which do not flower much. Most of these tiny plants reproduce asexually by budding. The mat seemed pocked with centimeter-high knolls, a dozen or so per ten square meters. It reminded one old Closeteer of the Yucatan's vast flat jungles growing from limestone. From cleared tops of restored Mayan ruins one can see many green knolls rising above the jungle, ruins not yet uncovered. We slowly approached the green mini-knolls of watermeal and duckweed; when within a few feet there were splashes and the bumps disappeared. What we were seeing were the tops of frogs' heads covered with the tiny plants they had pushed upward when rising and wore as camouflage. The edges of the huge impoundment must measure a mile or more. We tallied a score of heads in just 50 feet. There must be many tens of thousands of frogs in this impoundment alone. The place is truly alive from deep in the mud below to the insect- and bird-inhabited air high above. We roughly estimated 100 meal and duckweed plants per square centimeter of surface, each producing oxygen and habitat surface for microorganisms.

Priscilla Neal, a veteran of our Friday hikes, while returning across Second Pasture said something like, "How very peaceful it was there. I could have stayed all day. If it wasn't for the sound of unseen jets you'd think us truly far from humanity." While no one said, "Amen," I suspect we all agreed.

Thanks to Essex County Greenbelt, The Trustees of Reservations, state parks, Mass Audubon, and town conservation lands we are blessed with many such retreats. Beavers too deserve our gratitude; in balance their changes produce more diverse habitats. We are returning in many places to what it was like here when the Indians and beavers were the chief land-affecting inhabitants. The natives' purposely-set yearly fires landscaped the uplands; beaver impoundments, which certainly keep essential water in our watersheds longer, the lowlands.

Clean Water Lady

In the last years of the second millennium the Ipswich River Watershed Association (IRWA) sent the about-to-fledge Middleton Stream Team, average age then about 60, a girl engineer just out of MIT to help us fly. We old-timers three times her years were skeptical about Daniele Lantagne, a seeming hippie with the voice of a 12-year-old. Friendly, in careless loose clothing, and without airs, she quickly had us on her side and wanting to follow. We knew there was much more to this 21-year-old, who appeared 15, than what we with blinders first saw. The old lesson here, one we should have learned long ago, is not to judge.

It was long ago when this water sprite lightly bobbed up among us. Last week, Dr. Lantagne, Ph.D., from London School of Hygiene and Tropical Medicine, in her thirties returned to the Watershed Association's headquarters on the Ipswich River for a luncheon to renew acquaintances.

In high school she decided she wanted to be an engineer in order to do something practical for others. At some point she chose providing clean water. What goal could be more simple and important, yet hardly one that concerns most Americans? We have clean water at our beck and call from several household taps. Such abundance isn't the same in much of the world. An old Stream Teamer whose Navy ship visited postwar Hong Kong in the 1950s remembers people of all ages in a long line with buckets, pots and kettles awaiting their turns at a single tap in a city neighborhood square. Almost weekly we watch on TV villagers in poor African countries scooping cloudy water from shallow wells. Daniele knew where she was needed most; the next we heard of her after leaving the IRWA, she was in the hemisphere's poorest nation helping Haitians with their water problems. That, the first of subsequent visits there, was long before the earthquake. Engineer Daniele has since visited 27 countries around the world showing people how to have water free from cholera and typhoid bacteria. She says her reward is returning to be told stories of her team's successes in saving lives.

Some of us old admirers missed Daniele's visit here to see us, her early colleagues, then only ankle deep in the water field. We gave family obligations as excuses for not attending. Rather we should have dropped all else and brought families and friends to see her. How often does one get to meet and hear from such an energetic, altruistic person? We had mistakenly thought her a child not knowing that she was a purposeful woman long before we knew her. Would that she could visit all our schools to tell young folks what engineers can do. She has visited many. She certainly impressed us old-timers in whom, despite our efforts, cynicism sometimes leaks in and poisons. We need our blood cleansed of such contaminants. We don't use Daniele's purifying chemicals, pumps and filters but we do call up thoughts of her to clear our minds.

Clean water for all including plants and animals is a noble goal. We Stream Teamers and Closeteers are too old to follow Daniele the world over but we can certainly cheer her on and wish her and colleagues well.

On visiting the many websites about her we realize how little we know of Daniele first hand. She came to us when needed and then as young people do went out into the world to seek her fortune, not in money, but in her words of encouragement to students to "Love what you do." Certainly others love what she does. We are proud to have known her for a bit as she buoyantly flowed by. And speaking of buoyant and bouncy, one of her recreations is competitive Lindy Hopping. Google her name as we did and visit her page entitled "Engineer Your Life" and others. In addition we asked Kerry Mackin, Director of IRWA, for her impressions of her onetime assistant. Kerry's good response is paraphrased here as follows:

Dear Closeteers,

Daniele is that rare combination – a brilliant scientist and an outgoing "people" person; a high-energy, positive and prodigious worker who held several jobs while she worked with us. She built our monitoring, herring count, and stream team programs from scratch. Many of the volunteers she recruited back in 1997 are still with us. She wrote numerous reports about the findings of our programs. Her technical expertise is outstanding.

One of her priorities is to encourage girls and women to pursue careers in math and science. She recruited and trained our first intern, Kate Morkeski. Kate is now a research scientist at Woods Hole Marine Biological Lab.

See the YouTube video clip of Daniele inspiring people from Ipswich H.S. to distant countries.

She is active in Potters for Peace, an organization that has folks making ceramic pots for use as household water filters.

She was one of four people worldwide appointed by U.N. Secretary General Ban Ki-moon to investigate the source of post-earthquake cholera in Haiti.

[Note: Kerry could have gone on listing scientific papers by Daniele and her teams available online. We end here with portions of her last paragraph.]

Having said all this, my biggest impression of Daniele is that she is a person who loves life and lives it to the fullest, according to her values. She is certainly making a real difference in the lives of many people throughout the world.

Kerry

Thanks Kerry. In the Closet we are now toasting Dr. Daniele and you with glasses of clay-pot-filtered Ipswich River water.

AUGUST 2011

ICE CAP DOFFED IN FAREWELL

The other night we happened upon a CNN news report that showed a reporter visiting the North Polar ice cap by helicopter. A U.S. Navy submarine, as arranged, broke through several feet of ice nearby to receive him for a visit. As children we thought the ice cap a place where only daredevils and Eskimos ever go. Now visits by air and ships are becoming commonplace. Some of us in our few remaining years may live to see a planet without an ice cap floating on the Arctic Ocean. How very different the world will be for our children and for theirs. They may take holiday cruises where once only Richard Peary, Matthew Henson, Robert Byrd, Roald Amundsen and other explorers ventured. Polar bears may be gone. Water there will be in the liquid state year round from top to bottom except for icebergs calving off remaining glaciers. The Arctic Ocean is relatively shallow. Thousands of oil rigs may sprout up from the broad continental shelves and shallow seas. We old-timers of the Stream Team hope not, but will have no say, not that we have any now. Even after the BP disaster drilling at sea continues.

Our species is greedy and irresponsible. Collectively we want ours now, the devil with the world's environment. Some would say "'Tis too late. No sense crying over spilt oil and excessive heat." Perhaps they are right, but forgive us a few tears in waning years. We liked the time when there were places on our planet where only a few of the most adventurous would go, areas that were pretty much left alone year round. Where will Santa, assistants and reindeer go? How about the Eskimos and harp seals? There must be a thousand other species biologists can name that will be affected or even be gone largely because of one.

The climate change deniers may scoff at such whining. Let the good times roll for the rich. "Eat, drive and be merry while fossil fuels last. We worked hard to earn our 10 miles per gallon RV and it is our right to tear down our God-given superhighways towing a standby car." Despite all the warnings and pleas in the last few decades we see little change in a NASCAR nation. In the '50s, '60s and '70s our governments built a network of remarkable freeways and the people came. Fifty years ago, one Closeteer's wife, recently from Japan, where they have an efficient railway system, wondered out loud why crops weren't being grown on the shoulders and center strips of our superhighways. Maybe they will be someday and even where asphalt has been abandoned. We know it takes only a couple human generations for plants to take over rotting pavement not used. This could be the case after the oil runs out.

We'll not attempt to repeat any of the evidence for accelerated melting. It pours in from scientists around the world as fast as ice changes to liquid water. For the non-scientists like ourselves we have but to view satellite photos taken yearly of the rapidly diminishing Arctic ice cap to be convinced. One prediction read recently has the summer cap gone in this decade.

A few scientists think we have already reached the 'tipping point," the time when positive feedback systems have been triggered that will greatly accelerate the rates of warming and melting no matter what we do. We hope them wrong, but let us very reluctantly assume they are correct and that our grandchildren's generation will be migrating north into the changing boreal forests and tundra. Those future pioneers' grain belts will be sown in soil devoid of permafrost for the first time in tens of thousands of years. The spruce will give way to mixed hardwoods and cultivated fields. Human "snow birds" will retreat south in the winter to New England and the Great Lakes. Those fleeing summer's heat for cooler vacation spots like Maine and the Maritimes, escapes for us, may in the future travel north to Baffin Island and the Queen Elizabeth Islands.

Climatologists don't yet know what lands and seas will be like in the future. Rapid climate changes raise many unanswered questions about weather patterns and ocean currents. What places now dry will be wet and vice versa? Actually it all sounds quite challenging and exciting at least for a few. We of course must leave the changes for those younger to sort out. In the last couple decades we old-timers finally learned to easily say "Cool it" as the young had taught us. We might have had our chance to do so, but didn't. For them it is probably too late. As we prepare to leave we beg them to lay down their arms (many ours left over) and to consider other organisms as they adapt. It is in diversity that adaptation can take place.

FROM GERMANY TO PEABODY THEY CAME

John "Jack" "Red" Caulfield came to Middleton from some mean streets in Peabody. Bernd Heinrich came to Vermont from Germany. Red also came home from Germany after a stint in the Air Force. The other day Red brought the Closet a book by Bernd he thought we'd like. *A Year in the Maine Woods* is one of several the famous naturalist has written. It dawned on one old Closeteer while happily reading it that book-giver Red and the author have things in common. They are roughly the same age; both have roamed in woods, along streams and through fields since childhood. Both are fans of the wilds of Maine.

Red escaped a hardscrabble existence as a young boy in a city supported by tanneries, which to visiting outsiders often reeked of hides being cleaned and cured. Lucky Red ended up with people who took him under their wings in lucky-to-get-him Middleton. He became as familiar with the paths of our rural town as he was with the alleys around his childhood apartments. While raising a family here with good wife Joan he served on the appeals, planning and selectmen boards. We admire and like him because he is interested in all things and likes to share his knowledge. What we admire most is his helping others who need it most. On a minus-15-degree F morning in 1988 he dropped previous plans and spent the frigid day patching a friend's roof damaged by firefighters who had successfully fought an intense upstairs blaze in the predawn dark. In the spirit of the Water Closet we feel we must mention the fight ended with several inches of ice on the first floor. We could go on and on with examples of Red quietly helping others, most older and in need.

This Water Closet essay is not primarily about water; rather of men who while taking very different career paths have interests in common. If you study nature in New England, a place blessed with well over 40 inches of precipitation each year, or anywhere else for that matter, you can hardly separate water and the people who love the great outdoors. The two are interwoven.

That combination brings to mind another man, unknown to our 14-year-old Stream Team. The late Eben "Midge" Baldwin is a man who becomes the subject of almost any conversation with Red after a half hour of enthusiastic talk. Midge was a Middleton postal worker more known to strangers in town for his under-five-foot stature. He befriended boys in town and taught them to fish, to camp, and to properly interact with other folks. Red and others idolized their mentor. Midge gave them "quality time," a phrase that came later, one Midge didn't know. Those times are fresh in memories 50 years later. Red, probably six foot since a teen, looked up to Midge while looking down. Midge knew boys should be in and on the water swimming and fishing at every opportunity, ones that he provided.

So Bernd, naturalist extraordinaire, long-distance runner, scientist, and writer; Red, discerning reader, outdoorsman, family man, people helper and good citizen; and Midge, whom we hardly know except through Red, come together in our minds. We imagine them fishing together and hiking in pond-pocked northern New England. Bernd is identifying bird songs and tasting bugs, one of his favorite diagnostic techniques. We won't go on about his eating fresh road kill. He, a biologist, knows the proteins and fats are the same as market meats. Red is excitedly telling of what he has read and seen. Midge is trailing along, happy to have been transcended by this member of his young flock. They all have strings of fish, which will be eaten back at camp around a fire. As he eats Bernd will dissect, study and sketch his perch. Red will tell of past trips and what he has lately read. Thank you Red for Bernd's book and others loaned us. Thank you Midge for helping Red and other lads get to the water.

THE GREEN MANIFESTO

Nature writer David Gessner's most recent book, *My Green Manifesto*, is a conflicting yet provocative read. In an opening page he quotes Kermit the Frog as so many environmentalists do, "It's not that easy being green." He then goes on for over 200 pages showing the validity of Kermit's complaint.

Photo, courtesy of Andrew Richardson.

While on a strange canoe trip down the Charles River Gessner repeatedly whines about other environmentalists' whining. His main objections are to the doomsday warnings of many. He gores Al Gore several times, fortunately making sideswipes with a dull horn. Doesn't he understand that there is a spectrum of people in the environmental movement as in all political parties and movements? Excuse the use of "environmental" already three times in this paragraph. It is the word Gessner is trying to escape as he reminds us every few pages. He doesn't want to be called the environmentalist he clearly is.

Perhaps the strangest aspect of his manifesto is apologizing several times for being a bird lover. There are lots of us and no wonder. Birds are beautiful, they can fly and sing with infinite variations, and they have been around a very long time. Some tell us they are little dinosaurs. Yet Gessner seems ashamed of this love while he accuses those who he thinks don't have it of not being true advocates for nature. He repeatedly picks on "theorists" Ted Nordhaus and Michael Shellenberger, authors of a doomsday essay that makes him angry. He accuses them of not going forth as he does into the wild. "Wild" by the way is a favorite word, it must appear 100 times in his manifesto without, understandably, ever being clearly defined. He, while living a professor's life in Cambridge, was wild. Nordhaus and Shellenberger, who fret about huge environmental problems, are not. Another odd habit for someone of his intelligence is using the F word completely out place and not related to the basic verb. He must think it macho instead of stupid as it clearly is used in this book. Perhaps some imagined macho fear explains his need to explain away his fondness for birds.

Alas, Gessner is, as we guess manifesto writers should be, provocative and repetitious. Yet unlike the creators of *The Communist Manifesto*, the only other one we know, he is at times amusing and intriguing so we read on wondering where he'll take us next. He writes well between beers and the need to tell us several times of his coffee addiction. He, very well read, drops names throughout that should be dropped on us as he reviews, dare we say it again, the environmental movement. Thoreau, his hero and that of so many lovers of nature and good literature, is mentioned and quoted a score of times. John Muir and Rachel Carson are frequently called up also. To list all the others he reminds us of would fill a page. For someone entering the field or wanting a review of the movement, his mentioning so many in interesting ways is of value.

Dan Driscoll, champion of the Charles River, Gessner's paddling companion, while little known outside eastern Massachusetts, has famously restored portions of his river. Driscoll did and still does what we all should be doing according to admirer Gessner and that is falling in love and then fighting tooth and nail for our beloved. We Middleton Stream Teamers agree. Driscoll persevered in his love affair and fight and has done wonders restoring gritty parts of the Charles. Water Closet hero Marion Stoddart and team did it successfully for the whole Nashua River. Gessner surprisingly doesn't mention her. She is a perfect example of local action his manifesto is touting.

The value to us of Gessner's sometimes rocky rant is the turmoil he, as an environmentalist, feels as a fellow hypocrite, which he readily admits to being. One old Closeteer for a year had a large sign on his lawn: NO OCEAN DRILLING. A friend asked him, "Do you drive a car?" His basic meaning is clear. We environmentalists drive and even fly to distant meetings burning fossil fuel. We, like most of our countrymen, consume far more of everything than we need. Gessner is timid about chastising us for these excesses. He probably rightly rails against preaching. However, in his last two chapters his own preaching soars. We like it. He urges us to visit the patches of wildness we have left and to accept the fact that we too are animals, an underlying theme of the Water Closet in its six years. He wants us to love other species and their habitats. Amen.

We in the Closet recommend this book to all wherever they are on the spectrum: from those driving spikes in trees to those carrying green grocery bags. His words get the blood flowing and the mind working, as also happens during walks he advocates. If we only hiked and thought more about local problems like Driscoll and Stoddart we'd probably be inspired to get more done. Gessner urges us to act locally come what may. While resting between battles he'd have us in the wild away from the fray, our eyes out for birds. This new book by a conflicted soul, also a fine writer and teacher, may become an important one if widely read. For one old Closeteer it already is. His frustration while reading was not having the author around to argue with.

In his final chapters Gessner calms down and becomes softer on his contrived enemies. We guess he is a tolerant cuss who recognizes it will take all kinds to save bits and pieces of what he calls wild. Some with wider audiences may protect, conserve or restore on continental scales as did Teddy Roosevelt, Carson, and Wangari Maathai. Gessner's manifesto has sure got us here in the Closet trying to sort things out. Perhaps we'll come up with a shorter manifesto of our own, its language in ringing Churchillian phrases that Gessner recommends. He wisely makes the point that bureaucratic language just won't do. He asks for a return to Thoreau's and Emerson's "nonconformity." He like Driscoll urges practical action.

SEPTEMBER 2011

QUEST FOR HEADWATERS

In our quest to find the beginnings of the Ipswich River we go up where the waters of Maple Meadow Brook and Lubbers Brook join and flow together in eastern Wilmington. This is certainly not the beginning, but the beginning of a name that holds to the sea. What we'd really like is the Indian name that faded away long ago with them. We don't believe it was simply Agawam, the name, no doubt mispronounced, of the people in the lower watershed before the English. Someday we plan to seek the sources of Maple Meadow and Lubbers. In doing so we may find streamlets feeding them. Old now we will probably never find the headwaters; however, searches are important and true searches never end. Say we do find the springs that give rise to the smallest tributaries; if followed they would take us underground and then eventually into the air and back to sea. You see water goes round and round. We don't and finite be. That doesn't bother; others, DNA kin, will carry on the search.

Such whimsical thoughts flit in and out of the old Closeteer's mind as he paddles with a friend easterly from the convergence of the brooks down a scarce seen channel hidden by blooming water smartweeds, buzzing with bees, and drying reed canary grass. In just a quarter mile as a plane flies, from Woburn Street to Route I-93, we paddle and push a sinuous half mile through plants. We are slowly following the meanders toward the roar of traffic seen and heard so near. Finally we are in the shade of the tunnel under it. The morning light peeps in from the ends a football field apart. We exit into a seemingly different river dominated by buttonbushes. The smartweed population is diminishing. In relatively open water a few delicate yellow blossoms of horned bladderworts, new to us, stick into the air above their floating bases. We pass patches of cattails and low islands of willows on a pond-like stretch where once the shallow well pumps of Reading rendered the broad river here dry. A decade ago the old Closeteer and sister walked on dry bottom in late summer where now five feet of water slowly flows. Readingites are now drinking Quabbin water. The pumps, still maintained in their once noisy pump houses as standbys, lie silent. We suspect beaver dams not yet passed are keeping the substantial rainwater of August upriver longer. Hurricane Irene, predicted Sunday, may raise the water, making passage easier and faster; retired we are in no hurry. In this vast stretch between Reading Town Forest and North Reading's Riverside Industrial Park wildlife abounds as you might expect where there is now water year round. In a mile we spook a dozen Great Blue Herons, juveniles and adults. Four Belted Kingfishers and three cormorants are seen fishing in the open water. Two Green Herons and two Black-crowned Night Herons fly closely by. This wet place and Reading Town Forest, bounded by industrial parks, I-93, and downtown Reading not far south, are wonders of diversity. Continuing eastward we encounter our first low beaver dam of the day; more will follow. Their dams keeping back the water greatly enhance rich habitats. The first couple miles from our start at Woburn Street at times have not been easy. Shoulders ache from pushing and pulling at times through dense patches of plants. The effort has sure been worth it. We plan to return in the late fall and early spring when the water is higher and bird migrations peak.

As the sun climbs south we continue our pleasant paddle on a northeasterly course. Around almost every one of many curves are fallen trees or submerged snags we must consider. They don't bother much, rather just slow a bit allowing more observation time. Upland woods close in from north and south on a narrowing floodplain. A few beaver-drowned red maple trunks of once many still stand, perches for herons and kingfishers, and places for woodpeckers seeking insects. We pass our first cardinal flower of the day, the first of many, on a wet bank. There are a dozen blossoms on a single stem, a vivid red among the varied greens. Finally Mill Street, anticipated for half an hour, comes into view. Boulders, the rough floor of two large culverts, seem to cling to our vessel's smooth bottom despite good riffles over them.

It takes several minutes to pass 20 feet until free again in the woods between Mill and Route 28. At the highway, despite heavy traffic and commerce, we feel isolated on our lower water road screened by brush. Quickly we are within the wild again with few signs of people except sound which we can easily shut out and do. A patch of invasive Phragmites passes to port. It is the first we've noticed in our last two canoe trips on over 10 miles of the upper river. We pass but miss Bear Brook converging from the south between busy Route 28 and Park Street. This is not surprising; some major tributaries spread out into heavily vegetated wetlands upon approaching the river's floodplain. The Reading USGS map shows Bear Brook draining Cedar Swamp, a place like others we don't know but now want to explore. Perhaps in April or November when the water is higher we'll return and see if our canoe has water enough in the almost two-square-mile wet area that rivals the Great Wenham Swamp downriver in size. We could ask knowledgeable folks upriver as we thought of doing before this paddle. We are happy we didn't; it leaves more to discover.

Let us digress a moment to tell you where we are and have been on this voyage. Wilmington saw us for only half a mile. Since then we have been traveling on the river channel, which is also the North Reading-Reading line. Now moving east after Route 28 both sides are in North Reading. Since leaving Park Street a few minutes ago we are moving in the shade along the old Lowell-Salem railroad line. We didn't see the record Mother's Day Flood of May 16, 2006, up here, but from the USGS map we can roughly tell that the river and its floodplain appeared as a great lake a few hundred to 10,000 feet wide along the length of the three miles we will have traveled as the train went and the cars now go. The wandering channel has taken us by canoe about six miles.

The channel's curves in healthy red maple woods are more gradual now. It is cool and very pleasant in the dappled shade. We round a turn north to east and there not 50 feet away poised on a steep high bank, probably the old railroad bed, are two magnificent deer. We and they freeze, mama with left front foot up as if for escape and fawn, half her size with fading spots, just five feet down the bank has four legs spread but firmly planted. We expect they'll flee at any moment. They, glowing in good health, do not move their legs as we drift by within 20 feet. Their great lustrous eyes stare at us from heads turning toward us in passing. Beautiful antennae, four large ears, straight up, alert, are pointing directly at us. We leave with this tableau disappearing as we round another turn murmuring about the wonder of this encounter: two men, two deer not 400 feet from noisy Route 62 thrown together in dense forest. The scene will be with us forever.

Still joyfully recovering from our meeting we swiftly move on the current down under and between large pilings, which once supported a bridge that carried several passenger trains each day. In another five minutes we pass under Central Street and glide into North Reading's fine Ipswich River Park. We've reached the end of this day's journey. The hardest part is bending old knees on leaving the canoe. They'll mend; we shall return.

Goodnight Irene, We'll See You in Our Dreams

How fickle was Irene. Imagine a line of boys sitting on one side of a high school gym at a Sadie Hawkins Day dance of yore. (Old-timers, explain to the kids what this means. They may have trouble understanding why such days were needed before women's liberation.) A spirited girl approaches from the girls' side on a sinuous route designed to tease. Each lad hopes she'll ask him to dance yet is afraid. In the case of Irene we long saw her coming yet didn't know exactly where she would go. The satellite cameras showed a great whirling white disk larger than France moving easterly at a good jog upon the warm Atlantic. Heated air laden with water vapor rose lowering the air pressure. Highs around her edges rushed in bending right to coriolis forces so instead of directly approaching the center they combined to form a counterclockwise storm. Draw some diagrams, you'll see what we mean. In Irene's early days between Africa and the Caribbean she developed a great Cyclops eye clearly seen from cameras high above. In 1938 a then nameless cyclone followed very roughly the same route. Its track was not photographed but rather measured by a thousand barometers on ships at sea. Those close to the center recorded rapidly falling mercury and rising swells. Sailors faced the wind with right arm extending straight out to the side. They were then pointing at the eye. Try it next nor'easter or hurricane and you'll see. Those to the east of the center facing the wind point west; those to the west, east. If in port they cast off lines or weighed anchor and headed for sea to ride the hurricane out in deep water away from lee shores. One old Closeteer clearly remembers leaving Naha, Okinawa, in a hurry as his ship's radio warned of a typhoon, the Pacific name for hurricane. That night it struck and with each plunge of the bow water barely seen in the darkness washed knee deep over the bridge 20 feet above the ship's water line. Nearly the entire crew of 80 was sick in varying degrees. However, those on watch held tightly to something and carried on. In the pilot house the officer of the deck and helmsman kept the wind on the starboard bow as they fled the storm's center. At first light, swells six stories high were revealed. The ship and a great tanker seen nearby seemed to be climbing and descending hills of water. Fortunately the crests of those monster waves were several hundred yards apart. The sun, which had not been seen for a couple days, shone brightly; the wind shifting around from the west slacked off. The typhoon had curved northeast following the warm Kuroshio Current off the east coast of Japan. The path of that unnamed typhoon followed a very similar arc, half a world away and half a century earlier, to that of Irene's.

And so they come above warm water year after year following ocean-wide clockwise-flowing currents. Now, with yearly warmer water, heat their source of energy, we worry they might strengthen. In 1938 there was 12 feet of seawater in downtown Providence. Walls and floodgates were built at the head of Narragansett Bay soon after. How high and long can we build them? Do we have the will to Zuiderzee all our cities and low areas or should we accept what to some seems inevitable and retreat to higher ground as coastal residents of the mid to north Atlantic states were urged to do as Irene approached? My! My! What problems our grandkids face. Perhaps if people worldwide shift from making guns and bombs to doing whatever is needed to adapt to climate change, civilization, if that is the proper word, might carry on. FEMA has already floated a figure that Irene's cost to it might exceed three-quarters of a billion dollars, the amount spent in Iraq and Afghanistan every few days.

Irene's sisters and brothers will probably keep coming. Their visits are certainly exciting. The weather folks on TV never leave the cameras as they explain and warn while their colleagues, the news readers, embellish and titillate. We sit at home and watch the suffering of others. After the storms some public wallet watchers fret about paying taxes to help. We in the Closet would rather pay up front for natural storm damage and preparation than for manmade storms of bullets, explosions and fire.

On the beautiful morning after Irene we breathed scrubbed-clean fall-like air and ventured out on yards and roads littered with the prunings of the heavy-handed gardener. Twigs with leaves covered the ground. We here were largely spared; the lightly trimmed woods in Irene's wake are healthier. Alas, to the west in the Berkshires and on north into Vermont valleys weeping Irene wailed away a foot of tears that flushed out bridges and whole road sections reminiscent of '38. We now watch Katia and wonder about future tropical disturbances that will form in Columbo's wake. We as landlubbers can't weigh anchor or slip mooring lines.

A BEAUTIFUL SOUND

One definition of sound is a waterway between an island and the mainland. Moving water has beautiful sounds of another type not so easily described. In the past we in the Closet have challenged readers to tell us what they hear.

The Ipswich, Plum Island, Eagle Hill, Rowley and Parker rivers flow into Plum Island Sound en route the Atlantic, which in turn twice daily sends seawater up into them. This wondrous mixing can be viewed from marshes, dunes and drumlins that surround the scene.

Giovanni da Verrazzano, Samuel de Champlain, and John Smith sailed in the warmer months past the sand bar-braided entrance to the sound on their explorations. They and the fishermen that preceded them may have entered to careen their vessels on the low tide beaches and to dry salted cod on flakes above the tide. The explorers' logs recorded in Portuguese, French and English the beauty of this juncture of glacier-sculpted uplands, broad sound, tidal flats, soft green marshes, rivers and then the forested barrier island named for its plums. One old Closeteer exclaimed, while on a recent paddle in which his canoe partner was going on about the marvels of the scene, "This is as close to heaven as we'll ever get." He frequently visits the area year round with friends to dig clams. His fellow clammers know there is a lot more to his visits and theirs than clams. Soon after Smith returned to England with maps and praise for his finds, his countrymen came forth in great numbers. They, unlike the fishermen, stayed and farmed. They built their settlements where Indian towns surrounded by corn fields had been. Old World diseases had swept most of the natives away. They left no deeds and few names anyone cared to remember.

The drumlins surrounding the sound are Castle Hill and Steep Hill to the south with Crane Beach at their feet. Those to the west with the best views of the sound and the Plum Island River up to Newburyport are Little Neck and Great Neck.

The paddle mentioned above was led by Kerry Mackin, director to the Ipswich River Watershed Association. Monthly "Source to Sea" paddles that had started upriver in Reading in the spring were concluding this year on September 10 on the waters of the estuary. Fifteen kayaks and two canoes launched from the half tide cobbles of Pavilion Beach between Great and Little Necks. A cool northeast breeze across the blue-green seawater fresh from the ocean perked us up, igniting good spirits. Rounding Little Neck's steep east slope, left 12,000 or so years ago by a vertical half mile of ice, we passed close to huge hidden boulders rippling signals of alarm as each swell passed over. We were reminded of the sea's potential. Weather folks had told us that distant hurricane Katia's swells would be reaching the coast. The chop from diverging flood tide currents north to the Plum Island River and west to the Ipswich River and the scarce seen swells were nothing to fret about even in our tiny vessels with only a few inches of freeboard. From bucking the tide in the broad sound we passed easily into the Ipswich River. There the northeast breeze joined the tide flattening the surface. The sky above was a fine blue 3D canvas enhanced with wispy cirrus brush strokes.

Happy chatter passed back and forth between our vessels. The houses on Little Neck and plastic boats below in its anchorage for some of us disappeared. Eyes were on the flanking twice daily washed beaches and salt marshes, the drumlins, and the sky. Plants were greener than usual for this time of year. The generous rains of August had kept them so.

One of the Stream Teamers in the large canoe mentioned above drifted back to a time he'd only read about. The trees, buildings and molded boats disappeared. The hills became pastures; the salt marsh was dotted with large haycocks perched on staddles, circles of supporting cedar posts. The modern recreational sail and motorboats were replaced by working dories, sloops and schooners of wood. The dories were returning under oar from the clam flats. The sailors, with higher water soon on the tide's turn, would be tacking out the sound's mouth to the sea. The old Stream Teamer wandered even further back until half a millennium had passed. "Well-proportioned" fellow travelers were wearing less clothing. The faces of some were painted "black, red and white." Their hair and eyes were shiny black. Unpainted skins were shades of "olive." Their vessels were of two types about the length of our canoe. Some were of beautifully sewn birch bark, most are dugouts of pine or chestnut. They, like us 500 years later, were chatting happily. The daydreaming imaginer didn't understand a word yet the Algonquian sounds were pleasing to his ear. He thought the gist of what they were saying was about the air, water and passing birds, similar to our chatter.

Ooops! He, who was supposed to have been steering, cut off a modern kayak. He awakened and left the handsome people he had hoped to get to know. Alas, they'll remain a mystery, but he hopes his mind will again drift back. He'll return at different seasons when the summer folks have gone. Perhaps his companions for a bit will return and teach him about their fishing and their descriptive names of places.

PROMISED LAND BETWEEN TWO OCEANS

The Water Closet, an imaginary shack that moves from place to place along the Ipswich River, has no computer, TV, electricity or even phone. We like to think of ourselves on rude benches reading by sun or candlelight. Books we like and think are important we recommend to you here. Jay Parini, Middlebury College professor, poet, novelist and historian has had the audacity to select "thirteen books that changed America." The words in quotes are the subtitle of his 2008 book *Promised Land*. A few weeks ago Tom Ashbrook had him as a guest on his public radio show *On Point*. An old Closeteer obtained this book and is now happily reading his superbly well-organized, written, and argued chapters defending his selections. The thirteen are:

Of Plymouth Plantation by William Bradford

The Federalist Papers mostly by Alexander Hamilton and James Madison

The Autobiography of Benjamin Franklin

The Journals of Lewis and Clark

Walden by Henry David Thoreau

Uncle Tom's Cabin by Harriet Beecher Stowe

Adventures of Huckleberry Finn by Samuel Clemens (Mark Twain)

The Souls of Black Folk by W.E.B. Du Bois

The Promised Land by Mary Antin

How to Win Friends and Influence People by Dale Carnegie

The Common Sense Book of Baby and Child Care by Dr. Benjamin Spock

On the Road by Jack Kerouac

The Feminine Mystique by Betty Friedan

Just reading this list sets the mood for things Americana. We in the Closet see water everywhere. Some wag might say we are hydrocephalic. Let's see what we can wring from Parini's suggested homework.

William Bradford came early on from England across the sea. It took 10 weeks for the hundred, many seasick, Pilgrims to reach a shore unknown to them as winter loomed. They were greeted by an early snow. By spring there were but half a hundred left clinging to the coast. Bradford wrote well of that brave group and their generally good relations with the Indians. Parini is sorry that later arrivals and those who pushed on west didn't heed lessons in diplomacy from the Pilgrims led by Bradford.

The Federalist Papers we've heard of throughout our long lives, but hadn't read, are essays largely written by Alexander Hamilton and James Madison. John Jay wrote three of 85. Hamilton when young sailed up from the West Indies where he was born. Madison's people raised tobacco a few miles from Virginia's shores. These founders eloquently and successfully argued in writing for the acceptance of the new constitution. Scholars and others have been returning to their papers for more than two centuries as our once coastal country expanded on waterways across the continent.

The Autobiography of Benjamin Franklin is by a heroic genius out of two great ports, Boston and Philadelphia. He swam in the dirty waters of both harbors from an early age. Ships took him back and forth to and from the Old World on diplomatic missions. En route he studied currents and left us the first known map of the Gulf Stream. He lived long and accomplished much.

The Lewis and Clark journals need no reminders of water connections.

That brilliant team of co-captains traveled up the Missouri against strong currents, portaged over the Rockies in snow on foot, and canoed down the Columbia's then undammed rivers to the Pacific. In so doing they sealed the fate of a continent to Manifest Destiny. The many largely friendly Indian nations they encountered never really knew what hit them. Within a century most of them and their habitats were gone. Lewis and Clark and their men and woman were wet a good part of the time for the 28 months going and returning. Their notes, sketches, maps and measurements were somehow kept dry. Scholars in their research are still returning to them. In 1988 one old Closeteer and his good wife borrowed two great tomes, their abbreviated journals, from the Danvers library. In July and August, they, with tent, followed the Lewis and Clark route as closely as they could get by car from St. Louis to the mouth of the Columbia River. They read passages from the journals at appropriate spots along the way.

Now the old Closeteer is halfway though Parini's brilliant summaries and arguments wishing they would never end. He is with Henry David Thoreau and Parini at Walden. Thoreau, our neighbor just two watersheds west on the Concord River, is called a transcendentalist. Parini tries valiantly to explain what that means. Thoreau somehow experienced the world without much travel. His poetic and scientific observations spiced by original ruminations have flowed from the pond to folks around the globe. Walden Pond, relatively deep as New England ponds go, became ever deeper. Parini predicts Thoreau's millions of words will be forever fresh. Scientists as well as literary types and philosophers frequently return to his voluminous journals. Mahatma Gandhi, Martin Luther King Jr. and Nelson Mandela look lessons from him. Let us hope Thoreau's Walden never dries up. The fate of our species and others may depend on it.

Let's leave the list for now. We may return to the eight remaining books if needed and comment in a future Water Closet essay. We bet we can somehow squeeze water from them. It is surprisingly easy in a world inhabited by organisms made up largely of water that can't stray too far from it for long.

It is raining on the Closet roof as this is being written. The river just outside seen through the windows is flowing to the ocean where Bradford, Hamilton and Franklin sailed and Thoreau walked along its surf. We know it continues around the Horn and under the waning Arctic ice cap to the Pacific where the Corps of Discovery ended up the hard way. Thoreau journeyed even further, transcending them all.

OCTOBER 2011

HIGH-RUNNER TIDES

As kids we marveled at the "high-runner tides" that rose above our salt marshes each month. The greenish cold ocean water invigorated us at our swimming holes where at lows the brackish water was murky and sometimes lukewarm. For hours water flowed through small mosquito and natural ditches where it picked up heat and particles of debris. In the summer until old enough to work we visited the meandering flat marsh cricks several times a day to cool off and play. Occasional mud fights ranged over a quarter square mile of soft grasses. How wonderful to be bollocky-bare-ass, as we liked to say, running truly free with our companions. In and out of the cricks we'd seek shelter from peat-armed enemies. A group on one side of Pettengill's Crick would, when not attacking, defend its turf from amphibious assaults from the other side. At the end of sometimes long battles, truces would be declared and we'd all dive, splash and frolic together like otters. Girls, when approaching what we called the Dock through the surrounding upland woods would yell loudly, "Girls!" Boys would frantically run to find bathing suits, undershorts or pants. Once we were attired the bathing-suited girls would venture out on the marsh. In the evenings after work older youths and parents would sometimes join us.

During the twice monthly spring tides (more scientific name for "high-runners"), we'd experience seawater like found one mile east in the beach's surf. It came to us via the Merrimack River and tributaries. Some high-runner tides covered the marsh to depths of two feet. We could barely tell where our familiar cricks were. Thousands of acres of marsh became broad bays. Plum Island and Salisbury Beach were transformed into offshore islands. On the very highest tides, pushed up further by east winds, even the tall "thatch" grass, *Spartina alterniflora*, along the edges of the cricks disappeared. The temporary bays with long reaches developed whitecaps. And then the bays went away on the ebb; the cricks, in six and one-half hours, a dozen feet lower, became dark walled canyons. In them we could not see the level marshes above. Then, of course, as the tides waxed and waned there were all gradations between. At half tides when the flow was greatest we could barely swim against the tidal currents.

Last week all these memories flooded back as three one-time Salisburyites, brother, sister and cousin, who used to swim together six decades before in marsh creeks, paddled up the Parker River in canoe on a high high-runner tide. We meandered easily on the rising flood tide the three miles from Route 1A to Route 1 where salt hay had recently been cut from a few acres for mulch. Some had been stacked in several large cocks on circular arrangements of posts called staddles near the road so folks passing can see what the salt marshes of a hundred years ago looked like. Much of the hay then was used for feed. Despite the absence of any tide-enhancing east wind, the marsh grasses were almost covered as we easily returned against a slackening flood. According to the tide table it had turned, started to ebb, two hours before out at the river's mouth. There is an increasing lag as the tidal wave proceeds upriver. If you do this paddle and it is always a beauty, start from the Newbury Town Landing at Route 1 a little after high tide time at the mouth and you can ride the flood up and the ebb down. Tides have often been featured in Water Closet essays. You may remember hearing some of our childhood stories told here before. Forgive us if we repeat as old-timers tend to do.

Tides never cease to interest clammers, salt water fishermen, duck hunters, and us Closeteers. They offer changes every moment along our coasts, high - half - low - half - high - half - low at three and one-quarter hour intervals so timed on a spinning earth by a circling moon. At our latitude the range in elevation is from 13 to seven feet daily between the highs and lows, which are the crests and troughs of waves with half-world-circumference wave lengths. At full and new moons when the earth, moon and sun are aligned the so-called spring tides are higher and lower. The "neap" tides in between, when the bodies are at right angles to each other, don't rise as high or fall as low.

One old Closeteer claims that if he were dictator of our local schools these would be the first things kids would learn along with letters and numbers. They would do so on field trips to our estuaries. In early September and June they'd wade and swim at high and low tides; moon-sun-earth astronomy with a little fun. Teachers and pupils would dig a few clams on the lows and steam them for a snack over fires on the marsh edges. Crabs, snails and sea worms caught would be studied and released. No one would be given much attention if they complained about mud, bugs and sunburn. Let us dream.

IN THE SHADE WITH WANGARI MAATHAI

On September 21, far away across the Atlantic and North Africa, 2004 Nobel Peace Prize winner Wangari Maathai died. This memorial should have been written the day after. We were reminded again this week when the 2011 peace prizes for three other strong African women were announced.

In her 71 years Kenyan Wangari Maathai had been a superb student, anatomy professor, medical researcher, wife and mother, politician, champion for women's rights, environmental activist, and longtime thorn in the sides of corrupt Kenyan leaders. Her college education, undergraduate and graduate, was in the United States. Worldwide fame came to her as leader of Kenya's Green Belt Movement, a planter of trees to heal hurt land in her long agriculturally exploited country. Sources we found online had her many women followers establishing 6,000 tree seedling nurseries and planting over seven million trees. In their early years those needing it were lovingly watered.

Peace prize, you ask, what can trees have to do with peace? We in the Closet can think of nothing more peaceful than planting trees where badly needed for shade, for wood and work, for erosion prevention, for water retention and filtration, and for beauty. Maathai could have added another half-dozen reasons and often did in inspiring speeches.

We haven't had to plant here where rainfall is relatively high year round. Closet records show the five year average annual rainfall in the last 15 years since the Stream Team started paying attention and keeping records has gone from about 49 to 56 inches. Land was much exploited here too in the 17th to mid-20th centuries for agriculture, and the shipbuilding and charcoal industries. When wood for fuel and shipbuilding ran out it was imported from the far north and deep south. Paintings, old photos and written accounts show much of the countryside largely devoid of trees. Visit the Stream Team and we'll show you geologist John Henry Sears' snapshots taken here in Essex County early last century. With the advent of rail lines in the mid-19th century coal replaced wood and charcoal. Farming went west; forests came back and are thriving wherever land is left undeveloped. Before the colonists Indians burned land yearly so we may have many more trees now than in their time. We haven't needed a Maathai for trees but with rapid development we certainly need greenbelt movements and have them in the Essex County Greenbelt Association, The Trustees of Reservations and in state and town land conservation efforts such as Boxford Trails Association/Boxford Open Land Trust. We hope the same will continue in Maathai's Kenya and that other organizations will be started throughout the world. The following is from her Nobel acceptance speech to the world:

"We are called to assist the Earth to heal her wounds and in the process heal our own—indeed, to embrace the whole creation in all its diversity, beauty and wonder. This will happen if we see the need to revive our sense of belonging to a larger family of life, with which we have shared our evolutionary process."

We'd like to say much more about Maathai but don't really need to; it has been done many times and is readily available on the internet. Google noted over two million sites for her in 0.09 seconds! We read the first few to help us with this tribute. Wikipedia has a fair biography. One of the most compelling sites has many images of our hero. One old Closeteer scrolled on and on admiring photos of her strong round face flashing broad smiles. He asks us to look into her eyes where strength is clearly seen. Her husband divorced her for "being too strong" for a woman.

We don't know if she was cremated or buried. Either way her wonderful flesh, and ours after death, will break down largely to CO_2 and H_2O, some of which will end up in her trees. These are the main ingredients of photosynthesis. When the trees eventually die they too will decompose to CO_2 and H_2O, molecular immortality through recycling. She as a biologist understood this well and we bet loved the idea. While her body is gone her spirit will live on in millions. In some strong people, such as she was, it will inspire bold actions on behalf of the environment, which she saw as our first duty as educated animals. Here are a few more sentences from her Nobel acceptance speech in Stockholm that we think may explain much about her career:

"As I conclude I reflect on my childhood experience when I would visit a stream near our home to fetch water for my mother. I would drink water straight from the stream. Playing among the arrowroot leaves I tried in vain to pick up the strands of frogs' eggs, believing they were beads. But every time I put my little fingers under them they would break. Later, I saw thousands of tadpoles: black, energetic and wriggling through the clear water against the background of the brown earth. This is the world I inherited from my parents."

Today over 50 years later, the stream has dried up, women walk long distances for water, which is not always clean, and the children will never know what they have lost. The challenge is to restore the home of tadpoles and to give back to our children a world of beauty and wonder. (Go to the internet and see her deliver the entire speech in English and living color.)

We in the Closet much like the idea that we humans breathe the molecules of dead heroes and all fellow organisms that have passed on. We may have long been inhaling a few of those that were in Rachel Carson and Henry David Thoreau. In time the water passing by the Closet in the Ipswich River and in our tissues may have molecules that were part of Wangari Muta Maathai; however, what we really want is just a bit of her spirit.

BOLDLY GREEN

Presidents in the latter half of the 19th century, including Abraham Lincoln, and congresses joined businessmen in bold and massive ways to tie the nation together in a web of fast rail, fast compared with canal boat, horse and wagon. Generous subsidies were granted and loose laws passed to promote tracks and trains. The results were remarkable; in 40 years, 1850 to 1890, vast reaches were connected. We hesitate from the Water Closet to venture into the deep and mysterious seas of economics and business; however, it seems everyone else who frets about our economy does, so why not us environmentalists?

President Obama excited us greens in his presidential campaign. He saw, at least he said he did, that going green in a big way was a responsible and practical way to sail out of our economic doldrums. Alas, he soon ran upon the shoals of big oil and coal, which weren't about to help to fill any sails his crew might raise. They punctured and let the air out at every turn before even unfurled. Congress, long a champion of internal combustion engines, is sadly not about to go forth from lucrative black fuels to clean wind and sun. The latter are nice to breathe and bask in but they don't, ironically, in the short run fill wallets with green bills. There was a joke, perhaps still is, that arose from the "Keep Maine Green" signs that used to greet people upon entering the state. Wags would repeat the message with a smile while rubbing thumb and forefinger together as if counting paper money. Maine wanted tourists bringing in the green. Congress, and unfortunately the administration, smilingly talk green while rubbing together fingers holding cash reeking of oil. Look at what they did after the BP disaster. They allowed deep water drilling to resume. (By the way, since then someone took a long-standing NO OCEAN DRIILLING sign off an old Closeteer's lawn.) And now powers in Washington are planning to allow crude oil from Canadian shale to be piped down across our Bread Basket and bird migration routes to Gulf refineries. Even if it never leaks another pipe like that in Alaska from Prudhoe Bay to Valdez will be an in-your-face sign to the world of our arrogance and irresponsibility. "We want to keep our many big gas-guzzling vehicles," these pipes scream, "to hell with the air and water of the planet."

Would the person who took this sign from a Middleton Stream Teamer's lawn please return it, or better still take it to Washington and install on the White House lawn?

We Closeteers have been justly accused of hypocrisy when we rant on like this. Guilty. We too are Americans and have known the wonders of cars our entire lives. As kids, even if our parents had one, and many didn't, we got around by hitchhiking with someone else. Old-timers please explain what hitchhiking means to any youngster under 30. We had buses to get to school but often stuck out our thumbs instead. Now we notice two large parking lots at Masco that are daily filled with big cars. We are told the school buses we pay for are not filled. We hope that what the kids learn at school will wean them from fossil fuel burning engines. Jack Kerouac who famously wrote *On the Road* clearly knew that America was a car country. He, Ginsberg and Cassady rode back and forth across the continent, often, like we do, going nowhere. Another work of art, if you can call the movie *American*

Graffiti that, showed us how far we had gone in the ostentatious car department. Children filled the evening streets of our towns in great fin-fendered monsters showing off and looking for what they didn't quite know. Today our kids are never seen hitching or even walking our roads. Their parents take them everywhere until they have a ticket to drive. Last year one old Closeteer commented to a friendly Middleton librarian about all the cars in the parking lot of her spanking new library. She, quoting someone, said, "Build it and they will come." How true. We wonder if President Eisenhower didn't envision the same when he got the country to start the interstate highway system ostensibly for defense purposes in the 1950s. We came with a vengeance bypassing towns and passenger trains, which subsequently died. Shopping centers sprang up everywhere. Downtown stores boarded up their windows. Distant malls can't be easily walked to. There aren't even sidewalks to them. Drive-to gyms have taken the place of walking.

We've experienced all this and now watch the developing countries of the world seemingly aspiring to repeat our folly. Perhaps it is high time to step back on the ground. Rick Steves' popular public TV travel show would have us all flying to Europe on fossil fuel to quaint town centers and side alleys where people walk. On the positive side we see some moves back to our downtowns here. If people follow from the suburbs that were developed upon our little remaining farmland, the cities might recover. Boston now has the Greenway and public bicycles available throughout the city. A Boxford family just back from Washington, D.C., praised the city bicycles available there.

There are other good signs. Last night an old Closeteer happened upon a local TV station where the Ipswich Planning Board was hearing a wind turbine proposal. He was much impressed by the level of discussion and questioning by the board, applicant's representatives, and interested citizens. Wind power is coming. There is a wind turbine planned for Winter Island, Salem, now in the permitting process. If approved, it will be in the afternoon shadow of Salem's huge dirty coal-burning power plant. "Build windmills, wind will come." It always has. We just don't feel it with the car windows closed. While our descendants raze the coal power plants let them also turn the tens of thousands of miles of interstate highways into greenways. It won't cost much. After abandonment the weather will in a couple generations crumble the asphalt allowing seeds to sprout. We can

New snow on old ice, Prichards Pond, Middleton. Photo, courtesy of Pamela Hartman.

show you abandoned sections of road around our towns where in just 40 years plants, misnamed "weeds," have taken over. They've become good wildlife habitat. In a century, no time at all to a geologist, some will be hard to find.

We need leaders in our towns, states and country who understand the lessons from two centuries of profligate use of coal and oil. They were fun times for many but the hangovers inherited by our descendants will be severe. Please Mr. and Ms. future presidents around the world, boldly lead your flocks to greener pastures.

A Cap's Final Journey

Boston Brook, a major tributary of the Ipswich River, received a dirty cranberry-colored cap the other evening. Knitted into its front above the visor in once white letters are the words "Wetlands Preservation." An old Closeteer lost it while sweeping the brook's bottom with a net for insects and crustaceans from the Greenbelt's wooden bridge at the start of the rapids above North Liberty Street in Middleton. He and his seven-year-old grandson Django were sampling along edges of the brook in one of the few stretches of white water in town.

They put their catches in plastic bowls of water to study, identify and then release. While bending to make a pass with a net among the submerged boulders below the bridge, the cap, worn almost daily for 16 years, joined one of the streams its words boasted to protect.

Boy and grandpa moved quickly on down the narrow rough path on the south side of the brook in an effort to retrieve the half-sunken cap not easily seen in the darkening water and dim light of late afternoon. After a couple hundred feet it crossed in the turbulence to the north side where it looked like it might get hung up in some debris. The would-be rescuers ran back to the bridge and down the pathless north side of the fast-moving flow to no avail. The valued cap was lost, stuck unseen on bank or bottom or moving toward the distant sea.

Prior the incident, just upstream from the bridge, they had visited the ruins of a sawmill dam idle and unnoticed for over three centuries. Grandpa pointed out the remains of the earthen dam with overflow channel and sluiceway separated by an island, a portion of the dam, and tried to explain. Without a water wheel, mill pond and saw it seemed impossible although the boy listened attentively.

As the pair separated by 71 years hiked leisurely back to Prichards Pond they discussed the hat's likely fate. The old Closeteer hoped it would clear the thousands of obstacles between the rapids and Plum Island Sound 25 meandering river miles to the northeast and then make it on an ebb tide to the sea. The old man knew that in time it would join the ingredients of the river. Threads would decompose and in molecular form become a part of the water and soil. Django in some future visit, perhaps with grandchild, might admire a dragonfly with once hat atoms in it.

While walking back along the lovely path above the stream with bed of boulders the man remembered a time 40 years or so before when Django's mother, then about nine, slipped off one of the bank's moss-covered stones into the cold April water. Waist deep she was able to climb back out despite the strong flow. The Closeteer pointed to the spot and told the story. "That's where your mother fell in when a little girl." Django asked something like, was she scared? "No, a friend who was with us was impressed by how calm she was."

Same brook, one visited many times, brought memories of daughter, friend and scene clearly back. Now a battered but favorite hat has joined that section of a favorite brook. What does it all mean? Nothing, just chance, some things to fondly remember. We could stretch the story on downriver and south in the Atlantic and across the Pacific to where the daughter and her mother were born. Maybe Django will return with family and friends someday and remember the hat, the story of Mom's cold immersion, and we Closeteers hope "Ojii," Japanese for grandpa. If we really try to make connections, and we usually do here in the Closet, we can see how water connects us all through time.

By the way, Django and Ojii captured a dragonfly larva, a dozen whirligig beetles, a predacious diving beetle, several back swimmers and water boatmen, two species of small snails, numerous scuds, caddis fly larvae, and an isopod in their nets. We wonder if those caught are still wondering what hoisted them up and kept them in a white bowl for a while.

NOVEMBER 2011

WADING IN BANGKOK

TV certainly does bring the people of the world to us. This week we watch from our dry couches as thousands wade and paddle in Thailand's streets and fields. From their faces and body language we share their feelings and imagine ourselves and families leaving home and drowned crops for higher ground. We have vicariously participated in floods many times in the past decade. Much of the southern half of Bangladesh went under in 2005, 2007, 2011 and 20 times in the 20th century. The Indus River rose along its very long length in 2010 and inundated farmlands and beyond in Pakistan. In our country Katrina put our Gulf Coast and a much loved city under in 2005. We watched and wept as people waved for help from rooftops. Those victims in Thailand, Bangladesh, Pakistan and New Orleans are obviously kindred souls disrupted by too much water too fast.

As we old-timers often do in the Closet upon hearing of distant floods we open our National Geographic atlas, only two decades old, but already falling apart from use. The Closet lacking a computer doesn't allow us to Google Earth. We like our paper maps better anyway, all features are labeled and shading and colors have the mountains and other features standing clearly out. We became comfortable with paper maps in fourth-grade geography. For those not so old-fashioned, Google the Indian Ocean and Asia and see if you see what we do as southern Asia lies before us. Since childhood we've known of the mighty monsoons that sweep yearly up from the south collecting water from the warmest of oceans and leaving it as rain on land and as snow on the peaks of the Himalayas.

One old Closeteer tells of very hot days in Salisbury at the mouth of Merrimack. He worked all day in the gardens and hayfields knowing well there would usually be a break in the late afternoon. Warm air rose from the sun-heated land creating low atmospheric pressure. The cooler air above the sea just two miles away swept in to replace the rising warm air. Hundreds of folks who could drove downriver from the sweltering factory cities of Haverhill and Lawrence and slept upon the beaches cooled by soft easterly breezes. There was little air conditioning besides open windows then. We experienced mini-monsoons and never knew it. Monsoons in Asia bordering the sea last for several months. The dry land heats up for days on end in the summer. Land-heated air rises and vapor-laden air flows in off the warmest of oceans. As saturated air from the south ascends the rising continent clouds form and vapor condenses and falls as very welcome cooling rain. The countries fringing the Arabian Sea and Bay of Bengal and beyond depend on these rains for their agriculture. The vapor that makes it to the great wall of the Himalayas running east to west 3,000 miles falls as snow and rain, and upon melting descends back south via thousands of rivers, which converge making ever greater ones: the Indus, Ganges, Brahmaputra and Mekong to mention a few. In some monsoon seasons there is way too much from the skies above as rain and it comes down from the north as runoff. Banks overflow, crops and communities are inundated. Sometimes the monsoons' winds start to spin and typhoons form. Storm waves rise as bottom depth decreases, and surge along vast fronts such as happened with Katrina. Rhode Island's Providence received a 12-footer in September 1938. Our coastal towns each year get lesser surges with nor'easters. As this is being written, and the first snowstorm of the year covers still-green leaves, people are fretting about the sea walls in Scituate and the dunes at Plum Island and Chatham. Bangladesh gets monsoon surges from the South China Sea and flood water as runoff down from the northern mountains. As much as three-quarters of the country goes under. Now it is Thailand where people are shown suffering. Add to all this the fact that the oceans are yearly rising and extremes of precipitation in many areas are increasing.

When we look at the map of the Indian Ocean, we see huge funnels. The Arabian Sea has the Arabian Peninsula and India as side walls. The triangular funnel formed points north at Pakistan. The Bay of Bengal is flanked by India and Burma converging on Bangladesh. Thailand's funnel points down from the mountains. The other countries mentioned have runoff funnels from above also, so at times are deluged from both north and south. We have a similar situation in our country. The Rockies, Canadian Shield and Appalachians catch and send down runoff.

Let's return home and examine our perceived funnel, the Gulf of Mexico off the Caribbean, off the Atlantic. Our hurricanes (typhoons) originate over the warm westerly flowing North Equatorial Current just off Africa. When they come our way they bring tidal surges and torrential rains. Irina visited Mexico's Yucatan Peninsula last week.

Where is this well-known flow we are inflicting on you going? We know we'll see people wading somewhere each year again and again. Let ours, a very rich country, plan on it and help in ways other than we are using in Iraq and Afghanistan. What could the two billion dollars a week we spend in Afghanistan do if wisely used to help the Gulf Coast and Asian countries mentioned with their water woes? We too may need such help someday. Greenland, its ice several miles thick from past continental glaciers, mostly not land at all, looms melting above the sea. Other wild storms like Katrina will come.

White on Green

Our first snow came early on a strong nor'easter. Still-green leaves, sticky wet from the preceding rain, received and held it for a while. The rain came as predicted at 3 p.m. after a quiet morning without breezes beneath thickening clouds. Wind with snow soon followed. By evening thickly frosted limbs bowed, many broke. The barely freezing air didn't weld the wet snow to the leaves and twigs, so wind approaching blizzard force by early morning blew it off. The day dawned quietly; the storm passed leaving several inches of snow mixed with twigs and branches on still-green grass. Now several days later in early November our forests are still half green; leaves that have changed are of subdued colors compared with most autumns. Even the usually show-offy sugar maples have been uncharacteristically modest. The fall foliage of 2011 has been dull yet interestingly different, perhaps due to almost two feet of rain August through October.

A week has passed since the storm; patches of snow still linger in shady places. A walk in the woods reveals tracks of fellow mammals usually not so clear this time of year.

We old-timers still get excited as the first snow is forecast and then arrives. By the way, it is remarkable how close the meteorologists' calls come to pass. They tell us a day or two ahead amounts of precipitation and where. Could the excitement that they especially show be residual fear from when our ancestors approached the winter in caves, wigwams and drafty log cabins? How the new white world must have energized the wood gatherers, game hunters and children who hadn't seen snow for seven months. Another winter of possible starvation loomed. We Yankees feel for those in more southern climes who don't yearly experience these sights and feelings. Of course Snowbirds don't feel sorry at all; they flee south. We wonder if this early storm will shoo them off earlier.

In classrooms lessons cease in the minds of pupils as their eyes wander to the windows during even minor snow showers. Their bodies follow in classes where teachers allow. We wonder if it still happens in rooms where kids have computer screens as well as windows. In vicarious ways much of the world can enter the room and minds via flickering screens; the transparent windowpanes only allow local light. Our young have a dimension we didn't have. We had community prescribed by well-known people, town lines, streets and geological features. Computer-savvy folks have the planet's surface and many of its people at their fingertips, which, odd to us, has become their expanded community. It frightens many of us old-timers. But as the brother-in-law of one Closeteer said when he worried like this out loud, "That's the way it is." It was said in a tone that implied, quit your whining. We in turn ask, "Is that how it should be?" Brother-in-law repeats what he just said and shakes his head in disgust.

Funny what thoughts the first storm brings. Maybe subsequent storms will take down more wires and with that the internet and other electronic media. Kids will be sent next door to borrow candles so they can do homework while bundled up. Maybe they'll look up en route and without light pollution see the Milky Way. The refrigerator will be the whole house unless one has a wood stove or generator. Without power we'll all get a taste of what it was like before much winter outdoor life became short trips between heated cars and buildings.

Just in case the power does go out for long periods in subsequent storms, let's cut the fallen branches and trees for fuel that Mother Nature has pruned with wind and frozen water. It will be a good chance to explain natural selection. Over time beyond our ken the stronger woody plants have survived repeated drastic prunings. Those woody plants that lived to flower passed their better genes on. The trunks, branches and twigs of trees became ever stronger and more flexible. We feel sorry for, and not a little afraid of, those political candidates who deny evolution. We must invite them into the snowy woods after a storm and tell them of Charles Darwin. Only if we learn they still have the Earth in the center of the Universe will we give up trying to explain.

Goose Droppings

It is too bad such a noble bird as the Canada Goose has become famous for its excrement. In the days when almost all country and suburban folks had chickens no one fussed much about poultry poop. Soft turds, white-streaked with uric acid, were found in many yards. Now that we have lawns, golf courses and asphalt drives instead of fields and dirt yards their impressive offerings have become noticeable, especially to the squeamish. Friend of the Closet, naturalist Fred Gralenski, reminded us this week in his column "Quoddy Nature Notes," a feature of *The Quoddy Tides* newspaper, of magnificent *Branta canadensis* that we've come to take for granted and shouldn't. We thought we'd expand here in the Closet with recollections stirred up by his observations and research and bring the great bird closer home. We old-timers have been admiring Canada Geese for over seven decades. In our early years it was mainly twice a year as they passed through en route between feeding areas in southern marshes and fallow fields and breeding grounds, up to the tundra. James Michener in his best-selling novel *Chesapeake* spends many eloquent pages on their comings and goings. A half century earlier Edward Howe Forbush, a favorite ornithologist and crackerjack author, one we in the Closet often read and sometimes quote, outdid Michener in his old-fashioned way:

"Wild geese are the forerunners of winter and harbingers of spring, while ice still covers our lakes, before even wood frogs begin to croak, when the spring floods break up the frozen rivers, the geese are on their way; and when the flying wedge sweeps fast across the sky, it brings to all that see the promise of another spring. The farmer stops his team to gaze; the blacksmith leaves his forge to listen as the far-carrying clamor falls upon the ear; children leave their play and eagerly point to the sky where the feathered denizens of the northern wilderness press on towards the pole, babbling of the coming spring, carrying their message over mountain and plain to village, city and farm as far as open water can be found. Coming after the long cold winter, not even the first call of the Bluebird so stirs the blood of the listener. Again in autumn when the last great flight passes southward, flock after flock winging steadily on, we know the forest has closed the northern waters and that winter is at hand."

That is how we remember their flights as children. However, in just three human generations the migration patterns have dramatically changed. Large populations of the Canada Geese are now with us year around. They nest here in spring and early summer and graze upon our greens. We are told other Canada Geese populations still follow the long migration routes from Chesapeake estuaries to the tundra and back. We think we can tell the latter by their well-formed vees, Forbush's "flying wedges," beelining at high altitudes. Our locals fly from foraging areas to nearby open waters in low flights of roughly formed vees. Those folks living just east of Middleton center are treated to daily waves of them as they pass back and forth from Richardson Farm fields to Middleton Pond. On a recent late morning an old Closeteer estimated 300 passed for several minutes low over St. Agnes in about 20 waves on their way from leavings in harvested corn fields to the pond. They cleared the steeple and trees by only a few yards. Their flying chorus, we can't begin to describe, certainly "stirs the blood." Forbush says he can't hear any h's or k's in their honks. Sibley, in his wonderful picture book of all our birds, writes, "Familiar call a loud, resonant, and musical 'h-ront' and 'h-lent'; flock chorus gentle, slow-paced, mellow; no harsh or sharp notes." The old Closeteer noticed that a lady in the church parking lot on her way to the clothing collection bin didn't even look up. It just shows you how much we've gotten used to this common phenomenon.

Fred notes that he has never seen them poop in flight. The Closeteer under their daily flight path has never had to put on a hat upon hearing them coming. He almost wishes they would fertilize his garden, much in need of nitrogen.

The feisty geese we most like to remember, after those in striking high flights, are those in shiny courtship prime in winter and early spring. They seem so formal decked out in black and gray with white half collars. Later when five to nine eggs are snug in their nests, often atop beaver lodges along the river, we can get close in our canoes and are sometimes even attacked. They flatten their bodies and neck down with upper neck partly raised and hissing. One mother flew twice down at us and touched our raised paddles. We backed off and paddled on. Her nest was on the summit of a large lodge on the Ipswich River. We bet more than a couple dozen lodges, Wilmington to Ipswich, are so adorned in late spring. While Forbush reports up to nine eggs, we rarely see that many fuzzy yellow-gray goslings walking and swimming place to place between parents.   We've heard that snappers get some

Day after the storm. Photo, courtesy of Pam Hartman.

from below.

Take some time and go to fallow fields near your home to see them feeding. In Middleton and Danvers the best place may be along Gregory turned Dayton Street in the once Danvers State Hospital fields. Visit an open body of water and watch flocks swimming faces to the wind. Or better still just pause when they are passing overhead singing "resonant" and "slow-paced mellow."

Photo Contest

Each fall Middleton Stream Teamers, amateur photographers and friends gather in the Middleton Historical Society's meeting room to view photographs submitted to our annual contest and applaud contestants. The hour is a pleasant one in which beauty of Middleton waters captured over the past year is shared. We chat with friends, meet photographers we didn't know before, and leave contentedly knowing they've visited our precious swamps, streams and river, probably without backhoes or ATVs. Our long-time leader John Bacon greets folks and then introduces the team's photographer Judith Schneider who runs the contest and arranges for its annual completion. Winning photos are reproduced by Stream Teamers Katharine Brown and Millie Clark on fine note cards each with a map of Middleton's streams on its back. We are proud of these cards sold at Art of Framing, Mason & Madison, and town events. This year we had a table at the Middleton Farmers Market from which food for the soul was sold. The cards are a source of very little income. The team has proven over the past 14 years that much can be done without money. The Historical Society, Garden Club, Scouts, Chief Will's Day, Pumpkin Festival, Friends of the Flint Public Library, PTO and other groups we have not listed constitute a non-governmental web of volunteers that provide something deeply needed called community.

In our boasting about volunteerism and civic activity, something that should just happen and not be tooted about, we have strayed from the photographs. We'll very briefly comment on some here. We hope you will visit the bank/post office foyer in Middleton soon to see them in the Stream Team's display cabinet. Drop by almost anytime year round to see Judy's eye- and spirit-catching photo essays.

We hesitate to choose from the submissions for comment. We'll let you judge. Go to Judy's album at http://www.middletonstreamteam. org and click on the Photo Contest link. Three independent artist judges had high praise for the lot. We are glad not to have been in their shoes. However, we can't resist mentioning the infinite number of moods that water in its various forms evokes by pointing out a few.

Andrew Richardson, 10, perennial kid's contest entrant since six, this year gave us close-ups of a Great Blue Heron and a green frog. In the past he has submitted other crackerjack photos of frogs and turtles. His pictures enliven some of our most popular cards. Older contestants mostly go for scenery. We could go on about Andrew, long a pied piper for other kids on our Stream Team family hikes. He does 10 miles to our three, some in detours over high ledges and up trees.

Third prize winner Elaine Gauthier shares a lovely somber scene of beaver-drowned red maples in the Ipswich River as seen from Log Bridge park. She might have caught similar views in a score of other places around town. The beavers have returned in a big way after a four century hiatus.

Honorable mention winner Allison Colby-Campbell catches the ghostly mist among mature red pines planted by Stream Teamer Joan Cudhea's grandfather Charles Pritchard along the driveway to his house on Prichards Pond. Last week they were cut by loggers and hauled away. Joan will replace them with native trees and bushes attractive to wildlife. Allison's photo will be a record of their last days. Unlike hardwoods they won't send up shoots.

Lisa Campbell gives us a sunset off the calm waters of Middleton Pond. The Canada Geese flocks there each afternoon and early morning get to see such scenes daily, though never quite the same. Friends of the team Rita and Bob Kelley whose house is on the pond say goodbye to the sun each day as it shows off with a light show in farewell.

Pam Hartman, second prize winner, captured in two photos the wonder of freshly frosted trees after early snowstorms. She has been providing moving photos of our area as well as places the world around for years.

Jonathan Campbell, winner of first prize and an honorable mention, got down and close to less than a square meter of water featuring a white birch log framed by fallen leaves and still green duckweed. The shimmering water draws us near with him. We are blessed with an endless number of such scenes each fall as the trees and breezes sprinkle their dying leaves upon the water. We wonder if Jackson Pollock with dripping brushes wasn't inspired by them. Please submit your own watery pictures next year.

WATER RESOURCE AND CONSERVATION INFORMATION FOR MIDDLETON, BOXFORD AND TOPSFIELD

Precipitation data for month of	Aug	Sept	Oct	Nov
30 Year Normal (1971-2000) Inches	3.35	3.71	4.12	4.48
2011 Central Watershed Actual	9.69	4.38	9.92	2.96

IPSWICH RIVER FLOW RATE (S. MIDDLETON USGS GAGE) IN CUBIC FEET PER SECOND (CFS):

For Nov 29, 2011	Normal... 66 CFS	Current Rate ...165 CFS	*

DECEMBER 2011

CHANGES NEAR THE RIVER

Recently a retired conservation agent walked with Middleton's new agent along the Ipswich River. In the stretch from the Peabody Street fields upriver for a mile, Gould Hill, a 15,000-year-old or more drumlin broadly slopes to the floodplain's edge delineated by two-century-old stone walls. Tied to bushes above the walls are new pink ribbons. The agents were checking these "flags" placed there by a developer's wetland specialist. Finding the flagged lines marking the edges of the river's width and flanking wetlands essentially correct, their minds wandered to thoughts of the trees and ice-sculpted terrain. They guessed most of the hardwoods and pines are 50 to 60 years old. Just about all have single trunks, not clusters as would have come from cut stumps. Interspersed among the oaks and white pines are dead or dying red cedars about the same age. These clues, single trunks, each from a seed, and red cedars, told them that Gould's Hill was probably open pasture three human generations ago. The livestock gone, the plants were left alone. Red cedars grew up among the weeds and grasses. In partial shade, squirrel and Blue Jay buried acorns sprouted.

* The table above, with essay, is how The Water Closet appears weekly in the *Tri-Town Transcript*.

In time the slow-growing cedars were surpassed in their climb toward the sun. The faster oaks and pines pulled ahead and slowly shaded out the cedars. The area became a mixed hardwood and pine forest perhaps as it had been in the distant past before the Indians' annual burns and later English livestock. Cows eat seedling trees and woody bushes as well as grass. Forgive us for telling this story here in the Closet yet again. We want to emphasize changes here; the next, soon to come, may be the biggest since the continental glacier.

Just before the hike, the retired agent, standing in until the new agent was appointed, met with a developer's lawyer and engineers. They spread large plans for a 28-acre subdivision across the table and explained the locations of roads, houses and septic systems. These and lawns will replace the forest. At one point the enthusiastic young engineer said, "The houses/garages will probably not have the 6,000-square-feet floor areas shown here for planning purposes." The agent and chairman of the conservation commission shook their heads. Each had raised a family in a house with less than 2,000 and thought it plenty big enough. The lawns of the planned mansions will be artificially green monocultures kept so by fertilizers and herbicides. We see these strange fields without gardens, cows or even children playing on them all over town. In front of each will be an asphalt road over four cars wide that ends in a huge cul-de-sac.

Such were the melancholy thoughts in the mind of a least one agent as they walked in the woods along the now high river. The good news is that the Rivers Protection Act requires a 200-foot buffer measured out from each edge. We often paddle this section and even after leaves have fallen and before new leaves come out we see no houses. We hope the conservation commission will push for even wider buffers. The couple kids rattling around in each of the large houses will then have more protected woods near the river they can explore. Perhaps they will even fish, swim and paddle. We weep when we think of the scarcely to be used chlorinated pools that will be built after some of the houses. We want the kids in the sun, shade and river water with ducks, beavers, otters, muskrats and hundreds of other smaller creatures.

Why 6,000 square feet when 2,000 will more than do? Why foreign chemicals on yards that will grow lovely diverse mini-meadows without them? Why wide roads of impermeable asphalt with curbs, dangers to creatures passing to and fro? We guess in a culture fueled with lots of money people want to strut their stuff. Mansions, wide roads, pools and manicured lawns cared for by Spanish speakers are all part of the show. My oh my, what do we do? Are we emulating the British aristocracy we detached ourselves from long ago? We've been warned by the environmentalists, but can't stop. Of course we environmentalists, brought up in times high on the hog, also have trouble in this regard.

The 47-acre woodland, about which the meeting mentioned above was held, was owned by Middleton's most famous man in its three centuries. The late Norman Nathan relaxed from his brilliant radio career by raising pets in a clearing around his house. He also kept a close eye on his beloved woods. Alas, his only 40-year-old house will be razed and on its spot a mansion built. Norm, we hope your ghost is hanging out somewhere else.

* *This is how the Middleton Stream Team's Water Closet appears in the weekly* Tri-Town Transcript.

LAST PADDLE IN 2011, MAYBE

November ended in September heat. A few Stream Teamers took advantage and paddled down the Ipswich River in canoe and kayaks. The river was running high and fast. A dozen beaver dams were passed over without keels touching. We've done this Middleton stretch of river a hundred times and never find it the same. In a week there may be snow coating the "swamp dogwood" bushes, bending them to the water. In another month the surface is likely to be rock hard. Just over a month ago in the nor'easter, trees still dressed in leaves took on lots of wet snow, some fell, and many were broken. Twice we had to portage around downed great oaks. On encountering a third we cut our way though limbs with a bucksaw. Somewhat impatient, we chafed at the delay because dark was only three hours away and we had eight miles yet to go. Soon the calm water and soft air dampened our worries; we truly entered with the flow. By the end, in waning light, after an entire afternoon of non-stop paddling, we felt some regret at having to leave. It was warm and there was no danger; we could have gone on in the dim light of night. Had we done so we might have more interesting things to report. We would have had to negotiate the meanders south of the Masco campus in the dark among now naked "silver maples." Animals might have come out to join us.

We saw no other people on the river for the whole afternoon. It seemed entirely ours on what was probably our last paddle of 2011. Winter looms, yet our thermometers give little clue to date. Even the surprise October snowstorm was a relatively warm one. The phrase "global warming" haunts us. What if its effects come dramatically and there is no winter? Would we, used to winters, have the gumption to head north? These were some of the strange thoughts that whirled through one old Stream Teamer's mind.

In the channel's great meanders just south of Farnsworth Landing off Route 114 we came upon an unfamiliar duck. It, unlike those in the large flock of Mallards we had spooked earlier, held a swimming course away from us. We closed in time and let photographer Judy in her kayak take the lead. The duck turned toward our little fleet, leisurely off to the side, showing no fear. Later with bird book in hand we learned it is probably an immature White-winged Scoter perhaps en route the coast where scoters winter. Did it tire in the last few miles of its long migration from interior Canada where scoters breed? Were companions sad to see it leave the flock? Did they even notice? Is it sick, unable to fly? We could have checked more closely but rather left him or her as we passed on wondering of its fate. We hope it is now riding the salty waves with others along our beaches.

We mentioned the Mallard flock, largely male, that flew away north from us above the river. We'd seen large flocks before this time of year in Great Wenham Swamp, a six-hour paddle downriver. The other day's were hidden among acres of now brown reed canary grass and climbing hempweed. Where are the females? Are these Mallards fueling up before resuming migration? What are they eating? There are always more questions than answers. There are very few of the latter given which we completely trust. The variables along our rivers through time are a thousand fold. As said before, we never see the river, floodplain and flanking uplands exactly the same.

Another seeming change this year is the number of muskrat lodges. We must have passed a score near the channel in just a mile or so. Are we seeing more because it is later in the season than we usually paddle? Those we saw are nicely made of layered vegetable matter. They are smaller, steeper and softer than the familiar piles of sticks making up beaver lodges. Some cleverly take advantage of the bushes for framing and look almost like huge bird nests floating on the water. Actually they have firm foundations on the substrate. The residents enter from the water underneath. We'd like to vertically dissect one to study its internal structure of compartments and passageways. It would be heartless to do so now. We passed on, again with more questions than answers. We must ask friend Francis Masse, a hardy muskrat trapper as a boy long long ago.

We were treated with a surprise at the end of our journey. We hadn't had the river to ourselves! There resting at the Stream Team's Peabody Street landing were friend Xavier Chambers and his friend Robert. They, Eagle Scouts, unbeknown to us had preceded us downriver. With hardy good cheer they helped us pull our vessels from the water. Denny Chambers, Xavier's father, and Robert had paddled a canoe. Xavier and his lobsterwoman girlfriend and her dog had remarkably paddled the five miles standing on boards. While the air was warm, the water was cold. We less agile folks couldn't believe they were not wet. We had some nervous moments skirting tight places in our relatively high-sided vessels. They stood on their surfboard-like craft and propelled them with long-handled paddles. Amazing. You meet all kinds, including musicians like Xavier and his dad, a lobsterwoman out of Gloucester and a lone scoter, on the river.

We had paddled over three hours and never heard an engine or cell phone ring, or at least that we noticed. We passed under Routes 114 and 62 where there was plenty of traffic noise. Our thoughts were elsewhere and are again as we harken back to that Indian summer afternoon.

A Turk's Dream

What do you do if you are a middle-aged software and mechanical engineer dissatisfied with being cooped up in corporate offices all day? Rugged Erden Eruc, friend of a friend of the Stream Team, Al Rosner, decided to circumnavigate the globe on a very zigzag course under his own power fueled by food. More than a century ago Captain Joshua Slocum used wind as have many other "round-the-worlders." Joshua devised an automatic steering rig for his seaworthy sloop *Spray* and spent much of each day reading. High-tech athlete Erden disdains sail and uses oars, mechanical ones Joshua wouldn't recognize.

Al, long ago Erden's wrestling coach, from time to time tells us of

Erden's adventures; they unlike Joshua and friends can keep in almost daily touch. The 19th-century sailor's human contacts at sea were books. The lone rower's are the internet and cell phone. His vessel is loaded with electronic devices. The superstructure bristles with antennae, solar panels and weather-sensing gear. He knows where he is within a few meters constantly. Joshua, a crackerjack celestial navigator, knew within a few miles every few days.

We try hard to imagine Erden, now two months and 2,000 miles out of Namibia, coming this way on the South Equatorial Current. His physical world, disregarding the internet, the one he can see, is a disk of the South Atlantic seven miles in diameter circumscribed by the horizon. Except when a ship passes or a storm stirs the surface his briny surface is two-dimensional. Hour after hour, day after day his boat-centered circle slowly moves northwest under the pull of oars and the movement of currents. The unknown deep starts a few inches from his soles; the infinity of space extends above his soul. Unlike the sailors on wooden ships of yore he knows that below him at 200 meters it is pitch black, the water temperature a constant four degrees Celsius. He must often wonder about the three or so miles of water under him; at night his thoughts may be in the celestial sphere with the stars. There is no light pollution where he is. During alert, non-dreaming times, he must think a lot about his movement across the surface toward his present goal, the favorable currents flowing northerly off South America and on into the Caribbean Sea. We can but speculate, wish he were here or we there. We could perhaps call him through Al and ask questions, but strangers we would be penetrating his mid-ocean privacy. We await his book that may be titled after his project's good name, Around-n-Over; over the oceans by rowboat, over the continents by bicycle. We'll leave his dusty cycling to the landlubbers. This is the Water Closet. While our small vessels don't go out far in the deep our minds often do, especially when we have a brave dedicated friend of a friend like Erden who leaves a minuscule carbon footprint. We are sure the scientific Turkish rower, who by the way is fluent in English, could tell us almost exactly how much CO_2 he emits a day. We wonder if he weighs his food and then does the calculations.

The following is a portion of the latest dispatch we have from Erden. First we'll note his latest reported position: Day 62 (since leaving Namibia, Africa, 2,040 miles astern), Dec 11 2011, 6:00

GMT, 7:42:14S 8:44:42W (5,294 miles to Limon, Costa Rica, his destination):

Day 57, Dec 5. I was seeing more birds earlier on this crossing when I was closer to land (Africa) which included coastal species. Another reason for that was the nutrition rich waters that the cold upwelling from the deep (from Antarctica) brought to the surface forming the Beguela Current. This allowed plankton to flourish which in turn sustained a range of sea life from sardines to whales. The birds were there along with the seals to claim their part in this huge but still fragile eco-system while mankind did its very best to destroy by overfishing.

Erden then goes on to list and describe the bird species seen recently. He reports them to an ornithologist friend who tells him what he knows about them. You see, he is not just a rower, he is student of our planet. He is also a teacher; we and thousands who follow him via the internet are his pupils.

In 2004 an interviewer asked him, "What does having a dream mean to you?"

Erden's reply: "A dream is a goal glimmering in the distance; it is an inner calling which, when accomplished, serves as a rite of passage into wisdom." We are not fully sure what this means or whether it was said in Turkish or English. We like the poetry and much admire the dreamer who is making his dream real.

WORRIES ABOUT COD AGAIN

Once upon a time a magnificent fish filled the seas of our northern continental shelves. Brave men in tiny ships sailed across the ocean from the Old World to catch Atlantic cod, *Gadus morhua*, on offshore banks of the New. They preceded the English and French colonists by a century. We know little of them. They came in the spring and returned in the fall laden with valuable cargoes of salted fish. We offer their vague history as evidence of the enormous numbers of fish here. After literate colonists settled precariously along our New England and New France coasts we have records that the protein from our prolific seas saved many from starvation. Fish quickly became one of the bases of the colonial economy. Salted fish along with beaver pelts and sassafras were exported to home countries.

For three centuries bottom fish were commercially caught here with weighted hand lines. In the 19th century they shifted to "long lines" with multiple hooks. Several hundred feet of stout line with hooks on leaders every fathom or so were baited and neatly coiled in wooden tubs. These were dropped from dories manned by one or two men onto sandy and rocky bottoms for cod after an anchor and marker buoy were attached to an end. When most of the baited line was stretched out on the bottom a second anchor with buoy was attached and dropped at the end. Then another long line was set nearby. The dory returned to the first and brought it aboard starting at one end, taking off any fish caught. By mid-afternoon, after the second line was retrieved, the small seaworthy dories, filled almost to the gunnels, were rowed back to the mother schooner hovering nearby. Think about this method: a light line descended gently to the bottom doing no harm. Almost all the fish brought to the surface were target species; there was little "by-catch" to be thrown overboard dead or dying. While labor intensive, the damage done was minuscule compared with that of the great bottom-scarring trawls that replaced long lines in the last century and are still with us. The latter bring up almost everything that can't pass through the huge net's mesh. The catch is sorted on deck, the often large by-catch returned to the sea. The ocean bottom, supporting delicate layers of life, the sustenance of bottom fish such as cod, hake, haddock and halibut, is badly damaged.

In the 1950s through the 1970s vessels called factory ships with smaller catcher boats came from around the world to our waters. These high-tech fleets fished all seasons, night and day. One of their targets was cod spawning areas at times of spawning. This style, get as much as you can fast, of fishing was predominant in the wasteful latter half of the 20th century. In 1982 Canada and the United States extended their "exclusive economic zones" 12 to 200 miles out from shorelines. The foreign fleets left. Government subsidies, especially in Canada, stimulated high-tech fishing from larger boats. We copied the foreigners' methods. "Bigger is better," isn't that what the landlubbers also say? Witness our banks and corporations. By the early 1980s the small coastal fishermen in the Canadian Maritimes became greatly alarmed by the decline in cod populations. In 1992 Canada belatedly banned bottom fishing. Hundreds of coastal communities died. The fisher folks went on the dole. Around Newfoundland, populations of four-century-old villages were moved off islands and outposts and brought to the mainland where they could be provided for more efficiently. Despite the ban the expected return of cod and other bottom fish hasn't happened. The reasons are not well understood. Habitat and breeding cycle disruptions and especially "over exploitation" are thought to be the causes. On the fishing banks off New England catches of prolific medium- and large-size cod have also plummeted despite the 200-mile zone. Tallies in 2008 showed promising signs, but an article in the December-January issue of *The Working Waterfront* out of Rockport, Maine, has bad news from fish scientists yet again. The numbers expected for 2011 are not as predicted. They worry. We await their final report; reporter Craig Idlebrook just got some hints as to what it would contain. We won't go on; the media here have had frequent reports about our fishing woes.

Does this all sound familiar? Historians tell us that if we study the past we have less chance of repeating mistakes made. We old-timers in the Closet love history, but aren't so sure this happens, although we like to think they are right. Big fur trading in the 17th to 19th centuries came close to removing beavers and bison from this continent. Big whaling in the 19th and 20th centuries almost wiped out the Earth's most magnificent creatures. Big agriculture in the 20th has done away with small farmers. Big oil has covered our land with internal combustion engines and furnaces to the detriment of the world. Big banks have sucked up small local ones in which we knew the bankers. The largest are deemed "too big to fail," and yet they fail us. Big oil and big coal, despite claims to the contrary, harm the environment. Now perhaps the most important of sea animals, the cod, is threatened by the efficient methods of big boats. The first to suffer in all these takeovers are the little guys and gals. Our politicians daily praise small businessmen who "create jobs" while at the same time taking money from big corporations who can't but influence them in their policy making. Presidential candidate Dr. Ron Paul, who seems in some ways smart and wise, would have us do away with much of governments and their regulations. If this were done, we'd give our wetlands, streams, rivers and ocean fisheries little more than a few years. Big money, unchecked, as it once was, would do them in. Standard Oil types as in the 19th and early 20th century and Arthur Daniels Midland and BP, as in the 20th and 21st, would quickly move in and take over. We'd become dependent upon their philanthropy, by-catch from their tables. Paul and other "Live Free or Die" types are clearly wrong.

One of many examples is that of the Clean Water Act passed in 1972; within two decades the Merrimack, Androscoggin and many other rivers, long noxious sewers, were clean. Government accomplished these wonders. We could go on about President Teddy Roosevelt and national parks. Dr. Paul should read history.

What then are the answers to our environmental and fishery resource problems? We old-timers admit we don't have them, and our time is almost over. Positive proactive views of government instead of poisonous negative ones might be a good start. Isn't clean effective government what we really want, not necessarily less?

Back in hippie times there was a popular book *Small is Beautiful* by British economist E. F. Schumacher making the rounds; we've mentioned it here before. He, like Barbara Kingsolver with her gardens and farmers' markets, would have us do things locally so many more would have a stake in what is truly needed, made and raised.

Dear young people, our generation went the other way; big business was thought by many to be beautiful. It hasn't been. Read our sad environmental histories and take the historians' admonition to heart. We can't tell you how to solve the problems we bequeath you. However, we think "too big to fail" is not one of the solutions. Benign long lines, oars and sails weren't so bad. We urge you to create better modern equivalents and think seriously about settling with less of everything.

16653877R00255

Made in the USA
Charleston, SC
04 January 2013